Richard S. Ascough

Paul's Macedonian Associations

Richard S. Ascough

Paul's Macedonian Associations

The Social Context of Philippians
and 1 Thessalonians

WIPF & STOCK · Eugene, Oregon

Wipf and Stock Publishers
199 W 8th Ave, Suite 3
Eugene, OR 97401

Paul's Macedonian Associations
The Social Context of Philippians and 1 Thessalonians
By Ascough, Richard S.
Copyright © 2003 Mohr Siebeck All rights reserved.
Softcover ISBN-13: 978-1-7252-6752-7
Publication date 2/11/2020
Previously published by Mohr Siebeck, 2003

For Mary-Lynne

Preface

This book is a revision of my dissertation, completed under John S. Kloppenborg and submitted in 1997 to the Faculty of Wycliffe College and the Bibilical Department of the Toronto School of Theology in partial fulfillment of the requirements for the degree Doctor of Philosophy in Theology awarded by the University of St. Michael's College. Prof. Kloppenborg has been a constant source of methodological, bibliographical, and technical insight throughout his oversight of this project. As my Doktorvater and mentor he has provided ample inspiration and encouragement in the furthering of my career as a member of the guild of biblical scholars. I have much admiration and appreciation for his scholarship and example.

I have also benefited from the input of my other dissertation readers, Leif E. Vaage, L. Ann Jervis, and Michael G. Steinhauser, all of whom provided important comments, feedback, and support, both in the process of writing and at the final defense of the dissertation. I am particularly grateful to my external examiner, Robert Jewett, who provided challenging questions and enthusiastic support for the dissertation and was most helpful to me during my two-year sojourn in Chicago.

Much of my early grounding in the study of voluntary association inscriptions came through the Toronto School of Theology's Hellenistic Texts Seminar. I am particularly thankful for the use of our collective work to those who were members of the HTS during our "inscriptions" phase (1991-94): John Kloppenborg, Leif Vaage, Bradley H. McLean, Alicia Batten, Grant LeMarquand, Bill Arnal, and Philip Harland. The HTS inscriptions project received a three-year Social Sciences and Humanities Research Council of Canada grant, funding which allowed us to create an extensive database. It also allowed me, as a research assistant, to compile a subject index of all of our inscriptions, which has now been incorporated into the database. This database proved essential in the research for this dissertation. Thanks are also due to my research assistants Nancy Wilson and Erin Vearncombe who carefully proof read the final manuscript. Finally, I want to acknowledge the encouragement and input of those at Mohr-Siebeck, especially Prof. Martin Hengel, Prof. Jörg Frey, Dr. Henning Ziebritzki, and Ilse König.

I am grateful for the provision of funding and scholarships during my graduate studies from the Social Sciences and Humanities Research Council of Canada (a three-year doctoral fellowship) and the Catholic

Biblical Association (four years of Memorial Stipends). Subsequent support for this and related research projects has been provided by two Queen's University Advisory Research Committee grants, a Society of Biblical Literature's Research and Technology Grant, and a summer grant from the Wabash Center for Teaching and Learning in Theology and Religion.

Friends have played an important role both in my graduate experience and my early career. During my time in Toronto I have had the pleasure of meeting many talented individuals. Among the young scholars who have provided particularly important support and encouragement are John McLaughlin, Robert Derrenbacker, Tyler Williams, Alicia Batten, Caroline Whelan-Donaghey, James Beck, Paul Friesen, and Kenneth Fox. Colleagues at both the Institute of Pastoral Studies (Loyola University Chicago) and Queen's Theological College (Kingston, Canada) have been supportive throughout the various revision stages of this book. Friends from other walks of life who have been particularly gracious and tolerant, include Grant Cassidy, Lisa and Campbell Horn, John Inglis and Tanis Lockhart, and Brian Effer.

I also want to express my appreciation for the encouragement of my parents and my spouse's parents, who have seen our collective studies take us half-way around the world and back. My children, Hannah and Josiah, have been a constant source of joy and have provided many welcome diversions from my work. My wife, Mary-Lynne, has provided unfailing support throughout my academic endeavors, particularly during the years that I have labored with this project. I dedicate this book to her, with love.

Kingston, January 2003   Richard S. Ascough

Table of Contents

Preface vii

Acknowledgements xii

Abbreviations xiii

Chapter One: Introduction 1
   1. Pioneers and Proponents 3
   2. Problems and Prospects 10
   3. Outline of the Study 13

Chapter Two: Types and Functions of Associations 15
   1. The Rise of Associations 15
   2. Taxonomy 20
   3. Functions 24
   4. Founders and Foundations 28
       a) Private Associations 28
       b) Testamentary Associations 32
       c) Associations Founded by Divine Sanction 34
   5. Legal Status 42

Chapter Three: Membership and Its Requirements 47
   1. Social Location 47
   2. Gender 54
   3. Hierarchy and Egalitarianism 59
   4. Benefaction and Honours 61
   5. Finances 63
   6. Moral Ethos 65
   7. Cultic Activities 69

Chapter Four: Community Organization 71
   1. Self-definition Terminology 71
   2. Leadership and Officials 79
   3. Community Regulations 83
   4. Allegiance 87

Table of Contents

    5. Translocal Links 91
        a) Evidence from Associations 93
        b) Evidence from Judaism and Christianity 100
    6. Literary Production 108
    7. Conclusion 109

Chapter Five: The Philippian Christian Community 110
    1. Paul's Letter to the Philippians 115
    2. The Social Location of the Philippian Christians 117
        a) The Marketplace 118
        b) Prosopography 122
        c) Summary 128
    3. Philippians and the Associations 129
        a) Leadership Structure 129
        b) Internal Community Relationships 139
        c) Community Interaction with Outsiders 144
        d) Finances 149
        e) Further Implications for Community Structure 157
    4. Conclusion 160

Chapter Six: The Thessalonian Christian Community 162
    1. Paul's Letter to the Thessalonians 162
    2. The Social Location of the Thessalonian Christians 165
        a) The Thessalonians' Economic Situation 165
        b) The Thessalonians as Manual Laborers 169
    3. The Thessalonians and the Voluntary Associations 176
        a) Leadership Structure 176
        b) Internal Community Relationships 177
        c) Further Implications for Community Structure 184
    4. Conclusion 190

Appendix: Jewish Communities in Macedonia 191
    1. Literary and Archaeological Evidence 192
    2. Evidence From Paul's Letters 202
    3. Evidence From Acts 205
    4. Conclusion 212

Bibliography 213

Indexes 239
    1. Modern Authors 239
    2. Ancient Texts 241
        a) Hebrew Bible / LXX 241

    b) New Testament 242
    c) Early Christian Writings 247
    d) Other Greco-Roman and Jewish Writings 247
    e) Inscriptions and Papyri 249
3. Subjects 256
4. Place Names 259

Acknowledgements

Portions of chapter 4, section 5, were previously published as "Translocal Relationships Among Voluntary Associations and Early Christianity," *Journal of Early Christian Studies* 5/2 (1997) 223-41 and are republished here with the permission of Johns Hopkins University Press.

Portions of chapter 6 were previously published as "The Thessalonian Christian Community as a Professional Voluntary Association," *Journal of Biblical Literature* 119/2 (2000) 311-28 and are republished here with the permission of The Society of Biblical Literature.

Abbreviations

Abbreviations for collections of inscriptions follow those found in G. H. R. Horsley and John A. L. Lee, "A Preliminary Checklist of Abbreviations of Greek Epigraphic Volumes," *Epigraphica* 56 (1994) 129-69. In addition, the abbreviation "Pilhofer" refers to Peter Pilhofer, *Philippi*. Band II. *Katalog der Inschriften von Philippi* (WUNT 119; Tübingen: Mohr Siebeck, 2000). Abbreviations for classical authors and papyrological collections follow those found in Gerhard Kittel, ed., *Theological Dictionary of the New Testament* 1 (Grand Rapids: Eerdmans, 1964) xvi-xxxix. Abbreviations for biblical journals and related works follow the conventions found in *The Anchor Bible Dictionary*, ed. David Noel Freedman (New York: Doubleday, 1992). *The Anchor Bible Dictionary* itself is abbreviated as *ABD*.

Where possible I have used the inscription reference from the most significant corpus in which it appears. However, in some cases an inscription from Macedonia that is frequently referenced is not found in one of the common epigraphic works. For convenience, I have assigned a designator to such inscriptions following the form "IPlace-name" and a number. For example, IThessalonica 1 indicates an inscription from Thessalonica, the first to which I gave a number. Below I give the full bibliographical details for such inscriptions:

IAcanthus 1 = M. N. Tod, "Macedonia. Inscriptions," *Annual of the British School at Athens* 23 (1918-19) 85, no. 13.
IAmphipolis 1 = M. P. Nilsson, *The Dionysiac Mysteries of the Hellenistic and Roman Age* (Lund: Gleerup, 1957) 8, n. 11.
IAnthemonte 1 = M. B. Hatzopoulos and L. D. Loukopoulou, *Recherches sur les marches orientales des temenides (Anthemonte-Kalindoia) i* (Meletemata 11; Athens: De Boccard, 1992) 50-51, no. 5.
IAnydron = Panayotou, Anna, and P. Chrysostomou, "Inscriptions de la Bottiée et de l'Almopie en Macédoine," *BCH* 117 (1993) 370-72, no. 6.
IBeroea 1 = M. Tačeve-Hitova, "Dem Hypsistos geweihte Denkmäler in den Balkanländern," *Balkan Studies* 19 (1978) 72, no. 13.
IBeroea 2 = A. M Woodward, "Inscriptions from Beroea in Macedonia," *Annual of the British School at Athens* 18 (1911-12) 155 no. 22.

IBeroea 3 = G. H. R. Horsley, *New Documents Illustrating Early Christianity: A Review of the Greek Inscriptions and Papyri Published in 1979* (NewDocs 4; North Ryde, Australia: Ancient History Documentary Research Centre, Macquarie University, 1987) 215, no. 19.
IEdessa 1 = M. Tačeve-Hitova, "Dem Hypsistos geweihte Denkmäler in den Balkanländern," *Balkan Studies* 19 (1978) 72, no. 10.
IEdessa 2 = M. Tačeve-Hitova, "Dem Hypsistos geweihte Denkmäler in den Balkanländern," *Balkan Studies* 19 (1978) 72, no. 11.
IEdessa 3 = M. Tačeve-Hitova, "Dem Hypsistos geweihte Denkmäler in den Balkanländern," *Balkan Studies* 19 (1978) 71-72, no. 9.
IKalambaki 1 = P. Collart, *Philippes, ville de Macédonia, depuis ses origines jusqu'à la fin de la l'époque romaine* (Thèse. Université de Genève 85; Paris: Boccard, 1937) 271, note 2.
IPydna 1 = G. H. R. Horsley, *New Documents Illustrating Early Christianity: A Review of the Greek Inscriptions and Papyri* (NewDocs 1; North Ryde, Australia: Ancient History Documentary Research Centre, Macquarie University, 1981) 26-27.
IThessalonica 1 = E. Voutiras, "Berufs- und Kultverein: Ein ΔΟΥΜΟΣ in Thessalonike," *ZPE* 90 (1992) 87-96.
IThessalonica 2 = G. H. R. Horsley, *New Documents Illustrating Early Christianity: A Review of the Greek Inscriptions and Papyri Published in 1979* (NewDocs 4; North Ryde, Australia: Ancient History Documentary Research Centre, Macquarie University, 1987) 215, no. 17.
IThessalonica 3 = K. Rhomiopoulou, "New Inscriptions in the Archaeological Museum, Thessaloniki," *Ancient Macedonian Studies in Honor of Charles F. Edson*, ed. H. J. Dell, (Thessaloniki: Institute for Balkan Studies, 1981) 301-02, no. 6.

Chapter One

Introduction

As the twenty-first century opens increasing attention is being paid to the social contexts of early Christianity.[1] However, as Jonathan Z. Smith has argued, many biblical scholars continue to appeal to the "Jewish roots" of Christianity in order to insulate formative Christianity from its so-called "pagan" surroundings.[2] Smith shows how polemical agendas have been the context of the discussion and have skewed both the presentation of the "facts" and the subsequent analyses and conclusions. These observations extend to the debate over the use of models for understanding early Pauline community organization. Most scholars eschew models other than the synagogue for understanding Pauline Christianity. The synagogue model is often applied to all of the Christian communities with very little attempt to understand each of them in their own particular locale. Nor is there any sustained attempt to use models other than the synagogue such as philosophical schools, mysteries, or voluntary associations.[3] While we do not want to disparage the importance of formative Judaism and the synagogues for the understanding of early Christian communities, in this book we want to suggest that other models of community organization

---

[1] Unfortunately many studies of the socio-cultural context of early Christianity have been reduced to providing "background information," only sometimes deemed as significant for understanding the deeper ("more significant") theological truths of the texts (J. H. Elliott, *What is Social-Science Criticism* [GBS; Minneapolis: Fortress, 1993] 12). Too often exegetes are left to make the transfer from "background" to exegesis (e.g., E. Ferguson, *Backgrounds of Early Christianity* [Grand Rapids: Eerdmans, 1987]; C. K. Barrett, *The New Testament Background: Selected Documents* [2nd ed.; San Francisco: Harper Collins, 1987]). Fortunately, more recent social-scientific studies of the New Testament have advanced beyond this, providing solid exegetical insights based on a thorough understanding of the social world of the text.

[2] See J. Z. Smith, *Drudgery Divine: On the Comparison of Early Christianities and the Religions of Late Antiquity* (Chicago: University of Chicago Press, 1990) 83; also D. H. Wiens, "Mystery Concepts in Primitive Christianity and in its Environment," *ANRW* II.23.2 (1980) 1251; J. S. Kloppenborg, "Edwin Hatch, Churches and *Collegia*," in *Origins and Method: Towards a New Understanding of Judaism and Christianity. Essays in Honour of John C. Hurd*, ed. B. H. McLean (JSNTSup 86; Sheffield: JSOT Press, 1993) 226-28.

[3] There are exceptions; see R. S. Ascough *What Are They Saying About the Formation of Pauline Churches?* (New York and Mahwah: Paulist, 1998).

need to be considered seriously as part of the matrix of early Christian community formation, particularly the Macedonian Christian community.

Behind the reluctance to consider models other than the synagogue, Smith identifies a scholarly predisposition to equate comparison with inheritance. That is, when faced with similarities among two groups, movements, or even texts, scholars immediately determine that there is a genealogical connection.[4] They assume that one of the groups being studied must have "borrowed" from the other. As a result, they seem to fear that an admission that Christian groups have a relationship with something other than Judaism is an admission that it somehow became "corrupted."

Smith goes on to suggest that rather than seek, or even assume, such genealogical connections, the process should be one of analogical comparisons. In an analogical investigation the comparative process is not undertaken to find direct relationships. One is not looking for the "earlier" exemplar, nor is one trying to determine the direction of borrowing.[5] Rather, one type of association is compared to another in order to highlight both similarities *and* differences. Indeed, what is inherently interesting in the comparative process is not so much the similarities among various groups, although these are important, but the differences.[6] It is precisely in finding difference that one is invited into "negotiation, classification and comparison."[7] It is only in defining peculiarities that one is able to note what was distinctive about early Christian groups.

The comparative connections used rest in the mind of the interpreter and help the interpreter understand how things might be re-imagined or re-described. The comparison takes place around a set of options that the interpreter specifies. This approach does not preclude the borrowing of aspects from one religion to another – indeed, we have suggested as much in the case of some of the Pauline communities and the associations.[8] However, rather than simply explaining origins, Smith proposes that setting various facets of religion beside one another will lead to greater insight and awareness of all the groups being studied. It is with this foundational methodological commitment that we can turn to an investigation of Pauline Christian communities and the voluntary associations of antiquity.

In this book the voluntary associations of the Greco-Roman world are used as a comparative model for understanding early Christian community organization, with specific attention to Paul's Macedonian Christian

---

[4] Smith, *Drudgery Divine*, 47.

[5] Cf. Kloppenborg, "Edwin Hatch, Churches and *Collegia*," 228-30.

[6] Smith, *Drudgery Divine*, 42, 47.

[7] Smith, *Drudgery Divine*, 42.

[8] E.g., R. S. Ascough, "The Thessalonian Christian Community as a Professional Voluntary Association." *JBL* 119 (2000) 311-28. Also, see chapter 5 below.

communities. In the first instance, the book provides a comprehensive description of the range of voluntary associations, defined as groups "of men and/or women organized on the basis of freely chosen membership for a common purpose."[9] Drawing upon the comparative method outlined by Smith, the community language and practices reflected in Philippians and 1 Thessalonians are compared to that of the voluntary associations. Doing so helps to explain both Paul's language and the language and structure of the communities to which he writes. This book argues that many of the features of the two Macedonian Christian communities reflected in Paul's letters find ready analogies in voluntary associations. Thus, both of the Christian groups would have appeared to outsiders as associations and would have functioned internally as such.

1. Pioneers and Proponents

The research into the nature of voluntary associations has a long tradition.[10] The first essays on this theme originate from the sixteenth century, with others produced in the seventeenth and eighteenth centuries.[11] However,

---

[9] R. Ascough, "Associations, Voluntary," in *Eerdmans' Dictionary of the Bible*, ed. D. N. Freedman (Grand Rapids: Eerdmans, 2000) 117. In our investigation we will use the term "voluntary associations" or "associations" rather than the more specific "Roman *collegia*," which generally refers to Latin associations, most of them in the Western part of the empire. The term "voluntary association" is less than ideal but captures the essence of the type of group that we are discussing. That there was no one term used for associations in antiquity makes it difficult to find an antique name for them. Various definitions of these groups have been attempted: "voluntary associations of persons more or less permanently organized for the pursuit of a common end, and so distinguishable both from the State and its component elements . . . and . . . from temporary unions for transitory purposes" (M. N. Tod, "Clubs, Greek," *OCD* [1970²] 254); "An association is in general a group which a man joins of his own free will, and which accepts him of its free will, and this mutual acceptance creates certain obligations on both parties" (C. H Roberts, T. C. Skeat, and A. D. Nock, "The Guild of Zeus Hypsistos," *HTR* 29 [1936] 75; cf. W. A. Meeks, *The First Urban Christians: The Social World of the Apostle Paul* [New Haven: Yale University Press, 1983] 78); "a coherent group, which could be recognized as such by outsiders, with its own rules for membership, leadership and association with one another" (L. Gaston, "Pharisaic Problems," in *Approaches to Ancient Judaism*, ed. Jacob Neusner [Atlanta: Scholars Press, 1993] 85).

[10] The following is largely summarized from F. M. Ausbüttel, *Untersuchungen zu den Vereinen im Westen des römischen Reiches* (FAS 11; Kallmünz: Michael Laßieben, 1982) 11-13.

[11] Among the earliest to write on this topic, particularly the *collegia opificum*, were C. Sigonius, *De antiquo iure civumi Romanorum, Italiae, provinciarum, ac Romanae iurisprudentiae iudicis libri XI* (Frankfurt a. M, 1593), G. Pancirolus, *De magistratibus municipalibus et corporibus artificium* (Genf, 1623), E. Platnerus, *De collegiis opificum (Disputatio I und II)* (Leipzig, 1709) J. G. Heineccius, *De collegiis et corporibus opificum* (Halae Magdeburgicae: Litteris C. Henchelii, 1723), B. Brissonius, *Antiquitatum ex iure civili*

prior to Theodor Mommsen's pioneering work of 1843 studies had only pointed to isolated inscriptions, especially in the debate over the legal position of the *collegia* and *sodalicia*.[12]

Throughout the early 1800s the Berlin Academy published *Corpus Inscriptionum Graecarum* (*CIG*). Shortly after it was completed in 1877 the process was begun to replace it by *Inscriptiones Graecae* (*IG*), yet *CIG* remains the only modern *corpus* to cover the entire Greek world, as *IG* remains incomplete.[13] *CIG* was joined at the end of the nineteenth century by the publication of *Corpus Inscriptionum Latinarum* (*CIL*), which resulted in increased scholarly interest in Roman voluntary associations. The availability and fairly easy access to a number of association inscriptions in these volumes encouraged a number of important studies of voluntary associations.[14]

A number of collections of inscriptions from voluntary associations with accompanying studies were soon available.[15] W. Liebenam produced an inclusive study of all the extant evidence at that time for the professional associations.[16] Paul Foucart's *Les Associations religieuses chez les Grecs*

---

selectarum libri quattuor (Leipzig, 1741). W. Rein published a survey in the mid-nineteenth century: "Collegium." *PW* 2 (1842) 493-501. See Ausbüttel, *Untersuchungen*, 11 for details.

[12] Th. Mommsen, *De collegiis et sodaliciis Romanorum. Accedit inscriptio lanuvina* (Kiel: Libraria Schwersiana, 1843); Ausbüttel *Untersuchungen*, 11.

[13] Despite its incompletion as a series, *IG* has already undergone some revision. *IG* I, II, and III have become I^2 and II^2 (Attica); IV 1 (Epidaurus), IX (Aetolia, Acarnania, Western Locris) have been revised. These collections of inscriptions have a minimum amount of commentary. Other collections are more selective, classifying the inscriptions according to character; for a description of each volume see A. G. Woodhead, *The Study of Greek Inscriptions* (Cambridge and New York: Cambridge University Press, 1981^2) 103-07.

[14] See Ausbüttel, *Untersuchungen*, 11.

[15] H. C. Maué (*Der praefectus fabrum: ein Beitrag zur Geschichte des römischen Beamtentums und des Collegialwesens während der Kaiserzeit* [Halle: Niemeyer, 1887]) collected inscriptions relevant to the *fabri, centonarii* and *dendrophori* while T. Schiess (*Die römischen collegia funeraticia nach den Inschriften* [München: Ackermann, 1888]) worked on those of the so-called *collegia funeraticia*. Prior to 1914 there appeared in Germany further works on the Roman clubs including those of M. C. Cohn (*Zum römischen Vereinsrecht: Abhandlungen aus der Rechtsgeschichte* [Berlin: Weidmann, 1873]), O. Hirschfeld ("Der praefectus vigilum in Nemausus und die Feuerwehr in den römischen Landstädten" in *Gallische Studien* [Wein: C. Gerold's sohn, 1884]), B. Matthias ("Zur Geschichte der römischen Zwangsverbände," in *Festschrift zum fünfzigjährigen Doctorjubiläum von Dr. H. v. Buchka* [Rostock: Universität Rostock, 1891]), A. Müller ("Sterbekassen und Vereine mit Begräbnisfürsorge in der römischen Kaiserzeit," *Neue Jahrbücher für das klassische Altertum, Geschichte und deutsche Literatur* 15 [1905] 183-201), F. Neubecker (*Vereine ohne Rechtsfähigkeit* [Leipzig, 1908]), and A. Stöckle ("Berufsvereine [griechische]," *RE Suppl* 4 [1924] 155-211). Ausbüttel links the increased research in Germany to the German civil union movement which, prior to the first world war, raised a great interest among the middle class in the forms of earlier, private, self-organized groups (*Untersuchungen*, 12).

[16] W. Liebenam, *Zur Geschichte und Organisation des römischen Vereinswesens: Drei Untersuchungen* (Leipzig: Teubner, 1890).

(1873) is considered indispensable for particulars of Greek associations deeming themselves θιασῶται, ὀργεῶνες, and ἔρανισται.[17] The works published by Erich Ziebarth and Franz Poland focus on the Greek associations of the eastern areas, although Poland's book is regarded as an enlargement and completion of that of Ziebarth.[18] Poland's work has helped scholars to discuss Greek associations according to nomenclature, locality, and time.[19] Shortly after the publication of the works of Ziebarth and Poland, Mariano San Nicolò produced studies of Egyptian associations.[20]

In French scholarship Jean-Pierre Waltzing produced a four-volume work between 1895 and 1900 that collected both literary and epigraphical sources for Roman associations.[21] In the first volume he discusses the organization, activities, and development of the *collegia*. The entire second volume deals with the topic of associations as official institutions and the development of trade guilds. Volume three contains inscriptions while volume four organizes diverse information according to various criteria. Today his work, after more than one hundred years, remains an indispensable resource for researching Roman associations.[22] At the same time as Waltzing, Ernst Kornemann published a general, introductory article on *collegia*, and, fourteen years later Bernhard Laum published his analysis of voluntary associations, with the relevant inscriptions collected in the second part of the book.[23]

---

[17] P. Foucart, *Des Associations Religieuses chez les Grecs: Thiases, Éranes, Orgéons* (Paris: Klincksieck, 1873).

[18] E. G. L. Ziebarth, *Das griechische Vereinswesen* (Stuttgart: S. Hirzel, 1896); F. Poland, *Geschichte des griechischen Vereinswesens* (Leipzig: Teubner, 1909).

[19] W. S. Ferguson regarded it not as a history but as a (complete) collection of materials that would make a history of the Greek private associations' "community life" possible ("Review of Poland, *griechischen Vereinswesens*," *CP* 5 [1910] 228). The materials are "well mastered and admirably analyzed" with many new observations. Ausbüttel points out that despite the work of Ziebarth and Poland the Greek associations have not received as much systematic nor clear attention as the Roman clubs (*Untersuchungen*, 12 n. 5).

[20] M. San Nicolò *Äegyptisches Vereinswesen zur Zeit der Ptolemäer und Römer* (2 vols; Münchener Beiträge zur Papyrusforschung und antiken Rechtsgeschichte 2. Heft. München: C. H. Beck, 1913-15); "Zur Vereinsgerichtsbarkeit im Hellenistischen Aegypten" in *Epitymbion*, ed. H. Swoboda, 255-99 (Reichenberg: Stiepel, 1927). In other European countries ancient historians hardly engaged this topic. After the first-world war German historians produced only occasional monographs and essays on the ancient clubs and societies.

[21] J. -P. Waltzing, *Étude Historique sur les corporations Professionnelles chez les Romains depuis les origines jusqu'a la chute de l'Empire d'Occident* (4 vols. Mémoire couronne par l'Academie royale des Sciences, des Lettres et des Beaux-Arts de Belgique; Louvain: Peeters, 1895, 1896, 1899, 1900).

[22] Cf. Ferguson, "Review of Poland," 230. Waltzing's source material for the Eastern half of the empire is somewhat insufficient, according to Ausbüttel, *Untersuchungen*, 12.

[23] E. Kornemann, "Collegium," *PW* 4/1 (1900) 380-479; B. Laum, *Stiftungen in der griechischen und römischen Antike: Ein Beitrag zur antiken Kulturgeschichte* (Leipzig: Teubner, 1914).

During the 1930s and 1940s there was a resurgence of research into associations, particularly by Italian scholars.[24] For example, in 1934 F. M. de Robertis published a two-volume history of the Roman corporations, in which he focused primarily on the legal aspect of the corporations.[25] P. W. Duff devoted two chapters to a discussion of the legal status of *collegia* in Roman law.[26] Post-World War II research was published primarily as essays.[27] As in earlier works, the history of the Empire took predominance, with the socio-historical aspects of the associations being more or less neglected. The exception was the essays of Heinz Schulz-Falkenthal who used socio-historical analysis to examine workmen's *collegia* from a Marxist perspective.[28]

---

[24] Triggered, according to Ausbüttel, by the rise of Italian fascism and its emphasis on the corporate state (*Untersuchungen*, 13). Studies were produced by V. Bandini (*Appunti sulle corporazioni romane* [Fondazione Guglielmo Castelli 14; Milan: Giuffrh, 1937]), P. Leicht ("Lineamenti della introduzione storica al diritto corporativo" in *Atti del primo convegno di studi sindacali e corporativi*, 65-78 [Rome, 1930]; "Ricerche sulle corporazioni professionali in Italia dal secolo V all' XI," *RAL* 12 [1936] 195-241.), G. Monti (*Le corporazione nell'evo antico e nell'evo medioevo* [Bari, 1934]), and F. M. de Robertis (*Il fenomeno associativo nel mondo romano dai collegi della repubblica alle corporazioni del basso impero* [Naples: Liber Scientifica edifice, 1955]).

[25] F. M. de Robertis, *Storia delle corporazioni e del regime associativo nel mondo romano* (2 vols. Bari: Adriatica editrice, 1934).

[26] P. W. Duff, *Personality in Roman Private Law* (London: Cambridge University Press, 1938) 95-161; cf. D. Daube, "Review of Duff, *Personality in Roman Private Law*," *JRS* 33 (1943) 91-93 and 34 (1944) 128-29 for summary and analysis.

[27] Including the works of G. Alföldy ("Collegium-Organisation in Intercisa," *AAntHung* 6 [1958] 177-98), K. Kurz ("Methodische Bemerkungen zum Studium der Kollegien im Donaugebiet" *AAntHung* 8 [1960] 133-44), J. Linderski ("Suetons Bericht über die Vereinsgesetzgebung unter Caesar und Augustus," *ZGR* 79 [1962] 322-28; "Der Senat und die Vereine," in *Gesellschaft und Recht im griechisch-römischen Altertum*, 94-132 [Deutsche Akademie der Wissenschaften zu Berlin 52. Berlin: Akademie Verlag, 1968]), H. d'Escurac-Doisy ("Notes sur le phénomène associatif dans le monde paysan à l'époque du Haut-Empire." *AntAfr* 1 [1967] 59-71), G. Clemente ("Il patronato nei collegia dell'imperio romano," *SCO* 21 [1972] 142-229), M. Jaczynowska ("Le caratteristiche delle associazioni della gioventù romana (collegia iuvenum)," *AIV* 134 [1975/76] 359-81; *Les associations de la jeunesse romaine sous le Haut-Empire* [Wroclaw: Zaklad Narodowy Im Ienia Ossolinskisch, 1978]), and P. Kneissl ("Die Entstehung und Bedeutung der Augustalität," *Chrion* 10 [1980] 291-326; "Die utriclairii. Ihre Rolle im gallo-römischen Transportwesen und Weinhandel," *BJ* 181 [1981] 79-99); see Ausbüttel, *Untersuchungen*, 13.

[28] H. Schulz-Falkenthal, "Zur Frage der Entstehung der römischen Handwerkerkollegien," *WZ* 14 (1965) 55-64; "Zur Lage der römischen Berufskollegien zu Beginn des 3. Jhs. u.Z. (die Privilegien der centonarii in Solva nach einem Reskript des Septimius Severus und Caracalla)," *WZ* 15 (1966) 285-94; "Zur Frage der organisatorischen Vorbilder für den korporativen Zusammenschluss in den *collegia* opificium und ihr Verhältnis zu den mittelalterlichen Zünften," *WZ* 19 (1970) 41-50; "Gegenseitigkeitshilfe und Unterstützungstätigkeit in den römischen Handwerkergenossenschaften," *WZ* 20 (1971) 59-78; "Zur politischen Aktivität der römischen Handwerkerkollegien," *WZ* 21 (1972) 79-99;

In the last part of the twentieth century interest in voluntary associations has not been sustained, although there are a few full-length works of note.[29] Françoise de Cenival studied demotic texts from voluntary associations in Egypt.[30] Frank Ausbüttel's sociological study investigates the membership structure, the activities, and the social meaning and development of the Roman associations in the western part of the Roman Empire (Italy, North Africa, the Iberian Peninsula, Gaul, Britain, Germany and the Danube province) from the first century BCE up to the third century CE.[31] Onno van Nijf has published a comprehensive study of *The Civic World of Professional Associations in the Roman East*, a task Nicholas Jones has undertaken for the associations of classical Athens.[32]

The use of "voluntary associations" as a model for understanding early Christian community formation goes back more than a century. Indeed, if one were to include some of the earliest commentators on Christian groups, one could even argue that the use of this model goes back to the patristic period. We find there writers such as Tertullian, Celsus, and Alexander Severus using associations as the point of comparison for Christian groups.[33] However, it was with the studies of Mommsen and de Rossi that the associations were used by critical scholars as a means for understanding Christian origins.[34] From the latter part of the nineteenth century[35] through the early part of the

---

"Römische Handwerkerkollegien im Dienst der städtischen Gemeinschaft und ihre Begünstigung durch staatliche Privilegien," *WZ* 22 (1973) 21-35.

[29] For the most part, associations are discussed briefly as a small part of larger studies on Greco-Roman antiquity, or in articles on individual inscriptional finds.

[30] F. Cenival, *Les associations religieuses en Egypte d'après les documents démotiques* (2 vols. Publications de l'Institut français d'archéologie orientale du Caire. Bibliothèque d'étude, vol. 46; Caire: Institut français d'archéologie orientale, 1972).

[31] Ausbüttel, *Untersuchungen*, 13.

[32] O. M. van Nijf, *The Civic World of Professional Associations in the Roman East* (Dutch Monographs on Ancient History and Archaeology 17; Amsterdam: Gieben, 1997); N. F. Jones, *The Associations of Classical Athens* (Oxford: Oxford University Press, 1999). On the latter subject see also I. Arnaoutoglou, "Between *koinon* and *idion*: Legal and Social Dimensions of Religious Associations in Ancient Athens," in *Kosmos: Essays in Order, Conflict and Community in Classical Athens*, ed. P. Cartledge, P. Millett, and S. von Reden, 68-83 (Cambridge: Cambridge University Press, 1998).

[33] Tertullian, *Apologia* 38-39; Celsus in Origin, *Contra Celsum* 1.1; 8.17, 47; Alexander Severus, *Historia Augusta*, *Vita Alex.* 49.

[34] Mommsen, *collegiis et sodaliciis*, and G. B. de Rossi, *La Roma sotteranea cristiana* (Rome: Cromo-litografia Pontificia, 1864-77).

[35] E. Renan, *The Apostles* (New York: Carleton, 1866); G. Heinrici, "Die Christengemeinden Korinths und die religiösen Genossenschaften der Griechen," *ZWT* 19 (1876) 465-526; E. Hatch, *The Organization of Early Christian Churches: Eight Lectures* (Bampton Lectures; London: Rivingtons, 1881); idem, *The Influence of Greek Ideas on Christianity* (The Hibbert Lectures, 1888; London: Williams and Norgate, 1891). For a treatment of Hatch see N. F. Josaitis, *Edwin Hatch and Early Church Order* (Gembloux: Éditions J. Duculot, 1971).

twentieth century[36] associations continued to be profitably explored by New Testament scholars. However, from the twenties through to the sixties interest in the associations waned. Although it is difficult to document why (since no one seems to explicitly reject the model) it may have to do with loss of interest due to the discovery of Christian and Jewish documents such as the *Didache* and the Dead Sea Scrolls and, to a lesser extent, the Nag Hammadi codicies.

Edwin Judge was one of the first scholars in the modern era to bring the associations back into focus by suggesting that despite the differences, Christian groups would have been indistinguishable from other types of voluntary associations, both in their own minds and in the minds of the public.[37] This opinion was confirmed by others such as Robert Wilken, William Countryman, and Marta Sordi.[38] The most influential study of the last quarter of the twentieth century, however, was Wayne Meeks' *The First Urban Christians*. In eleven pages Meeks lays out four possible models for community formation that have become the reference point in the debate over the appropriate analogy for understanding early Christian communities: the household, voluntary associations, synagogues, and philosophical schools.[39] Meeks himself favours the synagogue model and offers reasons why the other models are not viable. His persuasiveness is shown in the number of studies that simply adopt his critique, particularly of the voluntary associations model, usually without an examination of any primary evidence.[40]

---

[36] E. G. Hardy, *Studies in Roman History* 1 (London and New York: Sonnenschein and MacMillan, 1906); M. Radin, *Legislation of the Greeks and Romans on Corporations* (Columbia University: Tuttle, Morehouse & Taylor, 1910); T. Wilson, *St. Paul and Paganism* (Edinburgh: T. & T. Clark, 1927).

[37] E. A. Judge, *The Social Pattern of Christian Groups in the First Century: Some Prolegomena to the Study of New Testament Ideas of Social Obligation* (London: Tyndale, 1960) 44-45.

[38] R. L. Wilken, "Collegia, Philosophical Schools, and Theology," in *The Catacombs and the Colosseum: The Roman Empire as the Setting of Primitive Chritianity*, ed. Stephen Benko and John J. O'Rourke (Valley Forge: Judson, 1971) 99-120; W. L. Countryman, "Patrons and Officers in Club and Church," in *SBL 1977 Seminar Papers*, ed. P. J. Achtemeier (SBLASP 11; Missoula: Scholars Press, 1977) 135-43; M. Sordi, *The Christians and the Roman Empire* (London and Sydney: Croom Helm, 1983) 147, 182-86.

[39] Meeks, *First Urban Christians*, 74-84. In my own work on this issue I suggest that the household is not a viable model as distinct from the other models, since the others are often based in the household. I point out that the other analogous model that is often used is that of the ancient mysteries. (Ascough, *Formation of Pauline Churches*, 7-9). For an alternative position see J. S. Kloppenborg, "Collegia and *Thiasoi*: Issues in Function, Taxonomy and Membership" in *Voluntary Associations in the Graeco-Roman World*, ed. J. S. Kloppenborg and S. G. Wilson (London and New York: Routledge, 1996) 23.

[40] For example, J. S. Jeffers, *The Greco-Roman World of the New Testament: Exploring the Background of Early Christianity* (Downers Grove: InterVarsity Press, 1999) 79-80; A. D. Clarke, *Serve the Community of the Church: Christians as Leaders and Ministers* (First-Century Christians in the Graeco-Roman World; Grand Rapids and Cambridge: Eerdmans,

Although Meek's study might have signaled the end of the use of the associations for understanding early Christian community formation, the issue was taken up as a five-year seminar by members of the Canadian Society of Biblical Studies (1988-1993), the published papers from which are edited by John Kloppenborg and Stephen Wilson as *Voluntary Associations in the Greco-Roman World*.[41] The articles in this volume represent a range of positions, from those who view the associations as an important analogue for understanding ancient Jewish and Christian groups to those who are more reserved in the application of the analogy. Whether as a direct result of the work of the CSBS or not (and in some cases a direct link can be made) a number of articles, both published and unpublished, have continued to investigate the relationship of the voluntary associations to early Christian communities. In Europe significant work that uses the voluntary associations as a lens to understand aspects of early Christian communities has been published, most notably by scholars such as Hans-Joseph Klauck, Peter Lampe, Matthias Klinghardt, and Thomas Schmeller, to name a few.[42] Others such as Peter Pilhofer and Lukas Bormann have used the associations profitably in their studies.[43]

Throughout the twentieth century many articles were published on individual voluntary association inscriptions. Nevertheless, Robert Wilken's observation from a quarter century ago is still apropos: "[t]he literature on associations is endless, very repetitive, and frequently preoccupied with questions of legal history."[44] This observation is being changed to a small degree by the recent New Testament scholars who are investigating the relationship of early Christian groups to the voluntary associations. However,

---

2000) 159-60. In both cases they spend considerable time describing the associations but in the end decide against adopting them as a model for understanding Christian community by citing Meeks' objections.

[41] J. S. Kloppenborg and S. G. Wilson *Voluntary Associations in the Graeco-Roman World* (London and New York: Routledge, 1996).

[42] H.-J. Klauck ("Die Hausgemeinde als Lebensform im Urchristentum," *MTZ* [1981] 32:1-15; *Hausgemeinde und Hauskirche im frühen Christentum* [SBS 103. Stuttgart: Katholisches Bibelwerk, 1981]; *The Religious Context of Early Christianity: A Guide to Graeco-Roman Religions* [SNTW; Edinburgh: T. & T. Clark, 2000]), P. Lampe ("Das korinthische Herrenmahl im Schnittpunkt hellenistisch-römischer Mahlpraxis und paulinischen Theologia Crucis (1 Kor 11,17-34)," *ZNW* 82 [1991] 183-213), M. Klinghardt (*Gemeinschaftsmahl und Mahlgemeinschaft. Soziologie und Liturgie frühchristlicher Mahlfeiern* [Texte und Arbeiten zum neutestamentlichen Zeitalter 13; Tübingen and Basel: Francke, 1996]), and T. Schmeller (*Hierarchie und Egalität: Eine sozialgeschichtliche Untersuchung paulinischer Gemeinden und griechisch-römischer Vereine* [SBS 162; Stuttgart: Katholisches Bibelwerk, 1995]).

[43] P. Pilhofer, *Philippi*. Band I. *Die erste christliche Gemeinde Europas* (WUNT 87; Tübingen: Mohr-Siebeck, 1995); L. Bormann, *Philippi: Staat und Christengemeinde zur Zeit des Paulus* (NovTSup 78. Leiden: Brill, 1995).

[44] Wilken, "Collegia," 290 n. 35.

much more work remains to be done both by New Testament scholars and scholars of Greco-Roman antiquity. Particularly desirable is a more comprehensive collection of association inscriptions and an updating of the discussion of the nature of associations.[45]

2. Problems and Possibilities

There are a number of areas where the associations are being used as a model for defining and understanding early Christian communities.[46] For example, a number of recent studies of Matthew's gospel have suggested that the model of voluntary associations is appropriate for understanding the community for whom the document is written. Dennis Duling suggests, "[t]he Matthean *ekklesia* can be described as a fictive kinship group or fictive brotherhood association," that is, it is a type of voluntary association.[47] Although not adequate for a full description of the Matthean community, he suggests that voluntary associations explain some of its features.[48] This is also the case with Anthony Saldarini, who states that "[w]ithin Greco-Roman society, Matthew's group would have been understood as a private, voluntary

---

[45] Much of the material remains in obscure, inaccessible works and many of the primary data sources, the inscriptions, remain untranslated. Most scholars of antiquity are still heavily reliant upon (and indebted to) Poland, *griechischen Vereinswesens*, and Waltzing, *corporations Professionnelles*. A current research project based in Toronto, Canada, hopes to rectify this situation with a two volume work provisionally entitled *Cultic Groups, Guilds, and Collegia: Associations in the Greco-Roman World*, edited by J. S. Kloppenborg and B. H. McLean. The second volume will prove particularly useful as it will include a number of texts and English translations, along with bibliography, from associations throughout the Greco-Roman world. Easier access to the primary data should allow for a more fruitful debate over the use of voluntary associations as a model for understanding early Christianity.

[46] Other areas of comparison include, Luke-Acts (R. S. Ascough, "Benefaction Gone Wrong: The 'Sin' of Ananias and Sapphira in Context," in *Text and Artifact in the Religions of Mediterranean Antiquity: Essays in Honour of Peter Richardson*, ed. S. G. Wilson and M. Desjardins [ESCJ 9; Waterloo: Wilfred Laurier University Press, 2000] 91-110) and the Book of Revelation (P. Harland, "Claiming a Place"; "Honouring the Emperor or Assailing the Beast: Participation in Civic Life Among Associations [Jewish, Christian and Other] in Asia Minor and the Apocalypse of John," *JSNT* 77 [2000] 99-121), and the Pauline communities (the topic of this book).

[47] D. C. Duling, "The Matthean Brotherhood and Marginal Scribal Leadership," in *Modelling Early Christianity: Social-Scientific Studies of the New Testament in Its Context*, ed. P. F. Esler (London: Routledge, 1995) 178, 163; idem, "Social-Scientific Small Group Research and Second Testament Study," *BTB* 25 (1995) 188. See also B. J. Malina, "Early Christian Groups: Using Small Group Formation Theory to Explain Christian Organizations," in *Modelling Early Christianity: Social-Scientific Studies of the New Testament in its Context*, ed. P. F. Esler (London: Routledge, 1995) 107, 108.

[48] Duling, "Matthean Brotherhood," 159.

association" and it is within this social context that it must be understood.⁴⁹ Michael Crosby likewise thinks that the household based, non-hierarchical voluntary associations are reflected in the house church envisioned by Matthew.⁵⁰

In his recent commentary Warren Carter has also proposes the model of the voluntary association for understanding the Matthean community. Having established that the Matthean group had separated from the synagogue in Antioch, he lists a number of features that the early Christian groups shared in common with the associations and concludes that "in terms of these features, Matthew's community(ies) look(s) like a voluntary association to outsiders, and feels like one to insiders."⁵¹

All four of these works suffer a similar lacuna – the offering of concrete evidence upon which to base their claim.⁵² Only Duling and Carter offer any evidence, although most often not based on a fresh examination of the texts. Yet the thesis that the Matthean community can be understood as a voluntary association can be strengthened when one takes account of a broader database of material from the associations. I have attempted to address this lacuna in a recently published essay on "Matthew and Community Formation" in which I trace the stages of Matthean community formation.⁵³

The analogy of the voluntary associations does have its detractors, both those who engage the idea as a possibility only to reject it, and those who argue against it in detail. Here we will turn our attention specifically to the Pauline communities. Bart Ehrman is one who considers the associations, specifically with respect to the Thessalonian Christian community. In his recent introductory textbook he points to social groups in the Greco-Roman world that "met periodically for worship and socializing" and notes that "we are especially well informed about ancient trade organizations and funeral societies."⁵⁴ He even includes the text of *CIL* XIV 2112 (Lanuvium) as an illustration and claims that "the church in Thessalonica may have been

---

⁴⁹ A. J. Saldarini, *Matthew's Christian-Jewish Community* (Chicago: University of Chicago Press, 1994) 197, cf. 120.

⁵⁰ M. H. Crosby, *House of Disciples: Church, Economics, & Justice in Matthew* (Maryknoll: Orbis, 1988) 104-10, cf. 29-31.

⁵¹ W. Carter, *Matthew and the Margins: A Sociopolitical and Religious Reading* (Maryknoll: Orbis, 2000) 49.

⁵² This is consistent with the most frequent problem of the scholarly enterprise in using the associations for understanding early Christian groups: a lack of use of the primary data.

⁵³ R. S. Ascough, "Matthew and Community Formation," in *The Gospel of Matthew in Current Study: Studies in Memory of William G. Thompson, S.J*, ed. D. E. Aune (Grand Rapids and Cambridge: Eerdmans, 2001) 96-126.

⁵⁴ B. D. Ehrman, *The New Testament: A Historical Introduction to the Early Christian Writings* (New York and Oxford: Oxford University Press, 1997) 282. His reference to "funeral societies," a category under much dispute of late, also shows that he is unaware of recent studies and suggests that he is, like many, reliant upon Meeks, *First Urban Christians*.

roughly organized like one of these groups."⁵⁵ However, he seems to immediately back away from using the associations as a model by stating, "on the other hand, given its central commitment to a religious purpose, it may have had some close organizational affinities with the Jewish synagogue as well, although the synagogue may have been much larger than the Christian group."⁵⁶ Ehrman sees the "religious purpose" of the Christian groups as disqualifying them as associations, despite the fact that associations formed primarily for cultic purposes are widely attested.⁵⁷ Even more problematic is his appeal to a "large" Jewish synagogue at Thessalonica, despite the lack of any archaeological or literary evidence outside of Acts 17.⁵⁸

In his recent book on early Christian leadership, *Serve the Community of the Church*, Andrew Clarke looks to a number of ancient organizations for leadership models, particularly civic structures, households, synagogues, and voluntary associations. He shows that the associations were the locus of exercising leadership and receiving honors for those who could not otherwise participate in the more public aristocratic system of honor exchange, namely, artisans, merchants, workers, and slaves.⁵⁹ However, when it comes to the use of the associations for understanding how early Christian communities were structured Clarke backs away. He admits that "it is not unreasonable that some of the earliest Christians were formerly, or continued to be, members of associations or at least familiar with such groups. Thus the associations exerted "direct or indirect" influence on Christian community.⁶⁰ However, Clarke thinks it remains "unproven whether the early Christian communities either viewed themselves as associations, or were expressly modeled on such social and religious groups."⁶¹ Yet despite his agnosticism he hints that the "significant differences" between the associations and Christian groups disqualify them as having influence. Clarke concludes his study by arguing that although Paul's communities attempted to reflect the organizational structures of their contexts, Paul's own counter-cultural stance meant that his pattern of Christian organization was *sui generis*.⁶²

Ehrman and Clarke are representative of other scholars who entertain the use of the associations as an analogy for early Christian groups only to reject it. In many (not all) cases the cause of the rejection is not a fresh investigation of the primary data but a reiteration of the problems raised by Meeks and, to

---

⁵⁵ Ehrman, *New Testament*, 282.

⁵⁶ Ehrman, *New Testament*, 282.

⁵⁷ See Kloppenborg, "Collegia and *Thiasoi*," 18-19.

⁵⁸ See the Appendix on "Jewish Communities in Macedonia"; cf. Ascough, "Thessalonian Christian Community," 313 and idem, "Voluntary Associations and Community Formation," 176-89.

⁵⁹ Clarke, *Serve the Community*, 59-77.

⁶⁰ Clarke, *Serve the Community*, 159.

⁶¹ Clarke, *Serve the Community*, 159-60.

⁶² Clarke, *Serve the Community*, 249-51.

some extent, those raised in an article by Barton and Horsley.[63] The issues they raise go right to the issue of methodology, since claims are made that the evidence does not support, or at least does not support without more serious nuance.[64] With this in mind, it seems best to address some of the major objections directly and bring them into conversation with the data from the voluntary associations.

3. Outline of the Study

This book attempts to summarize the nature of voluntary associations in antiquity and to raise and address a number of problematic areas for using the associations to understand the formation of Christian community, particularly Pauline communities. It gives particular attention to 1 Thessalonians and Philippians as these two letters are under-utilized for an understanding Pauline community formation and they provide a fruitful comparison with the associations.

Chapter two, "Types and Functions of Voluntary Associations," provides a taxonomy of ancient associations and describes the various social and political functions that these groups played in their contexts. It then describes the process by which these groups were founded and their standing in the Roman world. The third chapter, "Membership and Its Requirements," begins by describing the social location of the membership of voluntary associations. This leads into a discussion of the important area of hierarchy and egalitarianism in both the associations and the Christian groups. This is followed with a description of the place of benefaction and honors in the associations, which is also linked to the financial life of the associations. Finally, the moral ethos and cultic activities of the associations are described.

The fourth chapter takes as its focus "Community Organization." It begins with the terminology of self-definition found in the associations and then moves to the leadership structure. Next, community regulations are examined and, in particular, conflict and conflict resolution. Again striking similarities are found with the Macedonian Christian groups, although important

---

[63] Meeks, *First Urban Christians*, 78-80; S. C. Barton and G. H. R. Horsley, "A Hellenistic Cult Group and the New Testament Churches," *JAC* 24 [1981] 27-4. In the end, the differences prove too great for Meeks, who looks to the synagogues and the philosophical schools as the best model. Barton and Horsley suggest a combination of philosophical school and voluntary association ("Hellenistic Cult Group," 40).

[64] Recently, Kloppenborg has argued that Meeks has misread the evidence and effectively takes Meeks to task on a number of these differences ("Edwin Hatch," 231-37), as does R. S. Ascough, "Local and Translocal Relationships Among Voluntary Associations and Early Christianity," *JECS* 5 (1997) 223-41. Carter (*Matthew and the Margins*, 568 n. 252) notes Meeks' objections but apparently accepts my "effective refutation" of them (presumably in Ascough, "Local and Translocal Relationships").

differences are also noted. Other community organization issues are addressed such as maintenance of allegiance, translocal links among associations around the circum-Mediterranean, and the production of epigraphic and literary texts. These latter issues are important as they are often used to disqualify the associations as a viable analogue for early Christian groups. However, we argue that the differences have been exaggerated.

Having completed the descriptive process the final chapter examines, in turn, Philippians and 1 Thessalonians to show how Paul's language and assumptions in both letters reveals an awareness of the language and practices of voluntary associations. At the same time, it identifies instances in which Paul attempts to distinguish the Christian practices in some areas. At issue is both how the members of these groups would have constituted themselves (consciously or unconsciously) within the larger framework of group formation in Greco-Roman antiquity – how these groups would have appeared to outsiders and to what other type of groups at Thessalonica and Philippi would they have been compared?[65] We suggest that the Thessalonians were most analogous to a professional voluntary association while the Philippians were most analogous to a religious association. More importantly, we make suggestions as to how such a comparison can shed exegetical light on important texts.

---

[65] What is at issue is not what Paul himself would have been most familiar with, but what the groups that he formed in the Greco-Roman urban centers would have looked like, both to those who attended and to those on the outside – with what would persons in each category have most naturally associated the Pauline churches?

Chapter Two

Types And Functions Of Associations

1. The Rise of Associations

The primary source of information for voluntary associations comes from inscriptions in which the associations' membership, decrees, and statutes were engraved upon stone and set up for reading.[1] Such inscriptions, unlike papyri, have weathered fairly well throughout the Greco-Roman Empire.[2] It is from such inscriptions that we can form a general understanding of the history of voluntary associations in antiquity. We take on this task bearing in mind the warning of Fisher that "the overall picture is one of complexity, and no little contradiction."[3]

Voluntary associations of various sorts have a long history extending back to Archaic Greece.[4] At that time a number of groups flourished inside the city-states. These included groups that defined themselves in cult terms and shared common sacrifices and meals, groups that were organized on the basis of descent groups or φῦλαι (tribes), as well as groups based on localities, occupation, or shared activities. One of the fourth century BCE laws of Solon lists a number of social groups and organizations and it legislates that their own internal regulations are considered to be binding unless they contradict the city's written laws.[5] Groups listed include

---

[1] Cf. Schmeller, *Hierarchie und Egalität*, 24.

[2] In the case of Egypt there is some evidence for associations among the papyri. This confirms what is suggested in the inscriptional record: that associations would have also used other media for their record keeping and correspondence. Unfortunately, such media have not withstood the ravishes of time.

[3] N. R. E. Fisher, "Greek Associations, Symposia, and Clubs," in *Civilization of the Ancient Mediterranean: Greece and Rome*, ed. M. Grant and R. Kitzinger (New York: Charles Scribner's Sons, 1988) 1195.

[4] Much of the following information concerning the history of clubs is found in Fisher, "Greek Associations," and idem, "Roman Associations, Dinner Parties, and Clubs" in *Civilization of the Ancient Mediterranean: Greece and Rome*, ed. M. Grant and R. Kitzinger (New York: Charles Scribner's Sons, 1988). Two other important studies of the history and nature of voluntary associations are Poland, *griechischen Vereinswesens*, and Waltzing, *corporations Professionnelles*.

[5] See *Digesta* 47.22.4 (a fragment of Gaius' commentary on the Twelve Tables).

members of village communities, phratries, hero-cults, dining clubs, cult associations, "pirates," and merchants.[6]

During the classical period political associations (ἑταιρεία) operated in Athens. These were mostly used for securing certain results at elections and in the law courts and were not regarded as harmful or illegal.[7] In the fifth century there also seems to have been an increasing number of associations with a predominantly social and religious focus as well as the formation of various mining and trading companies.[8] During the fourth century BCE there was considerable development of such companies, including the increased organization of groups of foreign merchants. "What all such groups tend to have in common is a cult basis, a shared meal (at least annually, often more frequently), an elected organizing official or two, a shrine or cult premises, often with dining room and sometimes with a plot of land that could be leased out to provide income, and some limited concern for the well-being of members."[9]

From the Hellenistic period there is a marked increase in the epigraphical evidence for social and religious associations throughout the Greek-speaking world, due in part to the increasing use of this medium for the dissemination of decrees.[10] Yet it is clear that the voluntary associations began to grow in importance. Benefactors and patrons became an important source of funds at this time. The Hellenistic period also witnessed the creation of associations focusing on mobile groups such as traders and shipowners. These united traders were persons from one area who regularly did business elsewhere.[11] In the urban areas there were many

---

[6] See Radin, *Legislation*, 36-40; cf. Fisher, "Greek Associations," 1175; See further Radin, *Legislation*, 36-51. I. Arnaoutoglou points out that, "membership in demes was compulsory and patrilinear; while membership in phratries was patrilinear but its compulsory character is still debated; membership in other cult organisations may have been patrilinear but it was not compulsory" ("Associations and Patronage in Ancient Athens," *Ancient Society* 25 [1994] 12).

[7] See Thucidides 3.82-84; 8.54; 65; W. W. Fowler, "Club." *EncBrit* 6 (1910[11]) 564.

[8] See D. G. Rice and J. E. Stambaugh, eds., *Sources for the Study of Greek Religion* (SBLSBS 14; Missoula: Scholars, 1979) 140-43; cf. *IG* II² 1237; H. J. Edwards, "Commerce and Industry," in *A Companion to Greek Studies*, ed. L. Whibley (New York and London: Hafner, 1963³) 526.

[9] Fisher, "Greek Associations," 1186.

[10] M. N. Tod, *Sidelights on Greek History: Three Lectures on the Light Thrown By Greek Inscriptions on the Life and Thought of the Ancient World* (Oxford: Blackwell, 1932) 73.

[11] For example, on Delos there is evidence (inscriptional and archaeological) for second century BCE associations of warehousemen with a large clubhouse which served religious, social, and commercial purposes (Tod, "Clubs," 255; Fisher, "Greek Associations," 1195): the koinon of the Heraclesiastai of Tyre Merchants and Shippers (see IDelos 1519; B. H. McLean, "The Place of Cult in Voluntary Associations and Christian Churches on Delos," in *Voluntary Associations in the Graeco-Roman World*,

associations based on specialized workers such as clothes manufacturers, metalworkers, food retailers, barbers. However, in the Hellenistic period there is no good evidence for the associations of traders or manufacturers acting collectively in pursuit of their joint economic interests.[12]

The literary and epigraphical evidence also reveals the importance of associations in the Roman Empire. By the early fifth century BCE associations of men based on shared occupations, common cults, and/or shared localities existed in Rome.[13] In the Middle Republic there seems to have been a steady proliferation of voluntary associations (*collegia*), although the evidence is sketchy. They would have served a variety of purposes such as occupational associations, religious groups, and social and drinking clubs. There is some evidence of disruptions caused by certain associations in Rome during the Late Republic. The senate attempted to curb the operation of these associations in 56 BCE.

Most of the evidence for the organization and activities of the various associations comes from the Imperial period. Although the various restrictions placed on the formation of private associations were occasionally enforced, voluntary associations continued to flourish throughout the Empire, particularly professional associations. In Rome itself foreign collegia were plentiful and probably originated with the foreign merchants living in Rome who wanted to engage in their native cults.[14] Each was probably begun by a group of foreign individuals who maintained contacts with their homeland.[15]

Throughout the Roman Empire there seems to have been many professional associations, including bankers, doctors, architects, producers of woolen or linen goods, dyers, fullers, launderers, tanners, cobblers,

---

ed. J. S. Kloppenborg and S. G. Wilson [London and New York: Routledge, 1996] 191) and the koinovn of the Poseidoniastai of Berytos Merchants, Shippers, and Warehousemen (see IDelos 1772-96; McLean, "Place of Cult," 196-205).

[12] Fisher, "Greek Associations," 1195.

[13] The origin of workers' associations at Rome may go back to the seventh century BCE; see P. Louis, *Ancient Rome at Work: An Economic History of Rome from the Origins to the Empire* (London and New York: Kegan Paul, Trench, Trubner and Knopf, 1927).

[14] G. La Piana, "Foreign Groups in Rome During the First Century of the Empire." *HTR* 20 (1927) 240, 246; cf. 274.

[15] See, for example, the Tyrian merchants' inscription in *CIG* 5853. Often what began as a private society of merchants eventually became a public cult. For example, a private society of Egyptian merchants was formed in Eretria during the third century BCE. It grew rapidly and flourished, and by the third century CE it had become a public cult (T. A. Brady, "The Reception of the Egyptian Cults by the Greeks (330-30 B.C.)," in *Sarapis and Isis: Collected Essays* [Chicago: Ares, 1978] 18-19). Likewise, in Piraeus Phrygian merchants formed an association dedicated to the Mother of the Gods that was later opened up to citizens (*IG* II^2 1273; W. S.Ferguson, "The Attic Orgeones," *HTR* 37 [1944] 108-09).

workers in metal, stone and clay, builders, carpenters, farmers, gardeners, fishers, bakers, pastry-cooks, barbers, embalmers, and transport workers.[16] Most of the members of these associations were independent workers or employers of small bodies of slaves or free laborers. Their primary functions were cultic and social, not economic.[17] Occupational collegia were quite unlike modern trade unions.[18] Few benefited their members economically: "there are pitifully few cases – in the East and mostly during the later empire – when associations seem to have been seditious and refused to work."[19] However, by the Late Roman Empire some professional associations were transformed from voluntary associations into state-controlled guilds and workers had a more important part to play in society.[20]

Turning our attention to the area of Macedonia we find at least seventy-five voluntary association inscriptions which date from the Hellenistic and Roman periods.[21] They range in provenance from Kalliani and Stobi in the

---

[16] For details see A. H. M. Jones, "The Economic Life of the Towns of the Roman Empire," In *La Ville: Deuxième partie: Institutions économiques et socials*, vol 2., ed. Jean Firenne (Recueils de la Société Jean Bodin 7; Brussels: editions de la Libraire Éncyclopédique, 1955) esp. 170-86. For a list of industrial guilds and associations of traders in Roman Asia Minor see T. R. S. Broughton, "Roman Asia Minor," in *An Economic Survey of Ancient Rome* vol. 5, ed. Tenny Frank (Baltimore: Johns Hopkins University Press, 1938) 841-44.

[17] Tod, "*Sidelights*, 81; idem, "Clubs," 255; G. H. Stevenson, "Clubs, Roman," *OCD* (1970²) 256.

[18] Tod, *Sidelights*, 81.

[19] Fisher, "Greek Associations," 1222. On the increase in strikes in the later empire (after Hadrian's reign) see R. MacMullen, "A Note on Roman Strikes," *CJ* 58 (1962) 269-71, and B. H. Baldwin, "Strikes in the Roman Empire," *CJ* (1964) 75-76. W. H. Buckler discusses four strikes in the Roman province of Asia, three from the second century CE and one from the fifth century CE ("Labour Disputes in the Province of Asia," in *Anatolian Studies: Presented to Sir William Mitchell Ramsay*, ed. William H. Buckler and W. M. Calder [Manchester: Manchester University Press, 1923] 27-50; cf. Broughton, "Roman Asia Minor," 847-49).

[20] Countryman, "Patrons and Officers," 136; A. Burford, *Craftsmen in Greek and Roman Society* (Aspects of Greek and Roman Life; London and Ithaca: Thames & Hudson and Cornell University Press, 1972) 149-50.

[21] There exists no complete collection of voluntary associations inscriptions from Macedonia. Thus, one of the most difficult tasks one faces in undertaking a study of Macedonian voluntary associations is locating all of the relevant inscriptions among the numerous sources. *IG* X is meant to cover inscriptions from "*Epiri, Macedoniae, Thraciae, Scythiae*." The fasciscule covering Thessalonica and vicinity appeared in 1972 under the editorship of Charles Edson. Work on part II, fasc. 2 is, according to Woodhead as late as 1981, "proceeding" (*Greek Inscriptions*, 105) but has not yet appeared (on the delays in the publication of this volume of *IG*, which was first assigned to Edson in 1936, and problems with the one fasciscule published see Al. N. Oikonomonos in the preface to the republication of IMakedD [Chicago: Ares, 1978:xii-

South and North of the western part of the province respectively, to Philippi and its surrounding villages in the eastern part of the province. Most of the inscriptions come from cities such as Thessalonica and Philippi.[22] The finds in these cities reflect the fact that in large cities of the Greco-Roman world voluntary associations can be found in abundance. However, finds of voluntary association inscriptions in smaller Macedonian villages confirm that voluntary associations are not simply an urban phenomenon. There are a number of inscriptions from smaller villages, particularly those around Philippi such as Reussilova, Proussotchani, Alistrati, Podgora, Kalambaki, Raktcha, and Selian. While the villagers may have been imitating what was begun among their urban counterparts, the number of village associations suggests that voluntary associations were an important part of village life, at least during the Roman period.

The majority of the Macedonian inscriptions date to the common era, with most datable inscriptions coming from the second and third centuries CE (about the same time as we begin to find evidence for a Jewish presence in Macedonia). However, there are three dedications to Zeus Hypsistos dating from the second century BCE and a number from the first and early second century CE. Unfortunately many of the inscriptions cannot be accurately dated, but almost all of them certainly come from the Roman period (common era). Nevertheless, they can be helpful for understanding the nature of voluntary associations in Macedonia during the first century CE. Indeed, the diversity of the material suggests that associations of various types were common in Macedonia in all periods, as they were elsewhere throughout the Greco-Roman empire.[23] For this reason, we are confident in using them analogously for understanding Pauline community formation.

---

xiv]). Other collections from various locales in Macedonia are starting to appear. P. Pilhofer's recently published collection of inscriptions from Philippi is an invaluable resource for that city (*Philippi*. Band II. *Katalog der Inschriften von Philippi* (WUNT 119; Tübingen: Mohr Siebeck, 2000]). At a conference in 1987 P. Ducrey announced that a separate collection of inscriptions from Philippi is underway (see *BE* 1992:486 no. 324; Pilhofer, *erste christliche Gemeinde*, vii) but to my knowledge has not been published.

[22] This probably tells us more about archaeological excavations in Macedonia than about the distribution of voluntary associations. Thessalonica and Philippi have undergone significant archaeological exploration primarily, but not exclusively, due to their connection with the New Testament and early Christian history. Other Macedonian cities with a number of important texts include Edessa, Beroea, Kassandreia, and Amphipolis.

[23] The widespread dispersion of our texts should come as no surprise. The provenance and date of any local collection of association inscriptions will show that Macedonia is typical. This is the case with the large database (over 1000 inscriptions) compiled for a separate project by members of the Toronto Hellenistic Texts Seminar under the direction of J. S. Kloppenborg.

A number of different types of association inscriptions are found in Macedonia. Some inscriptions are honorific, bestowing honors on a founder (*IG* X/2 58), a member (Pilhofer 209), a patron (*IG* X/2 192, 220, IMakedD 1104, *SIRIS* 124), a civic benefactor (*SIRIS* 122; Pilhofer 697/2, 350), or even the Emperor (IAcanthus 1). Such honorary inscriptions usually follow an act of benefaction to the association. A good number of inscriptions are dedications or votives to a deity. A few are simply membership lists (*IG* X/2 244, Pilhofer 091), one with an account of dues given (*CIL* III 633). An interesting inscription from Thessalonica records the founding of an association of Sarapis and Isis in the Achean town of Opus (*IG* X/2 255).

Other inscriptions are dedications or votives given in thanksgiving for benefits bestowed. While most of the benefits in these inscriptions are unspecified, *IG* X/2 67 presents an interesting example of a votive set up after the dedicator has, as the result of a dream, avoided placing himself in a situation at sea that would have proved perilous. In contrast, IThessalonica 1 is a memorial to a less fortunate fellow who perished at sea.

2. Taxonomy

Various terms were used for voluntary associations in antiquity, originally with differing meanings, although these nuances began to fade over time.[24] Ὀργεῶνες was usually used in the plural of a group of sacrificing associates (from the fifth century BCE).[25] θίασος (plural θίασοι) was used of national / ethnic clubs which were originally formed to worship Dionysos, although the term came to be used more broadly for many types of associations. Ἔρανος (plural ἐρανισταί) was used of banquet/social clubs in the third century BCE to the second century CE. Roman associations were generally termed *collegia*. Other Greek terms used for associations or their members include ἔφηβοι, νέοι, (or νεώτεροι), ἐκκλησία, συναγωγή, σύνοδος, and κοινόν. Latin terms include *sodalitas*, *factio*, *curia*, and *fratres*. Due to this range of terms, and compounded by the type of evidence available, it is difficult to distinguish clearly the various types of associations on the basis of nomenclature alone.[26]

---

[24] See F. W. Danker, "Associations, Clubs, Thiasoi," *ABD* 1 (1992) 501; cf. Tod, *Sidelights*, 74-75.

[25] Ferguson points out that there is no corporate noun which corresponds to this word (such as θιασῶται to θίασος "Attic Orgeones," 61). The orgeones are not designated in ancient literature as a cult association but simply as participants in a cult (M. P. Nilsson, *Cults, Myths, Oracles, and Politics in Ancient Greece* [Lund: Gleerup, 1951] 160). They were devoted to the worship of deities and local heroes.

[26] Kloppenborg, "Collegia and *Thiasoi*," 18.

Using an analysis of function, three broad categories of associations are usually distinguished by modern commentators. The first is burial or funerary associations, or *collegia tenuiorum / funeraticia*, which are described as being organized to insure the proper burial of their deceased members. In exchange, members paid entrance fees and/or regular dues that would be pooled for the burials. However, Kloppenborg has cogently argued that associations formed solely for the burial of members did not exist until the second century CE (from the time of Hadrian and beyond).[27] In fact, even at that time they were a "legal fiction," a way of gaining legal recognition to meet as a group while another purpose (usually social) was the primary interest of the group. Nevertheless, many associations did undertake the proper burial of their members as one of the benefits of membership.[28] Another significant aspect of the connection between associations and funerary practices is found in a number of associations that were founded or endowed by a patron for the purpose of commemorating the anniversary of his or her death at the family tomb.

The elimination of the category of funerary associations leaves two types of associations: religious and professional. Religious associations had as their primary focus the worship of a particular deity or deities though cultic acts and special festival days. Such associations might also include a public procession. Some associations performed public functions in connection with worship, usually in public temples, while others were private associations that gathered most often in private shrines or homes.[29] These associations also had a significant social aspect to them. Most of the associations attested in Macedonia seem to be founded as religious associations. The following deities are attested in the inscriptions: Zeus Hypsistos, Theos Hypsistos; Dionysos (including once as Zeus Dionysos); Liber and Libera, Sylvanus, Herakles, Hero god, Sarapis, Isis, (in both occurances she is named with Sarapis), Anubis (once as Hermes-Anubis), Asclepius (as indicated by Asklepiastoi), Aphrodite, Diana, Nemesis, Cupid, Souregethes, Gods of Samothrace, the Emperor, and Cybele and Attis.[30]

---

[27] Kloppenborg, "Collegia and *Thiasoi*," 20-22. Cf. Ziebarth (*griechische Vereinswesen*, 17) and Poland (*griechischen Vereinswesens*, 56, 503-04) both point out the lack of evidence for the existence of associations devoted exclusively to the burial of members among the Greek associations; so also P. M. Fraser, *Rhodian Funerary Monuments* (Oxford: Clarendon Press, 1977) 58-70; see Kloppenborg, "Collegia and *Thiasoi*," 22 and 29 nn. 41 and 42.

[28] Kloppenborg, "Collegia and *Thiasoi*," 21.

[29] Roberts, Skeat, and Nock, "Zeus Hypsistos," 75.

[30] An inscription of a religious society devoted to Cybele and Attis was found in Philippi but is now, unfortunately, no longer legible (P. Collart, *Philippes, ville de Macédonia, dupuis ses origines jusqu'à la fin de la l'époque romaine* [Thèse; Université de Genève 85; Paris: Boccard, 1937] 455-56). The existence of an epitaph *dendrophorus*

There is considerable early evidence for the existence of voluntary associations formed on the basis of common occupation and formed by traders or specialized workers in both the Hellenistic and the Roman periods.[31] Large associations of foreign merchants and artisans were formed in almost all of the cities of the empire, and especially so in the larger commercial centers (e.g., Rome, Corinth, Ephesus). Since most artisans would live and work in one particular area of a city, it would be easy for them to form themselves into associations.

Among the professional associations from antiquity we have evidence of associations of Dionysiac artists, Roman veterans, hunters, gladiators, and athletes.[32] However, of more significance for our study are the professional associations of the artisans. A number of professional associations are evident in the inscriptional record from Macedonia. An association of purple-dyers is found at both Thessalonica (*IG* X/2 291) and perhaps Philippi (Pilhofer 697/1).[33] There is evidence for an association of yoke-makers at Thessalonica (IThessalonica 2).[34] Inscriptions of

---

Augustalis suggests that one association was at the same time dedicated to both Cybele and the imperial cult (Collart, *Philippes*, 270; cf. 456).

[31] See respectively Fisher, "Greek Associations," 1195 and Jones, "Economic Life," esp. 170-86.

[32] See Tod, "Clubs," 255; A. W. Pickard-Cambridge, *The Dramatic Festivals of Athens* (revised by J. Gould and D. M. Lewis; Oxford: Clarendon, 1968²) 281-85; M. Ginsburg, "Roman Military Clubs and Their Social Functions," *TAPA* (1940) 150-56; F. Chapouthier, "Némésis et Niké," *BCH* (1924) 300-01; Collart, *Philippes*, 381, 385-86; C. A. Forbes, "Ancient Athletic Guilds," *CP* 50 (1955) 238-39; H. W. Plecket, "Some Aspects of the History of the Athletic Guilds," *ZPE* 10 (1973) 197-227.

[33] The authenticity of Pilhofer 697/1 has been called into question. The inscription was found on a slab of white marble by Stauros Mertzides in 1872 in a miltary post which he claims was subsequently destroyed. The trustworthiness of this inscription has been questioned by L. Robert ("Hellenica V, Inscriptions de Philippes publiées par Mertzidès," *RPh* 13 [1939] 142, who points out that Mertzides is known to have fabricated evidence) but affirmed by P. Lemerle (*Philippes et la Macédoine orientale à l'epoque chrétienne et byzantine* [BEFAR 158; Paris: Boccard, 1945] 28-29), and Pilhofer (*erste christliche Gemeinde*, 179-82). The latter thinks that it must be authentic as a bold falsifier such as Mertzides was would have included the name of Lydia or even Paul had he invented the inscription. Pilhofer suggests that a note about seeing an inscription with the word ΘΥΑΤΕΙΡ(ΩΝ) suggests that this inscription was seen independently by G. Lampakes (*erste christliche Gemeinde*, 180-81). The existence of the association of purple-dyers at Philippi is thought by some scholars to be confirmed by the fragmentary Latin inscription reading [PU]RPURAI (*CIL* III 664). On purple-dyers in Macedonia see *CIG* 3496 (Thyatira) in which a guild of purple-dyers honors a Macedonian who acted as a benefactor towards their city. Also, Acts 16:11-15 which names Lydia the purple dealer as the the first Christian convert in Europe: she is a Thyatiran living and working in Philippi.

[34] An association (*fabri*) of carpenters is attested at Dyrrachium, which is the city at the beginning point of the Via Egnatia on the shore of the Adriatic Sea (*CIL* III 611).

associations of donkey-drivers were found at Beroea (IBeroea 2), copper smiths at Amphipolis (*Syll.*³ 1140), and silversmiths at Kalambaki (IKalambaki 1).³⁵ We have evidence for an association of merchants at Acanthus (IAcanthus 1). Other evidence for Roman merchants in Macedonia comes from Beroea, where οἱ ἐνκεκτημένοι Ῥωμαῖοι honor the proconsul Calpernius Piso (cf. IMakedD 58), and Edessa (ἡ πόλις καὶ οἱ συνπραγματευόμενοι Ῥωμαῖοι, IMakedD 3).³⁶ Associations of merchants (Asiani) are attested at Thessalonica (IThessalonica 3; *IG* X/2 309; 480).

Like the religious associations, members of a professional association would have been involved in the worship of a patron deity or deities. ³⁷ However, owing to the occasional nature of inscriptions, "one does not expect to find a description of the day to day religious life and belief of trade guilds."³⁸ For the most part, a professional association would usually take as their patron deity a god associated with the resources, tools, or products of their trade. Thus, we find an association of gardeners who erected a monument to Demeter, the goddess of the earth (*CIG* 2082; Pessionos [Phrygia];) and woodcutter's guilds dedicated to Sylvanus (*CIL* VI 642) or the Great Mother (*CIL* VI 641).³⁹ Other professional associations simply took on the name of the patron deity; e.g., "the *koinon* of the Beirut Poseidoniast wholesale merchants, shippers and receivers"

Although this area was ocasionally included within the provincial boundaries of Roman Macedonia, it is not generally considered to be part of the province.

³⁵ By the Byzantine period many of the streets of Thessalonica were designated by the particular trade which was undertaken in that area, a practice carried out in many Roman cities; see J. S. Kloppenborg, "ΦΙΛΑΔΕΛΦΙΑ, ΘΕΟΔΙΔΑΚΤΟΣ and the Dioscuri: Rhetorical Engagement in 1 Thessalonians 4.9-12," *NTS* 39 (1993) 274-75 and n. 35, cf. O. Tafrali, *Topographie de Thessalonique* (Paris: Geuthner, 1913) 148.

³⁶ See also Caesar, *BC* 3.103; Cicero, *In Pis.* 40.96. For a discussion of Roman merchants see J. M. R. Cormack, "L. Calpurnius Piso," *AJA* 48 (1944) 76-77; M. B. Hatzopoulos and L. D. Loukopoulou, *Recherches sur les marches orientales des temenides (Anthemonte-Kalindoia)* i (Meletemata 11; Athens: De Boccard, 1992) 51-52 no. A6; F. Papazoglou, "Quelques aspects de l'histoire de la province de Macédoine," *ANRW* II.7.1 (1979) 356-57; idem, "Macedonia Under the Romans," in *Macedonia: 4000 Years of Greek History and Civilization*, ed. M. B. Sakellariou (Athens: Ekdotike Athenon S.A, 1988) 196 and 539, nn. 23 and 24.

³⁷ Poland, *griechischen Vereinswesens*, 5-6; Duff, *Personality*, 102; Daube, "Review," 91; Kloppenborg, "Collegia and *Thiasoi*," 18.

³⁸ B. H. McLean, "Trade Guilds of Lydia and Phrygia," unpublished essay of 1995, prepared for *Cultic Groups, Guilds, and Collegia: Associations in the Ancient World*, ed. J. S. Kloppenborg and B. H. McLean, 19.

³⁹ Cf. *Syll.*³ 1140 from Amphipolis in which a member of the guild of copper workers makes a dedication to the Great Gods in Samothrace.

(IDelos 1520; 1774; 1778) or the guild of dockyard porters in Smyrna, known as Asklepiastai (ISmyrna 713).[40]

3. Functions

Although the two broad, general categories of "religious" and "professional" associations are helpful,[41] there was much crossing over and many associations functioned in a number of different ways. One of the primary functions of all associations was social.[42] Most met together for common meals, either on an entirely social basis, in connection with sacrifices to the god(s), or commemorating a deceased member or patron. Due to their social focus many associations were repudiated often for their indulgence in food and drink. Philo states of the associations that "you could find no sound elements but only liquor, tippling, drunkenness and the outrageous conduct they lead to" (*Flacc*. 136).[43] For example, an association at Lanuvium formed under the guise of the burial of members in 136 CE seems to have feasts and banquets as their overriding concern (*CIL* XIV 2112). Of the fifteen by-laws of the *collegium* only four concern burial while six concern banquets and festivals, with two others legislating when members have to donate an amphora of good wine.[44]

---

[40] See further Kloppenborg, "Collegia and *Thiasoi*," 18 and McLean, "Trade Guilds," 19.

[41] Kloppenborg adds a third type of association, the domestic *collegia* ("Collegia and *Thiasoi*," 23). However, since for the most part these were not formed simply as being part of the household but had as their focus the worship of a particular deity (although they also served some social functions) I would include them in the category of religious associations.

[42] Religious activity was part of every association, as it was of every aspect of Greek life; S. G. Cole, "Greek Cults," in *Civilization of the Ancient Mediterranean: Greece and Rome*, ed. M. Grant and R. Kitzinger (New York: Charles Scribner's Sons, 1988) 887; B. J. Malina, *Christian Origins and Cultural Anthropology: Practical Models for Biblical Interpretation* (Atlanta: John Knox, 1986) 97.

[43] See also Philo, *Legat*. 10.311-12; *Flacc*. 4; T. Seland, "Philo and the Clubs and Associations of Alexandria," in *Voluntary Associations in the Graeco-Roman World*, ed. J. S. Kloppenborg and S. G. Wilson, (London and New York: Routledge, 1996) 110-27.

[44] Cf. Kloppenborg, "Collegia and *Thiasoi*," 22. Other associations whose attention is given to banqueting include *CIL* VI 10234; *IG* II^2 1368; *Syll*.^{3} 1024; *P.Mich.Tebt*. 243; 244; *P.Lond*. 2710, in which participants are forbidden to "bring the drinking to naught"; *IG* XI/4 1299, in which a dining hall was constructed within a temple "for the feast to which the god invites us" (line 65). Further on banquets in associations see D. E. Smith, "Meals and Morality in Paul and His World," in *SBL 1981 Seminar Papers*, ed. K. H. Richards (SBLASP 20; Chico: Scholars Press, 1981) 323-24; Klinghardt, *Gemeinschaftsmahl und Mahlgemeinschaft*, 21-173; H.-J. Klauck, *Herrenmahl und*

Membership in an association gave a person a sense of belonging in an age where many were dislodged from the traditional security of family, friends, and homeland (primarily through either military service or trade).[45] Life could be more enjoyable through membership in an association as many associations provided a network of social support within the larger society. Some groups even contributed funds to members who fell on hard times.[46] However, there is little evidence of associations contributing to the needs of the poor who were not members.[47] Participation in an association allowed for the attainment of honor, prestige and authority through the replication of the organizational structure of the *polis*. A person could thus reach a status "to which he or she could never aspire outside of the association."[48]

Often membership offered the benefit of the guarantee of a decent burial with the possibility of the annual commemoration of one's death.[49] A good number of associations were involved in the burial of their members, which included the setting up of inscriptions in memory of their deceased. This is the case with the professional associations of donkey-drivers from Beroea (IBeroea 2), the associates of Poseidonios (set up in conjunction with the deceased's wife and son; IBeroea 3), and purple-dyers in Thessalonica (*IG* X/2 291). It is also the case with other associations such as the Thessalonian worshippers of Dionysos (*IG* X/2 503) and of Herakles (*IG* X/2 288 and 289), the Asiani (IThessalonica 1, *IG* X/2 309 and 480), and a Hero cult (*IG* X/2 821). A more elaborate funerary practice is described in the tomb epigram from Amphipolis (IAmphipolis 1) where the dances of the Bacchants are detailed. Some associations may have been involved in the actual burial of these members, as is the case with *SEG* XXXVII 559 (Kassandreia) and *CIG* 2000f (Hagios Mamas).

A significant number of association inscriptions indicate funerary practices of some sort, particularly memorials for the deceased. Often an already existing association is endowed with a bequest of money or property (e.g., vineyards or land), the income of which is to be used for a memorial at the tomb of the deceased. The remainder of the income, however, goes to the association for their own use, probably in social gatherings like banquets (see *IG* X/2 259). Occasionally an association is formed in order to keep an annual memorial for the deceased, as is the case with *CIL* III 656.

---

hellenistischer Kult: Eine religionsgeschichtliche Untersuchung zum ersten Korintherbrief (NTAbh 15; Münster: Aschendorff, 1982) 68-76.

[45] Kloppenborg, "Collegia and *Thiasoi*," 17-18.
[46] Cf. Renan, *Apostles*, 281.
[47] Danker, "Associations," 502.
[48] Kloppenborg, "Collegia and *Thiasoi*," 18.
[49] Cf. Renan, *Apostles*, 285-86.

Many of the Macedonian association inscriptions with funerary contexts indicate that the association was involved in a festival known as the *rosalia*:[50] from Philippi and its surrounding area we have *CIL* III 703, 704, 707; IMakedD 920; Pilhofer 133, 029/1. Many *viciani* (associations formed of members of a particular village) participated in the celebration of the *rosalia* or *parentalia*[51] at the tomb of the deceased.[52] The *rosalia* is also mentioned in a Thessalonian inscription; in *IG* X/2 260 a priestess of a θίασος bequeaths two plethra of grapevines to insure that festivities involving rose crowns are conducted.[53]

In Italy the rose played a significant role in the funeral cult – the Italians called their feasts of the dead the *rosalia*, or "day of roses."[54] The *rosalia* had two aspects to it: one was the commemoration of the deceased, the other was the joyous celebrations of the return of spring and summer with an emphasis on banqueting and fun.[55] Since there is little evidence that the connection between roses and funerary practices was indigenous to Macedonia or Thrace before the coming of the Romans, it is probable that when the Italian colonists came to Macedonia they brought many of their own practices and beliefs with them, including the *rosalia*. Since

---

[50] On the *rosalia* see P. Perdrizet, "Inscriptions de Philippes: Les Rosalies," *BCH* 24 (1900) 299-333; Poland, *griechischen Vereinswesens*, 511-13; Collart, *Philippes*, 474-85; A. S. Hoey, "Rosaliae Signorum," *HTR* 30 (1937) 22-30; Ch. Picard and Ch. Avezou, "Le testament de la prêtresse Thessalonicienne," *BCH* 38 (1914) 53-62. The festival was popular throughout the Roman empire. Poland notes that the evidence for associations involved with the rosalia comes primarily from Bithynia in Asia Minor and around Thessalonica and Philippi "in Thrace" (*sic*; see *griechischen Vereinswesens*, 511).

[51] The *parentalia* occurred for nine days in February (13-21). Temples were closed and marriages did not take place. The days were taken up with private celebrations for the family dead. The final day was a public ceremony called the *Feralia* in which a household made offerings at the graves of its deceased members (see further H. J. Rose, "Feralia," *OCD* [1970²] 434; idem, "Parentalia," *OCD* [1970²] 781). The *parentalia* is found in *CIL* III 656 from Selian; see also Collart, *Philippes*, 474-75 n. 3 no. 7.

[52] Collart, *Philippes*, 479-80.

[53] Perdrizet ("Inscriptions," 323) points to a large sarcophagus from Thessalonica (now in the Louvre) on the lid of which a man and wife are shown in repose. The wife holds in her hand a crown of roses. See further bibliography in Perdrizet, "Inscriptions," 323 nn. 1 and 2.

[54] The roses symbolized the return of "la belle saison" when the earth seems to burst into life.

[55] Hoey, "Rosaliae," 22.

Macedonia was famous for its roses[56] it is no surprise that the *rosalia* was imported by the Italian settlers.[57]

The *rosalia* took place at the end of the spring (May), when roses were in bloom. The particular day seems to have been the choice of the family or of the association.[58] On the chosen day each family, sometimes accompanied by members of an association, visited tombs of their dead, decorating it with roses.[59] They participated in a solemn banquet, and perhaps offered a burnt sacrifice.[60] Rose crowns were sometimes worn as part of the ceremonies.[61] A bowl was filled with wine in front of the grave and the grave itself was crowned.[62]

The festival of the *rosalia* was often celebrated by members of a voluntary association.[63] However, it was not always the case that the one for whom the *rosalia* was held was a member of the association involved. In fact, a number of Macedonian inscriptions suggest that the deceased was

---

[56] Ch. Edson, "Cults of Thessalonica (Macedonica III)," *HTR* 41 (1948) 169; Picard and Avezou, "testament de la prêtresse," 53-54. On the making of rose crowns in Macedonia see Theophrastus, *de Causis Plant.* 1.13.11 (Dion), *Hist. Plant.* 6.6.4 (the region around Philippi), and Herodotus 8.138.1 (below the eastern slopes of the Bermion range); see McLean, "Trade Guilds," 12 n. 100.

[57] However, it is interesting to note that although the Italian *rosalia* is celebrated, the Thracian Horseman often decorates the tombstones in Macedonian villages (Perdrizet, "Inscriptions," 320), obviously suggesting synchronistic funerary practices (see Pilhofer 029/1, IMakedD 920, and *CIL* III 704).

[58] Perdrizet, "Inscriptions," 300.

[59] In adorning the tomb of the deceased the Macedonians probably did not simply use roses but rather they used all kinds of flowers, particularly those in season (Perdrizet, "Inscriptions," 299). The rose itself symbolized for the Greeks a life too early finished, that is, those who die before their time (Perdrizet, "Inscriptions," 299). This can be seen in the epitaph of Soudios Paibilas, who predeceased his mother (Pilhofer 029/1).

[60] P. R. Trebilco, *Jewish Communities in Asia Minor* (SNTSMS 69; Cambridge and New York: Cambridge University Press, 1991) 80; Papazoglou, "Macedonia," 206. The roses themselves were probably not burnt in the sacrifices. H. C. Youtie ("A Note on Edson's Macedonica III," *HTR* 42 [1949] 277-78) notes that the theory of burning roses in the *rosalia* originated from a grammatical misunderstanding on the part of Picard and Avezou ("testament de la prêtresse," 38-62) which was corrected by Collart, *Philippes*, 474-85. The theory was again put forth by Edson ("Cults of Thessalonica," 169) but is corrected by Youtie.

[61] When a member of a Greek association died, his colleagues often funded the making of a crown. However, the inscriptions never stipulate that this crown must be made of roses (Perdrizet, "Inscriptions," 300).

[62] Edson, "Cults of Thessalonica," 175.

[63] Cf. Trebilco (*Jewish Communities*, 80) who mentions only the involvement of professional associations and suggests that these had constituted themselves as funerary associations.

not a necessarily a member of the association involved in the *rosalia*.[64] In order to pay for the festival the deceased left an association a plot of land, a vineyard, or a bequest of money to be invested. The revenues from a bequest provided the necessary funds for the *rosalia* to be carried out.[65] It was in the interest of the association to accept the bequest as they were able to fund not only the celebration at the deceased's tomb, but presumably the unused portions of the interest from the endowment went to the further social practices of the association (cf. *IG* X/2 260). To ensure that the wishes were carried out after the testator's death the bequest was made public through an inscription. Further insurance was sometimes provided by designating alternative recipients of the bequest, in whose interest it would be to watch the original association carefully to see whether they carried out the required activities (as is the case in *IG* X/2 260 and Pilhofer 133).

4. Founders and Foundations

There is evidence for a number of methods of forming and propagating voluntary associations in antiquity. Here we will simply highlight a few of the procedures whereby an association was formed, procedures which were subsequently referred to in inscriptions. These procedures incorporate actions that were taken by individuals (including testamentary foundations), groups of professionals, and the gods (dreams and visions, oracles). It should be noted from the start, however, that in many cases we simply do not know how an association was formed and propagated, and there may have been many other methods than those discussed below. However, these are representative of what we do know occurred among assocations in antiquity.

a) Private Associations

Private voluntary associations could be formed by an individual for a number of purposes, although the primary reasons seem to have been

---

[64] *CIL* III 703, 704, 707; Pilhofer 133, 029/1. In some of the Macedonian cases the testator may have been a member; these inscriptions leave his membership unclear. McLean reaches a similar conclusion in his study of guild inscriptions from Lydia and Phrygia, where in all but one of the cases where a guild is involved in commemorative rites there is no indication that the deceased was a member of the guild ("Trade Guilds," 13).

[65] Trebilco, *Jewish Communities*, 80.

performance of cultic rites and gathering for social interchange.⁶⁶ That individuals could form voluntary associations is clear from very early on, as is indicated in the law of Solon (c. 450 BCE):

If the people, or brothers, or those who are associated together for the purpose of sacrifice, or sailors, or those who are buried in the same tomb, or members of the same society who generally live together, should have entered, or do enter into any contract with one another, whatever they agree upon shall stand, if the public laws do not forbid it.⁶⁷

Often the association was named after the founder.⁶⁸ For example, a fragment from a second century BCE inscription from Kyme suggests that the members have named the association after the founder: "this stele belonging to the members of the association of Menekleides is sacred to Dionysos" (IKyme 30, lines 4-6).⁶⁹

Private associations took on many forms at their foundational stage. *IG* II² 1369 (II CE) suggests that the common bond among members of an association at Athens was friendship: "male friends convened an association (κοινόν) by common council and established an ordinance of friendship."⁷⁰ Similarly, *IG* II² 1275 records a law (νόμος) which, when ratified, will bind the members of the association to act to right wrongs done to fellow members and their "friends," to provide burial for deceased members and to attend the burial, and to notifiy relatives and "friends"

---

⁶⁶ Ziebarth, *griechische Vereinswesen*, 140; Poland, *griechischen Vereinswesens*, 271; Liebenam, *Geschichte und Organization*, 169; Waltzing, *corporations Professionnelles*, I.337.

⁶⁷ Solon, cited by Gaius [*Institutes* 4] and recorded in *Digest* 47.22.4.

⁶⁸ San Nicolò, *Ägyptisches Vereinswesen*, 2.7. Cf. Ausbüttel, *Untersuchungen*, 20; 31. That private persons founded associations is attested to in the Twelve Tables 12 (Daube, "Review," 91). Examples of groups named after founders might include the Epicureans (see N. W. de Witt, "Organization and Proceedure in Epicurean Groups," *CP* 31 [1936] 205), Pythagoreans, and the Christians (Cristianovi cf. Acts 11:26; 26:28; 1 Pet 4:16). A group's name might also be taken from the basis of their common association (i.e., Aigyptoioi, Salaminioi, Molpoi, Porphyrobaphon; R. L. Wilken, *The Christians as the Romans Saw Them* [New Haven and London: Yale University Press, 1984] 34-35, 44) or from their patronal deity (Dionysiastai, Herakleistai). For a more complete list of guild names which indicate religious activities or divinites see Poland, *griechischen Vereinswesens*, 33-46; 57-62. M. Weinfeld suggests that the "Teacher of Righteousness" was considered founder of the Qumran community, according to the Damascas Scroll (CD 1:9; *The Organizational Pattern and the Penal Code of the Qumran Sect: A Comparison With Guilds and Religious Associations of the Hellenistic Period* [NovT et orbis antiquus 2; Göttingen: Vandenhoeck & Ruprecht, 1986] 45).

⁶⁹ Text and translation in Horsley, *New Documents* 1, 21; see also *IG* XII/1 127.60; *IG* XII/3 1098.

⁷⁰ For "friends" as members of an association see also *SEG* XXIX 1188 and *SEG* XXIX 1195. See also *DÖAW* 80 (1962) 59; *ZPE* 44 (1981) 89 no. 19.

about the death. It is possible that this inscription began with an enactment formula like that found in *IG* II² 1369. This enactment then becomes the "law of the subscribers" and thus the foundational document for the association.

Friendship played an important role in Greco-Roman antiquity. The bond of friendship between males was, in many ways, stronger than that between husband and wife. While marital relations were sometimes political and often for procreative purposes, friends were those with whom one could grow and develop physically, mentally, and spiritually. Foundational for friendship was the exchange of services and often friends helped one another in times of financial need. A widely known and oft quoted slogan in Greek literature is "Among friends, everything is common" (τοῖς φιλοῖς πάντα κοινά or κοινά τὰ φίλων).[71] For the most part, this "community of goods" was not a legal arrangement, but a knowledge that affection for one's friends would move an individual to put their goods at their friends' disposal when the need arose. This relationship was temporary and served a different purpose than the patron-client relationship common in the Roman world.[72] These inscriptions suggest the strong bond of friendship in a more formal fashion by reflecting friendship as the basis for establishing an association.[73]

Small family associations could be the foundational basis of a cult. For example, the cult of Sarapis on Delos was founded as a small family association formed by an Egyptian priest who moved to Delos. An inscription commemorating the founding and growth of the cult reads, in part,

> Our grandfather Apollonios, an Egyptian of the sacerdotal class, having brought with him his god from Egypt continued to do service (for his god) .... My father Demetrios succeeded him next in succession and likewise did service for the gods .... After (Demetrios), I inherited the

---

[71] For example, Plato, *Resp.* 4.424a; 5.449c; Aristotle, *Eh. Nic.* 11.52 1168b; Diogenes Laertius, "Epicurus" 10.11; Philo, *Abr.* 235; *Vit. Mos.* 1.28.156; Cicero, *De Officiis* 1.16.51; cf. *Epistle of Barnabas* 19.8.

[72] On friendship in antiquity see further P. Garnsey and R. Saller, *The Roman Empire: Economy, Society and Culture* (London: Duckworth, 1987) 154-56.

[73] It is interesting to note that Luke's presentation of the foundational stage of the early Christian community at Jerusalem is couched in the language of friendship. The believers are said to hold "all things in common" (ἅπαντα κοινα;, Acts 2:44) which would bring to mind for the Greco-Roman reader the hellenistic *topos* of friendship; see J. Dupont, *The Salvation of the Gentiles: Studies in the Acts of the Apostles* (New York: Paulist, 1979) 91-95; L. T. Johnson, *The Literary Function of Possessions in Luke-Acts* (SBLDS 39; Missoula: Scholars Press, 1977) 187. This is also true for Luke's comment that the believers "were of one heart and soul" (ἦν καρδία καὶ ψυχή μία, Acts 4:32). See further Dupont, *Salvation*, 96-100.

sacred images and was appointed (to perform) diligently the divine services. (*IG* XI/4 1299, lines 2-12;166 BCE)
The inscription goes on to indicate that the god revealed to the writer that rented rooms were not adequate for worship and that a temple should be built (see below on dreams). After much legal negotiating[74] and with the assurance of the god, the family cult is able to secure its land and build its temple. The cult of Sarapis eventually grew to be one of the largest cult groups on Delos in antiquity.

Local private associations could also be formed from a larger, more established group. *IG* X/2 255 records the founding of an cult association of Sarapis and Isis. The cult is brought to Opus (in Eastern Locris) from Thessalonica as the result of a divine epiphany (see below). It is begun in the home of Sosinikē, who functions as the head or "high-priestess." The passing on of the priestly duties to Eunosta demonstrates that women had an important role to play in the cult of Sarapis and Isis well before the first century CE.[75] Sokolowski argues that the gods were first accepted as the family cult of Sosinikē and sometime later outsiders were invited to join (lines 18-19, 21-22).[76] However, Eurynomos is the one instructed to establish the cult and he does not seem to be related to Sosinikē at whose house the rites take place.[77] This suggests that the cult had a wider (although perhaps not larger) group of adherents in Opus from the beginning.

A private association could be formed within a larger public association in the same city. In *IG* X/2 58 (early II CE) Aulus Papius Chilon is honored for "establishing" the *oikos* of the association of "hieraphoroi table-companions (οἱ ἱεραφόροι συνκλίται)" in Thessalonica. The *oikos* was probably a small building in which the society could meet, presumably for their banquets. The title οἱ ἱεραφόροι συνκλίται indicates that these are individuals who have participated in the mysteries of the Isis cult in some special way and who have some formal duty involving the sacred cult

---

[74] For details see Brady, "Reception," 18.

[75] See also S. Dow, "The Egyptian Cults in Athens," *HTR* 30 (1937) 193-96; D. Fraikin, "Introduction of Sarapis and Isis in Opus." *Numina Aegaea* 1 (1974) 8. S. K. Heyob only allows for a women taking on the role of priestess from the first century CE (*The Cult of Isis Among Women in the Graeco-Roman World* [EPRO 51; Leiden: Brill, 1975] 58, 90). Cf. *IG* V/2 265 (Arcadia) "furthermore she (the priestess) received the goddess (Kore) in her own house as is the custom for those who successively become priests" (lines 21-23, text and translation in Ferguson, "Attic Orgeones," 90).

[76] F. Sokolowski, "Propagation of the Cult of Sarapis and Isis in Greece," *GRBS* 15 (1974) 444.

[77] She is certainly not his wife or sister as it is in her house, not his, that the cult is established and there is no indication that she is related to either Eurynomos or Xenainetos (cf. line 6). Eunosta is the (grand) daughter of Sosibas; the family relationship to Eurynomos and/or Sosinikē is left unclear.

objects.[78] This association was a private one created for social purposes, formed from members of the larger established cult. According to Edson, "the hieraphoroi were a well defined group of functionaries associated with the municipal cult of the Egyptian gods at Thessalonica who chose to form themselves also into a private association, as the hieraphoroi synklitai, for purposes of social intercourse under the tutelage of the god Anubis."[79] It is probable that the provision of the *oikos* coincided with the founding of the smaller association.[80]

b) Testamentary Associations

In antiquity an endowment could be made in order to secure that certain rites be performed in memory of an individual and his or her family.[81] There were two primary types of "foundations": private and public.[82] The latter foundations established a link between the civic magistrates and the deceased. In exchange for a significant bequest a perpetual memorial was established, with attendant priests and sacrifices. Of more interest for our purposes is the private or "familial" foundation whereby an association is formed (or and existing one endowed) in order to establish a memorial at the family tomb.[83]

---

[78] See Edson, "Cults of Thessalonica," 185.

[79] Edson, "Cults of Thessalonica," 186.

[80] Cf. Ziebarth, *griechische Vereinswesen*, 140, and Poland, *griechischen Vereinswesens*, 273-75, who note that a member of an existing association could also form a new association.

[81] For a comprehensive collection of such texts see Laum, *Stiftungen* (cf. A. Mannzmann, *Griechische Stiftungsurkunden: Studie zu Inhalt und Rechtsform* [Fonts et Commentationes 2; Münster: Aschendorff, 1962] 136-47). Laum's collection was given somewhat guarded praise by W. S. Ferguson, but he summarizes Laum's analysis of the inscriptions with "Anything less interesting and more stupid and useless the reviewer has seldom encountered" ("Review of Bernhard Laum, *Stiftungen in der griechischen und römischen Antike: Ein Beitrag zur antiken Kulturgeschichte* (Leipzig: Teubner, 1914)," *CP* 11 (1916) 109-10).

[82] P. Schmitt-Pantel, "Évergétisme et Mémoire du Mort: À propos des fondations de banquets publics dans les cités grecques à l'époque hellénistique et romaine," in *La mort, les morts dans les sociétés anciennes*, ed. G. Gnoli and J.-P. Vernant (Cambridge: Cambridge University Press, 1982) 177; C. P. Jones, "A Deed of Foundation from the Territory of Ephesos," *JRS* 73 (1983) 116-17.

[83] See discussion of Jones, "Deed of Foundation," 116-25. An interesting example of a foundation which benefits extant private (guild) associations and the city (IEphesus 3803) is discussed by T. Drew-Bear, "An Act of Foundation from Hypaipa," *Chiron* 10 (1980) 509-36. A private citizen of Hypaipa benefacts the wool-sellers and the linen-weavers with a sum of money and gives to these two guilds and four others the use of a vineyard which he donates to the city (Drew-Bear, "Act of Foundation," 515-16).

On the island of Thera in the third century BCE Epicteta bequeathed a large sum in order to begin a private association to honor the memory of her husband, her sons, and herself (*IG* XII/3 330).[84] The cultic aspect of the association has a mixed character: a funerary cult and a cult of the Muses.[85] It provides a social setting for the members to meet and eat together for three days every year. Epicteta is a widow and is still living. In her will, inscribed here, she writes that she will continue to administer her goods, but that should something happen to her, the inscription records how they are to be dispersed. Her son-in-law, Hyperide, acts as her guardian, or "Kyrios." This suggests that her sons have died, as well as her husband. At the same time, she mentions the consent of her daughter Epiteleia. The will aims to create a corporation of all male relatives of the founder, those living and those to be born. A list of 25 names is included, with the son-in-law and the adoptive brother at the head. Also admitted, however, are wives of the members, their daughters, and a number of specific women. In fact, it is not the association which inherits the majority of Epicteta's property, but her daughter Epiteleia.

The original bequest of 3000 drachmae is intended to pay for the expenses of the three day annual meetings. However, the association does not receive the capital, which remains in the possession of the inheritors, but only the interest. The usual rate on Thera before 200 BCE was seven percent, thus giving an annual income of 210 drachmae.[86] In addition, the priesthood of the new association is hereditary, beginning with the male descendents of Epicteta's daughter, Epiteleia. It seems that Epicteta is concerned about giving her daughter as much control as possible over the family possessions and the association.[87]

In a similar inscription, *IG* IV 840 (ca. III-I BCE), a woman named Agasicratis establishes funerary rites for her family with the deposit of 300

---

[84] Jones calls this a "perfectly preserved example" of the establishing of a private memorial association ("Deed of Foundation," 116). A similar inscription can be found in *Syll*^{3} 1106, the Foundation of Diomedon of Cos. The original deed of Diomedon is not included, but there are extant four columns, each being part of separate documents, "engraved at different, but not very distant times" (W. R. Paton and E. L. Hicks, *The Inscriptions of Cos* [Oxford: Clarendon, 1891] 74). For text and commentary see ICos 36. See also *IG* XII/7 515 (Aigiale, late II BCE); *IGR* 4.661; IEphesus 3214. Cf. also *SEG* III 674, which is a document of a funerary *koinon*, although not the foundational document.

[85] Poland, *griechischen Vereinswesens*, 272; F. Sokolowski, *Lois sacrées des cités grecques*, (École française d'Athènes. Travaux et mémoires, fasc. 18; Paris: E. de Boccard, 1969) 232.

[86] R. Dareste, B. Haussoullier, and T. Reinach, eds., *Recueil des inscriptions juridiques grecques: Texte, traduction, commentair* (SJ 6; Rome: "L'Erma" Di Bretschneider, 1965) 109.

[87] Cf. Dareste, Haussoullier, Reinach, *Recueil des inscriptions*, 106.

silver drachmae in the temple of Poseidon on the island of Kalauria.[88] From this money a sacrifice to Poseidon and another to Zeus Soter was to take place bi-annually "on the alter erected beside the statue of her husband" (lines 7-8). The principal amount, it seems, was placed in the possession of the priests in the temple. Agasicratis appointed trustees who would carry out the sacrifices and maintain the family statues. At the end of each sacrifice an account of their expenses was to be submitted to the priests. Anything remaining was then to go to the priests for use in the temple. Since Agasicratis' statue is already in the temple, this is probably not her first act of patronage. Certainly it indicates some social standing within the community. The similarities between this inscription and that of Epicteta of Thera suggest that this is the founding document of a private, family association, although there was some public involvement. A similar testamentary foundation from the same time and place can be seen in *IG* IV 841 (Kalauria, III BCE).

c) Associations Formed By Divine Sanction

Often the formation and propagation of assocations was given divine sanction, much like other major events in antiquity. The most popular methods for the gods to intervene were dreams, visions, and oracles.[89] In response to a visible manifestation of a deity via a dream or vision, an association might be formed to participate in the worship of that deity. According to Plato, dedications were made because of dreams and visions "especially by women of all types, and by men who are sick or in some danger or difficulty, or else have had a special stroke of luck" (*Leg.* 909E-910A). In the *Epinomis* Plato records that "many cults of many gods have been founded, and will continue to be founded, because of dream-encounters with supernatural beings, omens, oracles, and deathbed visions" (*Epinomis* 985C). Certainly the inscriptional evidence supports this prediction, as most inscriptions referring to such encounters date from the Hellenistic or Roman period.[90]

---

[88] For another association founded by a woman in a similar fashion see *CIG* 2562 (Crete).

[89] In general, dreams were a prominent source for gaining insight into the demands of a particular deity. In the Hellenistic period, "dreams rivaled oracles as a source of divine commands" (Ferguson, *Backgrounds*, 172).

[90] E. R. Dodds, *The Greeks and the Irrational* (Berkeley and Los Angeles: University of California Press, 1966) 108. It is also noteworthy that the majority of dedications are made to healing gods (Asclepius, Hygieia, Sarapis) or are made by women, further confirming Plato's observation (Dodds, *Irrational*, 125 n. 33). Dodds notes other inscriptions which refer to dreams which prescribe some sort of cultic act (*Irrational*, 125 n. 31). All of them are from Dittenberger, *Syll.*³ 1128, 1147, 1148, 1149,

An inscription from Philadelphia in Lydia (*Syll*³ 985) records the ordinances given by Zeus to a certain Dionysius while he slept.

> the ordinances given to Dionysius in his sleep were written up giving access into his *oikos* to men and women, free people and slaves .... To this man Zeus has given ordinances for the performance of the purifications, the cleansings and the mysteries, in accordance with the ancestral custom and as has now been written. (lines 4-6, 12-14)

The text is unclear as to whether the ordinances were given orally, through an appearance of the god, by letter, or by both, as is the case in *IG* X/2 255. Certainly line 12 suggests that Zeus appeared personally. The dream convinces Dionysius either to establish an association in his house or, more likely, to allow others to have access to an association already existing in his house.[91]

A number of gods are introduced into the worship of the association, including Zeus Eumenes, Hestia, and a number of minor deities who were divinized abstractions such as Wealth and Good Fortune. The dream sanctions the addition of a number of gods to the domain that was, until this point, the place of worship of Agdistis (lines 51-52), a native Asia Minor deity.[92] This is most likely a case of religious syncretism in which a private shrine is reconstituted as a cultic association.[93] What follows are the new purity regulations that members of the association are to observe along with the ancient regulations (lines 12-14), both while participating in the ritual life of the cult, and, perhaps more significantly, at all times.

Fragment B from an inscription from Ephesus (IEphesus 24) gives praise to Artemis, "leader" of the city, and records that "everywhere her shrines and sanctuaries have been established, and temples have been founded for her and alters dedicated to her because of the visible manifestations effected by her" (lines B.11-14). Thus, manifestations of the god can serve not only for the founding of a local association, but also work to propagate a cult in new areas.[94] So common were Artemis' epiphanies that one of her many epithets was ἐπιφανεστάτη.[95]

1150, 1152, 1151, 1153. Also see *MAMA* 5 (1937) 41; A. D. Nock, "Studies in the Graeco-Roman Beliefs of the Empire," *JHS* 45 (1925) 95-97; Sokolowski, "Propagation," 441-45.

[91] The admission of men and women, slaves and free, into a club is similar to Paul's words in Gal 3:28 concerning those who are Christians (cf. 1 Cor 12:13).

[92] Barton and Horsley, "Hellenistic Cult Group," 12.

[93] Barton and Horsley, "Hellenistic Cult Group," 12.

[94] Despite the claims of the decree concerning the festival of Artemis in Ephesus, imperial sanction was still required for the festival to be carried out fully (see fragment A).

[95] See R. Oster who cites its use in IEphesus 27.385. Artemis was also accessible outside physical manifestations, through prayer ("Holy Days in Honour of Artemis," in *New Documents Illustrating Early Christianity: A Review of the Greek Inscriptions and*

A first century BCE inscription from Thessalonica, *IG* X/2 255, is a fine example of the founding and propagation of an association as a result of dreams. [96] The inscription records the founding of a cult of Sarapis and Isis in the town of Opus. Sarapis twice appears in a dream to Xenainetos and enjoins him to deliver a message to his political rival Eurynomos.[97] The subject of the message is the establishment of the worship of Sarapis and Isis in the town of Opus, which is in the region of eastern Locris (on the Euboean gulf).[98] The message is given to Xenainetos both verbally and in the form of a sealed letter which he finds under his pillow after the second dream. When he has delivered his verbal message to Eurynomos, the letter is opened, and it confirms the divine source of the dream.[99]

In the cult of Sarapis and Isis dreams were important in revelations, prophecy, healing, and initiation.[100] The introduction of the cult of Sarapis and Isis to a new location was often inaugurated through a dream in which

---

Papyri Published in 1979, ed. G. H. R. Horsley [NewDocs 4; North Ryde, Australia: Ancient History Documentary Research Centre and Macquarie University, 1987] 81). Oster also notes her epithet ἐπιφανεστάτη in IEphesus 504 ("Holy Days," 80). For examples beyond Ephesus see F. Pfister, "Epiphanie," *RESuppl* 4 (1924) 298-306. Strabo (4.1.4, I BCE - I CE) mentions that Artemis is said to have manifested herself to a prominent Ephesian woman in a dream. At the same time an vision of Artemis was received on a ship of Phokaians sailing nearby Ephesus. As a result, new cults or Artemis are founded in Ionia and Iberia. For more on dreams in ancient Greek literature see Dodds, *Irrational*, 102-34.

[96] The inscription itself dates from the I or II CE but is a copy of an earlier text.

[97] Probably during a period of incubation, a time when a person slept in a shrine awaiting healing, advice, a prophecy, or a vision (G. H. R. Horsley, *New Documents Illustrating Early Christianity: A Review of the Greek Inscriptions and Papyri* [NewDocs 1; North Ryde, Australia: Ancient History Documentary Research Centre, Macquarie University, 1981] 31; see line 3; cf. W. Burkert, *Greek Religion* [Cambridge: Harvard University Press, 1985] 115). Xenainetos seems to have been in Thessalonica on official business as a representative of the city of Opus. It was not uncommon for a "god" to convey a message through multiple dreams (R. Merkelbach, "Zwei Texte aus dem Sarapeum zu Thessalonike," *ZPE* 10 [1973] 52). Cf. Three times the hero Naulochus and the Thesmophorio appear to a man of Priene, telling him to institute worship of the hero at a certain place (IPriene 139, no. 196, c.350 BCE; A. D. Nock, *Conversion: The Old and the New in Religion from Alexander the Great to Augustine of Hippo* [Oxford: Oxford University Press, 1933] 50).

[98] The ruins of Opus have not been identified with certainty.

[99] The use of a letter from heaven (Himmelsbrief) in the foundation and propagation of the cult was common. As in the case of *IG* X/2 255, the letter is most often associated with a dream in which the god appears. Sokolowski ("Propagation," 443; cf. Merkelbach, "Zwei Texte," 53) gives four examples of such occurrences in the cults of Sarapis (*IG* XI/4 1299.56-58; *P.Cair.Zenon* I.59034) and Asclepius (Aristides, *Sacred Talks* 2.394; Pausanias 10.38.13).

[100] V. T. Tihn Tran, "Sarapis and Isis," in *Jewish and Christian Self-Definition 3: Self-Definition in the Greco-Roman World*, ed. B. F. Meyer and E. P. Sanders (Philadelphia: Fortress, 1982) 111; Heyob, *Cult of Isis*, 57, 59.

the god appeared and gave instructions. In his account of the origins of the cult at the court of Ptolemy I, Tacitus (*Histories* 4.83) records that the god appeared to Ptolemy in two separate dreams before Ptolemy established the cult.[101]

Dreams play an important role in the expansion of the cult of Sarapis and Isis on Delos (*IG* XI/4 1299; Delos).[102] The cult was brought from Egypt by a devotee. Within two generations this family cult had outgrown the rented premises where the devotees met. The priest Apollonios records:

> the god (Sarapis) revealed to me in a dream that a Sarapeum must be consecrated to him alone, and that he is no longer to be in rented rooms as before, and further that he (Sarapis) will find the place where it (the temple) should be situated and will indicate the location with a sign. And this happened (as he promised). (lines 13-18)

We have here the move from a private association to a public cult, although it is probable that the private association continued alongside the public cult.[103] That there was a society of worshippers, called *Therapeutai*, connected with the Sarapeum is suggested by a number of inscriptions on stone benches in the Sarapeum naming particular men and by a dedication reading "The priest Apollonios and those of the *Therapeutai* who contributed, to Victory."[104] This latter inscription probably has to do with a legal dispute that arose over the temple. According to the larger inscription Apollonios was assured of victory by the god in a dream; this, of course, came to pass.[105]

In an inscription from Sounion (*IG* II² 1366) we may have another instance of an epiphany. The founder, Xanthos, claims that he did choose the god with which to align his association by stating that the god chose him (line 2). This is probably a reference to a divine epiphany. In Xanthos' telling, the god has appeared to him, either in a dream or "in person,"

---

[101] See also the letter of Zoilus to Apollonius (G. A. Deissmann, *Light From the East: The New Testament Illustrated by Recently Discovered Texts of the Greco Roman World* [New York: George H. Doran, 1927²] 152-55; cf. *LSAM* 20). Cf. Nock, *Conversion*, 49-50; Dodds (*Irrational*, 125, n.32) suggests that as Zolius seems to have been a building contractor, he "had thus every motive for dreaming that Sarapis required a new temple."

[102] Sokolowski ("Propagation," 443) briefly discusses this inscription and describes it as recounting the story of a man who, after having Sarapis come to him in his sleep, finds some writing hidden in the frame of the door which instructs him where and how to build the temple (lines 56-58), which Sokolowski connects to the use of *Himmelsbriefe*.

[103] Nock, *Conversion*, 55.

[104] Nock, *Conversion*, 52. Further on the Therapeutai see Philo, *De Vita Cont.*

[105] Further on the building of sacred places as a result of a dream see Pausanius 3.14.4 where the wife of an early Spartan king builds a temple of Thetis.

commanding him to build the sanctuary.[106] This would not be uncharacteristic of this god, as Men is known to have appeared in dreams elsewhere (e.g., *CMRDM* 4.137).[107]

It is interesting that Xanthos is specified as a Lycian. Cape Sounion, the location of this inscription, is on the tip of the Attica peninsula, about 70 km from Athens by the coastal road. It was an important port, which the Athenians fortified during the Peloponnesian War. Lycia, on the other hand, is the area in the south west corner of Asia Minor. Since the cult of Men was well established in Lycia it seems that Xanthos is transporting a cult from his place of origin to his new place of residence.[108] We may have another instance of a divine epiphany being used to legitimate the propagation of a foreign cult in a new area.

Occasionally associations were founded as the direct result of oracles. For example, an inscription from Tralles (ITralleis 1; II or III CE) seems to record the oracle of a foundation of a cult of Poseidon in Tralles. It seems that there was an earthquake which the city escaped. Since Poseidon himself was given the epithet of "earth-shaker," he was given thanks for protecting the city from the wrath of Zeus, which was manifested in the earthquake. The oracle was given by Apollo (Python) to a priest of Zeus named Kleitosthene.

A third century BCE inscription from Halicarnasus (*Syll.*³ 1044) concerning the establishment of an association (θίασος) consists of three parts: the record of an oracle, a mortgage, and a decree. Poseidonios receives an oracle from the Telmessian Apollo telling him that, in order to prosper, he should establish an association of present and future family members who will worship certain deities including Zeus, Apollo, the Mother of the Gods and the "good demons of Poseidonios and his mother." As a result, Poseidonios establishes an association of his extended family that will use the revenues from certain mortgaged lands for sacrifices. The eldest male child is to administer the lands and receive the revenues. He is

---

[106] Xanthos was seemingly a rich patron of the cult of Men, having himself dedicated a sanctuary. Both G. H. R. Horsley (*New Documents Illustrating Early Christianity: A Review of the Greek Inscriptions and Papyri published in 1978* [NewDocs 3; North Ryde, Australia: Ancient History Documentary Research Centre, Macquarie University, 1983] 23) and Sokolowski (*Lois sacrées*, 107) maintain that "Gaius Orbius" is Xanthos' *duo nomina*, indicating that he is a slave. While this translation is possible, the fact that Xanthos has dedicated a sanctuary suggests that he is a man of some wealth and status, an unlikely position for a slave; he is most likely a freeperson or perhaps a freedperson. Strabo (12.8.14) notes that in Psidian Antioch the cult of Men actually owned slaves and lands prior to colonization by the Romans (Horsley, *New Documents* 3, 30).

[107] Horsley, *New Documents* 3, 23.

[108] Sokolowski, *Lois sacrées*, 107. The cult of Men flourished in Lycia and central Asia Minor and, less so, in Attica and the Greek islands (E. N. Lane, "Men: A Neglected Cult of Roman Asia Minor," *ANRW* 2.18.3 [1990] 2163; Horsley, *New Documents* 3, 26).

to set aside four gold staters a year to pay for the sacrifices which were to be carried out by three functionaries who were chosen annually. At the time of the inscription these staters of Alexander would be worth 22 to 24 drachmae each, making the total revenue received about 100 drachmae. The eledest male child is also to serve as the priest of the temenos which is to be founded.[109]

It is clear from the evidence that there were a number of different ways and a number of different reasons that voluntary associations could be formed in antiquity. Once formed, they attracted members, often outgrowing their original meeting places. We do not have evidence for a strong missionizing tendency in any of the associations, but it is clear from a number of associations that they attracted new members and sometimes established new groups both in their home area and in other locales.

Once formed, many associations remained under the control of their founder.[110] In the previously mentioned inscription from Sounion (Attica; *IG* II² 1366) the founder, Xanthos, dedicated a ἱερόν.[111] Xanthos does not restrict membership in his association; anyone may enter, so long as they have been purified (cf. *Syll.*³ 985). It seems, however, that Xanthos was concerned to maintain control of the association, since no sacrifice was to be made if he was not present (lines 7-8). To prevent unauthorized sacrifice a curse formula is invoked which renders the sacrifice ineffective. Xanthos' concern for control is again evidenced only a few lines later where provision is made for a time when he might be incapacitated or absent. In such cases only his designated representative is to have any authority in the association. This regulation has been strengthened since the first draft of the inscription. There it reads: "But if he (the founder) dies or is sick or is traveling, let the one to whom he hands over (authority) serve the god" (see *IG* II² 1365). In the later inscription the phrase "serve the god" (θεραπευέτω τὸν θεόν) was replaced by "let no one have authority except the one to whom he hands it over" (μηθένα ἀνθρώπων ἐξουσίαν ἔχειν, ἐὰν μή, line 14). However, this concern is seemingly belied by the later comment that "those who wish may form an association for Men" (line 21). It seems that Xanthos is not concerned to control the worship of Men generally, but only his own association.[112]

---

[109] Cf. a three-part inscription records the foundation of a temple of Aphrodite in Anaphe as the direct result of an oracle (*IG* XII/3 248, II BCE). Further on oracles of Artemis see Oster, "Holy Days," 81.

[110] San Nicolò, *Äegyptisches Vereinswesen*, 2.7-8.

[111] Note, this is not an *oikos*; compare with *Syll.*³ 985 (Philadelphia) where Dionysos opens up his *oikos* to the cult association.

[112] On Xanthos' control of his own club, but his allowance for the formation of clubs dedicated to Men by others compare 2 Cor 10:16 where Paul speaks of not wanting to boast of work done in another's field – there is a sense that certain people have claims on

We see this again in *IG* II² 1297 where members of a θίασος vote in favour of publicly honoring their founder and patron Sophron.[113] Sophron "generously and enthusiastically organized the *thiasos*" (καλῶς καὶ φιλοτίμως συνήγαγε τὸν θίασον, lines 3-4), setting a high standard for other potential patrons of the association (lines 7-8). Not only this, he continues to act as their president (ἀρχερανιστής).[114] This can be contrasted with *IG* II² 1369 where the patron (προστάτης) and president (ἀρχερανιστής) are two separate individuals. In this latter inscription the patron holds his position for his lifetime, while the president is chosen yearly by lot.

In *IG* XII/7 58 a security of property is given to the founder of an association and his wife. It is unclear as to what the wife's role is, as only the husband is named as "founder" (literally, he "gathered together" [συνάγω] the association). That his wife is named might suggest that she is a co-founder or at least plays some part in the administration of the association. The founder is named as the president, again indicating some merging of roles.

These inscriptions reflect the fact that there was no consistent policy in the Greco-Roman world as to the role an individual could play in an association with which he or she was connected, whether as founder, patron, or president. Sometimes the founder could benefact and control an association; in other instances benefaction was accepted with no commitment to allow the patron to participate in the association. Elsewhere the patron shared control with either a founder or an appointed official.

As an association began to grow, a meeting place soon became important. In these meeting places both social and cultic gatherings would take place. The temple became one meeting location, particularly for established associations. The decree of the Athenian *boulē* regarding the founding of a temple to Aphrodite by the Kitian merchants in Piraeus (*IG* II² 337) records the two stage process required for obtaining a sacred place in fouth century Athens. The Kitians (Cyprus) merchants seem to have already been established as a group of resident aliens in Piraeus, but they petition to have land leased to them to build a temple to Ourania, their Semitic Aphrodite.[115] The Athenian Council first heard the petition, and then passed it on to the citizen Assembly for final approval. The Kitian

---

particular areas / congregations, although all are Christians. Sokolowski (*Lois sacrées*, 108) suggests of this inscription that "il s'agit de la fondation d'une association d'aide mutuelle pour faciliter l'affranchissement" (from slavery).

[113] Association members often honored a founder in various ways (Ziebarth, *griechische Vereinswesen*, 40).

[114] For another inscription in which the association remains under the control of the founder see *IGRR* I 1095.

[115] Nock, *Conversion*, 20.

merchants were granted their lease of land to establish the temple of Aphrodite "just as also the Egyptians established the temple of Isis" (lines 42-45). This final line indicates, at the very least, that this was a practice somewhat common in the port town of Piraeus.

Often associations were founded on a particular piece of land and decrees were established to indicate their founding. A letter from King Antiochus (293-61 BCE) which was later inscribed on a stele (*IGRR* 3.1020) notes the "power of the god Zeus of Baetocaece" and establishes a place in the village where "the power of the god issues" (a place of oracles?) for the establishment of a temple to carry out monthly and annual sacrifices and festivals. Produce from the land is to be used in the rituals.

A less elaborate, but no less interesting, example is that of the foundation of a small cult in Isthmos (*LSCG* 171, II BCE) in which a sacred precinct is dedicated to Artemis and Zeus and the "family gods." This precinct is clearly intended to endure for some time, as the inscription promises that if the prescribed sacrifices are performed life "will go well" for those presently involved and for their children "forever." Such is the importance of the establishment of this cult that a slave is freed in order to become a priest and oversee all the sacrificial duties and services.[116]

The establishment of foreign associations also provided local people with opportunities to contact groups of foreigners and to be introduced to foreign cults, thus propagating the cult locally.[117] The port town of Piraeus would have provided opportunities to contact many people (particularly merchants and sailors) from other locales. The establishment of a proper temple to Ourania (and Isis) might indicate the concern to attract others to the cult – others who can then return to their own land to establish the worship of the deity there.[118] In fact, Piraeus was such a popular place for the establishing of associations that the deme had to enact a decree (*IG* II² 1177) in the mid-fourth century BCE in order to control the unauthorized

---

[116] Buildings also play a part in the founding of a "false cult." The second century CE satirist Lucian of Samosata describes the founding of a new cult by Alexander "the False Prophet." As part of Alexander's strategy he buried bronze "prophetic" tablets in a temple of Apollo in Chalcedon which announced the coming of Asclepius to Pontus. When these were discovered the people immediately responded by laying the foundations for a new temple for Asclepius (Lucian, *Alex.* 10; LCL). Once Alexander had established himself as the prophet of Asclepius in his home town of Abonoteichus he was able to send out "missionaries" to foreign lands to tell of his shrine and the prophecies being uttered there. Thus the local temple, once founded, became the base for further expansion of the cult.

[117] Nock, *Conversion*, 20.

[118] Cf. *LSAM* 34; a Sarapis cult is transplanted to Magnesia on the Maeander but experiences resistance from the local council when it attempts to build a sanctuary there (see comments by Sokolowski, "Propagation," 445-48).

use of the Thesmophorion (the temple of Demeter) by the newly forming *thiasoi* made up of people from outside of Piraeus.[119]

5. Legal Status

Those outside a group did not often view members of voluntary associations as honorable. Most often the least impressed were the civic magistrates and the imperial governors from Rome. During the Roman period voluntary associations experienced sporadic official resistance.[120] There is some evidence of disruptions caused by associations in Rome during the Late Republic. In 186 BCE the Roman Senate suppressed the association of Dionysos worshippers (*Bacchanales*). In 64 BCE *collegia* became involved in political action and were dissolved by the senate, a policy reinforced by two further decrees in 56 and 55 BCE.[121] In 49 BCE Julius Caesar banned all associations except those which had been established for a long time.[122]

By the time of Augustus (28 BCE – 14 CE) the associations had proliferated once again and Augustus passed a law that every association must be sanctioned by the senate or Emperor (see *CIL* VI 2193 = *ILS* 4966).[123] Despite this, many illicit *collegia* continued to flourish.[124]

---

[119] Ferguson, "Attic Orgeones," 96. There are a number of extant fourth century BCE inscriptions from associations at Piraeus; see R. Garland, *The Piraeus: From the Fifth to the First Century B.C.* (London: Duckworth, 1987) 228-34, for a list and brief description of each.

[120] For details of the following summary see W. J. Cotter, "The Collegia and Roman Law: State Restrictions on Voluntary Associations 64 BCE - 200 CE," in *Voluntary Associations in the Graeco-Roman World*, ed. J. S. Kloppenborg and S. G. Wilson (London and New York: Routledge, 1996), 74-89.

[121] Duff, *Personality*, 107-08.

[122] Jewish groups were granted this status and exempted from the ban (Cotter, "Collegia and Roman Law," 76-78; G. P. Richardson, "Early Synagogues as Collegia in the Diaspora and Palestine," in *Voluntary Associations in the Graeco-Roman World*, ed. J. S. Kloppenborg and S. G. Wilson [London and New York: Routledge, 1996] 93), although it did not prevent them from occasionally being disbanded in later times (i.e., temporarily under Claudius; Cotter, "Collegia and Roman Law," 78).

[123] Suetonius reports that Augustus "disbanded all guilds (collegia), except such as were of long standing and formed for legitimate purposes" (*Caes.*, "Augustus" 32.1, LCL). However, *CIL* VI 2193 (= Waltzing, *corporations Professionnelles*, III.227 no. 852; Rome, early I CE) suggests that they could exist with senate approval and an undertaking of public service (Cotter, "Collegia and Roman Law," 78). The inscription reads, "Dis manibus. Collegio symphoniacorum qui sacris publicis praestu sunt, quibus senatus c(oire) c(ogi) c(onvocari) permisit e lege Iulia ex auctoritate Aug(usti) ludorum causa."

[124] Hardy, *Studies*, 136.

Associations seeking official permission to form were often already *de facto* in existence.[125] Official sanction only made them legal associations. In Egypt there are less literary and inscriptional references to associations obtaining official permission, but it is probable that the requirement to and procedure for obtaining permission was not significantly different from elsewhere:[126] "It is fair to say, even with such little evidence as this, that scrutiny of voluntary associations extended well beyond Rome's gates during Augustus' administration."[127]

Under Tiberius (14-37 CE) associations fared no better, although they continued to exist. Gaius (36-41 CE) seems not to have acted against the associations, but Claudius (41-54 CE) "disbanded the clubs (ἑταιρείας), which had been reintroduced by Gaius" (Dio Cassius 60.6.6, LCL). In fact, Claudius closed taverns in Rome and Ostia as part of his suppression of the associations.[128] Nero (54-68 CE) also acted against the "illegal" associations, showing that for a time they had continued to exist unabated.

Under Hadrian, an association of Dionysiac artists reaffirms the permissions and privileges first granted to it by Claudius.[129] The following second century CE exchange between Pliny, governor of Bithynia, and the Emperor Trajan over the formation of a firemen's guild illustrates that official wariness over such groups continued into the second century. Pliny is concerned because a recent fire in Nicomedia brought the lack of fire-fighting equipment and personnel to his attention. In writing to Trajan he asks,

> Will you, Sir, consider whether you think a company of firemen might be formed, limited to 150 members? I will see that no one shall be admitted who is not genuinely a fireman, and that the privileges granted shall not be abused: it will not be difficult to keep such small numbers under observation. (*Epistulae* 10.33.3; LCL)

Trajan's response expresses reluctance about such a plan:

> You may very well have had the idea that it should be possible to form a company of firemen at Nicomedia on the model of those existing elsewhere, but we must remember that it is societies like these which have been responsible for the political disturbances in your province,

---

[125] Waltzing, *corporations Professionnelles*, I.337.

[126] San Nicolò, *Äegyptisches Vereinswesen*, 2.10-16.

[127] Cotter, "Collegia and Roman Law," 79.

[128] Dio Cassius 60.6.6-7; W. J. Cotter, "*Our Politeuma is in Heaven*: The Meaning of Phil. 3.17-21," in *Origins and Method: Towards a New Understanding of Judaism and Christianity. Essays in Honour of John C. Hurd*, ed. B. H. McLean (JSNTSup 86; Sheffield: JSOT Press, 1993) 99, cf. idem., "Collegia and Roman Law," 80.

[129] See *BGU* 1074; cf. Cotter, "Collegia and Roman Law," 79, 86.

particularly in its towns.¹³⁰ If people assemble for a common purpose, whatever name we give them and for whatever reason, they soon turn into a political association. (*Epistulae* 10.34.1; LCL)

Trajan ends by suggesting that the fire-fighting equipment be made available and that property owners be made responsible for putting out the fires.¹³¹

In a separate exchange between Pliny and Trajan we find another illustration of official suspicion of associations. During his tenure as governor, Pliny was concerned about the formation of a "benefit society" (*eranus*)¹³² in Amisus (*Epistulae* 10.92). Since Amisus was a "free and confederate city," the people could govern all of their own affairs, with the exception of foreign policy.¹³³ In giving his reply, Trajan allows that the city could found such an association, "especially if the contributions are not used for riotous and unlawful assemblies, but to relieve cases of hardship among the poor" (*Epistulae* 10.93). However, Trajan goes on to make clear that this city has special status and such associations are forbidden in cities governed by Roman law. A common purpose "for the good of society" justifies the existence of this association for the Emperor and the Governor. However, it is likely that the actual purpose of the association may be quite different, either cultic or, more likely in this case, social.¹³⁴

It is often thought that the general imperial ban on associations caused a number of associations to take on the guise of a burial association in order to obtain senate approval for their existence.¹³⁵ Christianity itself is thought to have taken advantage of this by portraying itself as a funerary association. Evidence for the allowance of such *collegia tenuiorum* (or

---

¹³⁰ A. N. Sherwin-White points out that there had been much strife in the provinces, particularly between the rich and the poor. The rich were seen to have some advantage by being organized in their clubs (*The Letters of Pliny: A Historical and Social Commentary* [Oxford: Clarendon, 1966] 610).

¹³¹ Further on the firemen's guild see Waltzing, *corporations Professionnelles*, II.193-97.

¹³² Pliny employs the Greek word ἔρανος (latinized as *eranus*). This is different from his use of *heraeria* for the fire-fighter's club (*Epistulae* 10.33) and for Christian groups (*Epistulae* 10.96).

¹³³ Wilken, *Christians*, 14; cf. Sherwin-White, *Letters of Pliny*, 687.

¹³⁴ Hence Pliny's use of *eranus*, since ἔρανος was often used for a banquet / social club.

¹³⁵ Stevenson, "Clubs," 256; Wilken, "Collegia," 280-81; J. E. Stambaugh and D. L. Balch, *The New Testament in Its Social Environment* (LEC 2; Philadelphia: Westminster, 1986) 125; Danker, "Associations," 503. The evidence summarized above for the most part indicates the suppression of associations in Rome and its environs (e.g., Pompeii). However, the evidence for such in Egypt during the time of Augustus and for Bithynia during the time of Trajan suggest that the restrictions were in effect across the empire (so Cotter, "Collegia and Roman Law," 84).

collegia funeraticia) comes from a *senatusconsultum* quoted within the regulations of the *collegium salutare Dianae et Antinoi*, dated to 136 CE (*CIL* XIV 2112):

> Clause from the *Senatusconsultum* of the Roman People:
> These are permitted to assemble, convene, and maintain a society: those who desire to make monthly contributions for funerals may assemble in such a society, but they may not assemble in the name of such a society except once a month for the sake of making contributions to provide burial for the dead.

This probably reflects a general regulation rather than a special dispensation granted by the Senate to this association, for in the latter case that fact would have been specified.[136] Kloppenborg has shown that the evidence for the existence of *collegia tenuiorum* associations before the time Hadrian is lacking and in fact, the *senatusconsultum* probably only came into existence after 133 CE.[137] The association of *CIL* XIV 2112 itself illustrates the founding of a social association under the guise of a funerary association. Calling themselves a "benevolent society" (*collegium salutare*), an association was formed which purported to provide insurance for proper burial. In fact, a close reading reveals that their primary concern is with banqueting at their meetings. The regulation limiting the association meetings to once a month is circumvented by proclaiming certain festivals throughout the year and announcing a feast for each. They attempted to overcome disapproval of the senate by associating themselves with the worship of Antinous, the beautiful, young, male lover of the Emperor Hadrian who had died in 130 CE.[138] The same is true of the Roman collegium of Aesculapius and Hygia (*CIL* VI 10234, 153 BCE) which only refers to burial once and uses most of the inscription to discuss banquets and the distribution of funds.[139]

All of this suggests that during the first century, particularly the time of the formation of Pauline churches, care was required for those who gathered regularly for social or cultic purposes. Despite the prohibition against such associations,

> these measures do not seem to have been uniformly enforced. If Claudius, Nero, and Trajan are seen to suppress the collegia, it is because these clubs continued to spring up and grow whenever the political climate allowed them to do so.[140]

---

[136] Kloppenborg, "Collegia and *Thiasoi*," 20.

[137] Kloppenborg, "Collegia and *Thiasoi*," 20-22.

[138] Cf. Kloppenborg, "Collegia and *Thiasoi*," 22; S. Dill, *Roman Society from Nero to Marcus Aurelius* (London: Macmillan, 1905) 259.

[139] Kloppenborg, "Collegia and *Thiasoi*," 22.

[140] Cotter, "Collegia and Roman Law," 88.

In this general context of official suspicion of associations, alongside their continued existence, Paul's exhortation to the Thessalonians to live so as to gain the respect of those outside the group (1 Thess 4:12) can be seen not as a means to change the fundamental constitution of the group but to insure that the group continues to exist unhindered. The concern is not so much that they gain legal permission to exist as that they are not singled out in such a way that they must disband.

Chapter Three

Membership And Its Requirements

Voluntary associations were relatively small groups, although it would be unusual for an association to have fewer than 10 members. Only rarely did an association have more than 100 members, although evidence exists for associations of up to 300-400 members and even an association of 1200 members.[1] Usually associations had a membership of between 20 and 50 persons. Most associations were composed of persons from the lower ranks of society, although some members clearly came from the upper ranks. Women are attested as equal members in some associations. However, the membership of professional associations was more likely to be divided according to gender, with all-male professional associations affiliated with those professions dominated by men and all-female associations affiliated with professions dominated by women.[2]

1. Social Location

A hierarchical social ranking was held commonly throughout the Roman Empire, including Macedonia.[3] The Roman *ordo* ("rank") was as follows (in descending order from highest): senatorial, equestrian, decurion, freeborn, freed, slave. The first three orders were comprised of a small part of the population of the Empire considered the elite. "Below them in the official hierarchy came the great mass of the humble free, and at the bottom of the heap, the slaves."[4]

---

[1] B. H. McLean, "The Agrippinilla Inscription: Religious Associations and Early Church Formation," in *Origins and Method: Towards a New Understanding of Judaism and Christianity. Essays in Honour of John C. Hurd*, ed. B. H. McLean (JSNTSup 86; S Sheffield: JSOT Press, 1993) 257; Kloppenborg, "Collegia and *Thiasoi*," 30 n. 64.

[2] See C. F. Whelan, "Amica Pauli: The Role of Phoebe in the Early Church." *JSNT* 49 (1993) 75-76 and nn. 20-23; Kloppenborg, "Collegia and *Thiasoi*," 25.

[3] The following description of these ranks and their interrelationships is summarized from Garnsey and Saller, *Roman Empire*, 112-125.

[4] Garnsey and Saller, *Roman Empire*, 115. In the time of the emperor Hadrian there was a formal distinction between the elite (*honestiores*) and the masses (*humiliores*). The former category included those in the aristocratic ranks along with Roman veterans (as a reward for protecting the social order) while the rest of the free population comprised the *humiliores* (Garnsey and Saller, *Roman Empire*, 115-16).

The senatorial rank was the most prestigious, being limited to the members of several hundred families "perceived to be worthy by the traditional standards of birth, wealth and moral excellence."[5] Under Augustus a male was required to purchase his seat in the senate for a large amount (one million sesterces) and although it was not a hereditary rank, sons were encouraged to follow their fathers in joining the senate.

The equestrian rank was of the aristocracy, although the requirements of high birth, excellence, and wealth were somewhat lower than that required to qualify for the senatorial rank. The equestrian rank was much larger than that of the senatorial rank, with numbers in the thousands. During the Principate some equestrians began to hold administrative and military positions and some gained greater wealth than others, leading to a hierarchy within the rank itself. Within this rank the elite generally lived in Rome while the others, the majority, were local notables.

The rank of decurion or councilor required respectable birth, wealth, and "moral worth." Respectable birth was defined as the son of a freedman (to become an equestrian one had to be at least the grandson of a freedman or better). Members of this rank held political responsibility in the towns throughout the Empire and were required to contribute to the public treasury upon entering the council or the civic priesthood. It was expected that they would retain public favor through civic benefaction.

It is important to note that there was a vast gulf between the elite ranks and the rest of the population in terms of wealth. The majority of those in the category of freeborn and freed were not wealthy in comparison to the elites. In antiquity, "[t]here was no genuine 'middle class' in the sense of an intermediate group with independent economic resources or social standing."[6] Although some persons within the categories of freed did have considerable wealth, this was certainly not typical of persons in this rank.

There was a legal division of the category of free person between both freeborn and freed and citizen and non-citizen. A freeborn person had a higher rank than that of a freedperson, although a freedperson may in fact have more wealth, if he or she had worked for a wealthy master who allowed the personal accumulation of wealth.[7] Citizenship was important

---

[5] Garnsey and Saller, *Roman Empire*, 112.

[6] Garnsey and Saller, *Roman Empire*, 116; R. MacMullen, *Roman Social Relations 50 B.C. to A.D. 284* (New Haven and London: Yale University Press, 1974) 89-90.

[7] The *peculium* allowed slaves to have money for capital expenses and to own property and other slaves. Often slaves ran their master's workshop or commercial operation with a great amount of freedom and some slaves were able to amass great wealth; see Garnsey and Saller, *Roman Empire*, 119-20 for details.

as it provided legal protection from flogging, torture, execution, and arbitrary abuse by magistrates; non-citizens faced all of these. During the time of the Principate the distinction between citizen and non-citizen began to lose its significance and a growing number of persons within the empire held this legal status.

In the Greco-Roman period slavery "was a basic, structural element of the household, affording owners and their families the leisure to indulge in the good life, however they defined it."[8] Under Roman law slaves were not considered persons but property – a "speaking tool" (*instrumentum vocale*) or a living instrument. As such, they had no legal standing of their own and could be bought, sold, punished, or abused as the will of the master dictated.[9] They had neither power nor honour. Although the institution of slavery was generally accepted, there were some who voiced objections to it, resulting in explanations and justifications for its existence.[10]

The estimation of a person's status within society was tied in some ways to that person's rank, but was more dependent upon "the social estimation of his honour, the perception of those around him as to his prestige."[11] Status could transcend the boundaries set up by rank, and a person of elite rank could fall into poverty while a free or freed person could amass great wealth. Since wealth and how one used it was often the basis for gaining honour from others,[12] the accumulation of wealth by non-elites created some tension in the social order.[13]

---

[8] P. Garnsey, *Ideas of Slavery from Aristotle to Augustine* (The W. B. Stanford Memorial Lectures; Cambridge and New York: Cambridge University Press, 1996) 238.

[9] A slave was considered kinless. Slave families had no social reality; slaves were not married, they simply cohabitated. Often slave families were broken up and the threat of the break up of a slave's family was one of the most effective ways of keeping slaves under control. Nevertheless, the life of a slave was often better than that of free poor persons since a slave, particularly a domestic slave, had more security in terms of food and lodging (MacMullen, *Roman Social Relations*, 92-93).

[10] The evidence is presented in Garnsey, *Ideas of Slavery*, although he concludes that "the overt attacks on slavery are few and isolated, and their impact limited" (Garnsey, *Ideas of Slavery*, 238).

[11] Garnsey and Saller, *Roman Empire*, 118.

[12] Honour was pursued through public benefactions and conspicuous consumption and benefactions to individuals (cf. the *salutatio* in which clients of a benefactor would congregate at his residence to pay their respects in exchange for food, money, clothing, or other favours; Garnsey and Saller, *Roman Empire*, 122).

[13] Namely, when a person of former servile rank gained sufficient wealth to own great lands or provide lavish banquets, more so even than those of the elite ranks. For a satirical take on this phenomenon see Petronius' "Dinner with Trimalchio" in his *Satyricon*.

Social hierarchy and status among freeborn persons was determined by a number of factors including family background and occupation. One of the most significant divisions was between urban dwellers (the minority) and rural workers (the masses), with the former looking down upon the latter. Freedpersons were at a particular disadvantage in society due to their servile background; "[F]reedom, citizenship and wealth, it was claimed, could not change the uncultured, servile spirit of a former slave."[14] Slavery was stratified into those who worked in households or in their master's business, and those who suffered under conditions of manual labor.[15]

There was little social mobility between those of the lower ranks and the elite. Two groups seem to have been able to amass the wealth and status required to move upward. Those who served in the military were granted citizenship and were often discharged with enough money to establish themselves as landowners and take up political roles in their locale. Slaves who worked in commerce or manufacturing were also able, given the right incentives by their masters, to amass some wealth. Upon manumission they could purchase positions on local councils that were in need of an infusion of cash. Thus, they had a greater potential for movement than those born as free citizens.

Unfortunately little is known about the specific social conditions of the people in Macedonia during the Roman period. There were broad divisions of slaves and free as well as Roman and non-Roman. However, how these were interrelated is not known in detail except that the Romans led a privileged existence and that non-Romans viewed them as representative of the ruling powers. There is little evidence that has any bearing on the condition of farmers, nor on the artisan work-force and other laborers, although it is clear that under Roman occupation Macedonia enjoyed reasonable prosperity.[16] Nevertheless, it can be assumed that the Roman system of social ranking described above was extant in the region, as it was throughout the empire.

---

[14] Garnsey and Saller, *Roman Empire*, 120.

[15] Slaves could have any of a number of occupations: craftspersons (e.g., shoemakers, linen workers), builders, banking, book publishing, business, clerical occupations, entertainment, medicine, teaching, philosophy, public maintenance, urban peace-keepers, shop-keepers. The majority, however, were agricultural laborers and menial household servants. Household managers (οἰκονόμοι) were those slaves who worked as stewards of households or businesses, although it may refer to plantation managers or financial bursars (even those in the civic administration).

[16] See Papazoglou, "Macedonia," 200-01 for details.

Generally, the social location of the membership of voluntary associations was predominantly from "the urban poor, slaves, and freedmen." [17] Yet, as Steve Wilson points out, "this tells us only that they catered to all but an elite minority."[18] The Macedonian associations themselves seem to represent the cross-section found throughout the empire. The membership base of the Macedonian voluntary associations comes predominantly from the lower ranks of society, although in some cases upper rank or wealthy persons are patrons and / or members. For example, *IG* X/2 192 (III CE) attests to the association of Sarapidai erecting a *bomos* honouring their προστάτης with the consent of the βουλή and δῆμος of Thessalonica. Poplius Aelius Nicanor is named as a Macedoniarch, which indicates that he is an important official of the Synhedrion, the provincial council.[19] The inscription suggests that at least some of the members belonged to the municipal aristocracy.[20] However, we have no way of determining whether all of the members of this association were of the same status.

In *CIL* III 633 a freedman (*libertus*) who had become a Roman official, Publius Hostilius Philadelphus, acted as patron to an association of worshippers of Sylvanus. The membership list is all-male, most of whom are probably freedmen.[21] However, of the sixty-nine members named in the second inscription four are slaves of the colony (Orinus coloniae, Tharsa coloniae, Phoebus coloniae, Phoibus coloniae) and three are slaves of individuals (Hermeros Metrodori, Crescens Abelli, Chrysio Pacci). For the most part the members of the association seem not to be wealthy.[22] The third and fourth inscriptions were set in place with lists of new members as the association either grew or replaced deceased members. The first three

---

[17] Kloppenborg, "Collegia and *Thiasoi*," 23; cf. Foucart, *Associations Religieuses*, 7-12; Schmeller, *Hierarchie und Egalität*, 49. Danker's suggestion that few associations admitted slaves to membership, with the exception of household oriented groups, cannot be sustained as a number of inscriptions show that slaves were often part of an association and sometimes formed their own associations ("Associations," 502). See Foucart, *Associations Religieuses*, 7-12; Hatch, *Organization*, 31; cf. *CIL* III 633.

[18] S. G.Wilson, "Voluntary Associations: An Overview," in *Voluntary Associations in the Graeco-Roman World*, ed. J. S. Kloppenborg and S. G. Wilson, (London and New York: Routledge, 1996) 10.

[19] Edson, "Cults of Thessalonica," 187.

[20] Edson, "Cults of Thessalonica," 187.

[21] Pilhofer, *erste christliche Gemeinde*, 110. Caius Paccius Mercuriales is the only other member designated *l(ibertus)*.

[22] Waltzing, *corporations Professionnelles*, 3.73; Pilhofer, *erste christliche Gemeinde*, 112.

inscriptions are from the II CE while the fourth is from the III CE, indicating that the association was popular and persistent.²³ Other inscriptions from Philippi similarly show members of the lower ranks (*CIL* III 656; 704) as well as reliance on wealthy patrons (*SIRIS* 122; 123; 124). In Pilhofer 338 the name Marronia Eutychia may indicate former servile status in that the name may be derived from the geographical place Maroneia, a town 70 km east of Philippi.²⁴

A vinedresser from Kalliani consecrated to Zeus Hypsistos two rows of vines from his private property (*peculium*) "for the sake of his master" (IMaked 22, III CE). This inscription indicates the servile status of the dedicator.²⁵ Other inscriptions indicate the lower rank status of worshippers of Zeus Hypsistos, namely the two slaves named in IPydna 1 (lines 33 and 34). IBeroea 1 may name a female slave as the dedicator, Aglais.²⁶ At the same time, there are also worshippers of Zeus Hypsistos of a somewhat higher status, as is attested by the mention of civic position (IAnydron 1) or by the use of *tria nomena* (IEdessa 3; IPydna 1), an indication of Roman citizenship.²⁷ The inscription from Pydna records a membership of mixed rank (citizen and slave) and as well as mixed gender (three women are named among the thirty-one men; IPydna 1). Nevertheless, citizenship should not necessarily be taken as an indication of great wealth.

Slaves are attested in other associations. Of fourteen persons named in *IG* X/2 58, at least six were probably slaves or freedmen, as indicated by their names: Felix (2x), Primus, Secundus (3x), and at least two Roman citizens were also members, Aulus Papius Chilon and Apoleus Lucilus Kalistratos. In *IG* X/2 288 at least two of the members were slaves: Demas and Primitas,²⁸ although they both served as secretaries within the association alongside a citizen, Marcus Cassius Hermonus.

Isidorus, named as the deceased in *IG* X/2 506 (209 CE), was a modest civic official, a curialis, of the civic council. That he is commemorated by

---

²³ V. A. Abrahamsen, *Women and Worship at Philippi: Diana/Artemis and Other Cults in the Early Christian Era* (Portland, ME: Astarte Shell Press, 1995) 37.

²⁴ L. Portefaix, *Sisters Rejoice: Paul's Letter to the Philippians and Luke-Acts as Received by First-Century Philippian Women* (ConBNT 20; Stockholm: Almqvist & Wiksell, 1988) 101.

²⁵ Papazoglou, "Macedonia," 200.

²⁶ J. M. R. Cormack, "Dedications to Zeus Hypsistos at Beroea," *JRS* 31 (1941) 20.

²⁷ Garnsey and Saller, *Roman Empire*, 116-17.

²⁸ F. Bömer, *Untersuchungen über die Religion der Sklaven in Griechenland und Rom* (Akademie der Wissenschaften und der Literatur; Wiesbaden: Steiner, 1958-63) 4.238.

a *bomos* rather than a sarcophagus suggests that his family was of limited economic means.²⁹ The text indicates that he was a priest of two or more θίασοι, although it does not specify whether he was so simultaneously or successively. In contrast to most of the previous inscriptions mentioned, the inscription of *IG* X/2 220 is poorly executed, with a semi-literate text, suggesting a membership from the lower ranks of society.³⁰

The ethnic origin of the membership is known in a few cases. Of the thirty-four people named in IPydna 1 the only obvious Macedonian name is that of Alexander (line 36), although Paramonos (line 37) is common in Macedonia. The others are probably either foreign born or of immigrant families. For the most part the membership of the associations of Asiani are composed of non-Macedonians, usually artisans. However, the membership is not limited to those from Asia Minor, nor is it necessarily only for those of lower rank.

The funerary dedication to a fellow *mystes* named Makedon was inscribed by the θίασος of Asiani (*IG* X/2 309) and names their high priest, Publius Aelius Alexander.³¹ His name indicates status as a Roman citizen and he is at least a freedman.³² This name and the careful work on the monument suggest that the social standing of some of the members was higher than that of the labourer.³³ The name Makedon was a common proper name in Macedonia indicating that this particular person was a native of Macedonia. Thus, "the Asiani of Thessalonica did not limit membership in their θίασος to persons of Asianic origin."³⁴ We can conclude that the Asiani of Thessalonica were a doubly mixed group which included both higher and lower status people and those from Asia Minor along with native Macedonians.³⁵

The evidence of our inscriptions leads us to conclude that voluntary associations in Macedonia were composed of people of mixed social rank or lower social rank (freepersons, and especially freedpersons and slaves)

---

²⁹ Edson, "Cults of Thessalonica," 160.

³⁰ Edson, "Cults of Thessalonica," 187.

³¹ This may be the case with the fragmentary *IG* X/2 480, where a certain Cassia Antigona Memoni is named.

³² Edson, "Cults of Thessalonica," 157.

³³ Edson, "Cults of Thessalonica," 157.

³⁴ Edson, "Cults of Thessalonica," 155. An association of Asiani at Napoca in Dacia (*CIL* III 870) admitted natives (see Edson, "Cults of Thessalonica," 155 n. 3).

³⁵ *IG* X/2 480 suggests that the deceased was a member of both the Asiani and an association of Asklepiastoi.

and could include both foreign persons and ethnic Macedonians.[36] There is some evidence for the inclusion of persons who held civic positions, although this in itself does not make them part of the elite (Publius Hostilius Philadelphius was an *aedile* at Philippi and a *libertus*; *CIL* III 633). Most associations were composed of men, although some included women (IPydna 1; IAmphipolis 1; Pilhofer 338). The associations of workers and merchants would be predominantly lower ranking persons. The Roman merchants of IAcanthus 1 would fall into the lower ranks of society. Even when great wealth had been gained through trade, there continued to be a distinction between the mercantile class and that of the upper ranks. We have no example of an association with a membership limited to higher-ranking people.

A significant factor that arises from these inscriptions is related to the political history of the region. The dominating presence of the Romans after 168 BCE led not to a predominance of Roman *collegia* among the populace, but rather to a blending of Greek and Latin elements of small group formation. This can be seen in the interchange of certain vocabulary, such as the use of "collegium" in Greek (κολλήγιον, *CIG* 2007f) and the Latinization of θίασος as *thiasum* (Pilhofer 340, 095; cf. *CIL* III 703, 704). We see the blending of Roman and Greek elements in the combining of local religious symbolism with Latin festivals (the Thracian horseman and the *rosalia*; Pilhofer 029/1) or the depiction of Latin deities (Nemesis, Nike, and Mars) with accompanying Greek inscriptions (Pilhofer 143, 143, 144).[37]

2. Gender

Although there is a paucity of women in professional voluntary associations, this is not the case for the religious associations of antiquity, where women were not only members but played an active role, often

---

[36] Elsewhere we find a Macedonian listed as a member of an association in Piraeus; see *IG* II² 1335.

[37] Cf. F. Chapouthier, "Un troisième bas-relief du théâtre de Philippes," *BCH* 49 (1925) 243. Papazoglou ("Macedonia," 204) speaks of two religious conceptions coexisting in Macedonia. One was the Greek religion of the Macedonians that worshipped aloof and majestic gods. The other was the emotional religion of the indigenous population that included mystic rites and orgiastic cults. Eventually these two conceptions interpenetrated one another. They then seem to have been mixed again with the elements of Roman religious sensibilities.

serving as leaders.[38] Kloppenborg notes that "[t]he most inclusive type of voluntary association was probably the *collegium* organized around the cult of a deity" citing the formulaic description of *Syll.*³ 985 (Philadelphia, II BCE), "men and women, freeborn and slaves" (lines 5-6, repeated in lines 48-49).[39] The regulations of the private association worshipping Men Tyrannos (*IG* II² 1366 [Attica, II/III CE]) indicates that women participated in the rites alongside the men. One of the most important examples of the involvement of women in an association occurs in the regulations of the mysteries of Andania (*IG* V/1 1390, 96 BCE),[40] where we find evidence for women at all levels of the association: initiates, officers overseeing the ceremonies, priestesses, virgins, and the wife of the founder / patron who shares in some of his honours. An inscription from Thera (IApamBith 35, Imperial period) attests to an association of men and women (οἱ θιασῖται καὶ θιασίτιδες) who have sacrificed to the gods on behalf of their priestess.[41]

A number of membership lists from associations make it clear that women were involved independently of their husband or fathers:[42] for example, *IG* II² 2347 (Salamine, second half IV BCE) lists three women along with twenty-five men; *IG* II² 1297 (Athens, *c.* 237 BCE) lists twenty-one women and thirty seven men; *IG* II² 2354 (Athens, late III BCE) lists at least nine women among the twenty-three members of τὸ

---

[38] In addition, we might note that women could found or benefact such associations without being members; see for example, *IG* IV 840 (Kalauria [Peloponesse], III-I BCE); *IG* IV 841 (Klauria, III BCE); Foucart 51 (Rhodes), 55 (Citium [Cyprus], II/I BCE); IDelos 1522 (II CE); see further Poland, *griechischen Vereinswesens*, 293-96. Some groups restricted women to serving as priestesses (see Poland, *griechischen Vereinswesens*, 292-93, 95) and did not grant them full membership in the association (*contra* some of the examples given by Foucart, *Associations Religieuses*, 6).

[39] Kloppenborg, "Collegia and *Thiasoi*," 25. Whelan ("Amica Paul," 75 n. 20) makes the same point using this inscription but does not cite the formula. Instead she misunderstands the name Agdistas (line 46) as the name of woman of distinction; it is actually the name given to a deity, a Phrygian manifestation of the Great Mother; cf. Barton and Horsley, "Hellenistic Cult Group," 13.

[40] M. W. Meyer provides a translation of this lengthy text in *The Ancient Mysteries: A Sourcebook. Sacred Texts of the Mystery Religions of the Ancient Mediterranean World* (San Francisco: Harper and Row, 1987) 51-59.

[41] Foucart suggests that the θιασίτιδες are a separate section of a larger association ("elles formaient une section distincte," *Associations Religieuses*, 6).

[42] As indicated by the fact that they are not identified with reference to such (cf. unpublished comment by J. S. Kloppenborg on *IG* II² 1297).

κοινὸν ἐρανιστῶν.⁴³ The large household based Dionysiac θίασος that moved from Lesbos to Rome around 150 CE lists 402 members who contributed to the erecting of a statue of their patron and priestess.⁴⁴ Among these names twenty-seven percent are women (110 names). McLean notes that

> the statue includes only those names of people who made a financial contribution to the statue. Therefore, it is reasonable to assume that more women than men are omitted since women generally had lesser economic means.⁴⁵

Another second century Bacchic θίασος seems to include both men and women as it mentions a male founder (Amandos) and a Maenad, the overseer of a college of women (*IG* IX/1 670; Physcos). A number of Latin inscriptions list both men and women as members of the association: *CIL* III 870 (Napoca Bacchic association, 17 women and 27 men); III 7437 (Nicopolis Bacchic association, several women among 109 men); VI 261 (Roman Bacchic association); VI 377; V 992 (= 8307).⁴⁶ That women could be full members of associations is seen in two grave inscriptions from the Athenaistai in Boeotia who buried female members,⁴⁷ *IG* VII 687 (*ca.* 200 BCE) and 688 (after 175 BCE).⁴⁸

---

⁴³ It is not clear that all the members are women; *contra* Foucart, *Associations Religieuses*, 6. Ziebarth (*griechische Vereinswesen*, 143) and Poland (*griechischen Vereinswesens*, 292) suggest that thirteen are women. This is likely, as it would divide the membership list in two between the thirteenth and fourteenth name, the latter ten names being male.

⁴⁴ McLean, "Agrippinilla Inscription," 240-45.

⁴⁵ McLean, "Agrippinilla Inscription," 262.

⁴⁶ Waltzing (*corporations Professionnelles*, 4.256-57) notes the presence of women in youth associations, two of which may be composed entirely of females; see *CIL* X 5907 and Waltzing, *corporations Professionnelles*, 3 no. 2334.3. He points out an unknown type of association of slaves that includes five or six women (*CIL* II 5812; Waltzing, *corporations Professionnelles*, 4.256).

⁴⁷ Cf. also *IGRR* 796 (Apama [Phrygia]) records that a mother had a tomb made for her son, the president of the market-centre merchants, and for herself, and that the members helped her with it. Although it is unclear whether she was also a member of the association, it does seem that she had some relationship to the group.

⁴⁸ See the lists of Waltzing (*corporations Professionnelles*, 1.255-56) and Whelan ("Amica Paul," 75 n. 21) that give extensive examples taken from so-called funerary collegia. Cf. Liebenam, *Geschichte und Organisation*, 173-74. Those whose taxonomy includes three types of associations – professional, religious, and funerary – often cite the funerary associations as the exception in their inclusion of women; e.g., "sind Sklaven und Frauen eher in römischen als griechischen und eher in religiösen (*besonderes Begräbnis-*) als in Berufsvereinen anzutreffen" (Schmeller, *Hierarchie und Egalität*, 48

Private associations dedicated to the worship of Isis and Sarapis were inclusive of women. *IG* II² 1292 (Athens, 215/14 BCE) names a woman as the head (προερανίστρια) of both the male and female members of a private association of Sarapiastai.[49] Two private associations on Delos involved women: *IG* XI/4 1216-1222 (III/II BCE) names a woman as a member of an association of therapeutai,[50] and τὸ κοινὸν τῶν δεκαδιστῶν καὶ δεκαδιστριῶν lists among its members seven women and nine men (*IG* XI/4 1227; before 166 BCE). A first century BCE inscription from Eretria attests to an association of navarchs[51] dedicated to the Egyptian gods in which women were members; *SIRIS* 80 lists forty-five women and fifty men as members.[52] An undated inscription from Rome lists among the members of an association of melanephors[53] a freedwoman named Marcia Salvia (*CIL* VI 24627 = *SIRIS* 426).

A number of religious associations seem to have been composed exclusively of women. Waltzing cites five *collegia mulierum* (*CIL* V 2072; VI 10423; XI 5223; IX 4697; VI 2239) to which he adds an association of *cervae* (*CIL* III 1303).[54] *RIG* 993 (43 BCE) records the decree of an association of priestesses of Demeter at Mantinea (Arcadia). An honourific inscription set up in memory of Apollonis in Kyzikos (I CE) indicates that she was a member of an association composed exclusively of women,

---

[my emphasis], summarizing most earlier studies). However, since this designation should be eliminated (Kloppenborg, "Collegia and *Thiasoi*," 20-23) we need a re-evaluation of the place of women in the associations. Since most of those designated as "funerary" which include women are similar to "religious" associations, this opens the way for broadened understanding of the place of women in these associations.

[49] See Heyob, *Cult of Isis*, 105; Dow, "Egyptian Cults," 194-95; Foucart, *Associations Religieuses*, 6.

[50] Heyob, *Cult of Isis*, 106.

[51] "The navarchs were connected to the feast of *ploiaphesia*, though precisely how seems uncertain" (Heyob, *Cult of Isis*, 106); see further L. Vidman, *Isis und Sarapis bei den Griechen und Römern: Epigraphische Studien zur Verbreitung und zu den Trägern des ägyptischen Kultes* (RVV 29; Berlin: De Gruyter, 1970) 76-87.

[52] Another inscription, *SIRIS* 81 repeats four names from *SIRIS* 80 while *SIRIS* 82 records the dedication of a stele to the Egyptian gods by four persons, one of whom is a women. These inscriptions are summarized in Heyob (*Cult of Isis*, 106) who indicates that they are connected to the association of navarchs.

[53] Another type of association dedicated to the Egyptian gods, distinguished from others by the wearing of black garments in order to identify themselves with the mourning Isis; Heyob, *Cult of Isis*, 107.

[54] Waltzing, *corporations Professionnelles*, 4.205, 256. There are some professional associations composed of women; e.g., *CIL* VI 10109; IX 2480.

designated as the "Pythaistrides."⁵⁵ A fragmentary inscription from Alexandria, Egypt, records the dedication of a black granite statue by an association of women; τῇ Ἀπολλωνικῇ γυνακικήᾳ [συνοφδῳ] ἐκ κοινῶν (IAlexandria(K) 70; early I CE), which the editor suggests may be a women's chapter of an Apollonian association.⁵⁶

A few of the Macedonian associations attest to women members. In IPydna 1 three women are named among the thirty-one men as members of the association of Zeus Hypsistos (Aurelia Sabina, Aurelia Parthenope, Aurelia Atheno).⁵⁷ The tomb epigram of IAmphipolis 1 makes it clear that men and women are members in the Dionysiac association.⁵⁸ A private association dedicated to Sarapis is founded in Opus by a man but established in the house of a woman, with the administration of the mysteries and initiations falling to a succession of women (*IG* X/2 255; Thessalonica, *ca.* I CE). Pilhofer 340 records a dedication by a "thiasos of the distinguished maenads" (*thiasus Maenadarum regianarum*), indicative of an all female association.⁵⁹

Overall, Foucart may be overly optimistic in his assessment that such examples "suffiront d'autant plus que, même dans les cérémonies du culte public, une part considérable était accordée ou réservée aux femmes."⁶⁰ However, Dow's conclusion that "[w]omen had only a meager share in cult societies generally all over the Greek world in all periods"⁶¹ is only true insofar as one looks at the *proportion* of male involvement to female involvement. Yet women had almost no share in the political process generally, in the same way that most lower rank men were not given such opportunities. That the women had any involvement at all, especially in mixed gender voluntary associations, is significant insofar as such associations provided a location in which they could participate more fully in collective life than was usually allowed them in the Greek and Roman

---

⁵⁵ See Horsley, *New Documents* 4, 10-17.

⁵⁶ F. Kaysar, *Recueil d'inscriptions grecques et latins (non funéraires) d'Alexandrie Impériale (Iᵉʳ – IIIᵉʳ s. apr. J.-C.)* (Bibliothèque d'étude 108; Cairo: Institut Français d'archéologie orientale du Caire, 1996) 226; cf. IAlexandria(K) 65.

⁵⁷ Cf. IBeroea 1 may be a dedication of a female slave to Zeus Hypsistos.

⁵⁸ M. P. Nilsson, *The Dionysiac Mysteries of the Hellenistic and Roman Age* (Lund: Gleerup, 1957) 8.

⁵⁹ Perhaps the same group is responsible for Pilhofer 339 as it is dedicated to the same trio of deities (Liber and Libera and Hercules) and is set up under the auspices of a woman, Pomponia Hilara.

⁶⁰ Foucart, *Associations Religieuses*, 6.

⁶¹ Dow, "Egyptian Cults," 194 n. 47; cf. Poland, *griechischen Vereinswesens*, 296, 98; Schmeller, *Hierarchie und Egalität*, 48; Kloppenborg, "Collegia and *Thiasoi*," 25.

cities and villages.[62] Thus, the ratio of men to women involved in the associations should not obscure from view that women were sometimes involved in associations.

3. Hierarchy and Egalitarianism

A common critique of the use of the associations as an analogy for Christian groups is based on the latter being more inclusive in terms of social stratification than were the voluntary associations. That is, it is suggested that the associations tended to draw together people who were generally socially homogeneous while the Christian groups allowed for more equality within a group of varying social categories.[63] However, this notion of egalitarianism has been misrepresented on both sides of the argument.

Within many associations there were both hierarchy and equality.[64] The hierarchy existed between the founder and the officials of the association and the general membership. For example, many of the officials received larger portions of the meat from the sacrifices than the general membership. Among the members themselves, however, it is not uncommon to find citizens and non-citizens, masters and slaves, and men and women, rich and poor, all meeting together in one association. Professional/trade associations would be the most socially homogeneous; other types of associations less so.[65] Associations often presented themselves as egalitarian, despite the *de facto* hierarchy that gets reflected in their ordinances. Schmeller has illustrated that the associations were at the same time hierarchical *and* egalitarian – hierarchical with respect to

---

[62] Heyob's comment on the Egyptian cults generally is true for the associations: "The fact that women did participate in the religion even to the small extent that they did is in itself significant, however, since their participation in the Greek and Roman religions was very narrowly limited" (*Cult of Isis*, 110).

[63] Meeks, *First Urban Christians*, 79. So also G. Schöllgen, "Was wissen wir über die Sozialstruktur der paulinischen Gemeinden?" *NTS* 34 (1988) 74-75. Barton and Horsley ("Hellenistic Cult Group," 38-39) use the same principle as Meeks to differentiate Christian groups from the associations, but from a different perspective. They suggest that while both groups aimed at being egalitarian, the egalitarian nature of Christianity was undermined by the elevation of some members over others on the basis of their "spiritual gifts." Nevertheless, because Christianity aimed at egalitarianism it is still thought to be different than the associations.

[64] Cf. Schmeller *Hierarchie und Egalität*, 42.

[65] Schmeller, *Hierarchie und Egalität*, 49.

patrons and offices and egalitarian with respect to the general membership.[66]

In similar fashion, the Christian communities reflect both hierarchy and egalitarianism. Although we have evidence of Christian rhetoric of egalitarianism it often does not match with the actual practices that went on in the Christian communities.[67] For example, one senses that in the Christian groups it is unlikely that a slave who prophesied would be elevated to a higher status than his master who had a gift of hospitality. Egalitarianism was difficult to sustain in practice as can be seen from the divisions that arose in the Corinthian church (1 Cor 1-4) that manifested themselves as debates over meat eating (1 Cor 8-10), discord at the community meal (1 Cor 11:17-34), and trouble over spiritual gifts (1 Cor 11-14).[68]

Kloppenborg's recent examination of 1 Cor 6:1-11 shows that Paul's injunction against taking one another to court highlights a problem within the Corinthian congregation that is found within the voluntary associations and suggests that the early Christian communities were not as "egalitarian" as often claimed.[69] Legal action of the sort described in 1 Cor 6 presupposes that both parties are from the wealthy strata of society. Civil cases were brought to the courts by such people as a means of displaying status; "[t]he courts, as instruments of social control, were one way in which superior social status was displayed and maintained" in a public forum.[70] Paul's charge in 1 Cor 6 aims to curb such displays of competition for honour among the wealthy of the congregation. The regulations of a number of voluntary associations show that regularly occurring agonistic community interaction required that restrictions be placed on members who were challenging one another's honour, both during the meetings of the association and outside of the meetings. This sometimes manifested itself by members taking one another to court, a practice that some associations forbad. For example, in a set of

---

[66] See Schmeller, *Hierarchie und Egalität*.

[67] Cf. Schmeller, *Hierarchie und Egalität*, 92-93.

[68] See further the varying data Barton and Horsley put forth and Kloppenborg's response to Meeks that although membership within both types of groups was inclusive to some degree, the "inclusivity" of Paul's churches has been as exaggerated, as has the hierarchical nature of the associations ("Edwin Hatch," 234-36).

[69] J. S. Kloppenborg, "Egalitarianism in the Myth and Rhetoric of Pauline Churches," in *Reimagining Christian Origins: A Colloquium Honouring Burton L. Mack*, ed. E. A. Castelli and H. Taussig, (Valley Forge: Trinity Press International, 1996) 247-63.

[70] Kloppenborg, "Egalitarianism," 255-56.

regulations from an Egyptian religious association, a fine is levied upon a member who brings a complaint before the civic authorities before bringing it before the membership of the group (*P.Cairo.Dem.* 30606; 158-157 BCE). Thus we see a marked similarity between the Corinthian Christians and the voluntary associations in terms of both internal conflict among members and regulated conflict resolution over the issues of honour and "equality."[71] This mix of both hierarchy and egalitarianism reflects both the dominant cultural milieu of which the associations and Christian groups were a part and also offers some relief from it.

Overall, the relationship of the elite and non-elite in associations is a complex one. There are a number of associations in which the presence of the elite conferred various benefits on the association but also brought about some tensions, much like the mixture of elite and non-elite in the Corinthian community.[72] At the same time, some associations were composed exclusively of non-elite and developed strategies to protect themselves from exploitation, much like rhetoric of the letter of James.[73]

4. Benefaction and Honours

The sharp distinction between the rich and the poor and the concentration of wealth in the hands of a very small proportion of the population of the Empire contributed to the proliferation of a system of benefaction and patron-client relationships.[74] In most cases beneficence went from a person of higher social status and wealth to a person or

---

[71] In an independent study published about the same time Schmeller arrives at a similar conclusion (*Hierarchie und Egalität*, 86-87). We might consider Matt 5:25-26 in light of such injunctions.

[72] J. S. Kloppenborg, "Status und Wohltätigkeit bei Paulus und Jakobus," in *Von Jesus zum Christus – Christologische Studien: Festgabe für Paul Hofmann zum 65. Geburtstag*, ed. R. Hoppe and U. Busse, Ulrich (Berlin and New York: Walter de Gruyter, 1998) 135-46.

[73] Kloppenborg, "Status und Wohltätigkeit," 146-54.

[74] In general, "benefaction" applies to group situations while "patronage" occurs at the individual level: "A durable corporate group with fixed structural properties grants corporate honours and amenities to one who had benefited the group. Patron-client terminology generally reflects a more individualized phenomenon in which one party is bound to another through specific transactions or the assumption of particular obligations" (H. L. Hendrix, "Benefactor/Patronage Networks in the Urban Environment: Evidence from Thessalonica," *Semeia* 56 [1992] 40). However, these terms can be and are used interchangeably (see Hendrix, "Benefactor/Patronage Networks," 56 n. 1).

persons of lower status. No repayment of monies given was expected. However, the client was expected to "acknowledge and advertise his benefactor's generosity and power."[75]

In voluntary associations the role of the benefactor or patron was particularly important.[76] Although many associations collected membership dues, most were dependent upon patrons for a large part of their funds.[77] In exchange for large financial donations that allowed them to exist and to hold banquets and festivals, voluntary associations publicly honoured their benefactors, particularly with inscriptions or memorial services.[78] For example, the preamble of an inscription set up by an association of Dionysiac artists reads:

> Resolved by the artists around Dionysos and the Twin Gods. Whereas Lysimachos son of Ptolemaios, of the Sostratian demos, the cavalry commander and prytanarches for life, has shown devotion to the king and the latter's parents, before as well as now, in numerous ways; and is religiously and reverently disposed towards Dionysos and the other god; and treats the artists courteously in every respect; and voluntarily gives his assistance to each individual privately and to all publicly, having devoted himself without reserve to the advancement of the

---

[75] Garnsey and Saller, *Roman Empire*, 149. On a personal level this might be done by standing at a patron's door for the morning *salutatio*, accompanying him on his public rounds, and applauding his speeches in court (Garnsey and Saller, *Roman Empire*, 151). A group that receives benefaction (e.g., a voluntary association, a synagogue, even an entire city) might honour their patron with inscriptions, statues or public proclamation of the benefaction. The secondary literature on benefaction and patron-client relationships in antiquity has grown tremendously in the past decade. For a brief but thorough introduction to the practice see A. Wallace-Hadrill, "Patronage in Roman Society: From Republic to Empire," in *Patronage in Ancient Society*, ed. A. Wallace-Hadrill (Leicester-Nottingham Studies in Ancient Society 1; London and New York: Routledge, 1990) 63-87.

[76] On patronage in antiquity generally see Garnsey and Saller, *Roman Empire*, 148-59. For a large collection of translations of inscriptions attesting to the practice of patronage, including some from voluntary associations, see F. W. Danker, *Benefactor: Epigraphic Study of a Graeco-Roman and New Testament Semantic Field* (St. Louis: Clayton, 1982).

[77] Garnsey and Saller, *Roman Empire*, 157; F. W. Danker, "On Stones and Benefactors," *Currents in Theology and Mission* 8 (1981) 252; Schmeller, *Hierarchie und Egalität*, 33.

[78] See IMakedD 1104; *SIRIS* 122; 123; Pilhofer 209; *IG* II² 1271; 1273; 1278; 1292; 1329; 1327; 1343; *IG* XI/4 1061; *IG* XII/1 155; 937; *IG* XII/5 606; Foucart 59; *OGIS* 50; 51; IDelos 1519; 1520; 1521. Similar honourifics can be found among Jewish inscriptions; see IKyme 45; *MAMA* VI 264.

theatrical art; and (whereas) it is proper to honour such men as distinguished with the befitting honours.... (*OGIS* 51)

There then follows a list of honours to be granted Lysimachos, including a wreath and a painted portrait. Although this inscription dates from the third century BCE, the practice continued through to the first centuries of the common era.

The patron of an association could be a man or a woman, or at times even an entire family.[79] Often a single association could have several patrons, or a single patron could benefact several associations at once.[80] While some patrons took part in the association that was benefacted others did not. For example, an interesting Latin inscription from 153 CE records that a woman patron of a men's association was among those who received part of the cash generated from her foundational donation, but she was the only one "who did not take part in the drinking for which she had also paid."[81] A number of inscriptions suggest that often (although not always) a patron functioned as president and was active at meetings. A patron could determine how funds were to be disbursed (particularly in testamentary foundations) and could even appoint some of the officials (often from members of his or her extended family).

5. Finances

Voluntary associations concerned themselves with the collection of money through various means. The most obvious means was the collection of dues for membership in the association, either upon initiation or upon attendance at each meeting. Some even required dues if a member was absent from the meeting.[82] These membership dues would be used towards the social activities of the association (the most common being banquets and festivals), towards the burial of members, or towards general expenses. Many associations included the office of treasurer (ταμίας), indicating a

---

[79] On women patrons see Whelan, "Amica Paul," 76-77; Kloppenborg, "Collegia and Thiasoi," 25; cf. W. A. Meeks, "The Urban Environment of Pauline Christianity," in *SBL 1980 Seminar Papers*, ed. P. J. Achtemeier (SBLASP 19; Chico: Scholars, 1980) 117.

[80] Schmeller, *Hierarchie und Egalität*, 33.

[81] R. Duncan-Jones, *The Economy of the Roman Empire: Quantitative Studies* (New York: Cambridge University Press, 1974) 280 n. 1; see *ILS* 7213.

[82] Initiation: *IG* II² 1298; 1368; *IG* V/1 1390; Attendance: *IG* XII/1 155; *CIL* XIV 2112; IDelos 1519; 1521; *P.Mich.Tebt.* 243; *P.Cairo.Dem.* 30605, 30606; *in abstentia*: *IG* II² 1339, absent members paying a reduced rate.

concern for finances within the associations.[83] Money might be generated through the sale of offices and the honours that go with them, particularly that of the priesthood, although this would be more common for civic associations.[84]

Money was collected more generally in order to assist the association. For example, an association from Knidos lists a number of people who have "freely chosen to assist the association," including the amount of their donation.[85] The monies collected are not designated for any specific reason and presumably are to be used to support the general operation of the association, particularly in their social gatherings.[86] Money might be collected for special projects, as is the case in the large inscription of an association of Sylvanus from Philippi found engraved on the rock of the acropolis (*CIL* III 633/1, II CE). This inscription provides the names of those who have donated to the building and ornamentation of the temple of Sylvanus: "Publius Hostilius Philadelphus, on account of his public office of *aedile*, at his own expense had this inscription placed on polished rock and inscribed the names of the association members who made donations...." It appears to the right of another inscription from the same association that gives a more complete membership list (*CIL* III 633/2). The framework of the inscription that lists the donors was subsequently enlarged to the left (*CIL* III 633/3) and now takes up some of the space

---

[83] There is evidence for this office in a number of diverse associations from various times throughout the Greco-Roman empire: for example, IIlion 10 (77 BCE); IMylasa 861 (II BCE); 942; ISmyrna 653 (I-II CE); IDelos 1519 (153/52 BCE); *IG* II² (Attica) 1263 (300 BCE); 1265 (300/299 BCE); 1271 (298/97 BCE); 1284 (III BCE); 1291 (III BCE); 1292 (III BCE); 1317 (III BCE); 1323 (II BCE); 1325 (*ca.* 185/84 BCE); 1327 (II BCE); 1329 (175/74 BCE); 1333 (II BCE); 1335 (III BCE); 1339 (57 BCE); 1368 (II CE); 1369 (II CE); 1390 (I BCE); 2950/51 (II BCE); *IG* XII/1 677 (Rhodes, 300 BCE).

[84] On the purchasing of the office of the priesthood in a private association of θιασῶται see IKalkhedon 13 = *LSAM* 2 (III BCE). Examples from the civic cults include *LSAM* 1, 7, 23; *Syll.*³ 1009, 1012, 1014; IPriene 174, 201; IMylasa 942, although many more could be cited.

[85] IKnidos 23, II BCE. The list of thirteen names is interesting as they are given along with their place of origin, probably an indication of servile status. Only one is from Knidos itself. There are no Macedonians mentioned, although one person is from Thrace.

[86] See also *IG* II² 1327 (Piraeus, 178/77 BCE) wherein a treasurer is honoured because, among other things, he "organized the original collection of the common fund." Other associations had "common funds"; see *IG* II² 1263 (Piraeus, 300 BCE); IDelos 1520 (II BCE).

between it and the membership inscription further to the left. Presumably the space was originally left for the enlargement of the membership list.[87]

6. Moral Ethos

Scholars of Christian origins who reject the voluntary associations as a model for early Christian groups frequently accuse the associations of being disinterested in instructing their members in ethical principles. Usually, they are contrasted to Christian groups that concerned themselves with the behaviour of their members.[88] Barton and Horsley are among the more restrained in pointing out that there are *some* similarities in the moral code of the Pauline groups and that found in *Syll.*³ 985 (Philadelphia [Lydia], I BCE). However, they go on to suggest that the Christian groups were *more* rigorous in their moral injunctions, focusing not only on the suppression of vices but also on the exhibition of virtues.[89] However, it is questionable whether those in antiquity would have recognized this distinction. Some associations did advocate the exhibition of virtues among their members.[90] There may have been a difference in rhetoric – Pauline groups adopted the language of "sanctification" while other groups thought of more static qualifications such as the maintenance of moral purity in order to participate in the rituals. However, this is not a decisive

---

[87] Other connections with finances can be found among the association inscriptions. From the village of Kalambaki, near Philippi, we have a tomb epigram for a treasurer of an association of "silversmiths" (*argentarii*), probably those involved in minting money (IKalambaki 1); see Collart, *Philippes*, 271 n. 2; A. Salač, "Inscriptions du Pangée de la region Drama-Cavalla et de Philippes," *BCH* 47 (1923) 78. The word *argentarii* can mean either "silversmith" or "banker/money changer." Collart leans towards the former meaning in this inscription. Salač suggests that the members of the association were involved in the manufacture or trade of silverware ("Inscriptions du Pangée," 78). Clearly finance was the primary focus of both this particular member and the association to which he belonged.

[88] See W. A. Meeks, *The Moral World of the First Christians* (LEC 6; Philadelphia: Westminster, 1986) 114; Jeffers, *Greco-Roman World*, 80.

[89] Barton and Horsley, "Hellenistic Cult Group," 37

[90] Members could be noted for their piety (εὐσέβεια, see, for example, IPergamon 485 [I BCE]; IDelos 1016 [172-62 BCE]) although the outward expression of respect for the gods was often tied to financial contributions, either public or private benefaction (A. W. M. Adkins, *Merit and Responsibility: A Study in Greek Values* [Oxford: Clarendon, 1960] 135; A. Batten, "The Moral World of Greco-Roman Associations," unpublished paper presented at the Canadian Society of Biblical Studies 2001 Annual Meeting, Laval, Quebec, May 24, 2001, 4-5.

distinction phenomenologically; in both instances maintenance of moral codes was required.[91] Indeed, "moral language was used to promote internal order within the associations, an essential ingredient for their survival."[92]

The inscription of a private association of Zeus (*Syll.*[3] 985, Philadelphia, Lydia) is one of the most significant texts in terms of recording moral language. The text results from a dream experienced by the association founder in which Zeus establishes regulations around access to the household-based association dedicated to the savior gods.

> When coming into this *oikos* let men and women, free people and slaves, swear by all the gods neither to know nor make use wittingly of any deceit against a man or a woman, neither poison harmful to men nor harmful spells. They are not themselves to make use of a love potion, abortifacient, contraceptive, or any other thing fatal to children; nor are they to recommend it to, nor connive at it with, another. They are not to refrain in any respect from being well-intentioned toward this *oikos*.

Anyone who knows of any infraction of these regulations is to expose it. A male association member must only have sexual relations with his wife. Failure to follow this will result in severe penalties for both the man and the woman involved:

> Woman and man, whoever does any of the things written above, let him not enter this *oikos*. For great are the gods set up in it: they watch over these things, and will not tolerate those who transgress the ordinances.

A free woman who does not restrict her sexual practices to her husband faces even stiffer penalties; not only is she "defiled and full of endemic pollution" she is "unworthy to reverence this god" and barred from the rituals.[93] Failure to obey brings about:

---

[91] Barton and Horsley also suggest that the cult association at Philadelphia that they examined (*Syll.*[3] 985) sought salvation from Zeus in this world, while the Christian groups looked for salvation in the world to come ("Hellenistic Cult Group," 41). While this is true for the association they examine, a number of religious associations did look for betterment in the afterlife by choosing a particular patron deity (W. Burkert, *Ancient Mystery Cults* [Cambridge and London: Harvard University Press, 1987] 21-23; idem, *Greek Religion*, 293-95).

[92] Batten, "Moral World," 1. I am indebted to Alicia Batten for a number of these observations and am grateful for her permission to use her unpublished work here.

[93] That a free woman is specified probably recognizes that a female slave would have little control over how her master treated her. At the very least, there is a recognition in the regulations that free persons have a moral choice. Although slave

evil curses from the gods for disregarding these ordinance. For the god does not desire these things to happen at all, nor does he wish it, but he wants obedience. The gods will be gracious to those who obey, and always give them all good things, whatever gods give to men they love. The good things promised probably include some of those things named as the inscription breaks off: "good recompenses, health, salvation, peace, safety on land and sea...." The retribution of the gods on those who disobey is similar to (in fact, harsher than) Paul's warnings in 1 Thess 4:6b: "...that no one transgress, and wrong his brother in this matter, because the Lord is an avenger in all these things, as we solemnly forewarned you." In the case of both the associations and 1 Thessalonians the concern is not with personal sexual purity in and of itself but with the larger implications for the community to which the transgressor belongs. In the inscription sexual indiscretion seems to affect adversely the rituals (cf. also *LSCGSup* 91). Although the regulations of this inscription do not focus on morality, "they are not completely severed from it."[94] That is, although the regulations do not aim at conversion or even, necessarily, character transformation, they do reflect attitudes that suggest certain practices in the culture, which although common, "were not universally condoned."[95]

A similar attitude can also be seen in a number of other inscriptions. In *IG* II² 1366 (Sounion, Attica, II-III CE) there is a concern for purity that requires abstinence from certain practices and activities before participation in the rituals: "No one impure is to enter, but let them be purified from garlic and swine and women." Women who want to enter must wash themselves "from head to foot" for seven days after menstruation, ten days after contact with a corpse, and forty days after miscarriage/abortion (the text is somewhat unclear which is indicated). The concern for purity is not the only concern behind these injunctions. There is also a promise that the god, Men Tyrannos, will benefit those who approach him in "sincerity (ἁπλοῦς) of soul." Such "sincerity" is expressed with respect to the heart as a moral duty in Eph 6:5 and Col 3:22 (slaves obedience to masters "as to Christ") and in 2 Cor 11:3 in Paul's worry that the Corinthians' thoughts "will be led astray from a sincere and pure devotion to Christ."[96] Although within this association moral impurity

---

women have equal access to the association, they do not have equal choice due to their legal status as non-persons.

[94] Batten, "Moral World," 10.
[95] Batten, "Moral World," 10.
[96] Horsley, *New Documents* 3, 24.

can be cleansed through washings, there exists an "unforgivable" sin: "Anyone who meddles with the god's possessions or is a busybody, may they incur sin (ἁμαρτία) against Men Tyrannos which he certainly cannot expiate."[97]

In *P.Mich. Tebt.* 243 (I CE) a community regulation stipulates that "if a member ignores someone who is in distress and does not assist in helping him out of his trouble" he shall be fined. This stands out from the more typical regulations pertaining to fights over seating arrangements and failure to place a wreath on a tomb. In the case of mutual assistance, we come close to the charitable impulse that was an important part of early Christian ethics. In *IG* II^2 1343 (Athens, 37/36 BCE) the praise given to a priest resulting from his "not being one who loves money" suggests that "avarice was not admirable."[98]

If one defines the mysteries of Mithras as an association,[99] then one finds there the expression of moral codes. The initiates into the grade of "lion" are required to

> keep their hands pure of all that which is painful, harmful, or dirty, and since it is an initiate of cathartic fire those hands are being washed, they use appropriate substance and avoid water because it is inimical to fire. They also purify the tongue of sin by means of honey. (Porphyry, *Antr. Nymph.* 15)

This concern in the initiation process goes beyond simply maintenance of ritual purity and is suggestive of a transformation that includes a moral dimension.[100]

These inscriptions do not prove the case that all voluntary associations were concerned with personal moral codes. Indeed, it seems to be the exception rather than the rule. However, even these few examples suggest that one cannot simply eliminate the need for taking seriously the associations as an analogue for early Christian groups on the basis of some perceived lack of moral rigor. Unfortunately, Poland's warning in the early

---

[97] The reference to sin in an inscription associated with Men is not unique to this text; see Horsley, *New Documents* 3, 24.

[98] Batten, "Moral World," 6.

[99] As does R. Beck, "The Mysteries of Mithras," in *Voluntary Associations in the Graeco-Roman World*, ed. J. S. Kloppenborg and S. G. Wilson (London and New York: Routledge, 1996) 176-85.

[100] Batten, "Moral World," 2.

part of the twentieth century that the immorality of the associations was exaggerated has gone unheeded.[101]

7. Cultic Activities

The concern within the voluntary associations with conviviality and cult is highlighted by Barton and Horsley, who suggest that the early Christians' lack of mysteries, purifications, expiations, and sacrifices and the inclusion of prayers, hymns, teaching, and the sharing of a common meal sets them apart from the associations.[102] This critique of the voluntary associations as analogous to Christian groups is problematic on two accounts. First, Christian groups did include some rituals, particularly baptism and the meal of remembrance (Eucharist). As far as we can tell from early Christian sources, Christian baptism reflects the hallmarks of a ritual. While the New Testament texts themselves say little about the process of baptism, the late first century document *Didache* includes a number of details. Although *Didache* does not advocate one particular process of baptism (though it signals a clear preference) it does emphasize the proper preparation of the initiates, the use of appropriate overseers, and two ritual symbols: water and a formula invoking the name of God. More importantly, it is clear that all three stages of a ritual of status transformation – separation, liminality, aggregation – are present in the carrying out of a baptism.[103]

Likewise, the Christian eucharistic meal has a cultic function. All three synoptic gospels record Jesus' institution of this meal (Matt 26:26-30; Mark 14:22-26; Luke 22:17-20), and Paul gives some formulaic details that are surprisingly similar to Luke's account (1 Cor 11:23-26). In all cases, "on the one hand, they give the aetiological reason for the current practice of the church and lead it back to its sustaining foundation; on the other hand, they have received their shape and form from the liturgical

---

[101] Poland, *griechischen Vereinswesens*, 499-501. This is not true of the recent work of Batten, "Moral World."

[102] Barton and Horsley, "Hellenistic Cult Group," 39. They note earlier that the deity, while present in both groups, is not represented physically in the Christian groups as it is in the association, giving the Christian groups an unusual "non-cultic" character (p. 30). This is a similar objection to the one addressed here.

[103] For details see R. S. Ascough, "An Analysis of the Baptismal Ritual of the *Didache*," *StLtg* 24 (1994) 201-13.

practice of the church."[104] The institution of a commemoratory meal probably goes back to the historical Jesus but soon after his death cultic aspects became a separate rite.[105] Second, we can note that the language of mystery[106] and purification[107] occurs in a number of New Testament texts. Third, features such as prayers, hymns, teaching, and meals were part of the life of associations.[108]

---

[104] H.-J. Klauck, "Lord's Supper," *ABD* 4 (1992) 363; cf. B. Chilton, "The Eucharist: Exploring Its Origins," *BRev* 10/6 (1994) 36-43; F. G. Carpinelli, "'Do This as *My* Memorial' (Luke 22:19): Lucan Soteriology of Atonement," *CBQ* 61 (1999) 74-91. Acts also seems to include references to a shared meal (e.g., 2:42, 46; 6:1-2), as do *Didache* (chapters 9-10) and Ignatius (e.g. *Smyrn.* 7:1, 8:9), the latter two being much more explicitly *eucharistia*.

[105] Klauck, "Lord's Supper," 371.

[106] For example, Phil 2:17; 4:12; cf. Rom 16:25; 1 Cor 2:1; 4:1; 15:51.

[107] For example, Paul's concern with sexual purity; 1 Thess 4:1-8; 1 Cor 5:1-2, 9-13; 6:12-20; cf. Phil 1:1; 1:10; 2 Cor 11:3. On expiation see Rom 3:25.

[108] For example see on prayer: *IG* II² 1343; *Syll.*³ 694; IMagnMai 98; *LSAM* 19; cf. *IG* II² 4636, 4637. Hymns: IMagnMai 100 A; IPergamon 485; *LSAM* 28; *IG* XI/4 1299; there were even professional associations of musicians who took the name μολποί (see *LSAM* 50; 53; *LSS* 91; IEphesus 899; 900; 901; 903; 906). Teaching: legislative material in association inscriptions is akin to Paul's parenetic sections of his letter; *IG* XI/4 1299 includes a lengthy hymn in hexameter verse recounting the founding and development of the cult of Sarapis on Delos; an inscription commemorating the founding of an association dedicated to Poseidon celebrates the saving of the city with a hymn (*BCH* 5 [1881] 340-42 No. 1); these latter two cases seem to function in a didactic fashion similar to Paul's use of a hymn in Phil 2:6-11. Meals: *IG* II² 1366; 1368; IPriene 195; 205; LSCG 77; *Syll.*³ 1009; 1024; *IG* V/1 1390; *IG* XI/4 1299; IDelos 1520; *LSAM* 9; IEphesus 24; *P.Mich. Tebt.* 243; 244.

Chapter Four

Community Organization

1. Self-definition Terminology

One of the significant differences pointed to between ancient associations and the Christian groups is the "complete absence" of any common terminology.[1] Two elements need to be addressed in response to this issue: (a) the idea of "common terminology" between the associations and the Christian groups;[2] and (b) the Christian designation ἐκκλησία. First, there is the issue of common terminology. In the associations there is a wide diversity of titles.[3] In Macedonia we find a variety of names used for associations in the inscriptions. Θίασος is used of six associations (IThessalonica 3; *IG* X/2 309; 506 for two different associations; 260 for two different associations) and the Latinized *thiasus* is used of four associations (*CIL* III 703; 704; Pilhofer 338; 095). The corresponding Latin word *collegium* is used of two of the associations (*SEG* XXXVII 559; *CIL* III 633) and the Greek form of the word, κολλήγιον, is used once (*CIG* 2007f). We find the use of συνήθεια by four associations (IBeroea 1; IThessalonica 2; *IG* X/2 291; 933), along with συμποσία (Pilhofer 697/2), τέχνη (*Syll.*³ 1140 of a guild), and δοῦμος by an association of merchant marines (IThessalonica 1; cf. the term used in *IG* X/2 860).

More often an association is named according to its adherents. Μύσται is the most common name. It is used of six different Macedonian associations, four of them devoted to Dionysus (*IG* X/2 259; 260; IMakedD 920; 1104) and two of them associations of Asiani (IThessalonica 3; *IG* X/2 309, which may have worshipped Dionysus). "Maenads" is used of an association of women worshipers of Dionysus

---

[1] Meeks, *First Urban Christians*, 79; Jeffers, *Greco-Roman World*, 80.

[2] "Common terminology" is Meeks' term; we prefer "overlapping terminology."

[3] For a more complete list of guild names that indicate religious activities or divinities see Poland, *griechischen Vereinswesens*, 33-46; 57-62. Inscriptional evidence attests the fact that there is no standard nomenclature for the designation of associations. Even lawyers in ancient Rome used no single, clearly defined name for an association; in their writings they use synonymous words, particularly *collegium* and *corpus*, to indicate private associations (Ausbüttel, *Untersuchungen*, 16). Sometimes one association had several names; for example see the *lex collegi* from Lanuvium (*CIL* 2112; Ausbüttel, *Untersuchungen*, 19). Often the names of associations differed according to geographical location (Ausbüttel, *Untersuchungen*, 33).

(Pilhofer 338). *Consacrani*, the Latin equivalent of συμμύσται, is used once (Pilhofer 339).[4] Συνθιασίται is used once (IMakedD 284). Θρησκευταί is used in five inscriptions (IPydna 1; *IG* X/2 192; 220; *SIRIS* 123; 124) while *cultores* is used in three others (*CIL* III 633; *SIRIS* 122; Pilhofer 209).[5] The designation συνκλίται is used of two groups of associates (*IG* X/2 68; 58), while συνήθεις is used of four others (IEdessa 3; IBeroea 3; *IG* X/2 288; 289). Finally, a number of singular designations are used of an association indicating either a trade (e.g., purple-dyers, silversmiths, donkey-drivers) or some other form of identification (e.g., Asiani, Πρινοφοροι).

This diversity of group designators for associations suggests that there was no one designation by which all groups could be identified. If Christian groups are to be understood within the matrix of the associations, we would be amiss to demand of them that they "adopt" a particular title to identify themselves as an "association." Such a concern does not seem to be part of the fabric of ancient society. Thus, whatever a group's name, they could still be understood, both socially and legally, as what modern scholars call "voluntary associations." Although it is quite clear that members of an association might consider themselves better or more attractive than another association, it is a difference of degree, not of kind.

The second issue in need of being addressed vis-à-vis association terminology is the use of ἐκκλησία. This referent for the Christian community is widely attested in the New Testament. It is used throughout Acts to refer to the early Christian community and Matthew places it on the lips of Jesus three times in his gospel (Matt 16:18, 18:17). Paul uses the term in the plural to indicate Christian groups in various locations (e.g., Rom 16:16; 1 Cor 7:17; 11:16; 16:19; 2 Cor 8:1; 11:28; Gal 1:22) and in the singular to indicate the church universal (e.g., 1 Cor 10:32; 15:9; Gal 1:13; Phil 3:6).[6] It is used to refer to the local Christian community (e.g., Rom 16:1, 5; 1 Cor 1:2; 11:18). This is the sense in 1 Thess 1:1 when Paul addresses τῇ ἐκκλησίᾳ Θεσσαλονικέων. In Phil 4:15

---

[4] Collart, *Philippes*, 431.

[5] P. Lemerle suggests that associations of θρησκευταὶ are rare ("Inscriptions latines et grecques de Philippes," *BCH* 59 [1935] 142); cf. Poland, *griechischen Vereinswesens*, 36. All of our instances come from the III CE, which is late for such usage.

[6] Cf. Meeks, *First Urban Christians*, 42-43. Hainz is incorrect in suggesting that Paul's use of ἐκκλησία in the plural always refers only to the Jerusalem church (e.g., 1 Cor 11:16) while in the singular it refers to the local congregation (*Ekklesia: Strukturen paulinischer Gemeinde-Theologie und Gemeinde-Ordnung* [BU 9; Regensburg: F. Pustet, 1972] 229-55).

he writes "no ἐκκλησία entered into partnership with me ... except you only," implying the designation ἐκκλησία for the Philippians.

The LXX and the Greek civic context are often recognized as background for the use of the term.[7] The word ἐκκλησία is used over one hundred times in the LXX, in most instances as a translation for the Hebrew קהל. Few scholars address cogently the issue of why the Christian groups would choose to use ἐκκλησία over συναγωγή. Most often the LXX background is cited in order to show how the title was derived from the community's roots in Judaism.[8] Duling's comments are representative with reference to Matthew: "[g]iven the Septuagint rendering of Hebrew 'assembly' (*qahal*) as both συναγωγή and ἐκκλησία and the relation of these two terms to the 'house-synagogue' and the 'house-church,' it is naturally *the* central option for the Matthean group."[9] However, this assumption will not stand, for Matthew or for Paul, since ἐκκλησία is not the only option; συναγωγή is also an option. In fact, συναγωγή is the more

---

[7] See Schmidt, "ἐκκλησία," *TDNT* 3 (1965) 513, 530-31; W. J. Cotter, "Women's Authority Roles in Paul's Churches: Countercultural or Conventional?" *NovT* 36 (1994) 370; W. O. McCready, "*Ecclesia* and Voluntary Associations," in *Voluntary Associations in the Graeco-Roman World*, ed. J. S. Kloppenborg and S. G. Wilson (London and New York: Routledge, 1996) 60-61.

[8] For Paul see, for example, Schmidt, "ἐκκλησία," 516; McCready, "Voluntary Associations," 60-61; G. F. Hawthorne, *Philippians* (WBC 43; Dallas: Word, 1983) 134; P. T. O'Brien, *The Epistle to the Philippians: A Commentary on the Greek Text* (NIGTC; Grand Rapids: Eerdmans, 1991) 377; A. Plummer, *A Commentary on St. Paul's First Epistle to the Thessalonians* (London: Roxburghe, 1918) 3; B. Rigaux, *Les épîtres aux Thessaloniciens* (Ebib; Paris: Lecoffre, 1956) 348-49; T. Holtz, *Der erste Brief an die Thessalonicher* (EKK 13; Zürich: Benziger, 1986) 38; C. A. Wanamaker, *The Epistles to the Thessalonians: A Commentary on the Greek Text* (NIGTC; Grand Rapids: Eerdmans, 1990) 70; E. J. Richard, *First and Second Thessalonians* (Sacra Pagina 11; Collegeville: Liturgical Press, 1995) 38. J. Y. Campbell argues that the term does not come from the Old Testament as a designation for 'the true people of God,' but he does find the primary source for *Christian* usage in the Psalms and in Sirach ("The Origin and Meaning of the Christian Use of the Word ΕΚΚΛΗΣΙΑ," *JTS* 49 [1948] 130-43). R. F. Collins suggests that as a Christian community designator it originated among Jewish Christians in Jerusalem from which Paul "borrowed" it, although he goes on to suggest that in 1 Thess 1:1 it retains both the civic and the LXX sense (*Studies on the First Letter to the Thessalonians* [Louvain: Louvain University Press, 1984] 287). However, he emphasizes the LXX in suggesting "Paul enables us to see that his choice of the term ἐκκλησία was not simply a borrowing of traditional terminology but the deliberate application to the Thessalonians of a biblical model whereby he could interpret their experience. By using the idea of election in reference to this community, composed essentially of Gentiles, Paul inserts them into the context of salvation history."

[9] Dulling, "Matthean Brotherhood," 164.

frequently chosen word in the LXX as a translation of קהל in the Hebrew Bible.[10] Thus, συναγωγή would seem to be a more obvious choice if the LXX is viewed as the primary background.[11]

The term ἐκκλησία is found in a few instances as a designator for voluntary associations and their meetings.[12] For example, the decree of the Tyrian merchants and shippers begins:

> During the archonship of Phaedrius, on the 8th day of Elaphebolion, at the assembly (ἐκκλησία) in the temple of Apollo, Dionysios son of Dionysios the *archithiasites* made a motion: Whereas Patron son of Dorotheos who belongs to the *synodos*, has come to the assembly (ἐκκλησία) and has renewed the good will he has for the *synodos* and has unhesitatingly supplied many needs, and continues to speak and act in every way to the profit of both the *koinon* and the *synodos*....
> (IDelos 1519; 196 BCE)

While ἐκκλησία is not frequently the group referent, it is one of many designations that the associations have taken over from the civic government.[13] Thus, it is difficult not to agree with Kloppenborg that within the context of urban-based Christian communities the term ἐκκλησία would have been heard to be indicative of a voluntary association.[14] This is the view of Neumann who suggests "it would have

---

[10] McCready, "Voluntary Associations," 60; Schmidt, "ἐκκλησία," 513-14, esp. n. 25.

[11] Cf. Ascough, "Matthew," 112-14.

[12] See also Poland, *griechischen Vereinswesens*, 332 (Samos); *OGIS* 488 (Kastollos near Philadelphia, II CE); *IGLAM* 1381 (Aspendus [Pamphylia]); *IGLAM* 1382 (Aspendus). O'Brien is incorrect in stating that ἐκκλησία "did not designate an 'organization' or 'society'" (*Philippians*, 377 n. 61).

[13] See Poland, *griechischen Vereinswesens*, 152-68. The term ἐκκλησία is used one hundred and eleven times in the New Testament, although only three have the civic sense (Acts 19:32, 39, 41). Only one of these refers to a legal body (ἐκκλησία ἔννομος, Acts 19:39) and is presented in contrast to the ἐκκλησία that gathered without official sanction at the theater in Ephesus (W. D. Ferguson, *The Legal and Governmental Terms Common to the Macedonian Greek Inscriptions and the New Testament* [Historical and Linguistic Studies Second Series 2/3; Chicago: Chicago University Press, 1913] 54-55).

[14] Kloppenborg, "Edwin Hatch," 231. As I have suggested elsewhere (Ascough, "Matthew," 114), there is the possibility that at least in some cases the Jesus-communities wanted to somehow distinguish themselves from the non-Jesus-believing groups through their community designator, and thus chose ἐκκλησία over συναγωγή. This is likely the case with the Matthean group who had recently been separated from the synagogue (or are in the process). The Matthean Christians would hear ἐκκλησία as marking them off as distinct from the Jewish συναγωγή and as designating them as similar in structure to a voluntary association. This contrast is made even stronger

needed explanation if Greek Christians had not seen religious fellowships or *thiasoi* in their new associations."[15]

---

through the language of "their/your synagogues" (4:23; 9:35; 10:17; 12:9; 13:54; 23:34; all but the first unique to Matthew) and the synagogues of the "hypocrites" (6:2; cf.6:5, 23:13-26). In choosing ἐκκλησία Matthew wants the newly founded group to be readily understood as a different type of association than the Jewish associations from which he and his companions have been expelled (perhaps seen in the placement of *"my* synagogue" on the lips of Jesus in Matt 16:18). According to D. Georgi many of those Christians who came to embrace the "Easter experiences" as conveyed by Paul were not themselves Jewish ("The Early Church: Internal Jewish Migration or New Religion," *HTR* 88 [1995] 40). Undoubtedly some were, but in many cases not even a majority of a particular community were Jewish (i.e., Galatia, Philippi, Thessalonica). In these cases it is unlikely that in working out a self-identity they would have seen themselves in competition with Jewish groups but rather with any other groups in general. Thus, Paul's use of ἐκκλησία becomes more significant than Georgi allows. Georgi points out that Paul himself never uses the terms "Christian" or "Christianity," suggesting that he did not know these terms ("Early Church," 40). However, as Georgi admits, neither does Paul use συναγωγή or προσευχή. Georgi suggests that he uses ἐκκλησία to deliberately compete with the "assembly of free citizens meeting in the local theater" rather than to compete with local Jewish groups ("Early Church," 41). In so doing, however, Paul's groups would be competing with other small, non-Jewish associations ("voluntary associations") that often took their nomenclature from the civic institutions (and more often not in direct competition but in the sense of "imitation as flattery").

[15] K. J. Neuman, *Der römische Staat und die allgemeine Kirche bis auf Diocletian* (Leipzig: Veit, 1890) 46-7, quoted in Schmidt, "ἐκκλησία," 516 n. 36 (Neumann's work was not available to me). H. Lietzmann calls Poland's three citations of uses of ἐκκλησία in associations the exceptions that prove the rule ("die drei scheinbaren Ausnahmen ... bestätigen diese Regel") that the LXX is the source for the Christian use of the term: "Es ist ein in der Christenheit selbst entstandener Name der Gemeinde, der in der LXX seine Quelle hat" (*An die Korinther I/II* [HNT 9; Tübingen: Mohr Siebeck, 1969⁵] 4 n. 2) However, this view tends both to blur all of the Christian groups and ignore the context of how local recipients of Paul's letters would hear them (perhaps differently from place to place). Despite his agreement with Lietzmann, Schmidt ("ἐκκλησία," 514) admits that, "[s]ome Gentile Christian circles, which were not so well, or not at all, acquainted with the OT context, might have understood the term in the light of its immediate derivation and possible recollections of Greek fellowships. It is quite possible, and wholly natural, that many matters of organization in Christian congregations should have been regulated according to the pattern of contemporary societies." This is especially the case for the Macedonian context where there is no evidence for a Jewish presence before the end of the second century CE. Klauck notes that since outsiders might have perceived Christian groups as associations Christians might have called themselves ἐκκλησία in order to clear up the confusion (*Religious Context*, 54). However, this is predicated on his comment that ἐκκλησία does not occur frequently in association inscriptions as a result of "an awareness of the distinction between the private association and the public assembly" (*Religious Context*, 46). However, Klauck leaves two aspects unexplained: (a)

For other overlapping terminology we might look at the term ἀδελφός. The word literally means "sons of the same mother,"[16] although it occurs frequently as a fictive kinship term within a variety of Christian communities, especially the Pauline communities.[17] Although he provides no direct evidence himself, Plummer asserts that ἀδελφός is commonly used for members of voluntary associations.[18] As an illustration, we have an interesting inscription from an association of masons from mid-first century CE Rough Cilicia that lists the names of a number of unrelated men[19] who have joint shares in a tomb that belongs to a κοινόν (IKilikiaBM 2.201). Their regulations stipulate:

If any brother (ἀδελφός) should wish to sell his share, the remaining brothers shall buy it. If the brothers (οἱ ἀδελφοί) do no wish to buy the share, then let them take the aforementioned cash, and let them (all) withdraw from the association.[20]

---

why many associations would use other terms from public assembly quite frequently and (b) why the early Christians thought it better to be perceived as a public, civic assembly rather than a private association (the former most likely to be perceived as a challenge [at least at the level of honour] to the local authorities).

[16] LSJ s.v.

[17] Meeks, *First Urban Christians*, 86-89; cf. J. Z. Smith, "Here, There, and Anywhere," unpublished keynote address to the conference "Prayer, Magic and the Stars in the Ancient and Late Antique World" (University of Washington, Department of Near Eastern Languages and Civilization, March 3-5, 2000) 19; S. S. Bartchy, "Undermining Ancient Patriarchy: The Apostle Paul's Vision of a Society of Siblings," *BTB* 29 (1999) 68-78.

[18] Plummer, *Thessalonians*, 19. Plummer has probably overstated the case as it is not a particularly common designation (cf. Kloppenborg, "Egalitarianism," 259). Nevertheless, there is evidence for its use in associations; see Poland, *griechischen Vereinswesens*, 56; Bömer, *Untersuchungen*, 72-78; G. A. Deissmann, *Bible Studies: Contributions Chiefly From Papyri and Inscriptions to the History of the Language, the Literature, and the Religion of Hellenistic Judaism and Primitive Christianity* (Edinburgh: T. & T. Clark, 1901) 88; J. H. Moulton and G. Milligan, *The Vocabulary of the Greek New Testament Illustrated from the Papyri and Other Non-literary Sources* (London: Hodder and Stoughton, 1914) 9; A. D. Nock, "The Historical Importance of Cult-Associations," *CR* (1924) 105.

[19] The exceptions are two of the ten who are named as sons of the same father.

[20] The men named earlier in the inscription are not the entire κοινόν, just those who have a share in one particular tomb of the κοινόν. The regulation suggests that should one of these men withdraw the others must "buy-out" his share unless a replacement can be found. If they do not, they must withdraw (as a group) from the larger κοινόν, each receiving the stated amount of cash. However, the tomb remains the property of the κοινόν, which is not disbanded.

This is a clear, mid-first century CE example of how ἀδελφός refers to men in an association. Another example comes from third century BCE Manshiyeh, where members of an association of Dionysiac artists are named as ἀδελφοί (*OGIS* 51; cf. *OGIS* 50) although it is clear that they are not relatives.[21] The same term is used of members of a religious association formed within the Serapeum at Memphis (*P.Paris* 42; II BCE).[22] In Latin inscriptions there is reference to members of associations as *fratres*.[23]

Other overlapping terminology can be found: for example, the term πολίτευμα occurs in Phil 3:20 and in the verbal form in Phil 1:27. The word πολίτευμα can be used variously to indicate "political government," "commonwealth," "state," "citizenship," "colony of foreigners," or "colony."[24] However, there is clear evidence for its use as a group designator within voluntary associations. From Egypt there is evidence that part of the temple of the goddess Sachypsis was reserved for a private association named for both its founder (Harthotes) and for the goddess: "the area of the *politeuma* of the blessed Harthotes the Great of the supreme goddess Sachypsis" (IFayum II 121, 93 CE).[25] In three inscriptions from the temple complex of Zeus Panamaros near Stratonicaea, Caria, there is mention of τὸ πολείτευμα τῶν γυναικῶν, probably indicating "a temporary association lasting only for the time of the feast."[26]

---

[21] The association is dedicated to the Twin Gods (θεοὺς ἀδελφούς = the Dioscuri) as well as Dionysos. The Dioscuri were seen as prime examples of brotherly affection (Kloppenborg, "ΦΙΛΑΔΕΛΦΙΑ," 285, 287).

[22] Moulton and Milligan, *Vocabulary*, 9; cf. *P.Tor* I.I$^{i.20}$, II BCE.

[23] *CIL* VI 377, 406, 7487, 10681, 21812; see Kloppenborg, "Edwin Hatch," 216 n. 17, 237.

[24] See W. Ruppel, "Politeuma. Bedeutungsgeschichte eines staatsrechtlichen Terminus," *Philologus* 82 (1927) 268-312, 433-54, also summarized in H. Strathmann, "πόλις, κτλ.," *TDNT* 4 (1967) 519-20; P. Böttger, "Die eschatologische Existenz der Christen. Erwägungen zu Philipper 3.20," *ZNW* 60 (1969) 244-63; A. T. Lincoln, *Paradise Now and Not Yet: Studies in the Role of the Heavenly Dimension in Paul's Thought with Special Reference to His Eschatology* (SNTSMS 43; Cambridge: Cambridge University Press, 1981) 96-100; G. Lüderitz, "What is the Politeuma?" in *Studies in Early Jewish Epigraphy*, ed. J. W. van Henten and P. W. van der Horst (AGJU 21; Leiden, New York, Köln: Brill, 1994) 185-88; cf. Moulton and Milligan, *Vocabulary*, 525-26.

[25] Text and translation in Lüderitz, "Politeuma," 191, who notes that the understanding of πολίτευμα as "a club of the type often called σύνοδος or κοινόν ... is also the opinion of all scholars commenting on this inscription" ("Politeuma," 192).

[26] See Lüderitz, "Politeuma," 190; for texts "Politeuma," 189.

An inscription from the second or first century BCE indicates that there was a πολίτευμα of soldiers in Alexandria that was constituted like a association:

> To Zeus Soter and Hera Teleia, the *politeuma* of the soldiers brought to Alexandria, their chairman Dionysios of Callon and secretary Philippos of Philippos, the founders, ex voto, year 6.[27]

Four burial inscriptions from Sidon (II BCE) use πολίτευμα to indicate citizens of one city who have formed an association while living in another city. These groups were most likely formed of soldiers, but may have included civilian members.[28]

From Egypt four inscriptions attest to various ethnic associations each of which are designated as a πολίτευμα:[29] Cilicians (IFayum I 15, III-II BCE), Boeotians (Xois, 165 to 145 BCE; *SEG* II 871), Phrygians (Pompeii, 2 BCE; *CIG* 5866c),[30] and Lycians (Alexandria, 120 CE; *SEG* II 848). Further evidence comes from a papyrus fragment from the Fayum (145 BCE; *P.Mich. Tebt.* 1.32) that mentions a πολίτευμα of Cretans. In two of the inscriptions there is mention of a priest of the πολίτευμα (*SEG* II 871 and *CIG* 5866c), a position often found in associations.[31] In *SEG* II 871 there is the designation of the members as οἱ συμπολιτευόμενοι, a designation found elsewhere for members of a κοινόν (*OGIS* 143 and 145, both from Cyprus).[32] Overall, this cumulative evidence shows that πολίτευμα is applied as a designation for a variety of voluntary associations.[33]

---

[27] Text and translation in Lüderitz, "Politeuma," 192.

[28] See Lüderitz, "Politeuma," 193-95.

[29] Lüderitz argues against the *assumption* of E. M. Smallwood (*The Jews Under Roman Rule* (SJLA 20; Leiden: Brill, 1976) 225; cf. Strathmann, "πόλις," 520) and others that these *politeumata* enjoyed a special, legally recognized position by the local rulers and thus were public institutions rather than private associations; "This is not evident from the texts cited" ("Politeuma," 201).

[30] The inscription was found in Pompeii but is of Egyptian origin. E. L. Hicks suggests that this association of Phrygians "resided in some Egyptian town or district in the enjoyment of their own laws, religion, and administration of justice" ("On Some Political Terms Employed in the New Testament" *CR* 1 [1887] 7). This is unlikely in light of the evidence Lüderitz collects.

[31] Lüderitz, "Politeuma," 200.

[32] See Lüderitz, "Politeuma," 202.

[33] Cf. Lüderitz, "Politeuma," 202-03. Cotter ("*Politeuma*," 104) suggests that the community model used by the Philippian church was that of the voluntary associations. This is based on her analysis of the references to the practices of the associations, the use of the word πολίτευμα in Phil 3:20 and its verbal form πολιτεύομαι in Phil 1:27, and references to leaders using titles taken from the offices of both the city and the

2. Leadership and Officials

Officials were common in the associations and there was a "positive exuberance" with granting titles to functionaries.[34] Often these association officials imitated both the titles and functions of civic officials. Association officials were responsible for the sacrifices, banquets, and festivals (priests, priestesses), the collection and disbursement of money (treasurers), and the convening and chairing of meetings (presidents). A person might be elected to one of these positions or in some cases the office could be purchased by the highest bidder. Either way, serving in such a capacity could bring with it a heavy financial burden as the official was required to expend his or her own money in carrying out the requisite duties. In exchange, of course, he or she received multiple honours (statues, crowns, proclamations, inscriptions) from the association members.

A number of different officials are attested in the Macedonian voluntary association inscriptions. Some associations either have a priest, priestess, or both.[35] Many mention either a patron or a benefactor.[36] Quite a diverse number of other functionaries are mentioned: πατήρ,[37] ἐπιμελητής, λογιστής, ἄρχων, γραμματεύς, ἐξεραστής, ὑδροσκόπος, ἀρχινακόρος (ἀρχινεωκόρος), ἀρχιμαγαρεύς, γαλακτηφόρος, κισταφορήσασα, ὀργιοφάντης, ἀρκάρις, γυμνασιάρχης, ἀγωνοθέτης.

One of the most interesting titles is that of ἀρχισυνάγωγος, which is used in five non-Jewish association inscriptions in Macedonia.[38] The title

---

associations (ἐπισκόποις κιὰ διακόνοις, Phil 1:1). We have tried to expand both the general evidence and the details of this specific data. We look at Philippians more closely in the next chapter.

[34] Meeks, *First Urban Christians*, 134.

[35] Priest: IEdessa 3; *IG* X/2 259, 503, 309, 506; IThessalonica 2; *CIL* III 633; Pilhofer 142, 143, 147, 209; cf. *SIRIS* 124. Priestess: *IG* X/2 255, 260. Priest and Priestess: *IG* X/2 261.

[36] Patron: IPydna 1; *IG* X/2 192, 220. Benefactor: IMakedD 1104, *SIRIS* 123; cf. Pilhofer 095.

[37] Πατὴρ is not the equivalent of *patronus* (likewise ματὴρ and *patrona*; see Kloppenborg, "Collegia and *Thiasoi*," 25, *contra* Liebenam, *Geschichte und Organisation*, 218). Both πατὴρ and ματὴρ are used as titles of honour for those who are members of the association.

[38] T. Rajak and D. Noy, "*Archisynogogoi*: Office, Title and Status in the Greco-Roman World," *JRS* 83 (1993) 89-92 list of 30 Jewish inscriptions; cf. J. Juster, *Les Juifs dans l'empire romain: Leur Condition Jurdique, Économique et Sociale* (Paris: Paul

ἀρχισυνάγωγος is found in inscriptions dedicated to Herakles (*IG* X/2 288, 289; *CIG* 2007f) and Zeus Hypsistos (IPydna 1), as well as two memorial inscriptions for members of separate associations (συνήθεια; IThessalonica 2 and IBeroea 3). The ἀρχισυνάγωγος was the head of the association and oversaw most of the sacred rites, arranged for banquets and funerals, and enforced the regulations and decrees. He was generally rich and was expected to finance personally many of the association's activities in exchange for the honour of being named ἀρχισυνάγωγος.[39] This data shows that the Macedonian associations are typical of what can be observed generally from all of the epigraphical data from voluntary associations, namely that there is no consistency from one association to another in the titles used for officials.[40]

Among the leadership titles found in association inscriptions outside Macedonia is the term ἐπίσκοπος. Ἐπίσκοπος is used frequently in classical writings to indicate an official title of a man designated to oversee a new colony or serve as inspector in a foreign land.[41] It might "involve oversight of goods and possessions."[42] However, "the data

---

Geuthner, 1914) 406 n. 2. Of six non-Jewish ἀρχισυνάγωγος texts listed by Rajak and Noy ("*Archisynogogoi*," 92-93) five are from Macedonia while the other (no. 1) is from Perinthus, Thrace (*IGRR* 782; see also *IG* XIV 1890 and 2304, both from Italy; IAlexandria(K) 91 and IFayum I 9, both from Egypt). This latter inscription also refers to the association as a συναγωγή, although it is clearly not a Jewish association (unlike *CIJ* 694, 694b, 693a, *SEG* XLIV 556 (Thessalonica) which use συναγωγή in reference to a Jewish group). Both συναγωγή and ἀρχισυνάγωγος are used in connection with non-Jewish societies (Poland, *griechischen Vereinswesens*, 355-58). However, they are used "most frequently to denote a meeting of the society rather than the society as an entity" (Danker, "Associations," 502). G. H. R. Horsley suggests that the term ἀρχισυνάγωγος was first used in non-Jewish private associations and came to be used later by Jewish associations once the term συναγωγή had been adopted as the standard word for a Jewish meeting place (*New Documents Illustrating Early Christianity: A Review of the Greek Inscriptions and Papyri Published in 1979* [NewDocs 4; North Ryde, Australia: Ancient History Documentary Research Centre and Macquarie University, 1987] 219-20, against B. J. Brooten, *Women Leaders in Ancient Synagogues: Inscriptional Evidence and Background Issues* [Brown Judaic Studies 36; Chico: Scholars Press, 1982] 5, 23 with 228 n. 81). Once this had occurred (early I CE) there is a considerable drop in the use of συναγωγή in inscriptions of non-Jewish associations.

[39] D. M. Robinson, "Inscriptions from Macedonia," *TAPA* 69 (1938) 63.

[40] Cf. Kloppenborg, "Edwin Hatch," 232.

[41] J. B. Lightfoot, *Saint Paul's Epistle to the Philippians* (London: Macmillan, 1881[6]) 95.

[42] J. Reumann, "Church Office in Paul, Especially in Philippians," in *Origins and Method: Towards a New Understanding of Judaism and Christianity. Essays in Honour of John C. Hurd*, ed. B. H. McLean (JSNTSup 86; Sheffield: JSOT Press, 1993) 88.

assembled by Hans Lietzmann in 1914 and subsequently expanded by others make a far better case for *episkopos* as a supervisory office in the state, in various societies, and other groups in the Graeco-Roman world, often with financial responsibilities."[43] A review of the evidence of the associations shows this to be so.

'Επίσκοπος is used in an inscription from Thera where it indicates financial officers of an association (κοινὸν): "It is resolved that the *episkopoi* Dion and Meleippus shall accept the offer and invest the money" (*IG* XII/3 329, II BCE).[44] In *IGL* 1990 (Salkhat [Nabataea]), it is used of the financial officers of a temple,[45] as it is in other similar inscriptions (*IGL* 1989; 2298).[46] An inscription from Bostra (*OGIS* 614) names an ἐπίσκοπος as an official, as does one from Kanata (*OGIS* 611 8f, time of Trajan).[47] From an association on Myconos an ἐπίσκοπος of a σύνοδος is to transfer the care of an honourary deed, under threat of penalty (Poland B 186, end II BCE).[48] In a Thracian inscription ἐπίσκοπος is used as a title for a cult functionary (Poland B 79 = Cagnat I no. 682).[49] An inscription from Delos attests to a Dionysiac θίασος that was headed by an ἐπίσκοπος "who was responsible for proclaiming the honours bestowed upon benefactors" (IDelos 1522, lines 8, 10, 13, early II CE).[50] Overall, the evidence for the use of ἐπίσκοπος in associations is clear, but the specific function attached to it is ambiguous[51] as officials seemed to have held different job descriptions in different associations.[52]

---

[43] Reumann, "Church Office," 88; cf. E. Best, "Bishops and Deacons: Philippians 1,1," *SE* 4 (1968) 371.

[44] Renan, *Apostles*, 351 n. 35; Hatch, *Organization*, 37 n. 26 (text and translation); Lightfoot, *Philippians*, 95 n. 2 (who notes the accusative plural -ος is a dialectic form); Poland, *griechischen Vereinswesens*, 375 (B 221); M. Dibelius, *An die Thessalonicher I, II. An die Philipper* (HNT 11; Tübingen: Mohr, 1937³) 60.

[45] Noted by Hatch, *Organization*, 37 n. 26; Dibelius, *Thessalonicher/Philipper*, 60.

[46] Dibelius, *Thessalonicher/Philipper*, 60.

[47] Dibelius, *Thessalonicher/Philipper*, 60.

[48] Poland, *griechischen Vereinswesens*, 375; Dibelius, *Thessalonicher/Philipper*, 60.

[49] Poland, *griechischen Vereinswesens*, 375. Other inscriptions from associations indicate the existence of the title (Dibelius, *Thessalonicher/Philipper*, 60; cf. Deissmann, *Bible Studies*, 230-31; *IG* XII/1 49, 50, 731; *CIL* V 7914, 7870 (Nizza).

[50] McLean, "Place of Cult," 225 n. 148.

[51] So Dibelius, *Thessalonicher/Philipper*, 60-61; cf. A. von Harnack, "On the Origin of the Christian Ministry," *Expositor* 3/5 (1887) 339.

[52] Foucart (*Associations Religieuses*, 32) suggests that within the association inscriptions the same general functions were carried out by those entitled variously ἐπίσκοποι, ἐπιμεληταί, σύνδικοι, λογισταί. The negative response to Hatch (*Organization*, 26-39) by G. Salmon ("The Christian Ministry," *Expositor* [1887] 18-20) and W. Sanday ("The Origin of

Διάκονος has a wide range of designations in antiquity. It can mean "servant" in reference to one who waits on tables. It can indicate those who assist in the cult within the contexts of temples and religious associations.⁵³ Moulton and Milligan note that "[t]here is now abundant evidence that the way had been prepared for the Christian usage of this word by its technical application to the holders of various offices."⁵⁴ It is used of sacral officials in a number of inscriptions including IMagnMai 109 (*c*. 100 BCE), *CIG* 1793b, *IG* IV 774 (Troezen, Argolis, III BCE), 824 (Troezen, Argolis), *IG* IX/1 486 (II/I BCE). An inscription from Kyzikos names five διάκονοι among the functionaries at a thank offering to the Great Mother (*RIG* 1226, I BCE). In IMagnMai 217 (I BCE) διάκονοι are listed among those who set up a statue of Hermes.

From the private associations we find τὸ κοινὸν τῶν διακόνων of nine men dedicated to the Egyptian gods, one of whom presided as priest (*CIG* 1800, Ambrakia),⁵⁵ and an association which includes two male διάκονοι and a female διάκονος along with a priest and priestess of the twelve gods (*CIG* 3037, Metropolis, Lydia).⁵⁶ Similarly, Μουσεῖον 93 (Kyzikos) lists a female διάκων and five male διάκονοι along with a priest and priestess

---

Christian Ministry. II. Criticism of Recent Theories," *Expositor* 5 [1887] 98-100) is based more on Hatch's attempt to designate the ἐπίσκοποι as *financial* officers rather than his attempt to understand the associations as a general background for the Christian use of the title. This is also true of the discounting of the associations as an adequate background by E. Loening (*Die Gemeindeverfassung des Urchristentums: Eine Kirchenrechtliche Untersuchung* [Halle: Niemeyer, 1888] 47), J. Rohde (*Urchristliche und frühkatholische Ämter: Eine Untersuchung zur frühchristlichen Amtsentwicklung im Neuen Testament und bei den apostolischen Vätern* [Theologische Arbeiten 33; Berlin: Evangelische Verlagsanstalt, 1976] 55), and Hainz (*Ekklesia*, 94-96), all of whom point out the difficulty in determining the function of the ἐπίσκοποι in Philippians. Especially telling against the hypothesis that the Philippian ἐπίσκοποι were financial officers is the separation of the title (Phil 1:1) from Paul's thanks for the financial gift (4:10-20) within the structure of the letter; Hainz, *Ekklesia*, 93.

⁵³ LSJ *s.v.*; Ziebarth, *griechische Vereinswesen*, 153; Lietzmann, *Korinther*, 106-07; Dibelius, *Thessalonicher/Philipper*, 61; D. Georgi, *The Opponents of Paul in Second Corinthians* (Philadelphia: Fortress, 1986) 1986:27.

⁵⁴ The following information is presented variously by Moulton and Milligan, *Vocabulary*, 149; Dibelius, *Thessalonicher/Philipper*, 61; J. N. Collins, *Diakonia: Reinterpreting the Ancient Sources* (New York: Oxford University Press, 1990) 166-68.

⁵⁵ Collins (*Diakonia*, 167, following Poland, *griechischen Vereinswesens*, 165) suggests that this is not necessarily a formal association and points to another example of συμπορευόμενοι who describe themselves as a κοινόν. However, in both cases it is probably a formally constituted private association within the public cult, not unlike *IG* X/2 58 from Thessalonica.

⁵⁶ All the priests and priestesses seem to be related; Collins, *Diakonia*, 168.

while another inscription from Kyzikos mentions διάκονοι (Μουσεῖον 100).⁵⁷ Even Poland, who denies the connection between the Christian use of ἐπίσκοπος and the associations, is willing to entertain the idea that the Christian use of διάκονος was taken over from the associations.⁵⁸ However, he is rightly critical of Hatch's narrower view that their function should be seen as those who distribute food to others.⁵⁹

3. Community Regulations

According to Tuckman, groups go through a number of stages of development: "forming," "storming," "norming," "performing," and "adjourning."⁶⁰ The forming stage is that point at which members of a group first band together and recognize the benefits of mutual interdependence. The "storming" stage is the painful process of transition from a collection of individuals to a collective. At this stage there is conflict within the group as individual members assert their own needs through argument and criticism of the leaders.⁶¹

> The norming stage is marked by interpersonal conflict resolution in favor of mutually agreed upon patterns of behaviour.... norming involves group members in the attempt to resolve earlier conflicts, often by negotiating clear guidelines for group behaviour.⁶²

After these stages have been experienced the group is in a position to work co-operatively towards a particular goal – performing.⁶³ At this fourth stage the group has an ability to look outward beyond the formative stages of the group towards establishing the vision that first inspired the formation of the group.

---

⁵⁷ With no evidence Collins simply surmises that in *CIG* 3037, Μουσεῖον 93, and Μουσεῖον 100 the male and female διάκονοι are given "an occasional and privileged role" to serve at religious feasts (*Diakonia*, 168), presumably to underline his earlier point that "there is no reason to see anything more in the word than the designation of a ceremonial waiter" (*Diakonia*, 166; cf. Hatch, *Organization*, 50).

⁵⁸ Poland, *griechischen Vereinswesens*, 391-92, cf. 377.

⁵⁹ Poland, *griechischen Vereinswesens*, 392 n. *; cf. 534; cf. Hatch, *Organization*, 49-50.

⁶⁰ B. W. Tuckman, "Development Sequence in Small Groups," *Psychological Bulletin* 63 (1965) 384-99. See also Malina, "Early Christian Groups," 103-05.

⁶¹ Malina, "Early Christian Groups," 104.

⁶² Malina, "Early Christian Groups," 104.

⁶³ Malina, "Early Christian Groups," 105.

Members take social roles that make the group more rewarding to all. They work together co-operatively to achieve mutual goals.[64] Only when the group is no longer viable do they reach the fifth and final stage, "adjourning." This stage may be due to any number of reasons, including irresolvable conflict within the group, changing external contexts, or the fulfillment of the group's mandate.

Of course, the middle three stages never progress in the linear fashion that the model might suggest. Groups go through the various stages of "storming," "norming," and "performing" at various times. Internal divisions and external pressures can lead to a reassertion of "storming," the resolution of which can be reflected in a new or revised set of community regulations ("norming") that are perceived as necessary for the group to return to the performing stage. Some associations must also have disbanded, although there exists little evidence for this. Members of the association are not likely to recorded such an event, if for no other reason than to save face or save money.

Association regulations were often given highest authority, as seen in the preface of the regulations of a first century BCE Egyptian guild: "The law (*nomos*) that those of the association of Zeus Hypsistos made in common, so that it should be authoritative" (*P.Lond.* 2193). The text then records the names of the president and his assistant for the upcoming year. In this particular association, it seems, the roles of president and assistant rotated on a yearly basis. The law goes on to stipulate that obedience to these men is expected and one's presence at any special occasion is mandatory.

A lengthy papyrus from Tebtunis, Egypt, records "The law which has been adopted by the members of the association and the chief-priest of the crocodile," which include regulations around monthly contributions, the performance of sacrifices and libations for the Pharaoh, and burial rites for members (*P.Cairo.Dem.* 30606; 158/57 BCE). It even stipulates "if one of our members has a son who dies at a tender age, we shall drink beer with him and comfort his heart."

Such regulations were taken very seriously and some associations even made provision for punishing those who would speak out against them. For example, "if a member should either speak or act in contravention of the law, an accusation against him may be lodged by any of the members who so wishes; and if he convicts him, let the members assess the penalty, whatever seems appropriate to the association." (*IG* II^2 1275; Piraeus, III

---

[64] Malina, "Early Christian Groups," 105.

or early II BCE). One of the clearest attempts at establishing community norms can be seen in the requirements put in place for admission to membership in the association. The second century CE association of the Iobakkoi states clearly

> Let it not be lawful for anyone to be an Iobakkos unless he was first enlisted (on) the customary list in the presence of the priest and was approved by a vote of the Iobakkoi (as to) whether he appears to be worthy and suitable for the Baccheion. Let the entrance fee be 50 drachmae and a libation for one whose father was not a member. Similarly, those whose fathers were members should enlist, giving an additional 25 drachmae – half the usual rate – until puberty." (IG II^2 1368)[65]

A second century Athenian association is likewise concerned with membership:

> The law of the subscribers: It is not lawful for anyone to enter this most holy assembly without being first examined as to whether he is holy and pious and good. Let the patron, the president, the secretary, the treasurers, and the syndics examine (the candidate)." (IG II^2 1369)

Such requirements probably did not arise from an abstract reflection upon who might enter. Rather, they reflect a process of community boundary setting that must at times have involved decisions to exclude or include certain individuals.

Other issues could be legislated such as the calendar of sacrifices, as seen in an inscription from Myconos ($Syll.^3$ 1024, 200 BCE). However, what is abundantly clear from the inscriptions is that associations often struggled with the problem of disorderly behavior, so much so that legislation was introduced to limit it with fines and/or corporal punishment to enforce it. Although the papyrus is fragmentary, the laws of the Egyptian guild of Zeus Hypsistos make it clear that community conflict is not to be tolerated:

> It shall not be permissible for any one of them to . . . . . or to make factions or to leave the association of the president to join another brotherhood, or for men to enter into one another's pedigrees at the banquet, or to abuse one another at the banquet or to chatter or to indict or charge another or to resign for the course of the year or again to bring the drinking to naught. (*P.Lond.* 2193)

---

[65] On the reduction of membership dues for sons of members of associations see Ziebarth, *griechische Vereinswesen*, 156; on club fees in general see Poland, *griechischen Vereinswesens*, 488-98.

Penalties for breech of an association's regulations often included fines. In one second century BCE Egyptian association fines were stipulated for failure to pay dues, failure to join with the association in fulfilling funerary rites (members who are in jail or are soldiers stationed elsewhere are exempt from this), bringing a complaint against another member to the public courts without first bringing it before the association, insulting another member, striking another member, bribery, failure to appear at a tribunal of the association, and refusal to serve or attend meetings (*P.Cairo.Dem.* 30606). The ordinance of an association in Tebtunis stipulates that

> if a member gets drunk and misconducts himself, let him be fined whatever the association determines. If a member is sent an announcement of the meeting and does not attend, he shall be fined one drachma (if the meeting is) in the village and four drachmae if it is in the city.... If a member ignores someone who is in distress and does not assist in helping him out of his trouble, he shall pay 8 drachmae. Whoever at the banquets in taking his seat shoves in front of another shall pay an extra 3 obols to sit in his own place. If a member prosecutes or calumniates another (member), he shall be fined 8 drachmae. If a member commits intrigue against, or corrupts the home of another (member), he shall pay 60 drachmae. (*P.Mich.Tebt.* 243, reign of Tiberius; cf. *P.Mich.Tebt.* 244)

Disruption of meetings was a serious offense, as can be seen in the by-laws of an Italian association:

> It was further voted that any member who moves from one place to another so as to cause a disturbance shall be fined 4 sesterces. Any member, moreover, who speaks abusively of another or causes an uproar shall be fined 12 sesterces. Any member who uses any abusive or insolent language to a quinquennalis at a banquet shall be fined 20 sesterces." (*CIL* XIV 2112 [Lanuvium, 136 CE]; cf. *IG* II^2 1368)

Disrupting meals was likewise discouraged, as can be seen in *IG* II^2 1368 where unauthorized speechmaking at meals is prohibited. However, in some associations such disruption could bring about corporal punishment: "... and let the rod-bearers flog those who are disobedient or behave indecently" (*IG* V/1 1390).[66] At the same time as having to heed warnings against contravening the association's regulations, members could reasonably expect support from their fellow-members. This is articulated in a late third or second century BCE inscription from the Piraeus: "if a

---

[66] Perhaps also *IG* II^2 1369; cf. disruptions of processions in *CIG* 3599.

member should be wronged, they and all the friends shall come to his assistance, so that everyone might know that we show piety to the gods and to our friends" (*IG* II² 1275).

4. Allegiance

There is evidence that membership in one voluntary association did not preclude membership in another. For example, in the second century BCE (185/84) an Athenian named Simon of Poros became a charter member of a new *orgeones* dedicated to Dionysus (*IG* II² 1325; cf. *IG* II² 1326, 2948) while still a member of a separate association dedicated to the Mother of the Gods, suggesting that dual membership was allowed in both (*IG* II/1 1327, 1328).[67] In Ephesus a priest served both the *mystai* of Dionysus Pheos and an association devoted to Demeter. By the second century CE dual (or more) membership was even seen by officials as a problem, so much so that "Marcus Aurelius and Lucius Verus re-enacted a law to the effect that it was not lawful to belong to more than one guild."[68] Yet despite this law, the strict enforcement of it seems unlikely.[69]

Such evidence is sometimes used to suggest that Christian groups demanded exclusive allegiance in a way that the associations did not. According to Meeks, being "baptized into Christ" meant that the Christian community was the primary group for the members and demanded primary allegiance.[70] Similarly, Klauck quotes Philo's criticism of the associations of Alexandria:

> There exist in the city associations [θίασοι] with numerous members, and there is nothing healthy in their fellowship [κοινωνία], which is based on unmixed wine, drunkenness, feasts and the unbridled conduct which results from these.[71]

---

[67] Cf. *IG* II² 1361; Ferguson, "Attic Orgeones," 105, 117; Jones, "Economic Life," 173; Waltzing, *corporations Professionnelles*, 4.248-51.

[68] Cf. P. A. Harland, "Spheres of Contention, Claims of Preeminence: Rivalries Among Associations in Sardis and Smyrna," unpublished paper presented at the Canadian Society of Biblical Studies 2001 Annual Meeting (Laval, Quebec, May 24, 2001) 12; cf. *Digesta* 47.22.1.2.

[69] R. Meiggs, *Roman Ostia* (Oxford: Clarendon, 1960) 321-23; Harland, "Spheres of Contention," 12-13.

[70] Meeks, *First Urban Christians*, 78-79; see also Jeffers, *Greco-Roman World*, 79-80.

[71] *Flacc.* 4.136 in Klauck, *Religious Context*, 54.

Klauck writes that,
> after such a devastating judgment, need we look around for further testimony? There can be no doubt that the self-assessment of Judaism and Christianity prevented them from simply setting themselves on the same level as private cultic associations.[72]

Klauck's statement is problematic on two accounts. First, he assumes that there is such a thing as "Judaism" or "Christianity" in the first and second century CE that would allow a uniform type of judgment. Clearly, there is evidence to the contrary.[73] Philo's comments certainly indicate that he himself opposed Jews participating in associations in Alexandria. However, this is not necessarily the case elsewhere, nor for all people. Indeed, it seems that at Caesarea Maritima Jews participated in the sacrifice of animals in pagan rituals (see further below). Second, Klauck is unclear in what is meant by a group setting itself "on the same level" as another group. The inscriptional evidence suggests a high degree of inter-group rivalry among many associations, with claims and challenges around pre-eminence. It is unlikely that *any* association would see itself "on the same level" as another group. That is, one's own group will always be perceived as superior (in the same way that Philo sees his Jewish group as superior).

It is clear that for Paul being "baptized into Christ" generally excluded an individual from full participation in the religious life of other associations, yet this is not how the Corinthians understood it. In 1 Cor 8-10 Paul addresses the "strong" at Corinth who seem to be attending temple sacrifices and the subsequent banquet (1 Cor 8:10; 10:14) and Paul is cautiously affirming of the practice. Certainly participation in the civic cult would have been required of Erastus, the city treasurer in Corinth (see Rom 16:23). Thus, for some of the Corinthians Christianity was not initially understood as demanding exclusive allegiance.

There are exceptions to the "non-exclusivity" of the associations. While we have nothing to suggest that associations generally demanded exclusivity, it is reasonable to assume that, for the most part, they at least *de facto* received the primary allegiance of their members.[74] A number of reasons can be suggested. First, at least in the case of professional associations, they would gather persons in one particular urban area involved in a particular type of occupation. There would be no need (or opportunity) to join another professional association. Second, joining an

---

[72] Klauck, *Religious Context*, 54.
[73] Ascough, "Translocal Relationships," 234-41.
[74] Cf. Harland, "Spheres of Contention," 15.

association often involved dues and sometimes contributions to banquets. For most persons there would be little extra cash on hand to join a number of associations – only one would be necessary (and affordable) for the social interaction desired. Third, the competition for honour among associations and the claims to be the "best" of the groups would imply that members had no need to join a competing group, as to do so would be to join an inferiour group.

In Sardis we find a late first or early second century CE inscription that delineates that the temple warden θεραπευταί of Zeus the Legislator are not to participate in the mysteries of Sabazios, Agdistis, and Ma.[75]

In the thirty-nine years of Artaxerxes' reign, Droaphernes son of Barakis, governor of Lydia dedicated a statue to Zeus the Legislator. He (Droaphernes) instructs his (Zeus') temple-warden devotees who enter the innermost sanctum and who serve and crown the god, not to participate in the mysteries of Sabazios with those who bring the burnt offerings and (the mysteries) of Agdistis and Ma. They instruct Dorates the temple-warden to keep away from these mysteries.

This inscription is a Greek re-writing from an earlier Aramaic edict from ca. 365 BCE.[76] The primary deity in the latter inscription is Zeus Baradates ("the Legislator"), the epithet being a Greek translation of the name of a Persian deity (Ahura Mazda).[77] Both Sabazios and Agdistis are of Persian origin, while Ma is a Cappadocian goddess.[78] That an earlier text is later translated and re-inscribed shows the force of the prohibition despite a five hundred year period.[79] In the first or second century CE, a certain Dorates

---

[75] Horsley, *New Documents* 1, 22. Text in *CCCA* I 456; P. Hermann, "Mystenvereine in Sardeis," *Chiron* 26 (1996) 329-35. The following translation is from Horsley, *New Documents* 1, 21-22. See also Hermann ("Mystenvereine," 321-29) for other inscriptions testifying to the *therapeutai* of Zeus at Sardis, esp. ISardBR 22.

[76] That the text legislates against participation in the mysteries of these deities suggests that their cults existed at Sardis in the fourth century BCE.

[77] F. Gschnitzer argues against this interpretation, suggesting that Βαραδάτεω should be taken as a genitive (it is the normal Ionic form); "Eine persische Kultstiftung in Sardeis und die 'Sippengötter' Vorderasiens," in *Im Bannkreis des Alten Orients: Studien zur Sprach- und Kulturgeschichte des Alten Orients und seines Ausstrahlungsraumes*, ed. W. Meid and H. Trenkwalder (Innsbrucker Beiträge zur Kulturwissenschaft 24; Innsbruck: Institut für Sprachwissenschaft der Universitat Innsbruck, 1986) 46-7.

[78] Horsley, *New Documents* 1, 22.

[79] D. R. Edwards thinks it is more likely that the text retrojects backwards current concerns (*Religion and Power: Pagans, Jews and Christians in the Greek East* [New York: Oxford University Press, 1996] 32; cf. P. Briant, "Les iraniens d'Asie Mineure après la chut de l'empire achéméide," *DHA* 11 (1985) 167-95). Either way, it is the "current" concern that interests us.

transgresses the association's prohibition and the re-cutting of the stone is a means to bring him into line.[80] This entire scenario is interesting because it shows that a notion of religious exclusivity is not confined to Jewish and Christian groups.[81] A further spin-off of this inscription is the conservatism reflected in it. For at least this one association at Sardis, the second century CE was "not a period of syncretism of 'religious creativity' but of conservatism, reinforcing the piety of the past."[82]

Another important text that indicates an exclusive group is the papyrus text found in Philadelphia, Egypt, and dating from the first century BCE (*ca.* 69-58). The regulations of this association (κοινόν) stipulate that "it shall not be permissible for any one of them... to leave the brotherhood (φράτρα) of the president or to join another brotherhood" (*P.Lond.* 2193, line 14). The text cannot indicate that a person would leave one of the civic phratriae into which he was born, nor can it mean membership in another type of association, or a sub-group of the current association. Rather, as a synonym for σύνοδος the word φράτρα indicates that members could not join with another similar drinking club, of which there were likely many at Philidelphia.[83]

In claiming a difference between the associations and Christian communities based on the latter being "exclusive" and "totalistic," critics not only assume that some associations were not exclusive (a false assumption, as we have just demonstrated), but they ignore evidence that some Christian groups did participate in aspects of civic life, including cultic activities.[84] As we suggested, at Corinth some Christians seem to

---

[80] Horsley, *New Documents* 1, 23.

[81] Horsley, *New Documents* 1, 23. Hermann, "Mystenvereine," 329-35, esp. 334-35.

[82] A. T. Kraabel, "Paganism and Judaism: The Sardis Evidence," in *Diaspora Jews and Judaism: Essays in Honour of, and in Dialogue with, A. Thomas Kraabel*, ed. J. A. Overman and R. S. MacLennan (South Florida Studies in the History of Judaism 41; Atlanta: Scholars Press, 1992) 254. This is true in the case of a column that recreates the seventh century BCE features of a goddess, an image which is also represented on Sardian coins from the time of Hadrian and beyond; see Kraabel, "Paganism and Judaism," 254. The same image appears on coins from other Lydian cities at that time; Kraabel, "Paganism and Judaism," 254.

[83] Roberts, Skeat, Nock, "Guild of Zeus Hypsistos," 52.

[84] This is true for Jewish groups for which evidence is emerging that indicates that not all were exclusive; see Seland, "Philo and the Clubs,"; Ascough, "Translocal Links," 235-26; Harland, "Honouring the Emperor," 108; idem, "Spheres of Contention," 13-14. On Jewish defectors see S. G. Wilson, "ΟΙ ΠΟΤΕ ΙΟΥΔΑΙΟΙ: Epigraphic Evidence for Jewish Defectors" in *Text and Artifact in the Religions of Mediterranean Antiquity: Essays in Honour of Peter Richardson*, ed. S. G. Wilson and M. Desjardins (ESCJ 9; Waterloo: Wilfred Laurier University Press, 2000) 354-71.

have joined with non-Christians at communal meals in various contexts, including meals in pagan temples (1 Cor 8-10). In Asia Minor Christians are encouraged "to adopt the common conventions of praying for or honouring civic or imperial officials and emperors," a view that is also in evidence for church at Rome.[85] At least one Christian seems to have been a member of a shippers' guild at Ostia,[86] and thus presumably took part in the cultic life of the association. As Harland points out, "this evidence for dual affiliations or 'loyalties' (to use Meeks's term) on the part of Christians should not be passed off as an exception."[87] Indeed, "there is a sense in which we should be surprised if a person were to sever all such contacts with fellow-workers once affiliated with another group such as the Christians or the local synagogue; for removing oneself would sever the network connections necessary for business activity, thereby threatening one's means of livelihood."[88] We are not here arguing that the associations were exclusive, just that the *assumption* of their non-exclusivity needs more careful nuance before a legitimate contrast with Christian groups can be made.

5. Translocal Links

Although many scholars of the late nineteenth and early twentieth century favourably compared voluntary associations and early Christian groups without reference to the difference in "translocal" connections, there was a major shift in latter part of the twentieth century. It is now more commonly suggested that the associations did not have the extralocal linkages that characterize the Christian movement. In fact, it is precisely this difference of the *localized* nature of voluntary associations verses the *translocal* nature of Christianity which scholars most often point to as

---

[85] See Harland, "Honouring the Emperor," 115; Rom 13; 1 Pet 2:11-17; 1 Tim 2:1-2; Tit 3:1; Polycarp, *Phil.* 12.3; *Mart. Pol.* 10.2; *1 Clement* 60-61. See his earlier article for the argument that the significance of the imperial cult for the corporate lives of voluntary associations should not be underestimated; P. A. Harland, "Honours and Worship: Emperors, Imperial Cults and Associations at Ephesus (First to Third Centuries C.E.)," *SR* 25 (1996) 319-34.

[86] See *CIL* XIV 251, which lists a M. Curtius Victorinus in its membership list. A man of the same name is listed on a Christian epitaph (*CIL* 1900) and is thought to be the same person (Harland, "Honouring the Emperor," 110; Meiggs, *Roman Ostia*, 389).

[87] Harland, "Honouring the Emperor," 102.

[88] Harland, "Honouring the Emperor," 119.

indicative of the vast difference between Christian groups and associations.[89] It is noteworthy that in most scholarly work on this topic very little primary data is presented in order to substantiate the claim that the associations were local while the Christian groups were translocal.

Wilken maintains that Christianity is "a 'worldwide' sect whose adherents lived throughout the Mediterranean world and shared a common religious profession and style of life."[90] This is unlike the voluntary associations that "were not 'international.'" Using Wilken's descriptions as representative of the position of other scholars, we can investigate the two-fold assertion of his statement: that voluntary associations were local in a way that Christian groups were not and that early Christianity was a translocal movement in a way that the voluntary associations were not. With the evidence to be presented below, what is being called into question is both a common modern understanding of voluntary associations and a common modern conception of early Christianity. I would suggest that the evidence is such that we can no longer confidently assert that early Christian groups had, to use Tod's words, "national or

---

[89] See Meeks, *First Urban Christians*, 80. This is the most consistently cited and the most pervasive work among modern New Testament scholars. Those who oppose the analogy on the basis of local vs. translocal links include: Judge, *Social Pattern*, 44; Wilken, "Collegia," 287; idem, *Christians*, 35; Countryman, "Patrons and Officers," 136; Meeks, *First Urban Christians*, 80; Stambaugh and Balch, *Social Environment*, 141; L. Alexander, "Paul and the Hellenistic Schools: The Evidence of Galen," in *Paul in His Hellenistic Context*, ed. T. Engberg-Pedersen (Minneapolis: Fortress, 1995) 82; Pilhofer, *erste christliche Gemeinde*, 138-39; McCready, "Voluntary Associations," 63-64; S. Walker-Ramish, "Graeco-Roman Voluntary Associations and the Damascus Document: A Sociological Analysis," in *Voluntary Associations in the Graeco-Roman World*, ed. J. S. Kloppenborg and S. G. Wilson (London and New York: Routledge, 1996) 135-36. E. R. Bevan makes the *assumption* that Christianity was united as "the one Divine world-wide Church, the Body animated by the Spirit of Christ" in contrast to local associations ("Mystery Religions" in *The History of Christianity in the Light of Ancient Knowledge: A Collective Work* [London and Glasgow: Blackie and Sons, 1929] 108-09). However, this seems to be based mostly on his suggestion that the Christian churches were more like synagogues than associations and the assumption that Judaism in the early first century CE was a monolithic movement. Barton and Horsley ("Hellenistic Cult Group," 28) note that the cult groups tended to be localized while Christianity was more international in scope. While they do admit ("Hellenistic Cult Group," 28) that the local character of the Christian groups is much like that of localized cult groups, they emphasize Christianity's worldwide connections as a primary difference. Some (e.g., Stambaugh and Balch, *Social Environment*, 141; Schmeller, *Hierarchie und Egalität*, 17) simply rely on earlier assertions such as that of Meeks (*First Urban Christians*, 80) who does not provide any evidence and only gives the issue two sentences.

[90] Wilken, "Collegia," 287; cf. idem, *Christians*, 35.

even, to some extent, international" links any more than did the voluntary associations.

A close analysis of relevant material leads us to conclude that some voluntary associations in antiquity had translocal links *and* that Christianity was more locally based than is often assumed. Thus, both Christian congregations and voluntary associations were locally based groups with limited translocal connections. By establishing this, what is often thought to be the greatest obstacle to the use of the associations as an analogy for early Christianity will be overcome and the way will opened up for more fruitful use of associations for understanding the formation and organization of early Christian groups.

a) Evidence From Associations

An investigation of the evidence from voluntary associations shows that there were in fact stronger translocal links between some associations than is often admitted. Although the evidence is scattered both geographically and temporally there is enough to suggest that many associations had a history of translocal links that had not died out by the first century CE.

The most obvious place to begin when investigating translocal links between associations is to look to groups of "foreigners" (people of one ethnic background living in another locale) in the circum-Mediterranean world, as they often continued the worship of their homeland.[91] These groups are obvious for two reasons. First, the amount of contact with their native land will enlighten our discussion. Second, "foreigners" were often traders or artisans, precisely those people that are attested in numerous association inscriptions.[92]

Traders were, by definition, "on the move," traveling throughout the then known world. Traders from one area who did business elsewhere could be united in one association, as is seen in Athens. An association of Kittian merchants asked for, and received, approval from the Athenian *boulē* to set up a temple to Aphrodite (*IG* II² 337). In doing so, they cite the precedent of the granting of the same privilege to the Egyptians in

---

[91] Tod, "Clubs," 254-55; cf. Fisher, "Greek Associations," 1186-87.

[92] A further reason is that Paul himself was an artisian and seems to have worked in his trade as he traveled.

Athens.⁹³ In the Piraeus the situation seems to have been similar in terms of the formation of associations. The deme of Piraeus had to enact a decree (*IG* II² 1177) in the mid-IV BCE in order to control the unauthorized use of the Thesmophorion (the temple of Demeter) by the newly forming θίασοι made up of people from outside of Piraeus.⁹⁴

That a group is composed of foreigners does not necessarily mean that there are translocal connections between this group and another group or another location. However, there does seem to be an implicit translocal element in the existence of such associations with their inevitable orientation toward the place of origin. This relationship implies other translocal links, even where they are not specifically mentioned.

A number of groups throughout the Mediterranean seem to have maintained ties with another locale. On the island of Salamis three decrees of θιασῶται of Bendis have been found at the same spot (*IG* II² 1317, 1317b, and *SEG* II 10). Despite the association on Salamis differing in both name and organization (i.e., having a priest instead of a priestess and priest), this association seems to have had direct links to an association of Bendis in the Piraeus: Both groups met on the second day of the month, and it seems probable that they either celebrated the Bendideia on the island at the same time as in the Piraeus (19/20th of the preceding month) or that they had actually taken part in the celebration in the Piraeus.⁹⁵

On Delos there was a sizable group of traders called the Ῥωμαῖοι who had their own agora, temples, and associations (*ca.* I BCE - I CE). These associations list their members as Ῥωμαῖοι, but list their city of origin; many "were Greeks from Southern Italy and Sicily, or natives of Campania and Apulia and other Italian regions."⁹⁶ Clearly they felt some connection with the capital city of the empire (probably because they were "citizens").

---

⁹³ The precedent actually goes back to the third century BCE when the Athenian state allowed the Thracians the right to found a sanctuary of their national goddess (*IG* II² 1283, 261/60 BCE; Ferguson, "Attic Orgeones," 97-98). This was the first instance of an alien group being granted such a privilege.

⁹⁴ Ferguson, "Attic Orgeones," 96.

⁹⁵ Ferguson, "Attic Orgeones," 100 n. 45. Other groups were able to look to the Athenian ὀργεῶνες for their name and, probably, structure, even where there is no intervention on the part of the Athenians. Ferguson ("Attic Orgeones," 61 n. 1; cf. Poland, *griechischen Vereinswesens*, 15) illustrates this with two inscriptions in which the word ὀργεῶνες is used: *IG* VII 33 (Megara, "before imperial times") and *RIG* 1307 (Teos, ca. 150 BCE). In both cases the word is partially restored, but Ferguson suggests that the restorations are "not improbable." Thus we can see "connections" without direct "links," which may be true for Christianity.

⁹⁶ La Piana, "Foreign Groups," 251.

Also, on Delos the Greek and oriental slaves of the merchants formed an association patterned on the Roman *collegium*, thus using a "translocal" model for a "local" organization.[97]

In Rome itself, *collegia* existed among foreign merchants living in Rome who wanted to celebrate their native cults.[98] Often their religious practices served to give them a sense of cohesion and continuity with their homeland.[99] Regardless of how much they opened themselves up to other persons, they "did not entirely lose their national character and connections."[100] Associations of foreign merchants in Rome had an official character in their city or province of origin and sometimes in Rome itself.[101] An interesting inscription from Puteoli (*CIG* 5853) reveals the interconnectedness of two associations of Tyrian merchants, both to one another and to their home city. When the Tyrian merchants at Puteoli (the port of Rome) were not able to pay their rent they wrote a letter to the city of Tyre asking for funding to maintain their *statio* (their business and social headquarters). The Tyrian senate responded by reinstating an old custom of having the Tyrian association in Rome pay the rent of the association at Puteoli. Thus, "between the two stations there was a connection not only of commercial, but of social, moral, and religious interest, involving mutual obligations."[102]

Along with trade associations, the associations of the Egyptian gods present an interesting case study for translocal links.[103] The cult of Isis and Sarapis remained in the control of the Alexandrians and Egyptians even during the period of its greatest expansion.[104] It never became Latinized

---

[97] Cf. La Piana, "Foreign Groups," 252. Rhodes had a large group of Italian merchants, although it is unclear whether they had "translocal" connections to their homeland. Meeks (*First Urban Christians*, 32) discounts the Delian and Rhodian merchants associations too quickly by referring to them as having grown "far beyond the bounds of the private association" before the first century CE.

[98] La Piana, "Foreign Groups," 240, 246; cf. 274.

[99] La Piana, "Foreign Groups," 321. Cf. Brady who suggests that a club "must have always meant more to the person who was away from home, residing in a city whose citizenship he did not possess" ("Reception," 21).

[100] La Piana, "Foreign Groups," 323.

[101] La Piana, "Foreign Groups," 245-46.

[102] La Piana, "Foreign Groups," 258.

[103] On Egyptian guilds see Roberts, Skeat, and Nock, "Guild of Zeus Hypsistos," 39-88; A. E. R. Boak, "The Organization of Guilds in Greco-Roman Egypt," *TAPA* 68 (1937) 212-20; and more generally San Nicolò, *Ägyptisches Vereinswesen*; idem, "Vereinsgerichtsbarkeit"; de Cenival, *associations religieuses*.

[104] La Piana, "Foreign Groups," 304-05.

but always retained strong cultic and iconographic links to the temples of the Nile valley.[105] For example, on Delos a third century BCE cult of Sarapis founded by Apollonius the Elder remained private and "Egyptian" for more than a century (*IG* XII/7 506).[106] Throughout that time the association maintained ties to Egypt, as witnessed in the following second century BCE inscription:

> The priest Apollonios had this engraved according to the command of the god. Our grandfather Apollonios, an Egyptian of the sacerdotal class, having his god brought with him from Egypt, continued to do service (for his god) in accordance with tradition and purportedly lived to ninety-seven years of age. (*IG* XI/4 1299)

In Athens, when an association of Sarapiastai was opened up to Athenians they took on the administrative roles but the Egyptians maintained the religious aspects.[107] An association in Priene (Asia Minor) stipulates that the priest must provide an Egyptian so that the sacrificial rites will be properly performed (IPriene 195, *ca.* 200 BCE). This tells us two things: that not all of the priests of this cult of Sarapis and Isis were Egyptian and that there is nevertheless some connection with Egypt.[108] More significantly, an adherent of the cult of Isis and Sarapis was able to travel throughout the Empire and be received by the local Isiac group wherever he or she happened to be.[109]

---

[105] La Piana, "Foreign Groups," 308. There are indications that the worship of the Egyptian gods presumed some links to Egypt, particularly with respect to the water of the Nile. For example, Serapeum A on Delos had an underground crypt that was directly connected to the Inopus River. It was thought that this river had physical links with the Nile, thus the crypt was provided with authentic Nile water (R. A. Wild, *Water in the Cultic Worship of Isis and Sarapis* [EPRO 87; Leiden: Brill, 1981] 34-35).

[106] Cf. Dow, "Egyptian Cults," 230.

[107] Brady, "Reception," 21.

[108] Mixed ethnic backgrounds are attested in other associations: around 200 BCE three maenads were imported from Thebes to form three separate θίασοι of Dionysus at Magnesia ad Maeander (IMagnMai 215); an inscription from Thessalonica reads "To Makedon, the θίασος of Asiani, to their fellow mystes, Publius Aelius Alexander being priest" (*IG* X/2 309) – the use of a common Macedonian proper name in an inscription of a θίασος of people from Asia (Asiani) suggests that the θίασος was not limited to persons from Asia (cf. Edson, "Cults of Thessalonica," 155 incl. n. 3 for a similar situation at Dacia [*CIL* III 870]; see also Nilsson, *Dionysiac Mysteries*, 50, 55 n. 55).

[109] La Piana ("Foreign Groups," 337) illustrates this by citing Lucius' move from Africa to Rome after his initiation (according to Apuleius, *Met.* 19). Lucius undergoes the initiation rites again in Rome because the first initiation was deemed incomplete, not as a requirement to join the Roman group; see Nock, *Conversion*, 147-49.

Other inscriptions from associations dedicated to the Egyptian gods stand out as particularly informative for showing translocal links. An inscription from Thessalonica (*IG* X/2 255, I/II CE copy of an earlier text) records that Sarapis appeared twice to Xenainetos in a dream[110] and enjoined him to deliver both a verbal and written message to his political rival, Eurynomos, concerning the establishment of the cult of Sarapis and Isis in Opus, a town in the region of eastern Locris (on the Euboean Gulf). Since this copy of the inscription was found in the sanctuary of Sarapis in Thessalonica, Xenainetos' dream probably took place in Thessalonica.[111] After the cult was established in Opus, the story was inscribed for use by the association there and a copy was taken to the Thessalonian cult centre to become part of its local tradition. The inscription was re-inscribed in Thessalonica around the first to mid-second century CE by devotees of the cult in Thessalonica.[112] Clearly there is a connection between the group in Opus and that in Thessalonica, both in the founding of the association in Opus and the memory of that founding in the Thessalonian association.

Another example of foreign connections within the Egyptian associations comes from Magnesia. An inscription records that when a priest of the cult of Sarapis at Magnesia conflicts with the civic magistrates over the building site of a temple, a tribunal comes to Magnesia from abroad to clear up any misunderstanding (IMagnMai 99). This suggests both that the priest was a foreigner[113] and that control of his actions, at the very least, was still governed from outside his current place of residence.

At Corinth, according to Pausanias (2.4.6), one of the two sacred precincts of Sarapis at the base of the Acrocorinth was dedicated to

---

[110] Probably during a period of incubation, a time when a person slept in a shrine awaiting healing, advice, a prophecy, or a vision (Horsley, *New Documents* 1, 31). Cf. Acts 12.7-10; 23.11; Horsley, *New Documents* 1, 32; P. Sellew, "Religious Propaganda in Antiquity: A Case from the Sarapeum at Thessaloniki," *Numina Aegaea* 3 (1980) 16. Xenainetos seems to have been in Thessalonica on official business as a representative of the city of Opus. In the cult of Sarapis and Isis dreams were important in revelations, prophecy, healing, and initiation (Heyob, *Cult of Isis*, 57, 59; cf. Fraikin, "Introduction of Sarapis," 3). The introduction of the cult of Sarapis and Isis to a new location was often inaugurated through instructions given by the god in a dream.

[111] *Contra* J. S. Hanson, "The Dream/Visions Report and Acts 10:1-11:18," unpublished Ph.D. Diss. (Harvard University, 1978) 5.

[112] See Sellew, "Religious Propaganda", 17-19. Cf. the cult of Egyptian gods that came to Cius, in Bithynia, near the end of the third century BCE, probably not directly from Egypt but from its mother city Miletus, where Isis was the focus of a θίασος.

[113] Sokolowski, "Propagation," 446 n. 16.

"Sarapis called 'in Canopus'."[114] Canopus, slightly East of Alexandria along the Mediterranean shore, was the site of an oracular and healing shrine in antiquity.[115] Although the worship of Sarapis of Canopus is known elsewhere in the Roman world,[116] Corinth is the only place known to have had a temple for him.[117]

The guild of Dionysiac artists (οἱ περὶ τὸν Διόνυσον τεχνῖται) presents another interesting case study of translocal links.[118] This guild was one of the longest standing religious associations. It began in Attica around the third century BCE or earlier and can be traced to the end of the Roman Republic.[119] During that time the guild served not only to unite members of a common profession, but various states employed it in ambassadorial duties because of its members' wide-ranging travel.[120] They may even have had a hand in negotiating a treaty between Rome and Pergamon; the Pergamonian βουλή and δῆμος honour the Dionysiac artists in an inscription from 129 BCE which reads, in part,

> For the good fortune and salvation of our people and of the Romans and of the brotherhood of the artisans associated with Kathogemones Dionysus; let the friendship and alliance with the Romans remain with us for all time; and let there be the best possible sacrifice presented to both Demeter and Kore and the goddesses who defend our city and likewise to Roma and all other gods and goddesses. (*Syll.*³ 694)

There existed a κοινόν of several local Isthmian and Nemean σύνοδοι of Dionysiac artists, centered at Thebes, with branches in Argos, Chalcis, and elsewhere.[121] In the third century BCE this guild is attested in Asia Minor (the Ionia-Hellespont guild c. 235 BCE centered at Teos) and in Egypt and

---

[114] D. E. Smith, "The Egyptian Cults at Corinth," *HTR* 70 (1977) 210-11.

[115] Smith, "Egyptian Cults," 227-29.

[116] Including Delos (II BCE), Epirus (I CE), Rome (II-III CE), Veneventum (II CE), Beneventum (II CE) and Athens (III CE) (Smith, "Egyptian Cults," 227 n. 86).

[117] Smith, "Egyptian Cults," 227.

[118] Countryman ("Patrons and Officers," 136) cites the artists guild as the exception to the general statement that there were no translocal links between voluntary associations in the Early Empire. However, the "exceptional" nature does not seem consistent with other evidence.

[119] Tod, "Clubs," 255.

[120] See further Pickard-Cambridge, *Dramatic Festivals*, 281-85; cf. G. M. Sifakis, *Studies in the History of Hellenistic Drama* (University of London Classical Studies 4; London: Athlone, 1967) 136-71.

[121] Tod, "Clubs," 255; cf. Pickard-Cambridge, *Dramatic Festivals*, 285; cf. *IG* VII 2484, 2485. Cf. also a single society that unites several cults on Rhodes: κοινὸν Σωτηριαστᾶν Διοσξενιαστᾶν Παναθαναιστᾶν Λινδιαστᾶν (Tod, *Sidelights*, 76).

Cyprus under the Ptolemies (*OGIS* 50). It continued variously during the reign of the Romans.[122] On one occasion representatives were sent from the guild at Pergamon to secure favours from guilds at Teos and on Delos (*IG* XI/4 1061),[123] and on another occasion members of the Teos guild were sent to help out the guild at Iasos.[124]

A Roman decree in 125 BCE (confirmed in 112 BCE) gives the priests of the guild of Dionysiac artists the right to wear crowns of gold and purple robes in all cities, suggesting that there was some continuity among the various associations.[125] By the first century CE this guild is often referred to as τῆς οἰκουμένης, which we might translate as "universal" or "world-wide," as seen in the letter of Claudius from 43 CE[126] and IEphesus 22 from Nysa (142 CE).[127] This latter text comes from the second century CE when the evidence for the "world-wide" guild is most plentiful, revealing that there were branches throughout the empire with the headquarters in Rome.[128] Local Dionysiac associations probably existed alongside the larger, "world-wide" guild[129] although eventually most were absorbed into the world-wide guild.[130]

---

[122] See further Pickard-Cambridge, *Dramatic Festivals*, 286-91; W. S. Ferguson, *Hellenistic Athens: An Historical Essay* (London: MacMillan, 1911) 370-73.

[123] See Pickard-Cambridge, *Dramatic Festivals*, 292-93; 314-15, no. 10a.

[124] Pickard-Cambridge, *Dramatic Festivals*, 292-93; cf. A. W. Pickard-Cambridge, *The Theatre of Dionysus in Athens* (Oxford: Clarendon, 1940) 242-43.

[125] See Pickard-Cambridge, *Dramatic Festivals*, 290-91; *Syll.*³ 704H; *IG* II² 1134.

[126] Claudius writes τοῖς ἀπὸ τῆς οἰκουμένης περὶ τὸν Διόνυσον τεχνείταις ἱερονείκαις στεφανείταις καὶ τοῖς τούτων συναγωνισταῖς (see *BGU* 1074; cf. *P.Oxy.* 2476, 2610). Cf. an inscription from Miletus containing a letter from Claudius with similar language (Pickard-Cambridge, *Dramatic Festivals*, 297).

[127] Text in Pickard-Cambridge, *Dramatic Festivals*, 319-20; cf. 298-99; partial translation in R. MacMullen and E. N. Lane, eds., *Paganism and Christianity 100-425 C.E.: A Sourcebook* (Minneapolis: Fortress, 1992) 65-66. Cf. by the I BCE we have evidence for a "world-wide" association of athletes; see Pleket, "Athletic Guilds," 201-3.

[128] For example, the "world citizens" of the branch of an artists guild at Ephesus seem to be linked to the branch at Rome (Poland, *griechischen Vereinswesens*, 129; 146). See further Pickard-Cambridge, *Dramatic Festivals*, 297-302).

[129] Pickard-Cambridge, *Dramatic Festivals*, 298. Thus, the officers of the guild of artists of Dionysus "varied from time to time and place to place" (Pickard-Cambridge, *Dramatic Festivals*, 303).

[130] Although the Guild of Dionysiac Artists were a "huge international body" under the empire and had close ties to the emperors and other rulers, they seem to have declined after the Antonines (Radin, *Legislation*, 126). They are thought to have been amalgamated with another international guild, that of the International Athletic Union (Radin, *Legislation*, 126 nn. 44, 47); but see Pleket, "Athletic Guilds," 200.

A guild name might reveal a translocal connection. For example, a name is occasionally added to the designation of a Dionysian σπεῖρα,[131] suggesting that the local associations belonged to "a more comprehensive organization."[132] Nilsson cites a number of examples: altars are dedicated to Διονύσῳ Καθηγεμόνι, the ancestral god of the Pergamene kings (IPergamon 319), τῆι Μιδαπεδειτῶν σπείρηι (IPergamon 320), Erythrae, where a σπεῖρα Βραχυλειτῶν is mentioned (*JhOAI* 13 [1910] 48, no. 13) and a dedication to Βρόμιος Πακοριτῶν at Pergamon (IPergamon 297).[133] In the Piraeus there existed an association of Αἰγύπτιοι, an association of Κιτιεῖς, a group of Cyprian Σαλαμίνιοι, and a group of Σιδώνιοι. Even their names suggest a connection with a former place of residence.[134]

In this section we have raised the issue concerning the meaning of "translocal" when scholars argue that voluntary associations are local as opposed to "translocal." The data shows that it is not the case that all associations had little or no contacts outside of a local group. A number of inscriptions point to the maintenance of contact with the place of origin of the association and/or its members,[135] as well as contact between associations in various locales. Thus, there seems to be some translocal connections among some voluntary associations.

b) Evidence From Judaism and Christianity

If, as we have seen, some (but not all) voluntary associations had translocal connections, it does not necessarily follow that these, rather than the "local" groups, should be given priority in a comparison with early Christian groups. Hence, the second part of our argument involves showing that *early* Christianity should be viewed with an emphasis on its "local" character rather than its translocal connections. In this way, we will find a meeting ground between those who contrast solely "local" associations with "translocal" Christian congregations.

---

[131] Latin, *spira*. This term is generally used in a military sense, but is used by associations as a synonym for θίασος; other synonyms would include μύσται and κοινόν.

[132] Nilsson, *Dionysiac Mysteries*, 50.

[133] Βρόμιος is a name of Bacchus (Dionysus).

[134] Tod, *Sidelights*, 76.

[135] As a final illustration we might mention a third century BCE inscription from Attica recording the regulations of an association concerning dues. The decree stipulates "those of the Heroistoi away from home for whatever reason shall give three drachmae per month" (*IG* II² 1339 lines 8). Cf. *IG* II² 1361, 1368.

Before turning to Christianity, however, it is worth a brief detour into the Jewish communities as reflected in the Diaspora synagogues and the Dead Sea community. Many scholars who do not accept the analogy of the voluntary associations for Christian groups often suggest that Christian groups had much more in common with Jewish groups, particularly in regard to their requirement of exclusive adherence and their "translocal" connection to Jerusalem.[136] However, there is a growing body of literature that suggests that in fact the Jewish groups had much in common with voluntary associations.[137] If this is so, then the use of associations as an analogy to Christian groups is strengthened even more.

Studies of Diaspora synagogues have noted similarities to Greco-Roman voluntary associations.[138] For example, the Diaspora synagogues

---

[136] For example, Meeks, *First Urban Christians*, 80.

[137] Cf. so sure is Hardy (*Roman History*, 141) that Christian groups were associations that he states that if they "were affiliated to the Jewish synagogues, these latter were certainly regarded as θίασοι, and the Christians would therefore be ranked among them too." See also La Piana, "Foreign Groups," 349 and n. 17 for further bibliography and La Piana's assertion that the synagogues were not *collegia* (contradicted later [355 n. 23] in his statement that a number of synagogues "were really Jewish *collegia domestica*").

[138] See Hardy, *Roman History*, 141; La Piana, "Foreign Groups," 341-63; S. L. Guterman, *Religious Toleration and Persecution in Ancient Rome* (London: Aiglon Press, 1951) 130-56; H. Mantel, "The Nature of the Great Synagogue," *HTR* 60 (1967) 75-91; E. Schürer, *The History of the Jewish People in the Age of Jesus Christ (175 B.C.—A.D. 135). A New English Version*, rev. and ed. G. Vermes, F. Millar, M. Black, and M. Goodman. (Edinburgh: T. & T. Clark, 1979-87) 3/1.107-12 (but see n. 37); E. E. Ellis, *Pauline Theology: Ministry and Society* (Grand Rapids: Eerdmans, 1989) 122-45; L. M. White, *Building God's House in the Roman World: Architectural Adaptation Among Pagans, Jews and Christians* (ASOR Library of Biblical and Near Eastern Archaeology; Baltimore: Johns Hopkins University Press, 1990) 82; Richardson, "Synagogues as Collegia," 90-109; M. D. Nanos, *The Mystery of Romans: The Jewish Context of Paul's Letter* (Minneapolis: Fortress, 1996) 43-44. From the time of Julius Caesar the Romans probably classified synagogues as *collegia* (see Smallwood, *Jews Under Roman Rule*, 133; H. J. Leon, *The Jews of Ancient Rome: Updated Edition* (Peabody: Hendrickson, 1995) 9-11; Cotter, "Collegia and Roman Law," 76-78). Others have noted the similarities but suggest that ultimately the differences disqualify them from categorization as associations: Juster, *Juifs*, 1.413-24; Smallwood, *Jews Under Roman Rule*, 133-43; S. Applebaum, "The Organization of the Jewish Communities in the Diaspora," in *The Jewish People in the First Century: Historical Geography, Political History, Social, Cultural and Religious Life and Institutions*, ed. S. Safrai and M. Stern (CRINT 1; Assen and Philadelphia: VanGorcum and Fortress, 1974) 502; Meeks, *First Urban Christians*, 35, 80; J. T. Burtchaell, *From Synagogue to Church: Public Services and Offices in the Earliest Christian Communities* (Cambridge and New

adopted the "Greek nomenclature of the associations" which "included a great variety of terms in different places."[139] A number of studies have been produced illustrating the similarities between the Qumran documents and the community associated with them and the Greco-Roman voluntary associations.[140] Here we might simply note that the Dead Sea community definitely had translocal links, both to Egypt[141] and to various towns in Palestine.[142]

Along with the similarities between Jewish groups and voluntary associations there is some evidence that within Judaism there could exist an openness to participation in other forms of worship. In fact, it is no longer clear that Judaism was exclusive in a way different than other cult groups,[143] as we earlier illustrated with Philo's strong polemic against Jews

---

York: Cambridge University Press, 1992) 265-67. Ellis (*Pauline Theology*, 131) thinks that Guterman has adequately addressed the differences.

[139] La Piana, "Foreign Groups," 360. Recently M. H. Williams has suggested that even within Rome itself the synagogues evidence a variety of structures and titles of officials and were probably not homogeneous ("The Structure of Roman Jewry Reconsidered – were the Synagogues of Ancient Rome Entirely Homogeneous?" *ZPE* 104 [1994] 129-41).

[140] H. Bardtke, "Der gegenwärtige Stand der Erforschung der in Palästina neu gefundenen hebräischen Handschriften, 44: Die Rechtsstellung der Qumran-Gemeinde," *TLZ* 86 (1961) 93-104; C. Schneider, "Zur Problematik des Hellenistischen in den Qumrantexten," in *Qumranprobleme, Vorträge des Leipziger Symposions über Qumranprobleme vom 9. bis 14. Oktober 1961*, ed. H. Bardtke (Berlin: Akademie Verlag, 1963) 305-09; B. Dombrowski, "היחד in IQS and τὸ κοινόν: An Instance of Early Greek and Jewish Synthesis," *HTR* 59 (1966) 293-307; M. Hengel, *Judaism and Hellenism: Studies in their Encounter in Palestine During the Early Hellenistic Period* (Philadelphia: Fortress, 1974) 243-44; Weinfeld, *Organizational Pattern*. Walker-Ramish, "Voluntary Associations," argues against the connection. Cf. Kloppenborg, "Edwin Hatch," 226-28 and Smith (*Drudgery Divine*, 83) on the problematic use of Judaism to isolate Christianity from the Greco-Roman world.

[141] Cf. the "Damascus Document" found in three of the Qumran caves and the *geniza* of a Cairo synagogue; G. Vermes, *The Dead Sea Scrolls in English* (London: Penguin, 1987³) 81.

[142] Vermes, *Dead Sea Scrolls*, 15-18. Private associations in the form of "guilds" have a long history in Palestine, probably dating from before the Hellenistic period; see I. Mendelsohn, "Guilds in Ancient Palestine." *BASOR* 80/4 (1940) 17-21; cf. idem, "Guilds in Babylonia and Assyria." *JAOS* 60 (1940) 68-72, on guilds in Babylonia and Assyria. The *marzeah*, seen by many to be "a *thiasos* dedicated to a particular god in which the memorial rites are characterized by eating and drinking," has a long history at Ugarit, Palmyra, and in Palestine (J. Greenfield, "The *Marzeah* as a Social Institution," *Acta Antiqua Academiae Hungaricae* 22 [1974] 451).

[143] Some polemical writings indicate that many people still required exclusive worship within Judaism, but this tells us more about the actual problems that were being addressed.

who joined associations and partook of their social practices.[144] For Philo the actual problem with the associations is what goes on at the association meetings, as he goes on to suggest that Jews might join non-Jewish social associations that allow the Jews to keep their own customs and standards of behavior: "As for contributions and club subscriptions, when the object is to share the best of possessions, prudence [φρόνησις], such payments are praiseworthy and profitable" (*Ebr.* 20).[145] Yet there are no examples of associations that did not align themselves with any deity at all; it could be that Philo is here suggesting that Jews could be part of an association that had a "pagan" deity as its divine patron.[146] In fact, the rabbinic text *t.Hul.* 2.3 implies that Jews in Caesarea Maritima joined in pagan rituals:

If one slaughters an animal in order to sprinkle its blood for idolatrous purposes or to offer its fat parts for idolatrous purposes, such meat is considered as sacrifices of the dead. If it had already been slaughtered, and one sprinkled its blood for idolatrous purposes and offered its fat parts for idolatrous purposes.... This happened in Caesarea.[147]

These examples suggest that not all Jews in antiquity were against participation in the voluntary associations and its ritual practices.

The "translocal link" between Diaspora Jews and Jerusalem had its limitations. During the Palestinian uprising of the mid-first century CE the Jews of Rome (and elsewhere) "seem to have avoided entanglement in the rebellions and to have remained calm, saving their privileges and traditions."[148] Their links to Jerusalem were not so strong that they felt compelled to take a stand in support of their brethren on the other side of the Empire.

In turning to Christianity, we must evaluate what evidence there is that it was a "translocal" or "world-wide" religion. The translocal "link" for many scholars is Paul, since he is seen to "connect" the various

---

[144] See *Ebr.* 14; P. Borgen, "'Yes,' 'No,' 'How Far?': The Participation of Jews and Christians in Pagan Cults," in *Paul in His Hellenistic Context*, ed. T. Engberg-Pedersen (Minneapolis: Fortress, 1995) 45; *contra* La Piana, "Foreign Groups," 343.

[145] Translation in Borgen, "Participation of Jews," 46.

[146] Erastus, a member of the Corinthian congregation, would have been required to participate in cultic rituals at city council meetings due to his position as city treasurer (Rom 16:13). When writing to the Corinthians Paul does not limit the participation of Christians in pagan temple meals, except under certain conditions (1 Cor 8:1-13, 10:23-11:1; cf. Borgen, "Participation of Jews," 57-59).

[147] Translation in Borgen, "Participation of Jews," 42; see also L. I. Levine, *Roman Caesarea: An Archaeological-Topological Study* (Jerusalem: Institute of Archaeology, Hebrew University of Jerusalem, 1975) 45.

[148] La Piana, "Foreign Groups," 374.

congregations. Certainly he himself would like to think that the congregations are connected, but this may not have been the case. For example, the support of the Philippian church went to Paul, not the other congregations with which he worked (Phil 4:10-20). For the Christian groups themselves their first priority seems to have remained their own local congregations. This is best seen in Paul's attempt to collect money for the Jerusalem church. Meeks points to Paul's collection as indicating translocal obligations to other Christians.[149] However, Paul's troubles with raising the money promised, and his rhetorical strategies in his letters to the Corinthians (2 Cor 8:1-15; 9:1-5), suggest that they, at least, remained unconvinced that they had a social and religious obligation to an otherwise unknown group. What confuses the Corinthians is not the fact that they have to donate, but that the monies are going to Jerusalem rather than the common fund of the local congregation.[150] Also, the financial support for the Jerusalem church came from the newer, Pauline churches (not the reverse), which would have gone against expectations. In a translocal organization the established centre usually supports the struggling, newer organizations.[151]

---

[149] Meeks, *First Urban Christians*, 110.

[150] Kloppenborg, "Edwin Hatch," 237. La Piana ("Foreign Groups," 372-73) highlights the willingness of the Jews of the diaspora to contribute to the collection of funds for Jerusalem because of their strong translocal link to Jerusalem. If this is so, it contrasts with the attitude of the Corinthians who, given Paul's rhetoric and his repeated appeals, did not have such a feeling of obligation; they consider themselves to be a localized group, much like the associations. Priority may also have been placed on smaller groups within one urban centre (e.g., 1 Cor 1:10-17). Voluntary associations could have more than one local group. Cities with more than one grouping of a larger association include Thessalonica (Dionysiac, early III CE) and Magnesia ad Maeander (Dionysiac, III BCE).

[151] J. T. Townsend, "Missionary Journeys in Acts and European Missionary Societies," in *SBL 1985 Seminar Papers*, ed. K. H. Richards (SBLASP 24; Atlanta: Scholars Press, 1985) 437 n. 38. The local nature of Pauline Christian communities is noted by Hainz, who argues that Paul himself does not hold to any concept of the "church universal" but emphasizes each of the local churches as in itself the 'church of God': "Paulus spricht nicht von der 'Gesamtkirche'; d. h. ἐκκλησία τοῦ θεοῦ und 'Volk Gottes' sind für ihn keineswegs identische Größen.... Paulus spricht nur von konkreten Gemeinden, und seine Gemeindetheologie ist *primär* eine Komponente seines Apostolatsverständnisses; d. h. es muß als erste Grundbestimmung für die Gemeinde gelten: sie ist 'apostolisch'" (Hainz, *Ekklesia*, 359, his emphasis). This seems to be overstating the case for Paul, who did see some connections among his communities and among all of the Christian communities, including the one in Jerusalem, even if the local communities themselves did not perceive these connections.

Concerning both terminology for group designation and terminology for officers, Christian groups have similarities to voluntary associations not in particular usages, but in the diversity of usages among the groups. Local particularities of language can be cited for both Christian groups and associations. Dow points out that of eight societies of Sarapiastai throughout the Greek world, "there is no similarity of organization, so far as one can observe, between any two of them."[152] The same can be said of Pauline churches where it would be difficult to show a similar structure between, for example, the church at Galatia and the church at Corinth.

There is no a priori reason to assume that there was uniformity among the Pauline churches, any more than one should assume a uniform organizational structure in associations. On the contrary, titles were highly variable, local particularities abound, and in many instances, we have no indication of how officers were designated."[153]
In the case of Paul, and of the Sarapiastai, the "differences" are due to their varying locations in the circum-Mediterranean world.[154]

As we saw earlier, the term ἐκκλησία is used by Paul as a designation for his churches in both the singular and the plural. Paul's use of the word in the plural shows that in his mind there were connections among Christian groups within one or more provinces rather than simply within a town (e.g., Rom 16:16; 1 Cor 7:17; 11:16; 16:19; 2 Cor 8:1; 11:28; Gal 1:22; 1 Thess 2:14). However, both Paul and the Christian community used ἐκκλησία in the local sense (e.g., Rom 16:1, 5; 1 Cor 1:2; 11:18), much like some associations who used it as a self-designator.[155] While Paul may have used the term on the basis of the LXX,[156] "within the Greek speaking

---

[152] Dow, "Egyptian Cults," 191.

[153] Kloppenborg, "Edwin Hatch," 232. Cf. Vincent 1897:50: "The church was not one body, but only an aggregate of local communities; and the features of organization and government in any single community and the official titles which their administrators bore were not the same in other communities."

[154] Dow ("Egyptian Cults," 191) suggests that since it has proven unfruitful to compare various clubs of Sarapiastai throughout the Greek world, we would be better served to compare the Attic Sarapiastai to cult societies of all other kinds within Attica itself, a task that proves to be quite successful (see B. H. McLean, "For the Love of Dionysos: Five Forms of Dionysias Devotion" unpublished paper, 1995). The same could prove to be the case for Pauline churches; more local studies are needed before any solid conclusions are put forward.

[155] Liebenam, *Geschichte und Organisation*, 272-73; Hardy, *Roman History*, 141; Poland, *griechischen Vereinswesens*, 332.

[156] As Schmidt maintains ("ἐκκλησία," 513-14, esp. n. 25).

cities it would be understood as a term used by, among others, voluntary associations."[157]

When Countryman suggests that the associations were "strictly local" he goes on to state that "[i]n the church, however, the officers enjoyed life tenure and derived their authority from outside the congregation, either literally or in theory."[158] Yet this assumes much for Pauline churches. The disputes within the Corinthian congregation make it clear that there was no primary authority in the church that could oversee all aspects and negotiate between various factions. Paul attempts to take on this role as an external authority, but the letters of 2 Corinthians should show us that he was not always successful (1 Cor 9; 2 Cor 1:15-2:13; 2 Cor 10-13). The earliest that we might see some indication of Christianity as a "world-wide" phenomenon with a central seat of authority is the early to mid-second century in the writings of Ignatius and 1 Clement. Even here, however, the idea of the primacy of the bishop of Rome is not entirely clear.[159]

Meeks suggests that Paul and other "missionaries" actively sought to establish a notion of a "universal people of God"; "The letters themselves, the messengers who brought them, and the repeated visits to the local assemblies by Paul and his associates all emphasized this inter-relatedness."[160] Yet this assumption can be called into question. Certainly *Paul* refers to his "churches" and the common teaching and practices therein (1 Cor 4:17; 7:17; 11:16), but this does not necessarily represent a monolithic movement. The Corinthians may not have been impressed with Paul's rhetorical strategy; it is unlikely that they moved swiftly and eagerly to "correct" their practices in light of Paul's letters. Paul never assumes that his own communities were in contact with one another, even in 2 Cor 8, where the reference to the Macedonians is very general. If his aimed to establish a translocal, "world-wide" group, one would think that from the beginning he would be encouraging local leaders to meet with leaders from other locales or even go to Jerusalem.[161]

---

[157] Kloppenborg, "Edwin Hatch," 231.

[158] Countryman, "Patrons and Officers," 138.

[159] See R. E. Brown and J. P. Meier, *Antioch and Rome: New Testament Cradles of Catholic Christianity* (New York: Paulist, 1983) 164-66, on *1 Clement*. See W. R. Schoedel ("Ignatius, Epistles of," *ABD* 3 [1992] 386) and H. Chadwick ("The Silence of Bishops in Ignatius," *HTR* 43 [1950] 170) on Ignatius.

[160] Meeks, *First Urban Christians*, 109.

[161] Townsend's call for a re-evaluation of the consideration of Acts as presenting Paul undergoing "missionary journeys" is apropos ("Missionary Journeys"). He warns about (and illustrates) commentators "reading their own presuppositions back into apostolic times" in this regard ("Missionary Journeys," 436). It may be that neither Paul or his converts thought

Meeks' claims are again called into question when he states that it is "peculiar" that early Christian groups could emulate the "intimate, close-knit life of the local groups" and still be part of a much larger, worldwide movement.[162] It is unlikely that Paul's words that others "invoke the name of our Lord Jesus Christ in every place" (1 Cor 1:2) would have been any different than a similar claim of a priest of Isis or of Asclepius, the worship of whom was spread throughout the empire.[163] Meeks simply assumes this indicates "translocal connections"[164] before immediately turning to the "supralocal organization" of Christianity in the time of Constantine.

We see perhaps in the Dionysus artists' association an analogy to what may have occurred in Christianity. Over a period of three or four centuries this association grew from local groups with very loose translocal connections to the "worldwide" guild of artists (see above). Likewise Christianity did become a strong, well-defined global movement, but not until a few centuries beyond the foundations of the original groups. Christianity became a universal religion without national or racial connections only "[t]hrough a long and painful process of evolution."[165] Thus, the description of formative Christian groups as "universal" would certainly not be an apt description.

It is significant that early Christian and non-Christian writers "did not consider it incongruous to speak explicitly of the church as a *thiasos*."[166] When Trajan banned fraternities, Christian groups, at least in Bithynia,

---

of what they were "up to" as a mission (as L. E. Vaage has suggested; "Religious Rivalries and the Struggle for Success: Jews, Christians, and Other Religious Groups in Local (Urban) Settings (63 BCE - 330 CE)," unpublished Paper Presented to the Annual Meeting of the CSBS [Montreal, 1995]) or even as having any more translocal connections than other associations.

[162] Meeks, *First Urban Christians*, 70.

[163] Cf. The formula εἷς Θεός ("one God") is applied not only to the Christian God but to other deities such as Sarapis – εἷς Θεὸς Σάραπις ("one God, Sarapis"; see C. Bonner, *Studies in Magical Amulets, Chiefly Graeco-Egyptian* (Ann Arbor: University of Michigan Press, 1950) 10, 41, 46-47).

[164] Meeks himself points out that some scholars think that this phrase was added later to the Pauline corpus in order to "catholicize" it (*First Urban Christians*, 229 n. 155).

[165] La Piana, "Foreign Groups," 339.

[166] A. J. Malherbe, *Social Aspects of Early Christianity* (Philadelphia: Fortress, 1983²) 89. Cf. Hardy, *Roman History*, 141; Celsus in Origen, *Cels.* 3.2.3; Lucian, *Pergr. Mort.* 11; cf. Eusebius, *Hist. Eccl.* 6.19, 16; 7.32, 27; 10.1; Tertullian, *Apologia* 39 (refering to Christianity as *factio Christiane, corpus, secta Dei*, and other titles used of associations); *CIL* VIII 9585.

gave up their usual practices because they thought that the ban applied to them (that is, they fit the description of fraternities).[167] It is worth noting that Pliny's letter concerning the Christians in Bithynia does not reflect the governor's anxiety that the worldwide phenomenon might lead to rebellion but rather the local merchants' distress over the effect on their trade of masses of people joining Christian groups.

We can conclude that our survey of the available data reveals that some voluntary associations in antiquity had translocal links *and* that Christian groups were more locally based than is often assumed. There is no doubt that the *primary* basis for associations was local,[168] but, we would argue, this would be equally true for the Christian groups. Christian congregations and voluntary associations were both locally based groups with limited translocal connections.

6. Literary Production

One final issue of community organization needs to be addressed, primarily because it has been suggested as a difference between Christian groups and associations, namely, Christians production of literature and the lack of it among associations.[169] First, we should note that Paul's communities did not produce "literature," Paul did. Second, although we may not possess literature from the associations, that fact might be an accident of time. Most associations claimed a patron deity, many of whom did have much literary support that the associations may have used. It is only after initial Christian groups were founded that we get "literature" (Gospels), at the earliest in the 60s or 70s, probably later.

In associations we do know that written records were kept along with the inscriptions.[170] Letters to and from associations and their members and especially letters written by founders or patrons, are extant (see *P.Enteuxeis* 20; 21; *P.Karanis* 575; *P.Rainer* V 23). However, the nature of archaeological preservation places the bulk of surviving letters from antiquity in Egypt. Thus, we have evidence of letters concerned with

---

[167] Pliny, *Epistulae* 10.96; Judge, *Social Pattern*, 48.

[168] Fisher, "Roman Associations," 1209.

[169] Alexander, "Hellenistic Schools," 82.

[170] See *SEG* III 674 (Rhodes, II BCE); F. A. Pennacchietti, "Nuove iscrizion i di Hierapolis Frigia," *Atti della Accademia delle Scienze de Torino* 101 (1966) nos. 7, 25; IDelos 1521 (II BCE); 1522 (II CE); cf. IDelos 1520 (II BCE); *P.Cairo Dem.* 30605; 30606; *P.Lond.* 2710; *P.Lillie.Dem.* 29; *P.Mich. Tebt.* 243; 244; 248; *P.Ryl.* 580.

associations from this part of the Mediterranean. While this does not conclusively indicate that this was the case throughout the Empire, it certainly suggests that it is possible that the practice was followed. Some inscriptions do indicate that letters were exchanged, and a few even record the contents of such letters, as in the case of the Tyrian merchants in Ostia (*CIG* 5853).

7. Conclusion

We have now come to the end of our survey of various aspects of voluntary associations, particularly their functions, membership, and organization. It is with this data in mind that we turn in the next chapter to the Macedonian Christian communities to see what light the voluntary associations can shed on an interpretation of Paul's letters to these communities.

Chapter Five

The Philippian Christian Community

Among scholars of the New Testament there is a growing awareness of the importance of studies of early Christianity that take seriously local peculiarities. Exegetes recognize that New Testament texts must be read in the light of the social situation to which each was addressed if they are to be properly understood. Rather than read the social situation in terms of New Testament ideas alone, one must read the texts more widely by examining the social, political, economic, and ideological contexts, and, more narrowly, local situations.[1]

While most modern scholars acknowledge in theory the lack of a uniform local model for the church, in practice this importance has been overlooked. In general, scholarship that undertakes a social description of "Pauline Christianity" homogenizes all Pauline churches, generally treating 1 Corinthians as the model for all else.[2] This is both historically implausible and methodologically problematic. For example, much of the discussion of the social level of the early Christians is based on studies of the Corinthian Christian community, where the church is thought to be composed of members of all ranks save the very top and the very bottom of society.[3] It is clear, however, that the members of the Macedonian

---

[1] Judge, *Social Pattern*, 72; cf. H. Hendrix, "Thessalonians Honour Romans," unpublished Th.D. Thesis (Harvard University, 1984) 6-10; Kloppenborg, "ΦΙΛΑΔΕΛΦΙΑ," 267.

[2] For example, see R. Russell who uncritically reads information from Acts 17 into the situation at Thessalonica and then jumps to the following conclusion: "all of this essentially agreeing with Theissen's conclusions on the social makeup of the Corinthian church," which he takes to indicate the presence of some higher social elites in the Thessalonian congregation ("The Idle in 2 Thess 3.6-12: An Eschatological or a Social Problem?" *NTS* 34 [1988] 111).

[3] See Judge, Social Pattern; Malherbe, *Social Aspects*; Meeks, *First Urban Christians*; and especially G. Theissen on social status (*Social Reality and the Early Christians: Theology, Ethics, and the World of the New Testament* [Minneapolis: Fortress, 1992]; idem., *The Social Setting of Pauline Christianity: Essays on Corinth* [Philadelphia: Fortress, 1982]). The discussion is aptly summarized in C. Osiek where it is obvious that Corinth is the test case for all of Paul's churches; after almost exclusively discussing texts from Corinth she concludes that "[w]e have traced some of the social factors operative in the life of Paul and in the churches he founded. The evidence as illuminated by recent scholarship indicates gatherings of people from across the social spectrum, with the exception of the very lowest levels and the highest aristocratic orders"

churches were financially poorer than the members of the Corinthian churches.⁴ Failure to take seriously local peculiarities of each of Paul's churches and to read each of his letters in the light of the local social situation to which each was addressed will result in a misunderstanding of that particular Christian community.⁵

This leads us to the topic of the final two chapters of our investigation: putting Paul's Macedonian Christian communities in their local context. While scholarly attention has focused on the Corinthian congregations, little has been said of the social character of the Macedonian churches. Most commentaries are all too brief in attempting to place the letters of Paul to the Thessalonians in its context.⁶ It is usual for commentaries on 1 Thessalonians to rely upon the account in Acts 17:1-9, which leads

---

(*What Are They Saying About the Social Setting of the New Testament?* [New York and Mahwah: Paulist, 1992²] 70-71).

⁴ See 2 Cor 8:1-4; A. J. Malherbe, *The Letters to the Thessalonians: A New Translation with Introduction and Commentary* (AB 32B; New York: Doubleday, 2000) 65; cf. R. Jewett, *The Thessalonian Correspondence: Pauline Rhetoric and Millenarian Piety* (Foundations and Facets. Philadelphia: Fortress, 1986) 120-21. Cf. Schöllgen's critique of Meeks (*First Urban Christians*, 51-73): "Meeks behandelt nämlich nicht jede Gemeinde getrennt für sich, sondern wirft das Material aus allen paulinischen Gemeinden zusammen und verwertet es in einander ergänzender Weise" ("Sozialstruktur," 73).

⁵ In contrast, Horsley has produced a lengthy analysis of the inscriptions of Ephesus that seeks to establish the first century context for Christianity in that city ("The Inscriptions of Ephesos and the New Testament," *NovT* 34 [1992] esp. 157-58, 168). At the end of his study Horsley issues a *desideratum* for more studies of Ephesus in order to better understand that locale. Horsley's *desideratum* should not be limited to Ephesus alone as much social history remains to be done for all the cities in which Christian congregations were established.

⁶ For example, J. Eadie, *Commentary on the Greek Text of the Epistles of Paul to the Thessalonians* (London: Macmillan, 1877) 1-3; G. Milligan, *St. Paul's Epistles to the Thessalonians: The Greek Text with Introduction and Notes* (London: Macmillan, 1908) xxi-xxv; L. Morris, *The First and Second Epistles to the Thessalonians* (NICNT; Grand Rapids: Eerdmans, 1959) 15-19; E. Best, *The First and Second Epistles to the Thessalonians* (London: Black, 1972) 1-2. Jewett (*Thessalonian Correspondence*, 113 n.1) chides W. Marxsen (*Der erste Brief an die Thessalonicher* [ZBK NT 11/1; Zürich: Theologischer Verlag, 1979]), I. H. Marshall (*1 and 2 Thessalonians* [NCBC; Grand Rapids: Eerdmans, 1983]), C. Masson (*Les Deux Épitres de Saint Paul aux Thessaloniciens* [Neuchâtel and Paris: Delachaux & Niestle, 1957]), Best (*Thessalonians*), and F. F. Bruce (*1 & 2 Thessalonians* [WBC 45; Waco: Word, 1982]) for being too brief on the political and geographic setting of Thessalonica and for barely mentioning the available studies of the political, economic, and cultural situation of the city and the religious activity therein. This is not the case with Rigaux (*Thessaloniciens*, 11-20).

exegetes to assume that the church grew naturally out of the synagogue.[7] While some recognize that the Thessalonian church was composed primarily of Gentiles, they follow Acts in suggesting that Paul "stole away" a number of God-fearers and proselytes.[8] As with commentaries on 1 Thessalonians, those that exegete Philippians tend to provide the "historical setting" of the letters all too briefly and with too much uncritical reliance on the account of the founding of the church in Acts 16:11-40.[9] A typical example is Gordon Fee whose account of the history of the founding of the Philippian church consists of a reiteration of the account in Acts with little expansion of the details.[10] This reliance on Acts

---

[7] For example, Milligan, *Thessalonians*, xxvi-xxx; J. E. Frame, *A Critical and Exegetical Commentary on the Epistles of St. Paul to the Thessalonians* (ICC; Edinburgh: T. & T. Clark, 1912) 1-7; Rigaux, *Thessaloniciens*, 3-11, 20; Masson, *Thessaloniciens*, 5-6; Bruce, *Thessalonians*, xxi-xxviii; less so Best, *Thessalonians*, 2-7; Holtz 1986:9-10; Wanamaker, *Thessalonians*, 6-16; Malherbe, *Thessalonians*, 57-65. Also N. Hugédé, *Saint Paul et la Grèce* (Paris: Les Belles Lettres, 1982) 67-90.

[8] For example, Eadie, *Thessalonians*, 12-13; Frame, *Thessalonians*, 5-6; Rigaux, *Thessaloniciens*, 20; F. Laub, "Paulus als Gemeindegründer (1 Thess)," in *Kirche im Werden: Studien zum Thema Amt und Gemeinde im Neuen Testament*, ed. J. Hainz (Munich: Schöningh, 1976) 25; Holtz, *Thessalonicher*, 10. Malherbe (*Thessalonians*) is more cautious in that he recognizes the predominantly Gentile composition of the Thessalonian community, but he still suggests that there were some Jews in the community (p. 56), despite admitting that while "there might have been some Jews in the church" 1 Thessalonians "offers no evidence" of their presence (p. 66). B. R. Gaventa is much more cautious than most (*First and Second Thessalonians* [Interpretation; Louisville: Westminster John Knox, 1998] 4-5).

[9] See A. Plummer, *A Commentary on St. Paul's Epistle to the Philippians* (London: Robert Scoll, 1909) v-xi; P. Bonnard, *L'épître de saint Paul aux Philippiens et l'épître aux Colossiens* (CNT 10; Neuchâtel: Delachaux, 1950) 7-8; J. J. Müller, *The Epistles of Paul to the Philippians and Philemon* (NICNT; Grand Rapids: Eerdmans, 1955) 13; J.-F. Collange, *The Epistle of Saint Paul to the Philippians* (London: Epworth, 1979) 1-3; G. Barth, *Der Brief an die Philipper* (ZB NT 9; Zürich: Theologischer Verlag, 1979) 7-8; Hugédé, *Saint Paul*, 38-59; Hawthorne, *Philippians*, xxxii-xxxvi; M. Silva, *Philippians* (Wycliffe Exegetical Commentary; Chicago: Moody, 1988) 2-5; O'Brien, *Philippians*, 3-8; U. B. Müller, *Der Brief des Paulus an die Philipper* (THK 11/I. Berlin: Evangelische Verlagsanstalt, 1993) 1-4; C. Koukouli-Chrysantaki, "Colonia Iulia Augusta Philippensis," in *Philippi at the Time of Paul and After His Death*, ed. C. Bakirtzis and H. Koester (Harrisburg: Trinity Press International, 1998) 27. More skeptical of the Acts account is J. Gnilka, *Der Philipperbrief* (HThK 10/3; Freiburg: Herder, 1980³) 3. In most cases there is an implicit or explicit assumption of the presence of at least a small Jewish community at Philippi, an assumption that is not warranted by the evidence.

[10] G. D. Fee, *Paul's Letter to the Philippians* (NICNT; Grand Rapids: Eerdmans, 1995) 27-28. For Fee's understanding of the letter, more important than the social situation in Philippi itself is the situation of friendship that existed between Paul and the

is true of J. B. Lightfoot, although he takes more seriously than most the specific character of Philippi during Paul's time there (e.g., the strong influence of women; the collective conversion of households).[11]

Other studies of 1 Thessalonians and Philippians focus on theological or epistolographic issues, taking little interest in the local particularities of the recipient cities.[12] Fortunately, there are some notable exceptions to this generalization for both Thessalonica[13] and Philippi.[14] While these studies have proven useful for understanding the locale in which the church was formed they are not without their limitations.

Philippians and is reflected in the genre of Paul's letter, a "letter of friendship" (Fee, *Philippians*, 1 and more generally 1-14; so also B. Witherington III, *Friendship and Finances in Philippi: The Letter of Paul to the Philippians* [The New Testament in Context; Valley Forge: Trinity Press International, 1994]).

[11] Lightfoot, *Philippians,* 47-65.

[12] For example, J. Reumann, "The Theologies of 1 Thessalonians and Philippians: Contents, Comparison, and Composite," in *SBL 1987 Seminar Papers*, ed. K. H. Richards (SBLASP 26; Atlanta: Scholars Press, 1987) 521-36; N. T. Wright, "Putting Paul Together Again: Toward a Synthesis of Pauline Theology (1 and 2 Thessalonians, Philippians, and Philemon)," in *Pauline Theology 1: Thessalonians, Philippians, Galatians, Philemon*, ed. J. M. Bassler (Minneapolis: Fortress, 1991) 183-211; B. N. Kaye, "Eschatology and Ethics in 1 and 2 Thessalonians," *NovT* 17 (1975) 47-57; B. C. Johanson, *To All the Brethren: A Text-Linguistic and Rhetorical Approach to 1 Thessalonians* (ConBNT 16; Stockholm: Almqvist & Wiksell, 1987); R. Jewett, "The Epistolary Thanksgiving and the Integrity of Philippians," *NovT* 12 (1970) 40-53; R. Russell, "Pauline Letter Structure in Philippians," *JETS* 25 (1982) 295-306; B. Mengel, *Studien zum Philipperbrief* (WUNT 2/8; Tübingen: Mohr Siebeck, 1982); D. E. Garland, "The Composition and Unity of Philippians: Some Neglected Literary Factors," *NovT* 27 (1985) 141-73; P. Perkins, "Christology, Friendship and Status: The Rhetoric of Philippians," in *SBL 1987 Seminar Papers*, ed. K. H. Richards (SBLASP 26; Atlanta: Scholars Press, 1987) 509-20; D. F. Watson, "Rhetorical Analysis of Philippians and Its Implications for the Unity Question," *NovT* 30 (1988) 57-88; L. Alexander, "Hellenistic Letter-Forms and the Structure of Philippians," *JSNT* 37 (1989) 87-101.

[13] Hendrix, "Thessalonians Honour Romans"; K. P. Donfried, "The Cults of Thessalonica and the Thessalonian Correspondence," *NTS* 31 (1985) 336-56; Kloppenborg, "ΦΙΛΑΔΕΛΦΙΑ"; Jewett, *Thessalonian Correspondence*.

[14] Portefaix, *Sisters Rejoice*; Abrahamsen, *Women and Worship*; Bormann, *Philippi*; D. Peterlin, *Paul's Letter to the Philippians in the Light of Disunity in the Church* (NovTSup 79; Leiden/New York/Köln: Brill, 1995); Pilhofer, *erste christliche Gemeinde*; C. Bakirtzis and H. Koester, *Philippi at the Time of Paul and After His Death* (Harrisburg: Trinity Press International, 1998). These works are some of the more significant studies that note the significance of the local setting. For an evaluation of Abrahamsen, Peterlin, Bormann, and Pilhofer see R. S. Ascough, "Recent Books on Philippi," *TJT* 13 (1997) 72-77.

With this in mind, we turn to Paul's Macedonian letters themselves in an attempt to use the information gleaned in the preceding chapters to understand the organization of these communities.[15] Reading Paul's letters in light of the community practices and language of the voluntary associations will allow us to see typicality and particularity in a context that will bring a new sense to the Pauline texts. Illustrating the language and practices of 1 Thessalonians and Philippians by reference to the associations will help explain both Paul's language and, in turn, the language and structure of the communities to which he writes.[16] However, we want to be clear from the start that when we find analogous material in Paul's letters and the voluntary association inscriptions we are not suggesting that any particular inscription or association is the source of Paul's ideas and language (the "genealogical" argument). In fact, there is no foundational template of 'voluntary association' that explains all of the features of Paul's Macedonian letters. Rather, we want to show how Paul's choice of words and concepts reflects the structure and the ethos of the communities to which he writes. Although Paul founded each of the communities, the members of each must have had a part in determining salient features of their community interaction. To presume otherwise is to presume that the Macedonians did not know how to organize clubs. This is unlikely. Given the evidence for voluntary associations generally in the Greco-Roman world and more specifically in Macedonia, it is likely that both Paul and the Macedonian Christians share the same discursive field as the associations.

We are not attempting to conclude that the Macedonian Christian communities are now to be understood simply as Christian voluntary associations, as if that would explain the two Pauline letters *in toto*. Rather, we are concerned to show that many of the features of the two Macedonian Christian communities find ready analogies in voluntary associations, and thus would appear to outsiders as associations and would function internally as such. Comparison with a broad range of associations

---

[15] Second Thessalonians is deliberately excluded from the primary investigation due to the contentious nature of the letter in terms of both authorship and audience. See Jewett, *Thessalonian Correspondence*, 3-23 for a summary of the debate.

[16] Some of the concepts and language that we look at will have been familiar to most persons living in antiquity (what V. K. Robbins calls the "social intertexture" of texts in *Exploring the Texture of Texts: A Guide to Socio-Rhetorical Interpretation* [Valley Forge: Trinity Press International, 1996] 62-63). However, looking at the specific use in the associations and in 1 Thessalonians and Philippians can help us uncover resonance within the texts that have previously been overlooked.

enlightens various features of Paul's discourse and allows us to better understand how both the Thessalonian and the Philippian communities were organized.

1. Paul's Letter to the Philippians

Views on the authorship of Philippians vary widely. A number of scholars reject Pauline authorship primarily on the basis of the letter's use of "gnostic" ideas (particularly the hymn of 2:6-11) and its lack of anything distinctly Pauline.[17] A second view holds Paul himself wrote the entire work including the hymn found in 2:6-11.[18] Probably the most widely held position among modern interpreters is that Paul wrote Philippians but incorporated into it previously existing Christian material such as the hymn found in Phil 2:6-11.[19]

The literary unity of Philippians is subject to much debate. A number of scholars point to evidence that suggests that the letter is composed of more than one letter written by Paul to Philippi.[20] Some suggest that a later editor combined two letters, based on the shift in tone at 3:1-2. Paul wrote most of what follows, which is strong invective against his opponents, after he wrote the Philippians a thank you letter for money which they had sent him. The "three-letter hypothesis" breaks down the letter even further. The first letter is found at 4:10-20 and represents Paul's immediate acknowledgement of the monetary gift sent to him from the church. The second (1:1-3:1a; 4:4-7, 21-23) followed shortly afterwards and addresses some of the external problems faced by the Philippians and urges them to greater unity. The third letter (3:1b-4:3, 8-9) comes from a later time, perhaps after Paul's release from prison and visit to Philippi (cf. 2:24; 1:26; Acts 20:1-2). In this letter Paul addresses the threat to the church posed by the Judaizers who are among them. A later redactor has taken these letters of Paul and pasted them together, although not very neatly.

---

[17] Summarized in O'Brien, *Philippians*, 9-10.

[18] Cf. Fee, *Philippians*, 43-46.

[19] Paul not only uses his hymn within the rhetoric of chapter 2, but also echoes themes from it in 3:20-21; see N. Flanagan, "A Note on Philippians 3,20-21," *CBQ* 18 (1956) 8-9.

[20] Such claims are bolstered by Polycarp's letter to the church at Philippi between 98-117 CE. Polycarp, Bishop of Smyrna, speaks of Paul's letters (plural) to the Philippians (*Phil* 3.2). However, internal evidence is the primary reason for suggesting separate letters.

The position of those who hold to the unity of the letter is somewhat more straightforward – the letter we have in our canon reflects the letter sent by Paul to Philippi. However, this position has been argued variously with no agreement on the unifying elements within the letter. Russell appeals to ancient letter structure as a means for arguing for the unity of Philippians.[21] Garland uses literary and rhetorical features to undergird the unity of the letter.[22] Watson argues for the letter's unity on the basis of his rhetorical analysis of the letter (although he differs from Garland on the identification of some of the rhetorical features).[23] Wick suggests that Philippians is composed of ten blocks of material representing five distinct occasions, but that Paul set up the entire letter using linguistic parallels, the themes of the first five parts of the letter being paralleled in the second five parts of the letter.[24] Black uses text-linguistics as a precursor to rhetorical analysis to show the unity of Philippians.[25] Luter and Lee attempt to highlight a chiastic structure in Philippians as a means to show its literary integrity.[26]

It is beyond the scope of this book to detail all of the arguments for and against the multiple letter hypotheses.[27] The assumption made herein is that the canonical form of Philippians reflects a single letter written by Paul. While this is far from an assured conclusion, we are more persuaded by those who hold to the unity of the letter on thematic grounds.[28] Even the

---

[21] Russell, "Letter Structure," 295-306.

[22] Garland, "Composition and Unity," 141-73.

[23] Watson, "Rhetorical Analysis," 57-88.

[24] P. Wick, *Der Philipperbrief: Der formale Aufbau des Briefs als Schlüssel zum Verständnis seines Inhalts* (BWANT 7/15; Stuttgart: Kohlhammer, 1994). For my analysis of Wick's arguments see my review in *JBL* 114 (1995) 750-52.

[25] D. A. Black, "The Discourse Structure of Philippians: A Study in Textlinguistics," *NovT* 37 (1995) 16-49.

[26] A. B. Luter and M. V. Lee, "Philippians as Chiasmus: Key to the Structure, Unity and Theme Questions," *NTS* 41 (1995) 89-101.

[27] For more details see B. Byrne, "The Letter to the Philippians," in *The New Jerome Biblical Commentary*, ed. R. E. Brown, J. A. Fitzmyer, and R. E. Murphy (Englewood Cliffs, NJ: Prentice Hall, 1990) 791-92 or J. Murphy-O'Connor, *Paul: A Critical Life* (Oxford: Clarendon, 1996) 215-30, both of whom hold to the three-letter position. The debate is summarized in Hawthorne (*Philippians*, xxix-xxxii) O'Brien (*Philippians*, 10-18), and R. P. Martin, *Philippians* (NCBC; London: Oliphants, 1976) 10-21, all of whom argue for the integrity of the letter.

[28] In drawing this conclusion we are in good company among some recent writers on Philippians. Both K. L. Berry, ("The Function of Friendship Language in Philippians 4:10-20," in *Friendship, Flattery, and Frankness of Speech: Studies on Friendship in the New Testament World*, ed. J. T. Fitzgerald [NovTSup 82; Leiden, New York, Köln: Brill,

advocates of the compositional theory admit that the individual letters would have been written and received in fairly close proximity (within a couple of years). Thus, whichever compositional conclusion is accepted, it is agreed by most that the entire content of the canonical form of the letter comes from the hand of Paul and was written to the church in the city of Philippi around the same time.[29]

2. The Social Location of the Philippian Christians

Throughout Philippians Paul exhorts the Philippians to live a corporate life "worthy of the gospel" (1:27). Paul's subtle references to the Philippian Christians' social status are used to affirm rather than denigrate the Philippians' corporate life. Paul's rhetoric allows the Philippians to see that they are already well on their way to fulfilling the ideal of this "life worthy of the gospel."

1996] 121) and A. J. Malherbe ("Paul's Self-Sufficiency (Philippians 4:11)," in *Friendship, Flattery, and Frankness of Speech: Studies on Friendship in the New Testament World*, ed. J. T. Fitzgerald [NovTSup 82; Leiden, New York, Köln: Brill, 1996] 128) see the *topos* of friendship throughout the canonical form of the letter as indicative of its unity. N. A. Dahl ("Euodia and Syntyche in Philippians," in *The Social World of the First Christians: Essays in Honour of Wayne A. Meeks*, ed. L. M. White and O. L. Yarborough, [Minneapolis: Fortress, 1995] 3-15) and Peterlin (*Disunity*, 217) have independently used the theme of unity in the letter to suggest the literary integrity of the letter. J. T. Reed has suggested that 3:1 is actually a "hesitation formula" and not a badly made seam ("Philippians 3:1 and the Epistolary Hesitation Formulas: The Literary Integrity of Philippians, Again," *JBL* 115 [1996] 63-90). See also Jewett ("Epistolary Thanksgiving," 49-53) whose most persuasive argument is the point that topics announced in the thanksgiving (Phil 1:3-11) are connected with each succeeding part of the letter.

[29] A mid-50s CE date is most often held for this letter, based on it being written from Ephesus. Those who suggest a Caesarean or Roman imprisonment maintain a later date, the early 60s. Either way it is among the later of Paul's letters. Paul's ministry in Philippi was earlier than this, perhaps in the early 50s. In Phil 4:15 Paul talks about his work in Macedonia as the "beginning of the Gospel." Most have taken this to indicate that Paul's time in Macedonia represented a renewal for his zeal for the Gospel (J. B. Lightfoot, *Biblical Essays* [London: Macmillan, 1893] 237), or the beginning of a new phase of his own ministry (Collange, *Philippians*, 152). However, J. M. Suggs ("Concerning the Date of Paul's Macedonian Ministry," *NovT* 4 [1960] 60-68) has argued that from Paul's letters alone (i.e., without Acts; see Phil 1:5; 4:15-16; 2 Thess 2:13) we would be compelled to conclude that Macedonia was Paul's first mission field. This being so, Paul's mission in Macedonia would need to be dated in the early 40s. This seems to me unlikely and I would place Paul in Macedonia in the early 50s.

There are a number of indications in the text that suggest that the Philippian Christians were not particularly well-off despite their generous contributions to Paul and to the collection for Jerusalem. In fact, Paul makes explicit reference to their poverty in 2 Cor 8:1-2, where he points out that the churches of Macedonia contributed despite their "extreme poverty" (ἡ κατὰ βάθους πτωχεία αὐτῶν ἐπερίσσευσεν). In Philippians itself, Paul's assurance that God will supply "all their needs" (πληρώσει πᾶσαν χρείαν ὑμῶν, 4:19) suggests that they have material needs to begin with.[30] Furthermore, Paul's statement of contentment when facing "poverty[31] ... hunger and ... want" (4:12) may suggest that the Philippians need to possess such contentment, while the larger context implies that it is contentment in "want" not "wealth" that they must possess.[32] This can be coupled with Paul's comment on their willingness to share his θλῖψις (4:14) by giving money; in this context his θλῖψις is clearly his impoverishment.

a) The Marketplace

Paul uses a number of metaphors taken from the world of the marketplace and trade when writing to the Philippians. These metaphors show a concern not with the high finance of the elite but with the ordinary practices of common merchants. Marketplace metaphors predominate in chapter three of Philippians. In the midst of his encomium of self-recommendation (Phil 3:2-17) Paul makes extensive use of marketplace language. Three times he uses ἡγέομαι ("regard"), a word that can be used in contexts of accounting.[33] This context is confirmed by Paul's use of κέρδος and ζημία and the cognate verbs κερδήσω and ἐζημιώθην, which involve loss-gain language reminiscent of bookkeeping.[34] The word ζημία

---

[30] The parallel with "my need" (χρείαν μοι) in 4:16 indicates that the reference in 4:19 is to the Philippians' material needs similar to the needs of Paul which were fulfilled with the Philippians financial contribution; so Hawthorne, *Philippians*, 207-08.

[31] Ταπεινοῦσθαι is a "socio-economic term" indicating poverty; P. Marshall, *Enmity in Corinth: Social Conventions in Paul's Relations with the Corinthians* (WUNT 2.23; Tübingen: Mohr Siebeck, 1987) 235.

[32] That Paul faces poverty, hunger, and want is probably due to his lower status and life as an artisan, compounded by his itinerancy. Times of "plenty" would result from certain benefactions from others, including perhaps the Philippians.

[33] H. Schlier, "κέρδος, κτλ.," *TDNT* 3 (1965) 672.

[34] The terms were commonly used outside of the marketplace, but were clearly recognized as coming from that world. Aristotle states, "The terms 'loss' (κέρδος) and

generally indicates "disadvantage," but in settings of the marketplace it indicates loss or damage in money or material goods.[35] Its use here in the singular is contrasted with the plural use of κέρδος; Paul regards his former "gains" as one great loss in the light of Christ.[36] Paul uses the word κέρδος one other time, in Phil 1:21, where it refers to the result of his death.[37] Here the clear implication is that Paul will be given rest from his present troubles of earthly existence.[38] The use of the word in Phil 1:21 is clearly drawing on the imagery of the marketplace, where Paul states that it is more "profitable" for him to die.

Returning to Phil 3:7-8 we note that Paul continues to use the loss-gain language through the verb ζημιόω in the phrase τὰ πάντα ἐζημιώθην (3:8). The form used, ἐζημιώθην, is found only in the passive elsewhere in the New Testament,[39] but here it should probably be understood as the middle with the action ascribed to Paul himself. Paul has not been deprived of everything so much as he has willingly given up all things.[40] Here the thought is even more intensified through the use of this verb and the addition of σκύβαλον to the equation.[41] Continuing with the metaphor of

---

'gain' (ζημία) in these cases are borrowed from the operations of voluntary exchange" (Eth. Nic. 5.4.13, 1132b, LCL). "Paul is using the figure of a balance-sheet, showing Assets and Liabilities" (F. W. Beare, *A Commentary on the Epistle to the Philippians* [London: Adam and Charles Black, 1959] 110; cf. Hawthorne, *Philippians*, 135). For illustrations see Moulton and Milligan, *Vocabulary*, 273.

[35] Moulton and Milligan, *Vocabulary*, 273; O'Brien, *Philippians*, 385. The only use of ζημία outside of Philippians is Acts 27:10 and 21, where Luke presents Paul twice noting that the sea voyage to Italy would involve injury and "much loss" of ship and cargo. Indeed, the cargo was thrown overboard and the ship wrecked on some rocks at Malta (Acts 27:18).

[36] O'Brien, *Philippians*, 385. The plural of κέρδη is often used of money; Moulton and Milligan, *Vocabulary*, 341.

[37] The only other New Testament use of κέρδος is Tit 1:11 where it is used of false teachers who teach "for base gain" (αἰσχροῦ κέρδους χάριν).

[38] D. W. Palmer, "'To Die is Gain' (Philippians 1:21)," *NovT* 17 (1975) 203-18. For a more fully developed theological investigation of Phil 1:19-26 see T. F. Dailey, "To Live or Die: Paul's Eschatological Dilemma in Philippians 1:19-26," *Int* 44 (1990) 18-28.

[39] Matt 16:26; Mark 8:36; Luke 9:25; 1 Cor 3:15; 2 Cor 7:9. The passive used with τὰ πάντα would indicate "I have been fined everything" or "I have been deprived of all that I have" (O'Brien, *Philippians*, 389).

[40] Plummer, *Philippians*, 73; Collange, *Philippians*, 130; Hawthorne, *Philippians*, 135; O'Brien, *Philippians*, 389. Against Bonnard, *Philippiens*, 64; Beare, *Philippians*, 115; F. F. Bruce, *Philippians* (NIBC 11. Peabody: Hendrickson, 1983) 118.

[41] The term σκύβαλον is "vulgar" and expresses "the force and totality of his renunciation" (Hawthorne, *Philippians*, 139). In the larger context of the encomium it is

exchange, in 3:8 Paul outlines what he has received by giving up his former achievements, this time using κερδήσω, a cognate of κέρδος. In the language of market exchange, Paul was able to have a net gain far surpassing the value of his former achievements – a relationship with Christ.[42] However, when Paul does a final calculation he still has not attained that to which he is called. Again, his "calculation" is noted using a commercial term, λογίζομαι (3:13).

Paul uses commercial metaphors extensively in Phil 4:14-20.[43] The language of exchange is found in the phrase εἰς λόγον δόσεως καὶ λήμψεως ("in the account of giving and receiving," 4:15). Εἰς λόγον is found in many business transactions from antiquity and is probably a technical phrase meaning "to the account of."[44] The two nouns δόσις and λῆμψις "refer to monetary transactions on two sides of a ledger."[45] Even the word κοινωνέω used here could denote a business transaction.[46]

The word καρπός used in 4:17 can be used to indicate the profit that comes from a business transaction or more specifically as "interest."[47] This latter sense is more likely the case here since the following word is πλεονάζων ("continuing to multiply"), a word which can indicate

---

used in a comparative manner. Paul's former achievements are not "refuse" in and of themselves, they are "refuse" in comparison with what Paul now has.

[42] See O'Brien, *Philippians*, 387-88; Beare, *Philippians*, 115.

[43] Recognition of the commercial nature of this passage goes back at least until the fourth century and the Homilies of John Chrysostom; see H. A. A. Kennedy, "The Financial Coloring of Phil. 4.15-18," *ExpTim* 12 (1900-1901) 43; B. J. Capper, "Paul's Dispute with Philippi: Understanding Paul's Argument in Phil 1-2 from his Thanks in 4.10-20," *TZ* 49 (1993) 198.

[44] Moulton and Milligan, *Vocabulary*, 379; Beare, *Philippians*, 151; Marshall, *Enmity in Corinth*, 158-59; O'Brien, *Philippians*, 533.

[45] O'Brien, *Philippians*, 534.

[46] So O'Brien, *Philippians*, 534. This is probably the case in this context, although it has even stronger resonance within the contexts of comparison with the voluntary associations. What we do not have here is any clear evidence that κοινωνέω should be taken in a technical sense to indicate that the Philippians entered into a formal *societas* relationship with Paul, as J. P. Sampley suggests ("*Societas Christi*: Roman Law and Paul's Conception of the Christian Community," in *God's Christ and His People: Studies in Honour of N.A. Dahl*, ed. W. A. Meeks and J. Jervell [Oslo: Universitetsforlaget, 1977] 158-74; idem, *Pauline Partnership in Christ* [Philadelphia: Fortress, 1980]). See also Witherington, *Friendship and Finances*, 118-19. Marshall suggests that the entire phrase should be understood as an idiomatic expression indicating friendship (*Enmity in Corinth*, 163).

[47] Beare, *Philippians*, 155; Kennedy, "Financial Coloring," 43. The word καρπός appears in Phil 1:11 and 1:22, but less obviously as a commercial metaphor.

compounding interest.⁴⁸ Paul's use of εἰς λόγον again further confirms the business context. In acknowledging the receipt of the Philippians' gift, Paul uses ἀπέχω ("received") in 4:18, a word very common in business transactions, to indicate the receiving of money or goods. The word ἀπέχω was often written at the bottom of a receipt.⁴⁹ It was "a word as unmistakable as the mark of a rubber stamp on a bill, PAID."⁵⁰ Its use in the phrase ἀπέχω δὲ πάντα καὶ περισσεύω ("and I have everything and more") clearly indicates that Paul expects nothing else from the Philippians. In the concluding thoughts of this passage Paul assures the Philippians that "God will supply (πληρώσει) every need of yours" (Phil 4:19). The verb πληρόω can indicate "fill" but is commonly used as "pay."⁵¹ Thus, God will pay for what the Philippians need, keeping with the theme of the marketplace.

This extensive use of the language of the marketplace has implications for the type of audience Paul addresses, as it does for Paul himself. The appeal of Paul's metaphors rests not on the familiarity of the audience with business transactions (most people in antiquity would have been familiar with such) but on the positive place that such language plays in his rhetoric. Paul's dealings with the Philippians over their financial contribution and especially his account of the Christian life indicates that the world of business is not denigrated but held up as a positive metaphor for what takes place among Christians. Elites held the marketplace, and small-scale traders generally, in low regard.⁵² Cicero reflects this attitude:

Trade, if it is on a small scale, is to be considered vulgar; but if wholesale and on a large scale, importing large quantities from all parts of the world and distribution to many without misrepresentation, it is not to be greatly disparaged. Nay, it even seems to deserve the highest

---

⁴⁸ See Beare, *Philippians*, 155; Berry, "Function of Friendship," 119.

⁴⁹ O'Brien, *Philippians*, 540 n. 180; Berry, "Function of Friendship," 120.

⁵⁰ Beare, *Philippians*, 150; cf. 156. For evidence of this use see *BGU* II 584.5-6; 612.2-1; U. Wilcken, *Griechische Ostraka* (Leipzig: Von Gisecke & Devrient, 1899) 1.80-87; Deissmann, *Bible Study*, 229; idem, *Light From the East*, 110-12; Moulton and Milligan, *Vocabulary*, 57 (cf. Matt 6:2, 5, 16; Luke 6:24).

⁵¹ Moulton and Milligan, *Vocabulary*, 520.

⁵² S. R. Joshel, *Work, Identity, and Legal Status at Rome: A Study of the Occupational Inscriptions* (Norman and London: University of Oklahoma Press, 1992) 63-69; R. M. Grant, *Early Christianity and Society: Seven Studies* (New York: Harper and Row, 1977) 81. For Roman satirists "lying, cheating, vulgar tradesmen are stock figures along with rich, obnoxious freedmen, greasy foreigners, decadent nobles, needy clients, insensitive patrons and unchaste women" (Joshel, *Work, Identity, and Legal Status*, 63).

respect, if those who are engaged in it, satiated, or rather, I should say, satisfied with the fortunes they have made, make their way from the port to a country estate, as they have often made it from the sea into port. (*Off.* 1.151, LCL)[53]

Slaves were those whom an elite would send to transact daily business.[54] Although this reflects the position of the minority elite, it would have been the culturally dominant position; that is, persons involved in trade would have been aware of the general denigration of their professions. Those who gained great wealth through trade and were able to purchase their way into elite networks adopted this elite attitude towards the marketplace and its traders.[55] For Paul's rhetoric of the marketplace to be effective, therefore, his audience would be predominantly non-elites, either slaves or freed and free persons, for whom participation in the marketplace was an everyday experience and an integral part of their social world.[56]

b) Prosopography

At a number of points in Philippians Paul draws attention to others by name. Timothy is included along with Paul as a slave (δοῦλος) of Christ in the opening greeting of the letter (1:1)[57] and serves with Paul as a son does

---

[53] Cicero (*Off.* 1.150-51) catalogues respectable and base trades and occupations, but even those that are respectable are only so for those whose rank suits the occupation: "Although retail trading is vulgar, commerce on a large scale that involves importing and wholesale distribution, if not entirely respectable, ought not to be extensively criticized. It does not require deceit and, like medicine, architecture, and teaching, has a social utility" (Joshel, *Work, Identity, and Legal Status*, 67). See MacMullen, *Roman Social Relations*, 115-16.

[54] The marketplace itself was a venue for the display of the wealth and benefaction of the elite and the place for social and philosophical discourse and the elite would not have avoided going there (cf. F. Dupont, *Daily Life in Ancient Rome* [Oxford: Blackwell, 1992] 162). However, the actual purchasing of goods would have been the task of the household slaves.

[55] Garnsey and Saller, *Roman Empire*, 44-45, cf. 115.

[56] Cf. C. S. de Vos, *Church and Community Conflicts: The Relationships of the Thessalonian, Corinthian and Philippian Churches* (SBLDS 168; Atlanta: Scholars Press, 1999) 256-62.

[57] Phil 1:1 is the only occurrence of the ascription of δοῦλος to someone other than Paul in a Pauline letter opening. Paul claims this designation in Rom 1:1 In that instance Paul's status as ἀπόστολος is added; this is not so in Phil 1:1. In Gal 1:10 Paul makes reference to his position as "slave"; cf. Eph 6:6; Col 4:12; 2 Tim 2:24. The writers of James (1:1), 2 Peter (1:1), and Jude (1) claim the designation δοῦλος.

with a father (2:22). Thus Timothy, who will be sent to Philippi to act as Paul's representative (2:19), occupies the same social location as Paul.⁵⁸ As we saw earlier, the position of slave brought with it very little status in antiquity. When Paul willingly identifies himself as a "slave of Christ," the position of "slave" brings with it no immediate sense of honour.⁵⁹ In fact, the very use of this word would repel, rather than attract, any listener who is part of the upper ranks of Roman society.⁶⁰

---

⁵⁸ Black suggests, "in 1:1 Paul breaks with his normal procedure and condescends to grant Timothy the same title as himself (δοῦλοι)" ("Discourse Structure," 23). Paul is not "condescending" to do so, but is affirming Timothy's position alongside himself in order to support his recommendation of Timothy who will be coming to Philippi in his stead.

⁵⁹ Sass argues that Paul's use of δοῦλος rests on the LXX background of God's chosen messenger (e.g., Moses, Joshua, David, Jonah) and as such is an honourific title for those who serve God ("Zur Bedeutung von δοῦλος bei Paulus," *ZNW* 40 [1941] 24-32, also summarized in Beare, *Philippians*, 51; so also J. H. Michael, *The Epistle of Paul to the Philippians* [Moffatt NT Commentary. London: Hodder and Stoughton, 1928] 2-3; Barth, *Philipper*, 14; Gnilka, *Philipperbrief*, 31-32; W. Schenk, *Die Philipperbriefe des Paulus. Kommentar* [Stuttgart: Kohlhammer, 1984] 77). Even if this is the case, Paul would not have been unaware of its effect on the largely non-Jewish Philippian Christians, who would have understood it in the common sense of "slave" (cf. Collange, *Philippians*, 36; Bruce, *Philippians*, 26; Hawthorne, *Philippians*, 5; O'Brien, *Philippians*, 45). It certainly would not have been immediately understood as a title of honour (Bonnard [*Philippiens*, 13] and Fee [*Philippians*, 63] understand both connotations to be present). Hawthorne's suggestion (*Philippians*, 4, building on Collange, *Philippians*, 36) that Paul shares "his otherwise carefully and jealously guarded uniqueness" as a δοῦλος of Christ with Timothy in order to teach the Philippians a lesson in humility makes little sense, not only because nowhere else does Paul seem to be jealously guarding the title, but also because he invites all of the Philippians to imitate him (3:17), and thus become slaves of Christ. It is more likely that Timothy is included in order to enhance his status in light of his forthcoming trip as Paul's representative.

⁶⁰ D. P. Martin argues that for Paul Christians are to be good slaves, and in being such, find the means of salvation (*Slavery as Salvation: The Metaphor of Slavery in Pauline Christianity* [New Haven and London: Yale University Press, 1990]). Martin focuses on the possibility of upward mobility of slaves and shows how some were able to attain quite high status. In this context slavery can be understood as a positive aspect of the Christian life (cf. Martin [*Slavery as Salvation*, 130-31] on Paul's use of the slave metaphor in Philippians). However, in assessing the evidence Garnsey thinks that it is unlikely that Paul associated slavery with an ideology of success and that overall it was a highly undesirable position to be in (*Ideas of Slavery*, 186-87). "In so far as Paul (and his followers) had something positive to offer the good (Christian) slave *in this life*, it boiled down to the message that a slave could be assured that in rendering good service to his master, good or bad, he was serving Christ – and even following Christ's example, where he was suffering under a cruel master" (Garnsey, *Ideas of Slavery*, 186-87). To those in the Greco-Roman world, the predominant image evoked by identifying oneself as a slave would be lower-rank status and powerlessness. If Paul is making any status claims it is only insofar as one serves an honourable master (God/Christ; Martin, *Slavery as Salvation*, 51; cf. 47-48; Garnsey, *Ideas of Slavery*, 184-85).

Epaphroditus was a member of the Philippian Christian community who was sent to Paul with a monetary gift (4:18) and whom Paul now sends back, presumably with the letter (2:25). Epaphroditus is not known outside of Philippians.[61] His theophoric name is formed from the name of the Greek goddess Aphrodite, and may indicate that Epaphroditus came from a family devoted to her cult.[62] If so, Epaphroditus was a Gentile and probably a convert to Christianity.[63] The name, which means "lovely," "charming," or "amiable," was common during the first century,[64] particularly among those in the lower ranks of society, namely slaves or freedmen.[65] Thus, neither of these representatives of Paul who receive his recommendation come from the upper ranks of society. For them to be effective leaders within the Christian community lower status members must compose most of the congregation.

It is unfortunate that we only know a few names of other members of the Philippian Christian community. In each case, however, these names point to lower status persons. In Phil 4:2 Paul names two prominent

---

Nevertheless, this type of designation "slave of so-and-so") would only be viewed positively among other slaves (Martin, *Slavery as Salvation*, 46-47). We should note that Paul and his followers nowhere seem to be challenging the prevailing social structure of slavery outside the boundaries of corporate Christian life (cf. Gal 3:28; Garnsey, *Ideas of Slavery*, 187-88).

[61] Epaphras is a shortened form of the name, but there is no reason to identify the Epaphras mentioned in Col 1:7; 4:12 and Phlm 23 with the Epaphroditus of Philippi (Bruce, *Philippians*, 99; Horsley, *New Documents* 4, 22).

[62] Beare, *Philippians*, 98. Gender had little bearing on theophoric names; a male could be named after a goddess or a female after a god.

[63] The time period does not allow for him to have been born and raised in a Christian family. His theophoric name is an unlikely one if his parents or his master were Christian.

[64] F. Preisigke, *Namenbuch enthaltend alle griechischen, lateinischen, ägyptischen, hebräischen, arabischen, und sonstigen semitischen und nichtsemitischen Menschennamen* (Amsterdam: Hakkert, 1967) 100. Horsley (*New Documents* 4, 21-22) calls the name Epaphroditus; "exceedingly common" and notes that it is "the thirteenth most frequently attested Greek personal name" at Rome (294 attestations from I BCE – II/IV CE, most of them in I CE). Josephus' patron was called Epaphroditus (See *Ant.* 1.8; *Vit.* 420; *Ap.* 1.1; 2.1, 296), although this does not mean that he was not a freedman (cf. Bruce, *Philippians*, 99; O'Brien, *Philippians*, 329).

[65] L. Reilly, *Slaves in Ancient Greece: Slaves from Greek Manumission Inscriptions* (Chicago: Ares, 1978) 40-41; G. H. R. Horsley, *New Documents Illustrating Early Christianity: Linguistic Essays* (NewDocs 5; North Ryde, Australia: The Ancient History Documentary Research Centre, Macquarie University, 1989) 112, although some Roman citizens bore the name (see the list in Horsley, *New Documents* 4, 21-22).

women within the community: Euodia and Syntyche.⁶⁶ We do not know anything of either women outside of Philippians.⁶⁷ The name Euodia is well attested⁶⁸ and means "success" or, more literally, "prosperous journey."⁶⁹ Syntyche is likewise a well-attested Greek name.⁷⁰ The name means "Lucky" and is a derivative of τύχη, the Greek goddess of fortune or fate (cf. Latin *Fortuna*) who played a significant role in everyday life in antiquity.⁷¹ In the case of Syntyche at best we can conclude that she is from a pagan background and that either her parents or her owners wished the best for themselves in naming her.⁷²

In the same passage Paul names Clement (4:3), which is a Greek form of a very common Latin name (*Clemens*).⁷³ In fact, "Clement" is a common slave name.⁷⁴ Although Clement was a fellow-worker of Paul's at

---

⁶⁶ Although some have attempted to read these as masculine, the αὐταῖς in 4:3 clearly indicates that they are women (Fee, *Philippians*, 390). Some scholars have attempted to show that the two names Euodia and Syntyche represented two competing factions in the church (Jewish-Christian and Gentile-Christian) but their thesis is not widely held (O'Brien, *Philippians*, 478).

⁶⁷ Attempts to link either Euodia or Syntyche (and even the γνήσιε σύζυγε of Phil 4:3) with Lydia of Acts 16:14-15 (reading her name there as "the Lydian") are conjectural at best; we lack any solid evidence for such a connection (Dahl, "Euodia and Syntyche," 4).

⁶⁸ Moulton and Milligan, *Vocabulary*, 263; Preisigke, *Namenbuch*, 112; Reilly lists one instance as a slave name (*Slaves in Ancient Greece*, 49).

⁶⁹ Fee, *Philippians*, 390 and n. 29.

⁷⁰ Moulton and Milligan, *Vocabulary*, 615. There may be one instance of Συνγύχη as a slave name; see Reilly, *Slaves in Ancient Greece*, 115. Since Euodia and Syntyche may be slave names it may indicate current servile status. If they had been freed they might have taken on another name, one not commonly associated with servile status, as was sometimes the practice. However, the evidence is not clear enough for either name as a widely attested slave name so it is difficult to judge their exact status.

⁷¹ Cf. Fee, *Philippians*, 390 n. 30. In the association inscriptions from antiquity Tyche is invoked frequently with the formulaic ἀγαθῇ τύχῃ that precedes declarations and decrees made by the associations; see *IG* II² 1298; 1329; 1366; 1368. The other common invocation is Θεοί; see *IG* II² 1256; 1283; 1297; 1323; 2499; *IG* IV 840.

⁷² Cf. Fee suggests that Syntyche's (and Euodia's) parents named her with *her* interests in mind, a less likely interpretation (*Philippians*, 390).

⁷³ Moulton and Milligan, *Vocabulary*, 346; Preisigke, *Namenbuch*, 1176; Lightfoot, *Philippians*, 169; Gnilka, *Philipperbrief*, 168. The last of the 69 names in the membership list of Philippian association dedicated to Sylvanus is Valerius Clemens (*CIL* III 633/II), certainly not the same man as our Clement but indicative of the name in Philippi, albeit from the second century.

⁷⁴ Dahl suggests he was a descendant or a freedman/client of the Roman veterans settled at Philippi by Antonius or Octavian ("Euodia and Syntyche," 3).

Philippi it is not stated clearly that he was from Philippi or that he was resident there.[75] Paul's reference to him simply shows the Philippian's familiarity with him. However, most commentators assume that he is present there. If so, he clearly is not in a position of leadership, especially over Euodia and Syntyche, as Paul does not appeal to him to intervene in the conflict between the two women.[76]

Paul indicates, but does not identify by name, another person in 4:3: ναὶ ἐρωτῶ καὶ σέ, γνήσιε σύζυγε. This person is to intervene in the dispute between Euodia and Syntyche, indicating some authority within the community. Some have taken σύζυγε as the proper name Syzyrus.[77] If this is the case there is a pun on the name Σύζυγος in that it means "yokefellow," and he is described as being truly so with Paul (γνήσιε).[78] There is evidence of its use as a proper name in analogous compound names such as Συμφέρων.[79] It is more likely that Paul is describing an unnamed colleague here as there has yet to be found a single example of Σύζυγος as a proper name in antiquity.[80] This has led to a number of speculations as to this person's identity: Timothy, Epaphroditus, Silas, Luke, the entire Philippian congregation, and even Paul's wife.[81] However attractive any

---

[75] Lightfoot, *Philippians*, 168; Hawthorne, *Philippians*, 181; O'Brien, *Philippians*, 482; Müller, *Philipper*, 193-94; Fee, *Philippians*, 395; M. R. Vincent, *The Epistles to the Philippians and to Philemon* (ICC; Edinburgh: T. & T. Clark, 1897) 132. More problematic is whether he is a Philippian native or one of Paul's fellow itinerants who is presently in the city (Fee, *Philippians*, 393).

[76] There have been some attempts to connect the Clement of Philippi with Clement the writer of *1 Clement* and an early bishop of Rome. However, there are a number of difficulties with this theory, not least of which is the differences in location (Clement was connected with Philippi, while *1 Clement* was sent from Rome to Corinth) and date (Clement was a leader in Philippi in the 50s CE or earlier while *1 Clement* was written around 96 CE). For an elaboration of the arguments for connecting the two Clements and the evidence against it see Lightfoot, *Philippians*, 168-71.

[77] So Michael, *Philippians*, 191; Gnilka, *Philipperbrief*, 166-67.

[78] See Michael (*Philippians*, 191) who suggests the translation "you who are a Synzygos (comrade) not in name only but also in very deed." Cf. Paul's pun on the name Onesimus in Phlm 11.

[79] O'Brien, *Philippians*, 480-82.

[80] Cf. Paul's predisposition to use συν- compounds, four of which occur in this verse (Fee, *Philippians*, 393).

[81] Timothy: Collange, *Philippians*, 143; W. Schmithals, *Paul and the Gnostics* (New York: Abingdon, 1972) 76-77, 252. Epaphroditus: Lightfoot, *Philippians*, 158. Luke: O'Brien, *Philippians*, 8; Fee, *Philippians*, 394-95 [cautiously]). The entire Philippian congregation: Hawthorne, *Philippians*, 180. Paul's wife (Lydia?): Clement of Alexandria (*Strom.* 3.6.53.1); see Bruce, who points out the impossibility of the

one of these hypotheses, the fact remains that the "true yoke-fellow" remains unknown to us (although perfectly obvious to the Philippians) and as such is no help in our prosopographic study.[82] We can asertain that this person does not stand "over" Euodia and Syntyche as Paul tells him to help them, not command them, to be reconciled.

Finally, Paul sends greetings from "those of Caesar's household" (Phil 4:22), suggesting some affinity between those at Philippi and those with Paul. The *familia Caesaris* would have numbered in the thousands in Rome itself. Outside of Rome there would have been thousands more employed in the civil service of each town and city. The reference here is not to members of the imperial family but to those employed in the domestic and administrative aspects of the Empire. The majority of such people would be slaves and freedpersons, a number of them being from eastern provinces such as Greece, Anatolia, Syria, and Egypt.[83] To be a slave or freedperson within the *familia Caesaris* was to be better off than to be of the same status within the general population of the empire.[84] Many of the members of the *familia Caesaris*, held important administrative positions such as *dispensatores, arcarii, vilici, exactores*, and *contrascriptor*, all of whom were responsible for imperial funds in some way.[85] However, many of the imperial slaves held domestic positions, serving either the elites or the freedpersons and slaves who held

---

hypothesis because of the masculine adjective γνήσιε modifying σύζυγε (*Philippians*, 140; cf. Michael, *Philippians*, 190; G. Delling, "σύζυγος," *TDNT* 7 [1971] 749).

[82] Cf. Bonnard (*Philippiens*, 74), Beare (*Philippians*, 145), and O'Brien (*Philippians*, 481), who note the impossibility of determining the identity of this person. Barth (*Philipper*, 71-72) and Bruce (*Philippians*, 140) point out that the Philippians would have known to whom Paul was writing.

[83] Beare, *Philippians*, 158; Meeks, "Urban Environment," 116; more thoroughly P. R. C. Weaver, *Familia Caesaris: A Social Study of the Emperor's Freedmen and Slaves* (Cambridge: Cambridge University Press, 1972). According to Plummer (*Philippians*, 107), among the many members of Caesar's household there were a number of Jews, some of whom might have become Christians. However, it is not necessary for an understanding of Philippians to promote their Jewish background; without denying the possibility that some were Jews, non-Jews might have converted to Christianity.

[84] Horsley, *New Documents* 3, 8.

[85] See Weaver, *Familia Caesaris*, 200-06. Weaver divides the administrative professions of the *familia Caesaris* into two categories: *vicarii* and *vicariani*, both having to do with finances, the latter being one grade higher in legal and social status (see *Familia Caesaris*, 200-06 and 212-23 respectively). On the various administrative grades within the *familia Caesaris* see Weaver, *Familia Caesaris*, 227-94.

administrative positions.⁸⁶ Thus, even within the *familia Caesaris* itself there was social differentiation:

> Those in the clerical-administrative service, whether through background or connections within the *Familia Caesaris*, patronage, training or ability, began their professional careers early and were distinctly superior to those who spent their lives in sub-clerical or domestic occupations. With the exception of posts of special opportunity or responsibility within the Palace, there was little chance of crossing the occupational dividing line upwards into the administrative service.⁸⁷

One might expect that greetings from a group of slaves and freedmen would be most appropriate if the recipients were of the same social makeup. That is to say, freeborn and elite persons were not likely to welcome familiar greetings from slaves and freedborn, even those of the imperial household.⁸⁸ Nevertheless, we cannot necessarily infer from this that the Philippian Christians were all from the lower ranks, since the egalitarian thrust of early Christianity might have included the overcoming of this barrier.

c) Summary

Paul's extensive use of marketplace metaphors suggests that this is the arena in which the Philippians are most comfortable, an indication that they are not primarily from the elite ranks. The composition of the Philippian Christian community from the lower ranks is indicated in the few names that are mentioned in the letter (Epaphroditus, Euodia, Syntyche, possibly Clement) and the reference to affiliation with members of Caesar's household. The lack of Paul's specific mention of anyone of

---

⁸⁶ See Weaver, *Familia Caesaris*, 207-11. Weaver suggests, "personal slaves of Imperial slaves must have existed in considerable numbers" (*Familia Caesaris*, 207). This is evidenced in the case of "Musicus Scurranus *dispensator ad fiscum Gallicum* at Lugdunum, who was attended on his journey to Rome, where he died, by no fewer than sixteen personal slaves, including cooks, footmen, butlers, secretaries, and so on" (Weaver, *Familia Caesaris*, 201).

⁸⁷ Weaver, *Familia Caesaris*, 295.

⁸⁸ If Paul is writing from Ephesus, not Rome, those who send greetings are not from the very top of the administrative workers within the *familia Caesaris*, as those persons would be found in Rome (with the exception perhaps of the higher level freedmen who moved frequently from one provincial centre to another (cf. Weaver, *Familia Caesaris*, 295).

higher status probably indicates that no such persons existed within the Philippian Christian community. If they did, one would expect that Paul would take note of them, especially in the context of acknowledgement of monetary support as higher status persons would presumably have contributed more to the fund.

3. Philippians and the Associations

We suggested that the Philippian Christians were generally of lower status, and perhaps some of them were artisans and merchants. This is similar to the typical makeup of the voluntary associations, both in Macedonia and elsewhere. Thus, we are in a good position to read Philippians in light of the data from the voluntary associations to see what difference it might make to our reading of that letter.

a) Leadership Structure

In Philippians Paul singles out the leaders of the community as ἐπίσκοποι καὶ διάκοονοι (1:1),[89] Paul's only use of these titles together in any of his letters.[90] The separate designations for the two offices has led most scholars to suggest that the former indicates a supervisory role while

---

[89] Although there is no text critical justification for it, some scholars see this as a later gloss; so Schenk, *Philipperbrief*, 78-82. Schenk's argument, and the arguments against it, is summarized by Peterlin, *Disunity*, 20-21. The assumption that the phrase refers to later church offices and thus cannot be present in a letter written by Paul in the mid-fifties is directly countered by the argument below that these offices represent a local manifestation of leadership titles and do not represent ecclesial offices within the church universal. Some textual witnesses do read συνεπίσκοπος (B² Dᶜ K 22 1241ˢ 1739 1881 it arm Chrysostom Euthalius Cassiodorus Theophylact) but this makes for an awkward construction and the reading "is to be rejected" as it "arose no doubt from dogmatic or ecclesiastical interests" (B. M. Metzger (*A Textual Commentary on the Greek New Testament* [London: United Bible Societies, 1971] 611), notes that Theodore of Mopsuestia rejected it). These are clearly titles of certain functionaries and not an address to the entire congregation (Dibelius, *Thessalonicher/Philipper*, 60).

[90] The title ἐπίσκοπος only occurs in later New Testament documents (1 Tim 3:2, Tit 1:7; Acts 20:28; 1 Pet 2:25). Διάκονος as a title is used elsewhere for men and women in Christian service; Rom 13:4; 15:8; 16:1; 1 Cor 3:5; 2 Cor 3:6; 6:4; 11:15, 23; Gal 2:17; 1 Thess 3:2; cf. Eph 3:7; 6:21; Col 1:7, 23, 25; 1 Tim 3:8, 12; 4:6. For some methodological cautions in studying ecclesiastical offices in Paul, and especially the fallacy of reading later church practices into the letters, see Reumann, "Church Office."

the latter is one of service.[91] However, nothing else in the letter indicates what functions these officers might have had.[92] Our interest is in the use of titles for officers within the congregation and the use of these titles in particular.

The verb ἐπισκοπεῖν is common in the LXX as a translation of בקר and פקד. The noun ἐπίσκοπος is used primarily as an official designation for an overseer or inspector of some type. This is a common source appealed to for the use of ἐπίσκοπος in Phil 1:1.[93] Other commentators point to the background in the use of מבקר in the Dead Sea Scrolls, particularly the Damascus Document (1QS 6.12-20).[94] In the Damascus Document מבקר is described as "shepherding the flock and returning the lost" (CD 13.7-9)

---

[91] Peterlin, *Disunity*, 22. Some suggest that the phrase reflects a single office and should be designated "*episkopoi* who are deacons" or "*episkopoi* who serve" (Collange, *Philippians*, 39; Hawthorne, *Philippians*, 9-10; see critique in O'Brien, *Philippians*, 48-49 n. 21). Moulton and Milligan (*Vocabulary*, 245) suggest that the phrase in Phil 1:1 be translated "with them that have oversight, and them that do service [minister]" so as to reflect a description of the function and not a designation of office because in the New Testament the words have a "distinctive use." The use of the terms for offices in the larger cultural context, however, makes this latter claim less likely.

[92] Peterlin, *Disunity*, 22. These offices are different than those held in other Pauline Christian communities (cf. B. H. Streeter, *The Primitive Church: Studied With Special Reference to the Origins of Christian Ministry* [Hewlett Lectures for 1928; London: Macmillan, 1929] 53-65; J. Hainz, "Die Anfänge des Bischofs- und Diakonenamtes," in *Kirche im Werden: Studien zum Thema Amt und Gemeinde im Neuen Testament*, ed. J. Hainz [Munich: Schöningh, 1976] 103). Reumann is correct in his assessment that "[e]ach congregation seems to develop *ad hoc* and on its own, with what Collins calls in Philippi 'local idiosyncrasy'" ("Church Office," 89-90, citing Collins ("Diakonia," 236) who refers to H. von Campenhausen, *Ecclesiastical Authority and Spiritual Power in the Church of the First Three Centuries* [London: Adam and Charles Black, 1969] 69). Dibelius attempts to connect these functionaries with the gathering and distribution of funds at Philippi (*Thessalonicher/Philipper*, 62; hinted at by Beare, *Philippians*, 49; Reumann, "Church Office," 90; see further Hatch, *Organization*, 38-46 who describes the distribution of funds as the task of the ἐπίσκοπος in the later Christian church).

[93] For example, O'Brien, *Philippians*, 47.

[94] See B. Reicke, "Constitution of the Primitive Church," in *The Scrolls and the New Testament*, ed. K. Stehdahl (New York: Harper, 1957) 143-56; H. Braun, *Qumran und das Neue Testament* (Tübingen: Mohr Siebeck, 1966) 329-32; J. A. Fitzmyer, "Jewish Christianity in Acts in the Light of the Qumran Scrolls," in *Studies in Luke-Acts*, ed. L. E. Keck and J. L. Martyn (Nashville: Abingdon, 1966) 247-48; J. Jeremias, *Jerusalem in the Time of Jesus: An Investigation into Economic and Social Conditions During the New Testament Period* (Philadelphia: Fortress, 1969) 260-61; B. E. Thiering, "*Mebaqqer* and *Episkopos* in Light of the Temple Scroll," *JBL* 100 (1981) 74; Hawthorne, *Philippians*, 8.

which has affinities to the ἐπίσκοποι in Acts 20:28.⁹⁵ These Jewish analogies are not the most obvious background, however, for how the predominantly non-Jewish Philippians would understand ἐπίσκοπος.⁹⁶ This is also true of the word διάκονος, which has a wide range of designations in antiquity. It can mean "servant" and often is used to refer to one who waits on tables. Although there have been many attempts to find support for prototypes in Jewish literature, "these pale for Philippian use in the face of references to *diakonoi* in Greek guilds and societies."⁹⁷

It is more likely that at Philippi the leadership structure of the Christian community has adopted nomenclature that would immediately be understood in light of its use among voluntary associations.⁹⁸ The titles

---

⁹⁵ Weinfeld, *Organizational Pattern*, 20.

⁹⁶ See Ascough, "Translocal Relationships," 176-89; idem, "Thessalonian Christian Community," 311-13. See also Haniz, "Diakonenamtes," 98-102 who is skeptical of the connection of מבקר with ἐπίσκοπος, although he judges it more likely than the voluntary associations. The overall similarities of the Qumran sect with the voluntary associations suggest that there is probably no direct influence of the sect on Christianity, nor Christianity on the sect, but that the practices and languages of the voluntary associations influenced both, not necessarily in terms of direct borrowing but through a shared milieu with the associations in which the pattern for communal organization was already in place.

⁹⁷ J. Reumann, "Contributions of the Philippian Community to Paul and to Earliest Christianity," *NTS* 39 (1993) 448; cf. idem, "Church Office," 89.

⁹⁸ Cf. Reumann ("Church Office," 90): "The Philippians chose their terms for leaders from a world they know, of government, guilds, societies and the *oikos*" (also Reumann, "Contributions," 449). Although Reumann points to the background of the titles in the voluntary associations, he does not expand much on it. Others who allow for the associations as background for this use in Philippians include Vincent, *Philippians*, 45 (with caution); Fee, *Philippians*, 68 n. 50. The connection is denied by many; see the summary in Kloppenborg, "Edwin Hatch," 217-20. Those who deny the connection re: ἐπίσκοπος, seem to be reacting against the later Christian evidence of a monoepiscopate and a universal application of the title ἐπίσκοπος within Christian churches: Sanday, "Christian Ministry," 98-100; R. Sohm, *Kirchenrecht* (Berlin: Von Duncker & Humblot, 1923) 1.87 n. 13; Ziebarth, *griechische Vereinswesen*, 131; Poland, *griechischen Vereinswesens*, 377; Rohde, *Urchristliche und frühkatholische Ämter*, 55-56. E. Dassmann ("Hausgemeinde und Bischofsamt," in *Vivarium: Festschrift Theodor Klauser zum 90. Geburtstag* [JAC Ergänzungsband 11; Münster: Aschendorff, 1984] 82-97) and G. Schöllgen ("Hausgemeinden, *oikos*-Ekklesiologie, und monarchischer Episcopat," *JAC* 31 [1988] 74-90) move quickly from positing the οἶκος as the background to Paul's communities to using Ignatius of Antioch to explain the rise of the monoepiscopate and the function of presbyters and deacons, without pausing to discuss the local peculiarities of leadership expressed in Paul's letters (Dassmann does suggest that the *paterfamilias* of the house based Christian community would become the leader of the group, but he does not show why this would lead to the titles ἐπίσκοπος and διάκονος at Philippi

ἐπίσκοπος and διάκονος themselves are only used in a few voluntary associations. However, there is no consistency in the use of titles for officials within the association inscriptions. For example, we note a mid-II CE inscription from a large voluntary association of over 400 members that was grounded in a single household.[99] It had been moved from Mitylene to the Roman Campagna *en masse* and seemed to have attracted some new adherents from those who came into contact with the head of the household and his wife (Gallicanus and Agrippinilla). Like the early church, this association was of mixed membership, male and female, slaves, freedmen, and masters. In total, twenty-two different offices, most with titles, are reflected in the inscription, many of them held by women.[100] The association's use of titles was extensive but differed greatly from those used in other associations, even ones dedicated to the same deity, Dionysus.

In light of the evidence from associations it seems unnecessary to go to the lengths of Lightfoot to prove that πρεσβύτερος is a synonym of ἐπίσκοπος and that Paul intended to use the former term in his address to the Philippians, despite only writing ἐπίσκοποι καὶ διάκονοι (Phil 1:1).[101] While Lightfoot is correct in suggesting that in the Jewish synagogues πρεσβύτερος and ἐπίσκοπος go together, the lack of the former term in Philippians is indicative of the lack of a significant Jewish presence in the church and that the titles have resonance elsewhere.[102] In fact, Lightfoot himself suggests that the use of ἐπίσκοπος in the voluntary associations would make it the most obvious choice for the "presiding members of the

---

["Hausgemeinde," 89-90]). Dibelius (*Thessalonicher/Philipper*, 61) points out that at the earlier period there does not seem to be consistency in the application of titles within the Pauline churches, citing the titles in 1 Cor as different than those in Philippians. He points out that Polycarp's letter to the Philippians shows that even in the early second century CE the Philippians do not have a monoepiscopate as do some communities in Asia Minor (Dibelius, *Thessalonicher/Philipper*, 62). Polycarp speaks of πρεσβύτεροι and διάκονοι (where πρεσβύτερος is not synonymous with ἐπίσκοπος; see Vincent, *Philippians*, 47).

[99] Text and translation in McLean, "Agrippinilla Inscription," 240-45.

[100] See McLean, "Agrippinilla Inscription," 262.

[101] Hatch, *Organization*, 96-99; cf. 194.

[102] Lightfoot suggests that the office of πρεσβύτερος is "essentially Jewish" as distinct from ἐπίσκοπος that is best understood by looking at works "chiefly among heathen nations" (*Philippians*, 96). However, πρεσβύτερος is also attested as a title in some associations; see *CIG* 2221; Poland, *griechischen Vereinswesens*, 98-102; Deissmann, *Light From the East*, 156-57, 223-35. Lighfoot's argument also falters by the fact that nowhere in the authentic Pauline letters is πρεσβύτερος used as a title; it only occurs in 1 Tim 5:1, 2, 17, 19 and Tit 1:5 within the larger Pauline corpus.

new society."[103] He states that although the infant church would appear to the Jew as a synagogue, to the non-Jew it would appear as a "confraternity."[104]

Within the Christian communities themselves we find no consistency for titles of officials and we might suggest that they were as diverse as those within the associations, at least within the Pauline period.[105] In choosing particular titles for their leaders the Philippians are like the associations. We will look in vain for any "standard" titles among the associations that could be expected in a Christian "association." Nevertheless, the titles chosen for leaders at Philippi reflect those in use within at least some associations.[106] The exact nature of these offices remains obscure.[107]

---

[103] Lightfoot, *Philippians*, 194.

[104] Again, our goal is not to disparage the Christian connection with Judaism but rather to open up a conversation that suggests a much broader, albeit messier range of relations.

[105] Kloppenborg, "Edwin Hatch," 232. Cf. Streeter (*Primitive Church*, 53-65) who points out that Paul's churches did not follow a uniform pattern with regard to church leadership; while the Corinthians regarded "apostles, prophets, and teachers" as leaders, the ἐπίσκοποι and διάκονοι led the Philippians. For the diversity of terms used for officials in the voluntary association inscriptions see the lists in Liebenam, *Geschichte und Organisation*, 164-69, 199-220; Poland, *griechischen Vereinswesens*, 337-423; Kloppenborg, "Edwin Hatch," 232; Ellis, *Pauline Theology*, 136; cf. the conclusion of Arnaoutoglou on the use of ἀρχερανιστής in inscriptions from associations in Athens and Rhodes: "Associations were not monolithic groupings, but groups which would adapt to new developments by transforming their structure, or more often, their nomenclature; the semantic variety of the term ἀρχερανιστής reveals that what is true for one region of the Greek world is not necessarily valid for another" ("ΑΡΧΕΡΑΝΙΣΤΗΣ and its Meaning in Inscriptions." *ZPE* 104 [1994] 110).

[106] Fee (*Philippians*, 67) points out that the use of σύν indicates that when the leaders are singled out they are "not 'over' the church, but are addressed 'alongside of' the church, as a *distinguishable* part of the whole, but as *part of the whole*, not above or outside it." J. Ernst is correct in that "[d]ie Voraussetzungen für ein entwickeltes Kirchenverständnis waren noch nicht gegeben" but goes too far in suggesting "daß es in der Gemeinde von Philippi neben der Autorität des Paulus keine konkurrierenden 'Ämter' gegeben hat" ("Von der Ortsgemeinde zur Grosskirche – dargestellt an den Kirchenmodellen des Philipper- und Epheserbriefes," in *Kirche im Werden: Studien zum Thema Amt und Gemeinde im Neuen Testament*, ed. J. Hainz [Munich: Schöningh, 1976] 126).

[107] Cf. Hainz ("Diakonenamtes," 107): "So bleibt auch die Bedeutung dieser Ämter unbestimmbar." At the same time we must acknowledge that there are some titles frequently used in associations that do not seem to be evidenced in Pauline Christian groups, titles such as "priest/priestess" (but see Rom 15:16) and civic leadership titles (e.g., "president"; "treasurer"). It is unclear whether this pressure is due to a deliberate

We noted earlier that women could be full members of religious associations and could function in various leadership roles within them. One of best examples of this was the mid-second century CE inscription from Torre Nova in which a number of officials of household-based religious associations are indicated.[108] Women are named as holding a number of official positions including that of torchbearer and priestess, the second and third highest positions in the association.[109] We noted *IG* X/2 255 from Macedonia in which an association of Sarapis and Isis founded at Opus by men included women as officials within the cult. Other inscriptions make it clear women could function alongside men within an association as priestesses and priests.[110]

It is, therefore, no surprise to find that there is evidence that women played a significant role in the leadership of the Philippian Christian community. Thomas, citing the lack of any restrictions being placed on women in the epistle, argues that the women in the church at Philippi played a prominent role.[111] The very fact that Paul's appeal to Euodia and Syntyche (Phil 4:2) is included in the general letter which would be read before the whole church suggests that, "it is unlikely that the mutual antagonism was a private difference of opinion."[112] Rather, since it seems that their differences had ramifications for the entire church it is likely that it concerned a question of belief, worship, or ethics; they may even reflect two rival groups.[113] Thus, these two women were probably leaders at

---

choice to avoid such titles (Matt 23:6-12) or whether it is only later that such titles come into use within Christianity (see 1 Peter 2:9).

[108] McLean, "Agrippinilla Inscription," 240-43.

[109] McLean, "Agrippinilla Inscription," 262.

[110] On priests and priestesses serving together in the same association see *IG* II² 1361 (Piraeus, IV BCE); IMagnMai 98 (197-96 BCE); *LSAM* 48 (Miletus, 276/75 BCE); *LSCG* 124 (Eresos, II BCE).

[111] W. D. Thomas, "The Place of Women in the Church at Philippi," *ExpTim* 83 (1972) 119.

[112] Thomas, "Place of Women," 119.

[113] Dahl, "Euodia and Syntyche," 5:6; Hawthorne, *Philippians*, 179; Witherington, *Friendship and Finances*, 108. Cf. Paul's use of παρακαλῶ, "a polite yet urgent form of request" (as Dahl himself points out, "Euodia and Syntyche," 5), the same word he uses in his opening comments to the rival factions at Corinth (1 Cor 1:10). However, as Cotter ("Women's Authority Roles," 353) points out, the issue "cannot be so severe as to destroy the community because Paul is clearly refraining from giving advice on the specific matter at issue" yet "the situation is serious enough to warrant a public note in this community."

Philippi.¹¹⁴ Paul does not suppress the right of the two women to express themselves; he only asks that their differences be resolved.¹¹⁵

Paul notes the importance of these women to his ministry in Philippi; they have "labored side by side" (συλλαμβάνου) with him and he numbers them among his "fellow workers" (συνεργοί; Phil 4:3).¹¹⁶ In using συνήθλησαν Paul draws upon the metaphor of an athlete, suggesting that these women had a similar dedication in their "zeal for the victory of the Gospel at Philippi."¹¹⁷ Malinowski suggests that συναθλέω is used here in the sense of striving side by side in the face of the opposition being experienced at Philippi (cf. Phil 1:27, the only other use of this word in the New Testament), and, thus, the two women are singled out among the "company of the bravest" who stood by Paul in his struggle for the Gospel.¹¹⁸ He assumes that they did not exercise any official ministry of preaching or presiding, but were "brave Christians, unafraid of being humiliated, injured, and killed in witnessing to the Gospel" when Paul was exercising his ministry at Philippi.¹¹⁹ Thus, for Malinowski, women did not exercise leadership roles at Philippi. Malinowski does not deal with Paul's note that they were μετὰ καὶ Κλήμεντος καὶ τῶν λοιπῶν συνεργῶν μου (Phil 4:3). Clearly the phrase is to be connected with the statement "they fought side by side with me."¹²⁰ Paul seems here to be including both Euodia and Syntyche with those who were involved in an active ministry for the Gospel at Philippi. Paul uses the same term (συνεργός) of Prisca (Rom 16:3),¹²¹ indicating that he included women among his "fellow workers."

---

[114] So also Lightfoot, *Philippians*, 158; Gnilka, *Philipperbrief*, 166; Silva, *Philippians*, 221; Witherington, *Friendship and Finances*, 105-06; Fee, *Philippians*, 389-98; Peterlin, *Disunity*, 104-08. O'Brien (*Philippians*, 478) softens this, calling them "active members of the congregation" (cf. Bonnard, *Philippiens*, 74).

[115] Thomas, "Place of Women," 119.

[116] Interestingly, συνέργοι is used as a designator for members of professional associations; see ISmyrna 218, 715, 721; IEphesus 444, 454, 2976, 2078, 2079, 2080; *IGRR* 907; *SEG* XXIX 1184; *ZPE* 36 (1979) no. 31.

[117] Thomas, "Place of Women," 119.

[118] F. X. Malinowski, "The Brave Women of Philippi," *BTB* 15 (1985) 62.

[119] Malinowski, "Brave Women," 62.

[120] So Hawthorne, who discusses how others have [unsuccessfully] attempted to circumvent this connection (*Philippians*, 180). Cf. also F. M. Gillman, *Women Who Knew Paul* (Collegeville: Liturgical Press, 1992) 46-47.

[121] To be sure, Paul was not adverse to women working with him in his ministry, as is seen in the case of Phoebe (Rom 16:1; see Whelan, "Amica Pauli") and Prisca (Rom 16:3; 1 Cor 16:19; cf. 2 Tim 4:19; Acts 18:2, 18, 26). Other women workers of whom

Many commentators point out that the women of Macedonia had a reputation and tradition of initiative and influence; they "played a large part in affairs, received envoys and obtained concessions for them from their husbands, built temples, founded cities, engaged mercenaries, commanded armies, held fortresses, and acted on occasion as regents or even co-rulers."[122] However, an even better place to look for analogous material is in the specifically religious milieu of Philippi. After discussing the prominence of women leaders in the cults of Diana and Isis at Philippi Abrahamsen suggests that "it is hardly likely that the growing Christian religion could have ignored women accustomed to being in leadership roles unless it eliminated their roles by coercion."[123] Such elimination and coercion does not seem to have been the case within the Philippian Christian community.

The nature of the evidence for the participation of women in leadership roles within the cultic activity at Philippi is stronger for the public sphere than for private religious associations.[124] Nevertheless, it is possible to suggest that women undertook leadership roles in the associations at Philippi since it would be consistent with their roles otherwise at Philippi and consistent with the pattern of leadership found in religious associations throughout the Greco-Roman period. As such, these associations provide a fitting backdrop to the role of women in the Philippian church. Women's leadership would not have been seen as radical or counter-cultural but would have been accepted and expected as part of corporate religious life at Philippi.[125]

Paul has some knowledge include Junia (Rom 16:7), Mary (Rom 16:6), Tryphaena and Tryphosa (Rom 16:12), Persis (Rom 16:12), Chloe (1 Cor 1:11); see Gillman (*Women*, *passim*) for descriptions of these women, along with other women associated with Paul in Acts, the deutero-pauline letters, and the Pastorals. See Cotter, "Women's Authority Roles," 350-72.

[122] W. W. Tarn and G. T. Griffith, *Hellenistic Civilisation* (London: Edward Arnold, 1952^3) 98. This description would be particularly apt for women at Roman colonies such as Philippi, which could take advantage of the *ius italicum* (Dahl, "Euodia and Syntyche," 4). There is evidence for families of great wealth at Thessalonica, Beorea, and Philippi; see Papazaglou, "Macedonia," 201.

[123] V. A. Abrahamsen, "Christianity and the Rock Reliefs at Philippi," *BA* 51 (1988) 30.

[124] But see Pilhofer 338, 339, 340.

[125] In discussing the term ἐκκλησία in the Pauline letters Cotter ("Women's Authority Roles," 370) correctly suggests that it indicates "a civic seriousness to the assembly." However, she goes on to suggest that the presence of women in associations represents a counter-cultural challenge to the ruling authorities (Cotter, "Women's Authority Roles," 370). The claim is made on the basis of (mis-)reading the term

A brief examination of material from a later period confirms that women were involved in leadership within the Philippian church. The letter written to the church at Philippi written by Polycarp, Bishop of Smyrna, between 98-117 CE[126] seems to indicate that "Polycarp knew the relative freedom and respect accorded to the women at Philippi."[127] Polycarp places great emphasis in telling women to behave themselves suggesting that women played a active role within the life of the church, a role with which Polycarp is not entirely happy.[128] The letter indicates that there were Christian widows who were part of a special group who had a ministry in the church as well as a strong ascetic movement among virgins, married women, and widows.[129] In the final remarks of the letter (14.1) Polycarp commends the sister of Crescens who will be visiting Philippi. His singling out of this woman suggests that she was not merely moving to Philippi but that she had a significant role in the ministry of the larger church and was coming to Philippi to exercise that role.[130]

Inscriptions from the site of the city of Philippi suggest that during the Byzantine period (until the sixth century) women continued to serve in their churches. Graves associated with the basilicas in Philippi refer to various women as "deacon" (διάκονος, used even after διακόνισσα came

---

ἐκκλησία as a civic term that the associations did not adopt and thus misses the implications of her earlier note that "it was not at all unusual to create offices similar to those at city hall" ("Women's Authority Roles," 370). Women are involved in the leadership of associations that adopt other civic titles, but such associations were not seen to be directly countering the civic structure of the city (neither generally or in Cotter's outline). We do not see why it should be so in the case of ἐκκλησία. This is not to deny that the roles given to women in associations that used civic nomenclature would have allowed the women a sense of participation in the civic process denied to them outside the group. Our disagreement is with Cotter's *implication* (through the use of the word "counter-cultural") that these associations are presenting a threat to the civic structure. Although the associations were sometimes perceived as a political threat, it was not due to their leadership structure. In fact, there is probably an attempt on the part of the associations to appeal to the civic leaders by imitation.

[126] See Portefaix, *Sisters Rejoice*, 155 n. 3, for this dating; on the authenticity and integrity of the letter see B. Dehandschutter, "Polycarp's Epistle to the Philippians: An Early Example of 'Reception'," in *New Testament in Early Christianity*, ed. J.-M. Sevrin (BETL 86. Leuven: Leuven University Press, 1989) 276-79.

[127] Thomas, "Place of Women," 119.

[128] V. A. Abrahamsen, "Women At Philippi: The Pagan and Christian Evidence," *JFSR* 3 (1987) 18.

[129] Thomas, "Place of Women," 119-20 (cf. 1 Tim 5:3-10); Abrahamsen, "Women At Philippi," 19.

[130] Cf. Thomas, "Place of Women," 120.

into use in the third and fourth centuries), "canoness" (κανονική), and "servants" (δοῦλος, *servus*, used of both men and women).[131] The evidence suggests that despite not attaining the position of presbyter (seemingly the highest position in the later church at Philippi), women did play an influential role in the administration of the church.[132] While far from conclusive by itself, this evidence provides secondary support the contention that women had a prominent role to play in the church in Philippi.

Paul's letter to the Philippians indicates that the Christian community there had male leaders alongside the female leaders. In thanking the Philippians for sending Epaphroditus to him in his ministry (Phil 2:25-30) Paul describes him as an ἀπόστολος (Phil 2:25), a title that elsewhere Paul only uses in reference to himself.[133] Other male leaders include the unnamed "true yoke-fellow" and Clement, both mentioned by Paul in 4:3. At least some of the female and male leaders at Philippi bore the title ἐπίσκοπος or διάκονος.[134] This situation is similar to situations often found among the leadership structure of the voluntary associations where we find male and female leaders serving together.[135]

---

[131] For details see Abrahamsen, "Women At Philippi," 23-28. Cf. Horsley (*New Documents* 1, 121) for evidence for women office-holders in the church elsewhere.

[132] Abrahamsen, "Women At Philippi," 28. Abrahamsen relates this influential role in the church to the prominent role women took among the cult officials in the worship of Isis and Diana at Philippi ("Women At Philippi," 29).

[133] Although clearly Paul is aware that he does not have exclusive rights to the title, as he recognizes it as the primary category of church leadership instituted by God (1 Cor 12:28) and considers himself to be the "least" of the apostles (1 Cor 15:9).

[134] That is, both men and women could have these titles and either title might have been carried by Euodia and/or Syntyche; cf. Fee, *Philippians*, 69. Peterlin narrows the leadership titles of the women to διάκονος based on the lack of "biblical or extra-biblical evidence for the ascription of the title ἐπίσκοπος to a woman in either the apostolic or early post-apostolic church" (*Disunity*, 107; cf. Lightfoot, Philippians, 158; Hawthorne, *Philippians*, 179). However, his assumption about the earlier period based on the latter is surprising given his careful argument about the use of διάκονος for both men and women in the church, which attempts not to read back from a later period. The absence of ἐπίσκοπος applied to women at a later period and in other locations should not *de facto* rule out the possibility that Euodia and Syntyche held these positions at Philippi. On the masculine form of words applied to women see Peterlin, *Disunity*, 107-08.

[135] Cotter, "Women's Authority Roles," 369.

b) Internal Community Relationships

Philippians reflects a concern with internal community relationships in that Paul's emphasis on the communal dimension of the Philippians' life can be found throughout the letter. For example, Paul notes that "God is at work among you" (2:13), in reference to working out one's salvation. This is not individualism but an emphasis on a corporate sense of identity. Paul is "concerned with the Philippian church in its corporate life and its corporate activity."[136]

Commentators often note the warm relationship between Paul and the Philippians (e.g., 1:8; 2:2-4; 4:1) and Philippians is frequently referred to as a "letter of friendship."[137] We noted earlier explicit friendship language in some voluntary associations (e.g., *IG* II² 1369, 1275). Paul does not use the terms and rules of friendship in Philippians, thus "[a] 'society of friends,' Greco-Roman style, is not Pauline ecclesiology."[138] Yet voluntary

---

[136] Beare, *Philippians*, 91.

[137] For a comprehensive survey of the history of scholarship on the issue of Philippians as a letter of friendship see J. Reumann, "Philippians, Especially Chapter 4, as a 'Letter of Friendship': Observations on a Checkered History of Scholarship," in *Friendship, Flattery, and Frankness of Speech: Studies on Friendship in the New Testament World*, ed. J. T. Fitzgerald (NovTSup 82; Leiden, New York, Köln: Brill, 1996) 83-106. Reumann doubts that there is enough internal support to classify the letter as a ἐπιστολὴ φιλική, but does recognize that there is an influence from the vocabulary of φιλία and the friendship *topos* in Paul's letter ("Letter of Friendship," 105). A number of recent works have highlighted the language of friendship in Philippians: S. K. Stowers on Phil 1:19-26 ("Friends and Enemies in the Politics of Heaven: Reading Theology in Philippians," in *Pauline Theology I: Thessalonians, Philippians, Galatians, Philemon*, ed. J. M. Bassler [Minneapolis: Fortress, 1991] 107-21); L. M. White on Phil 2:6-11 ("Morality Between Two Worlds: A Paradigm of Friendship in Philippians," in *Greeks, Romans, and Christians: Essays in Honour of Abraham J. Malherbe*, ed. D. L. Balch, W. A. Meeks, and E. Ferguson [Philadelphia: Fortress, 1990] 201-15); Berry on Phil 4:10-20 ("Function of Friendship," 107-24); on the letter as a whole: J. T. Fitzgerald ("Philippians in the Light of Some Ancient Discussions of Friendship" in *Friendship, Flattery, and Frankness of Speech: Studies on Friendship in the New Testament World*, ed. J. T. Fitzgerald [NovTSup 82; Leiden, New York, Köln: Brill, 1996] 141-60); Malherbe ("Paul's Self-Sufficiency," 127-28), and A. C. Mitchell ("'Greet the Friends by Name:' New Testament Evidence for the Greco-Roman *Topos* on Friendship," in *Greco-Roman Perspectives on Friendship*, ed. J. T. Fitzgerald [SBLRBS 34. Atlanta: Scholars Press, 1997] 233-36).

[138] Reumann, "Letter of Friendship," 106. M. Ebner argues that Phil 4:10-20 uses commercial and friendship language to reflect the ideal of a community of friends (*Leidenslisten und Apostelbrief: Untersuchungen zu Form, Motivik und Funktion der Peristasenkataloge bei Paulus* [FB 66; Würzburg: Echter, 1991] 58-63, 352-58). At

associations use a spectrum of friendship language from "fellow-workers" (συνεργοί), to "sacrificing associates" (ὀργεῶνες), to "friends" (φίλοι), to "brothers" (ἀδελφοί). It is clear that the Philippian community (and that of the Thessalonians) fits well within this spectrum.

Indications of a strong communal bond among the Philippians is manifested through Paul's use of κοινωνία and its cognates.[139] There are two ways in which these words are used in the letter. First, they are used to underline a relationship with the divine realm. Paul writes of his own κοινωνίαν παθημάτων of Christ (3:10).[140] There is a communal aspect to this relationship with the divine realm, which Paul expresses as κοινωνία πνεύματος (2:1) and συγκοινωνούς μου τῆς χάριτος (1:7). In both cases the Philippians are indicated together in their experience of the divine realm. The second sense in which κοινωνία is presented in Philippians is the human relationship the Philippians share with Paul. In Phil 4:14 Paul notes that πλὴν καλῶς ἐποιήσατε συγκοιωνήσαντές μου τῇ θλίψει. He states that they have had a κοινωνία in the gospel with him from the beginning (1:5) and that from that time οὐδεμία μοι ἐκκλησία ἐκοινώνησεν εἰς λόγον δόσεως καὶ λήμψεως εἰ ὑμεῖς μόνοι (4:15).

Sampley points to these latter two verses to suggest that Paul is here referring to the creation of a legally recognized contractual partnership (a *societas Christi*) with the Philippians.[141] Within this relationship, the Philippians were expected to reimburse Paul for expenses incurred during his evangelistic efforts. A Roman consensual *societas* was "a verbal, legally binding, reciprocal partnership or association made between two or

---

Philippi Paul first established a community of friends, a position that was modified later in his ministry (post Corinthian problems) to the point that in writing to the Philippians Paul emphasizes his self-sufficiency. Also summarized in Mitchell, "Greco-Roman *Topos*," 234-36).

[139] The nature of Paul's concept of κοινωνία has generated much literature, although one of the most comprehensive studies is that of J. Hainz, *Koinonia: "Kirche" als Gemeinschaft bei Paulus* (BU 16; Regensburg: Pustet, 1982). On the various uses of κοινωνία and cognates in classical literature see J. Y. Campbell, "ΚΟΙΝΩΝΙΑ and Its Cognates in the New Testament," *JBL* 51 (1932) 352-60.

[140] Vincent (*Philippians*, 105) suggests that this is a "mystical union with Christ," which Beare (*Philippians*, 123) broadens to include both the mystical experience and experiences in this world. This is an interpretation with which Hainz (*Koinonia*, 98-99) is sympathetic.

[141] Sampley, *Pauline Partnership*, esp. 51-72. He argues a similar case for Paul's relationship with Philemon, but suggests that these are the only two letters that reflect this type of relationship between Paul and his converts.

more people regarding a common goal."¹⁴² It did not require witnesses, written documents, or notification of any authorities. The partnership lasts as long as the parties remain of the same mind, with each party contributing property, labor, skill, or status for the accomplishment of the goal and neither turning the *societas* to his own ends. Anyone may participate, even slaves, and a partner is entitled to remuneration for expenses incurred on behalf of the *societas*. The agreements of a *societas* are subject to enforcement by the courts.

Sampley sees the *societas* relationship operative in Philippians in a number of ways. Paul's use of commercial terms in Phil 4:10-20 is consistent with the provision of a *societas* that a partner is due reimbursement for expenses. Paul preached the gospel elsewhere on behalf of the Philippians and their gift can be seen as a response to a request that he made to them for support (Phil 2:25; 4:16, 19), as was his legal right within the *societas* relationship. Paul's uses the term κοινωνία, an equivalent for the Latin term *societas*, and he uses other *societas* phrases such as "be of the same mind" (Phil 2:2; 4:2). Samply concludes that the reason Paul sets up this relationship with the Philippians and no other church is because the Philippian community was stable and unified.¹⁴³

Sampley's description does not detail actual community structure so much as Paul's possible relationship with the community. Recently, Peterman has highlighted a number of problems with Sampley's thesis.¹⁴⁴ For example, Paul's use of financial terms in Phil 4:10-20 can be understood metaphorically and the section need not be labeled as a "receipt" for the Philipppians' reimbursement for services, as Sampley designates it. The "partnership in giving and receiving" in 4:15 may indicate a social relationship, not a financial one.¹⁴⁵ The argument from terminology is also weak as *societas* is only one possible analogue for κοινωνία. That κοινωνία can indicate "partnership" does not mean that Greek speakers used it as a label for the formal relationship of a Roman *societas*.¹⁴⁶ Peterman suggests that Sampley has exaggerated the unity of the Philippian community as tensions still remain within the community. What distinguishes the Philippians from the Corinthians is absence of

---

¹⁴² G. W. Peterman, "'Thankless Thanks': The Epistolary Social Convention in Philippians 4:10-20," *TynBul* 42 (1991) 123. The following is a summary of Peterman, "Thankless Thanks," 123-25.
¹⁴³ Sampley, *Pauline Partnership*, 104.
¹⁴⁴ Peterman, "Thankless Thanks," 125-27.
¹⁴⁵ Cf. Marshall, *Enmity in Corinth*, 157-64.
¹⁴⁶ Reumann, "Church Office," 441 n. 14.

conflict with Paul himself, not the absence of conflict with one another. Finally, nowhere does Paul suggest that he is the Philippians' *representative* in working to spread the gospel and thus working on their behalf. They are "fellow-workers" in the gospel. Berry has pointed out that, "the language which Sampley sees as the technical terminology of legal partnerships is used with reference to the broader range of social relations encompassed by φιλία and *amicitia*."[147] Thus, while Paul and the Philippians have established some sort of arrangement, it is not understood simply as a financial one.[148]

Examining the voluntary association inscriptions may help to shed some light on Paul's choice to use κοινωνία and its cognates. One common title used for associations is that of τὸ κοινόν.[149] It can stand as the title given for the collective membership of an association. For example, an inscription from Athens (237/36 BCE) records the honours the members gave to the founder and benefactor of a θίασος. The earlier part of the inscription can be translated,

> Whereas Sophron has generously and enthusiastically organized the *thiasos* and provided it with a stele to be set up in the temple, wishing to enhance the *koinon* at his own expense; and in order that there might be a rivalry among those who wish to be benefactors to the *koinon* and that they might know that they shall receive thanks; for good fortune, it has been resolved by the members of the *thiasos*.... (*IG* II² 1297)

We find a similar use of θίασος for the association and τὸ κοινόν for the membership in the regulations of an association from second century CE Physcos (*IG* IX/1 670). Paul's use of κοινωνία and its cognates would underline the Philippian Christian community's self-understanding as an association.[150]

In each case, Paul's use of the word or its cognates involves the community's relationships, either with one another or with Paul. "In 2:1 Paul appeals for unity and harmony on the basis of their experience of κοινωνία πνεύματος, i.e., either their 'joint-participation' in the Spirit or their 'fellowship' created by the Spirit."[151] In 3:10 κοινωνία is used of

---

[147] Berry, "Function of Friendship," 118.

[148] Cf. Campbell, "KOINΩNIA," 371; White, "Paradigm of Friendship," 210-12.

[149] See Poland, *griechischen Vereinswesens*, 163-68; see esp. *IG* II² 1291 (Piraeus); 1327 (Piraeus, 177/76 BCE); 1368 (Athens, 178 CE); *IG* XII/3 330 (Thera, 210-195 BCE).

[150] For a more complete discussion of Paul's conception of κοινωνία throughout his letters see Hainz, *Koinonia*, and Campbell, "KOINΩNIA."

[151] Berry, "Function of Friendship," 118.

Paul's sharing in Christ's sufferings. It is linked to the communal aspect of the Philippians though 4:14 and 1:7 where συγκοινωνέω and συγκοινωνός are used respectively of the Philippians sharing in Paul's troubles and God's grace to him in such troubles.[152]

One of the most interesting places in the letter where unity is emphasized is in the hymn of Phil 2:6-11. The introductory verse (2:5) suggests that the hymn is setting up the basis upon which the community is to relate to one another. As Beare translates it, "Let this be the disposition that governs in your common life, as is fitting in Christ Jesus."[153] The hymn that follows emphasizes humility and service within the community; "The model of selflessness, the willingness to give up one's own status and share another's troubles, is the ultimate sign of true friendship."[154]

Paul's exhortation to "do all things without grumbling or questioning" (2:14) attempts to legislate (in a mild way) how the members of the Christian community should interact with one another. Recall our earlier examples of attempts voluntary associations to regulate themselves: the Athenian association that stipulates that anyone who attempts to introduce legislation which goes against that already agreed upon by the membership is to be fined (*IG* II^2 1361; see also *IG* II^2 1275), or the rules of the Iobakkoi that censure anyone who should "sing or cause disturbances or applaud" and demand that they "speak or do their part with all decorum and quietness" lest they be subject to expulsion and/or fines (*IG* II^2 1368).[155]

In contrast to the imposition of steep penalties, which indicate that the conflict within a group was a serious concern for the membership, Paul only mildly exhorts the Philippians not to "grumble or question." He is rather mild in his attempt to unite Euodia and Syntyche and generally speaks well of the Philippians' ability to get along. Unlike the Corinthians, the Philippians have no need to be told to take turns in prophesying (1 Cor 14:26-33) or even to be silencet during worship (1 Cor 14:34-35),[156] and

---

[152] *Pace* Berry who excludes 3:10 from contexts of social relations ("Function of Friendship," 118).

[153] Beare, *Philippians*, 73.

[154] White, "Paradigm of Friendship," 212, cf. 212-15.

[155] Cf. *IG* V/1 1390 lines 39-44; see also *LSAM* 9; *P.Lond.* 2710 in which members are forbidden "to make factions... to enter into one another's pedigrees at the banquet, or to abuse one another at the banquet or chatter or to indict or charge one another or to resign during the course of the year or to bring the drinking to naught."

[156] Although the latter verses are probably best omitted on text critical grounds; see Fee, *Philippians*, 699-708, but see L. A. Jervis, "1 Corinthians 14:34-35: A

certainly have not sunk so low as to be taking one another to court (1 Cor 6:1-8).[157]

Alongside unity and cooperation, voluntary associations emphasized interpersonal rivalry and competition, with particular attention to φιλοτιμία. Such "love of honour" was the motivating factor for many benefactors of the associations.[158] In contrast to this striving for honour in the associations, Paul's injunction that the Philippians "do nothing from selfishness or conceit" indicates that they are not to compete with one another but "in humility count others better" than themselves (2:3).[159] Nevertheless, Paul's hope not to be put to "shame" (1:20) and his reference to a "crown" (4:1) do recall the language of honour/shame as expressed within the associations.

c) Community Interaction with Outsiders

The concern with outsiders in Philippians is also well-served through a comparison with the voluntary associations. In Phil 1:15-18 Paul describes a group that is preaching the gospel of Christ not out of love but rather envy and rivalry. Their aim is to make things worse for Paul in his imprisonment. Clearly there is some sort of inter-group rivalry among the Christians at Ephesus.[160] However, Paul goes on to speak of the opponents (ἀντικείμενοι) of the Philippians (1:28) with whom they are engaged in conflict. The Philippians observed Paul engaged in conflict and now hear that he is still engaged in this type of conflict (1:30). This conflict is not his imprisonment, but the competitive groups which "preach Christ from envy and rivalry" (1:15) which the Philippians have just heard about in the

---

Reconsideration of Paul's Limitation of the Free Speech of Some Corinthian Women," *JSNT* 58 (1995) 51-74, for an alternative view.

[157] On the disruptions experienced in the voluntary associations as a suitable background for understanding 1 Cor 6:1-8 see the independent studies published by Kloppenborg, "Egalitarianism," 247-63 and Schmeller, *Hierarchie und Egalität*, 86-87.

[158] For example, see *IG* II² 1263; 1271; 1291; 1292; 1317; 1327; 1369.

[159] This injunction may apply directly to Euodia and Syntyche (so Beare, *Philippians*, 143; Peterlin, *Disunity*, 101-02; Murphy-O'Connor, *Paul*, 219, 224), but does not preclude application to others in the community.

[160] Assuming that this is Paul's place of imprisonment (Fee, *Philippians*, 770-71; G. F. Snyder, *First Corinthians: A Faith Community Commentary* [Macon: Mercer University Press, 1992] 204-05). For an overview of the arguments for Rome, Caesarea Maritima, and Ephesus see J. T. Fitzgerald, "Philippians, Epistle to the," *ABD* 5 (1992) 322-23.

reading of the letter.[161] Members of these groups "look after their own interests, not those of Jesus Christ," as Paul comments of the opposing groups at Ephesus (2:21).[162] Such groups need not be large or even well established, but under the banner of "Christ" they create problems for Pauline groups.[163] Such inter-group rivalry seems to have been active at Philippi.[164]

Inter-group competition among those claiming allegiance to the same deity is a known phenomenon, particularly among voluntary associations. A number of inscriptions honour benefactors who have enhanced the reputation of the group, presumably with the aim of proclaiming, like the Iobakkoi of Athens, "now we are the best of all" (*IG* II² 1368). It is noteworthy that the Iobakkoi do not proclaim that they are the best of all possible groups, but that they are the best of all the Bacchic groups (the text reads, νῦν πάντων πρῶτοι τῶν Βακχείων).

Euphronsyne, a priestess of Dionysus at Thessalonica, uses such rivalry to her advantage in insuring the *rosalia* is performed at her grave. Her testamentary inscription stipulates that if the designated θίασος of

---

[161] Against the interpretation of Beare, *Philippians*, 69; Hawthorne, *Philippians*, 62; Bruce, *Philippians*, 58-59; O'Brien, *Philippians*, 161-62, all of whom point to the authorities imprisoning Paul and persecuting the Philippian Christians. On our reading, it is not necessary to understand these "Christian" opponents as the Judaizing Christians Paul addresses in 3:1-17; for those who hold this latter view see O'Brien, *Philippians*, 153.

[162] R. Jewett shows the connection between 1:15-18 and 2:21 ("Conflicting Movements in the Early Church as Reflected in Philippians," *NovT* 12 [1970] 369-70). Jewett argues that rival itinerant Christian missionaries who have a divine-man theology (similar to those in 2 Cor) oppose Paul and the Philippians ("Conflicting Movements," 366-71). However, in Phil 1-2 Paul does not present his arguments as a defense of his own position but as a warning against others – the threat does not seem as immediate as in 2 Cor or even as immediate as the threat of the Judaizing Christians of Phil 3.

[163] This is not meant to imply that the alternative groups at Ephesus and at Philippi are somehow connected or that there is some sort of conspiracy. Paul is simply drawing attention to the fact that the phenomenon at Philippi is like that which he is experiencing at Ephesus. Rival Christian factions are clearly present at Corinth, although, as with Philippi, Paul holds out hope that reconciliation is possible there.

[164] Perhaps this is what Paul fears will result from the conflict between Euodia and Syntyche if it is not addressed. *Pace* Dahl who suggests, "there is no evidence that there existed opposing factions within the congregation. The only conflict about which we get any information is the disagreement of Euodia and Syntyche" ("Euodia and Syntyche," 10); we hear of conflict at Ephesus (1:15-18), "opponents" at Philippi (1:28), and potential conflict with the Judaizers (3:1-17). Paul's "incomplete joy" (Phil 2:2) over the conflict between the two women (Dahl, "Euodia and Syntyche," 10, 14) has connections with the wider context of the letter.

Dionysus does not properly fulfill her wishes, then the bequest is to be transferred to a different θίασος of Dionysus (*IG* X/2 260). The second group is sure to be watching the first carefully in order to find some flaw in their execution of the ceremonies. Likewise, the association of the god Souregethes at Philippi would be sure to carry out the request of Valeria Mantana lest they be fined, with the money going to the association at the shrine of the Hero (Pilhofer 133). Paul's reference seems to suggest that other groups claim Christ as patron deity in order to oppose the Philippian Christians to whom he writes.

Paul addresses another challenge to the Philippian Christians in Phil 3:18-21[165] where he refers to a group or groups resident in Philippi.[166] Paul describes them and their practices variously. They are "enemies of the cross of Christ" who "glory in their shame." Their minds are set on "earthly things" with no thought for God as "their god is their belly." For Paul, the cross on which Christ died represented the humble, servile position that Christians must take toward one another. Using the oxymoronic "glory in their shame" (3:19) Paul draws attention to this group of opponents' focus on "glory" (δόξα) or "honour" (τιμή).[167] They are proud of doing what others would be afraid of admitting to and their minds are set on "earthly things" with no thought for God. As we saw above, one of the principal concerns of the voluntary associations was the attainment and ascription of honour to members and patrons. By suggesting that the Philippians' πολίτευμα is in heaven (3:20), Paul contrasts immediate honour promised in this life with a promise of much greater honour in the future, the transformation of the Philippians' "body of humiliation" to a "body of his [Christ's] glory" (3:21).[168]

---

[165] A separate group from the Judaizing Christians.

[166] Against D. J. Doughty who not only argues that there are no particular opponents being addressed in this passage but suggests that Paul himself did not write 3:2-21; it is deutero-Pauline ("Citizens of Heaven: Philippians 3.2-21," *NTS* 41 [1995] 102-22). Jewett ("Conflicting Movements," 376-77) notes that the imperfect ἔλεγον ("I told you," 3:18) suggests that "these enemies had been present during Paul's ministry at Philippi." However, they need not have left the community Paul founded but may have attempted to claim this new, powerful deity for themselves without ever having been part of the Christian community.

[167] Words which can be used synonymously; see J. P. Louw and E. A. Nida, *Greek-English Lexicon of the New Testament Based on Semantic Domains* (New York: United Bible Society, 1988) 734-35.

[168] Paul uses the hymn of Phil 2:6-11 as a basis for combating the attraction of the honour system of associations by alluding to it and expanding on it in the final two verses of 3:18-21. Cf. Flanagan, "Note on Philippians," 8-9. Meeks points out that this

The associations are illuminating because they were often repudiated for their indulgence in food and drink and banqueting and would clearly fit Paul's description in 3:19.[169] Recall Philo's accusation concerning the associations that "you could find no sound elements but only liquor, tippling, drunkenness and the outrageous conduct they lead to" (*Flacc.* 136).[170] Paul contrasts the Philippians' communal life with that of their opponents by suggesting that ἡμῶν γὰρ τὸ πολίτευμα ἐν οὐρανοῖς (3:20). The pronoun ἡμῶν used in the initial position suggests that Paul is using the terminology of his opponents.[171] Since he uses the verbal form πολιτεύεσθε in Phil 1:27 it is clear that Paul is "using language that reflects the particular interest of the Philippians themselves".[172] This is Paul's only use of these words suggesting that it is connected to the specific situation of the Philippians themselves.[173]

Paul clearly uses πολίτευμα metaphorically here. Many commentators understand it to be used as "citizenship" or "colony" and relate it to the situation of Philippi itself which was constituted as a Roman colony whose freepersons would have the rights of Roman citizenship and whose laws

---

echoing of the hymn of 2:6-11 in 3:20-21 is now commonly recognized by most commentators ("The Man From Heaven in Paul's Letter to the Philippians," in *The Future of Early Christianity: Essays in Honour of Helmut Koester*, ed. B. A. Pearson [Minneapolis: Fortress, 1991] 333). For the parallel Greek terms see Lincoln (*Paradise Now*, 88) or Hawthorne (*Philippians*, 169).

[169] Cotter, "Polituema," 98-100. Against the more common interpretation that understands the opponents in this passage as Christian. See the summary and critique of such positions in Cotter, "Politeuma," 92-96.

[170] See Philo, *Legat.* 10.311-12; *Flacc.* 4; Seland, "Philo and the Clubs," 110-27. Cotter incorrectly attributes Philo, *Flacc.* 136 to Varro, *R.R.* 3.2.16 ("Politeuma," 99).

[171] Böttger, "eschatologische Existenz," 260; Lincoln, *Paradise Now*, 97; Cotter, "Politeuma," 101. Cf. the play on the word περιτομή when polemicizing against the Judaizing Christian opponents in 3:2 (Cotter, "Politeuma," 102; Lincoln, *Paradise Now*, 97).

[172] Cotter, "Politeuma," 102. The pronoun ἡμῶν used in the initial position suggests that Paul is using the terminology of his opponents; Böttger, "eschatologische Existenz," 260; Lincoln, *Paradise Now*, 97; Cotter, "Politeuma," 101. Cf. the play on the word περιτομή when polemicizing against the Judaizing Christian opponents in 3:2 (Cotter, "Politeuma," 102; Lincoln, *Paradise Now*, 97).

[173] Most commentators recognize this. This is the only use of πολίτευμα in the New Testament. The cognate verb πολιτεύομαι occurs at Phil 1:27 (and once more, in Acts 23:1). Other related words in the New Testament are πολίτης (Luke 15:15; 19:14; Acts 21:39), πολίτης (Acts 22:28; Eph 2:12), and πολιτεία (Acts 17:6, 8), none of which occur in the authentic Pauline letters.

were enacted as if the citizens were living in Rome itself.¹⁷⁴ Lincoln suggests a more nuanced view by suggesting that it is better rendered "state" or "commonwealth" as a "constitutive force regulating its citizens."¹⁷⁵ Lüderitz's definition of πολίτευμα supports this: "*Politeuma* as a technical term for an institution within a πόλις stands for the ruling class as a sovereign body with specific rights, voting procedures, etc."¹⁷⁶ Thus, Phil 3:20 is best translated, "[f]or our state and constitutive government is in heaven."¹⁷⁷

In the previous chapter we noted evidence for the use of πολίτευμα as a group designator within some associations. Cotter suggests that voluntary associations modeled themselves on the civic structure in order to present themselves as a "civic entity" which implied with it "citizenship."¹⁷⁸ That

---

¹⁷⁴ Dahl, "Euodia and Syntyche," 8.

¹⁷⁵ Lincoln, *Paradise Now*, 99-100), followed by O'Brien, *Philippians*, 460; Witherington, *Friendship and Finances*, 98; Fee, *Philippians*, 378 n. 17; cf. Lightfoot, *Philippians*, 156.

¹⁷⁶ Lüderitz, "What is the Politeuma," 187-88.

¹⁷⁷ Lincoln, *Paradise Now*, 100. Cf. the common Macedonian designation πολιτάρχης for civic administrators; see G. H. R. Horsley, "The Politarchs," in *The Book of Acts in Its First Century Setting 2: The Book of Acts in Its Graeco-Roman Setting*, ed. D. W. J. Gill and C. Gempf (Grand Rapids and Carlisle: Eerdmans and Paternoster, 1994) 419-31.

¹⁷⁸ Cotter, "Politeuma," 103-04. The Stoics, who saw themselves as holding "citizenship" in a separate "state" from that of the ordinary Greek or Roman citizens, used πολίτευμα in a similar way; see Lightfoot, *Philippians*, 156; T. Engberg-Pedersen, "Stoicism in Philippians," in *Paul in His Hellenistic Context*, ed. T. Engberg-Pedersen (Minneapolis: Fortress, 1995) 264-69. Some scholars suggest that Paul is making reference to the specific privileges that Jewish groups enjoyed in the Roman Empire under the banner of πολίτευμα, which were not shared by other groups (e.g., Lightfoot, *Philippians*, 156; E. C. Miller, "Πολιτεύεσθε in Philippians 1.27: Some Philological and Thematic Observations," *JSNT* 15 [1982] 86-96). Although some Jewish groups did carry this title, the prevailing view that they are distinct from all other types of groups has been challenged. Most notably, Zuckerman "attacks this 'historiographic legend' and argues that there is no reason to think that politeumata differed from other clubs. According to him these were in fact private, voluntary associations" (Lüderitz, "What is the Politeuma," 185, citing C. Zuckerman, "Hellenistic Politeumata and the Jews: A Reconsideration. Review of *The Jews in Hellenistic and Roman Egypt: The Struggle for Equal Rights, by Aryeh Kasher*," *Scripta classica Israelica: Yearbook of the Israel Society for the Promotion of Classical Studies* 8/9 [1988] 180, 184; I was unable to obtain the latter work). Lüderitz suggests that the Jewish πολίτευμα in Berenice, represents a special form of political institution and is a "local peculiarity of the Jewish diaspora in Cyrenaica" ("What is the Politeuma," 222; cf. *SEG* XVI 931 [I BCE]; *CIG* 5136 [43 BCE]) which should not be assumed for Jewish groups elsewhere in the diaspora (which are Jewish associations; Lüderitz, "What is the Politeuma," 214). He

is, by joining an association, one takes on an identity with respect to the others in the association (fellow-members), has rights and responsibilities within the association, is governed by officials with civic titles, and sometimes takes on such roles for oneself. In Phil 3:20 Paul contrasts the Christian πολίτευμα, which is in heaven, with both the Roman πολίτευμα, which is in Rome, and, more immediately, the voluntary associations' πολίτευμα, which is in "this world" (that is, it resides within the local group).

In making these references to the voluntary associations in Phil 3:18-21 Paul seems to pick up on the practices and the vocabulary of this set of opponents and use them to reaffirm the Philippians' calling to a greater honour in the future.[179] Paul writes to them as he does in order to warn them that despite being similar to the associations as a community they are not to adopt the behavior typical of voluntary associations."[180]

d) Finances

We saw earlier that metaphors taken from business language figure prominently in Philippians.[181] Commercial terms are found in the

---

suggests that a misinterpretation of the evidence by Perdrizet ("Syriaca, part 2." *RArch* 35 [1899, 3rd ser.] 42-48) led to a perpetual misunderstanding of the implications of πολίτευμα: "The irony then is, that whereas scholars dealing with the history of the Jews usually point to the non-Jewish politeumata in order to substantiate the cause of a special legal position of these institutions, this very idea – that politeumata were sort of public institutions with special rights – was originally deduced from a misconception of the legal position of the Jews" (Lüderitz, "What is the Politeuma," 203-04).

[179] de Vos (*Community Conflicts*, 276-77) argues that in Phil 3:20-21 Paul is warning the Philippians not to join *collegia* that worship the Emperor. This seems to us to be too specific a connection.

[180] Cf. Cotter, "Politeuma," 104. We do not find convincing the arguments of M. Tellbe that the Philippians were faced with an "impending clash with the Roman authorities" (pg. 116) and were attempting to pass themselves off as "Jewish" in order to take advantage of the recognition of Judaism as a *religio licita* ("The Sociological Factors Behind Philippians 3.1-11 and the Conflict at Philippi," *JSNT* 55 [1994] :97-121). Two unsubstantiated assumptions are being made; 1) that there was a significant group of Jews at Philippi that were already making this claim, thus paving the way for the Christians to do so at Philippi, and 2) that the authorities would not actually see through such a ruse (nor does Tellbe suggest how the local Jews [if there were any] might have reacted to such a claim by the Gentile Christians).

[181] Unlike Philippians, there is no indication in 1 Thessalonians about finances or money.

voluntary associations inscriptions from Philippi and the surrounding area. A sarcophagus inscription from Reussilova records that money was given to the *thiasos* of Liber Pater Tasibastenus, the interest from which (*ex quorum reditu*) is to go towards holding a banquet at their funerary monument on the day of the *rosalia* (*CIL* III 703; also *CIL* III 707; cf. *CIL* III 704). A similar situation is established in Selian, where the income from bequeathed lands (*ex reditu eorum*) is to be used for the *parentalia* (*CIL* III/1 656). Mention of interest being used for the *rosalia* occurs in a Greek testamentary foundation from Philippi itself (Pilhofer 133). In each of these cases the interest accrued is used for the benefit of those who originally gave the money, as is the case with Paul's mention to the Philippians of "the interest that accrues to your account" (Phil 4:17).[182]

From Paul's comments to the Corinthians we learn that the Macedonian Christians contributed generously to Paul's collection for the church in Jerusalem.[183] Paul views the collection as a religious duty and his rhetoric suggests that this duty must be carried out in the same manner as one would carry out a religious duty within the voluntary associations.[184] In the context of his argument in 2 Cor 8 Paul invokes the Macedonians as an example in order to encourage a rivalry concerning the giving. Such rivalries were common among associations; many inscriptions include a formula to the effect that things are to be done "so that there may be a rivalry among those who wish to benefact the association, knowing that each will receive thanks in proportion to their benefaction" (IDelos 1519).[185]

In his attempt to shame the Corinthians, Paul's rhetoric hyperbolically emphasizes the generosity of the Macedonians by suggesting that they have gone beyond what would normally be required for contributions; they have given not only "according to their means" (κατὰ δύναμιν) but "beyond their means" (παρὰ δύναμιν, 2 Cor 8:1-5; cf. Rom 15:26-27). A second century BCE inscription from Magnesia ad Maeander concerning the ceremonies celebrated on the occasion of the installation of the statue of Artemis Leucophryene reads

It is good for the owners of houses or for those who have built workshops to provide (κατασκέασασιν) according to [their] means (κατὰ δύναμιν) for the decoration of the altars before the [temple]

---

[182] Translation by O'Brien, *Philippians*, 538.

[183] The following two paragraphs are adapted from R. S. Ascough, "The Completion of a Religious Duty: The Background of 2 Cor 8:1-15," *NTS* 42 (1996) 584-99.

[184] For details see Ascough, "Completion of a Religious Duty."

[185] See also *IG* II² 1263; 1273A; 1292; 1297; 1329 1337; 1369; 1375; *IG* XII/5 606.

entrance, and for those who make inscription[s] for Artemis Leukophryene Nikephoros. And if someone should fail to accomplish (ἐπιτελέσῃ) [these things], it will not be good for him. (IMagnMai 100 lines 86-90)

By using παρὰ δύναμιν in 2 Cor 8:3 Paul shows that the Macedonians were considerably generous with their funds.

Where the Macedonians' contributions differ from the collection of money within associations is in the sending of money outside of the community. Although such a practice is attested, it is rare. The association of Tyrian merchants at Ostia were able to secure the contributions of another association of Tyrian merchants at Rome in order to maintain their business and social headquarters (*CIG* 5853, II CE). However, in this particular case the Roman Tyrian association was constrained to contribute to the Ostian association by a decree of the Tyrian senate. Paul gives no indication of any constraints put on the Philippians, but suggests that their gift was given willingly.

The Philippians gave personal monetary support Paul (see Phil 4:16; 2 Cor 11:9). In Phil 4:10-20 he acknowledges the Philippians' most recent contribution. The nature of Paul's "thanks" is somewhat obscure and has created a number of exegetical problems. Paul seems less than enthusiastic about the gift, so much so that this passage has been deemed a "thankless thanks."[186] Paul does not use a term of "thanks" but opens with "I rejoice (ἐχάρην) in the Lord greatly that now at length you have revived your concern for me" (4:10). Some see his expression of joy as communicating his thankfulness while others see the phrase "now at length" (ἤδη ποτὲ) as indicating frustration on Paul's part that their gift was so long in coming. However, the recognition that the Philippians "had no opportunity" to help Paul nuances any potential frustration with the Philippians.

A number of conjectures have been proffered for this lack of opportunity including the poverty of the Philippians (cf. 2 Cor 8:1-2), the lack of someone to carry the gift to Paul, Paul's lack of need,[187] and Paul's restrictions on their giving in order both to deflect criticism that he was

---

[186] "Danklose Dank," Dibelius, *Thessalonicher/Philipper*, 73-74; cf. Fee, *Philippians*, 422 nn. 2 and 3, who disputes this; but see Peterman, "Thankless Thanks." Paul makes the claim that with or without the money he can be "content." In fact, he has learned self-sufficiency (αὐτάρκεια) in both wealth and poverty. This notion resonates with the Stoic and Cynic notion of αὐτάρκεια, although Paul's notion differs in that his is not truly "self"-sufficiency but an independence of external things because of a dependence on God (O'Brien, *Philippians*, 521).

[187] O'Brien, *Philippians*, 519.

simply preaching for gain and to channel funds towards the Jerusalem collection.[188] Whatever the reason, clearly the Philippians monetary support for Paul has now been resumed. Paul's continued good relationship with the Philippians is confirmed in the expression "you have revived your concern for me" (4:10). Furthermore, in thanking the Philippians Paul uses a Latinized form in the vocative plural to address the Philippians – Φιλιππήσιοι (4:15, from the Latin *Philippenses*).[189] This echo of the Philippians' status as citizens of a Roman colony emphasizes Paul's affection for the Philippians[190] as well as his gratitude for the gift.[191]

The amount of the support given to Paul remains unknown. Paul indicates that the support began shortly after his initial visit to Philippi.[192] Since it has continued until the time of the letter, it lasted at least five years.[193] All of this financial support given to Paul and to the Jerusalem collection indicates that the Philippians had money that they could send to Paul, or at least that they felt they needed to do all that they could to send money to him. It is clear that they were not a wealthy congregation and that at times it might have been difficult to raise the necessary funds (cf. 2 Cor 8:1-2 and perhaps Phil 4:10).[194]

The voluntary associations did often contribute money for their founders. For the most part it is honourary; money is spent on crowns and

---

[188] Summarized in Bruce, *Philippians*, 148-49; see further possibilities in Hawthorne, *Philippians*, 197.

[189] The more regular form would be Φιλιππεῖς or Φιλιππηνοί (O'Brien, *Philippians*, 531 n. 115).

[190] Collange, *Philippians*, 151. Cf. similar usage in 2 Cor 6:11 and Gal 3:1 in addressing the recipients there.

[191] O'Brien, *Philippians*, 531.

[192] This is the most likely meaning of the difficult phrase ἐν ἀρχῇ τοῦ εὐαγγελίου, ὅτε ἐξῆλθεν ἀπὸ Μακεδονίας (4:15). See O'Brien, *Philippians*, 532-32 (cf. Hawthorne, *Philippians*, 204) for other possible interpretations. This view is supported by Phil 1:5 where we find a similar reference to the Philippians' κοιωνία, ἀπὸ τῆς πρώτης ἡμέρας ἄχρι τοῦ νῦν.

[193] If not longer, depending on how one solves the question of dating, provenance, and unity. We take Paul to have first been in Philippi in 50 CE and to have written to the Philippians around 55 while imprisoned in Ephesus.

[194] Some commentators have understood this giving of money as a contractual obligation wherein Paul is required to preach the gospel and others pay in exchange. This conjecture is based on Paul's use of the language of exchange in 4:15 (so Sampley, *Pauline Partnership*, 51-77; Capper, "Paul's Dispute"). Others take this metaphor within the context of friendship discourse, showing that it is common to use the language of marketplace exchange within such contexts (e.g., O'Brien, *Philippians*, 534-35; Fee, *Philippians*, 440-47).

inscriptions honouring the founder/patron.[195] Paul's use of the financial support to found other communities was not a usual practice among associations. The Philippians do seem to have defined themselves from their formative stage as being involved in supporting their founder in his efforts to found other communities (4:15) by entering into some kind of relationship (κοινόω) with him (4:15, cf. 1:5 κοινωνία; 4:14 συγκοινωνέω).[196] While it might have been more typical to use the money to honour Paul within the community, this is not the case at Philippi. However, for Paul it is the Philippians themselves who are his crown (4:1) but not a material crown – a clear contrast between Paul's attitude towards what constitutes honour and that so deemed by the associations.[197] That Paul mentions that they are his crown may indicate the need to keep his relationship with the Philippians in proper perspective, an issue which will become more important in the latter part of Philippians 4.

The sending of money to a founder or to another group is somewhat different from the usual practice of associations. Paul himself recognizes that what the Philippians have undertaken is not normative for the groups with which he is involved. In discussing this issue with the Corinthians he claims to have "robbed other churches by accepting support from them in order to serve you," shortly thereafter naming the Macedonian churches as those "robbed" (2 Cor 11:8-9). Paul notes the atypical nature of such support by stating emphatically that no other community gave him monetary support (εἰ μὴ ὑμεῖς μόνοι, Phil 4:15).[198] The Philippian context is understood as somewhat irregular.

We noted that in voluntary associations the role of the benefactor or patron was particularly important. Although many associations collected membership dues, most were dependent upon patrons for a large part of

---

[195] Crowning was a frequent honour bestowed not just for athletic victories but for significant benefactions within voluntary associations. Such an honour was noted on their inscriptions; IDelos 1061; 1519; 1520; 1521; 1522; 1523; 2081; Foucart 48; 56; 59; 64; 65; *IG* II² 1256; 1263; 1271; 1273; 1277; 1278; 1291; 1292; 1297; 1314; 1315; 1317; 1327; 1329; 1334; 1343; 2347; *IG* IV 840; *IG* V/1 1390; *LSAM* 1; 8; 11; 13; 15; 38; IPriene 174; *Syll*³ 1009. The benefactor of an association at Thessalonica requires that the members wear a crown of roses during the ceremony at her tomb (*IG* X/2 260).

[196] The "partnership" is not *simply* monetary or contractual.

[197] Paul notes his "crown of boasting" in 1 Thess 2:19, reflecting the practice within associations of granting crowns to those who have given benefaction to an association as a means to promote φιλοτιμία.

[198] Against Reumann, "Contributions," 440. This is not to deny that individuals from other communities patronized Paul: Phoebe in Cenchrea; Gaius in Corinth; Philemon (in Colossae?).

their funds.[199] Understanding the financial contribution of the Philippians to Paul in light of patron-client relationships helps us better understand Paul's reticence in acknowledging the Philippians' gift (4:10-20; cf. above). Since he is in prison, he is not in a position to refuse the gift. His means of self-support, his trade, would no longer be available to him and, like most prisoners, he would be reliant upon friends or family for decent food and clothing, which would require disposable finances.[200] Under these circumstances the financial contribution of the Philippians would have placed Paul in a position of client with the Philippians acting collectively as patron.

Lukas Bormann suggests that the principle of reciprocity operative at Philippi is based on the Roman idea of *amicitia* or *beneficia* as described by Seneca in *De beneficiis* and *Epistulae morales*.[201] This led to the expectation on the part of the Philippians that Paul would repay them. Paul's thanksgiving letter (4:10-20) is his attempt to show that he has not entered into such a relationship with them; in fact, it is God who will repay his debt. While it is clear that Paul's language in Phil 4:10-20 suggests this, Bormann somewhat overlooks the significant part honour played in Greco-Roman patronage relationships, an aspect that would strengthen his case.[202] In Philippians 4:10-20 Paul seems to recognize that the result of the Philippians' gift places him in the role of client, but his debt would be one of having to honour the Philippians, an awkward social position for the founder of a community. Paul's language in Phil 4:14-19 is aimed at not allowing the Philippians to think that a patron-client relationship has been established with him in their debt.[203] He makes it clear that he did not complain of his current condition (4:11)[204] nor did he ask them for help (4:16).[205] This is an important clarification, as most benefactions in

---

[199] Garnsey and Saller, *Roman Empire*, 157; Danker, "Stones and Benefactors," 252; Schmeller, *Hierarchie und Egalität*, 33.

[200] See B. Rapske, *The Book of Acts and Paul in Roman Custody* (BAFCS 3; Grand Rapids and Carlisle: Eerdmans and Paternoster, 1994) 210.

[201] Bormann, *Philippi*, 171-205.

[202] Bormann, *Philippi*, does not explore why Paul's gratitude is given with reserve.

[203] The concealment of such benefaction is common in antiquity; "Some Romans tried to conceal the favours done for them precisely to avoid the implication of social inferiority arising from the fact that they had to turn to someone else for help" (Garnsey and Saller, *Roman Empire*, 149). Patronage is concealed with the language of friendship, a common theme in Philippians.

[204] Paul makes it clear that through Christ he has learned to contend with any situation of want or plenty (4:11-13).

[205] Nor is he hinting at future help; see Schenk, *Philipperbrief*, 44-46.

antiquity came about as a result of the client requesting funds from the patron. Paul makes it clear that he is self-sufficient (αὐτάρκης, Phil 4:11). In Phil 4:19 Paul notes that God is acting on Paul's behalf in meeting the needs of the Philippians.[206] In doing so, the Philippians have access to the "riches" (τὸ πλοῦτος) of God that will fulfill (πληρώσει)[207] all of their needs (πᾶσαν χρείαν ὑμῶν). The most obvious sense is that Paul wanted to convey to the Philippians that God will meet their immediate physical needs. While the Philippians have sent money that can help with some of Paul's needs, Paul is able to reciprocate with a much greater gift through God – meeting *all* their material needs.[208] To do this Paul has access to God's "riches in glory in Christ Jesus" (πλοῦτος αὐτοῦ ἐν δόξῃ ἐν Χριστῷ Ἰησοῦ). Paul often uses πλοῦτος for the riches of the Christian life (1 Cor 4:8; 2 Cor 4:7; 6:10; 8:2, 7, 9) and for God's riches (Rom 2:4; 9:23; 10:12; 11:33).[209] It is the commonly used word for "wealth," and a term whose

---

[206] Cf. Fee, *Philippians*, 452. O'Brien (*Philippians*, 545; also Vincent, *Philippians*, 151) notes that Phil 4:19 follows the previous verse with δέ functioning as a connective not an adversative particle. Thus it does not mean "but," suggesting that God's benefaction is compensation for the Philippians' gift to Paul. Rather, it means "and," indicating that their offering has met with God's approval. The remainder of the sentence indicates that compensation is what Paul has in mind.

[207] On external grounds alone πληρώσει is to be preferred over πληρῶσαι. Despite this, O'Brien (*Philippians*, 545) chooses to interpret this verse as a "wish-prayer" or petition; "may my God fill your every need...." The future indicative is better translated as a promise or declaration; "my God will fulfill your every need." Some commentators have been reluctant to accept this as a promise and see it rather as a petition, fearing that such a concrete promise would surely lead to disappointment and questioning when not met (Hawthorne, *Philippians*, 208). "Possible" theological and social difficulties, however, are no reason to reinterpret what seems to be clear in the text itself.

[208] On the use of the phrase πᾶσαν χρείαν ὑμῶν to indicate material needs (see Hawthorne, *Philippians*, 207-08; Fee, *Philippians*, 452 n. 12). O'Brien (*Philippians*, 547; cf. Plummer, *Philippians*, 105; Beare, *Philippians*, 156) attempts to broaden this to include the Philippians' "spiritual concerns" (i.e., standing firm in the faith, not being frightened, shining as lights, pressing on to the heavenly goal). Yet the examples of "spiritual" needs that O'Brien provides from Philippians and from New Testament use of χρεία elsewhere all can be realized in the physical realm: baptism, repentance, witnesses, teaching, patience, encouragement (see *Philippians*, 547 n. 223). There is no eschatological dimension to "all these needs" – Paul is promising benefits in the here and now.

[209] See O'Brien, *Philippians*, 548. This fulfillment of their needs comes "through" Christ (O'Brien, *Philippians*, 549). The designation ἐν δόξῃ should not be taken as indicating a future age but adjectively, qualifying πλοῦτος ("glorious wealth," Bruce, *Philippians*, 156) or perhaps adverbially, qualifying πληρώσει ("will fill your needs gloriously," Beare, *Philippians*, 156; Hawthorne, *Philippians*, 207; O'Brien, *Philippians*,

implications would be obvious to the community members who had just given money to their founder.

As founder of the community, Paul should function as one of its patrons.[210] However, he is not in a social or financial position to take up this aspect of the role. The Philippians' monetary contribution should reverse these roles, making Paul the client of the Philippians. Paul attempts to avoid this by referring to the Philippians' financial contribution as a "gift" (δόμα, 4:17), not once making explicit mention of money (e.g., ἀργύριον, χρυσίον).

This use of δόμα in 4:17 is often understood in a "friendship context" of gifts of reciprocity.[211] Others suggest that the δόμα is a "payment" or "salary" rather than "gift."[212] Another context for interpretation is possible. Δόμα is a synonym of other words which also indicate a "gift" – δῶρον, δωρεά. These words are used in the context of honours for benefactors of an association in association inscriptions.[213] For example, an inscription from Alistrati, near Philippi, records that a benefactor of an association was honoured with a gift (δῶρον) from the members of the association (IMakedD 1104). "Gift" can be used of the money paid out for the expense of crowns made to honour members who have served as officials in the association (e.g., *IG* II² 1317; Piraeus, III BCE). In using δόμα in reference to the Philippians' financial contribution Paul might be underlining the fact that as founder of the community such is his due. He is careful to maintain

---

548). This is not to deny a future aspect to this fulfillment, but it is not simply the promise of an eschatological fulfillment; see Fee, *Philippians*, 452 n. 12. On salvation as benefaction see F. Danker and R. Jewett, "Jesus as the Apocalyptic Benefactor in Second Thessalonians," in *The Thessalonian Correspondence*, ed. R. F. Collins (BETL 87; Leuven: Leuven University Press, 1990) 490.

[210] Paul might be bolstering his position as founder/patron with his references to his own "righteousness" which comes "from God" in 3:9. The "truly public-spirited citizen or benefactor" aspired to the virtue of Δικαιοσύνη (Danker, *Benefactor*, 669).

[211] O'Brien, *Philippians*, 537; Fee, *Philippians*, 447 n. 34.

[212] Sampley, *Pauline Partnership*, 51-77; Capper, "Paul's Dispute," 198-99. Both LSJ (*s.v.*) and Moulton and Milligan (*Vocabulary*, 168) cite *P.Petri.* III 42 C 1.4 (255 BCE), which deals with the payment of some quarry men.

[213] The opposite situation is possible. In a testamentary inscription from Thessalonica (*IG* X/2 260) a female benefactor stipulates that should a person not wear a crown in the ceremony of the *rosalia* at her graveside, then they forfeit their share of her "gift" (μὴ μετεχέτω μου τῆς δωρεᾶς, left side, lines 6-8). In *IG* XII/1 736 (Embona, Rhodes, III BCE) δωρεά is used three times to describe a burial plot, a parcel of land, and a sanctuary, all given to an association. The adjectival form is used six times in *IG* XII/3 330 (Thera, 210-195 BCE) to describe those who must officiate in the association "without charge" (line 27, 31 [2x], 47, 50, 91).

the "gift" in its proper perspective (as an honourific) and not to lose his standing in the community. By promising greater "riches" to come to the Philippians from God Paul upholds his side of the reciprocal κοινωνία that he has established with the community.[214]

e) Further Implications for Community Structure

As a religious association the Philippian community worshipped a God who is made known through the Saviour Jesus Christ. This particular aspect of the religious life of the community is worth comparing to the practices of voluntary associations. In Phil 3:20 Paul refers to Jesus as σωτήρ. Since this is the only time in the genuine letters that Paul ascribes this epithet to Jesus,[215] its significance might be sought in the context of Philippi. The title is used of various saviour figures in the LXX (including humans and YHWH).[216] Many interpreters look to the LXX as the appropriate background for Paul's use.[217] Yet this is unlikely to have been

---

[214] This interpretation finds some support in the argument of Peterman ("Thankless Thanks") who suggests that social conventions of the "thankless thanks" are at work in Philippians. Other ancient letters show that verbal gratitude is not expected among those who are intimate and, if offered, carries with it an expression of debt or expectation of repayment. By accepting the Philippians' unsolicited gift in the way he does, Paul is indicating that he has not become socially obligated to them. However, Paul still finds it necessary to indicate that benefits will arise from their gift, albeit from God. Although Peterman recognizes this ("Thankless Thanks," 270), he still maintains that the Philippians would not have expected reciprocation. I would argue that they would and did, so Paul counters their expectation on two fronts: by using a "thankless thanks" *and* by placing the reciprocating obligation on God. Cf. Hainz (*Koinonia*, 114): "Gemeinschaft ist für Paulus eine Beziehung, die durch gemeinsame Teilhabe an etwas vermittelt wird und in konkretem Anteil-geben und Anteil-nehmen Ausdruck findet. Dieser Konkretisierungen und Aktualisierungen kann Gemeinschaft nicht entraten; sie lebt vom Wechsel des Gebens und Nehmens." See further Hainz, *Koinonia*, 91-92.

[215] It is not a common title in the New Testament. There are only twenty-three other occurrences, ten in the Pastoral epistles, five in 2 Peter, two in Acts, and one each in Luke, John, Ephesians, 1 John, Jude. A much more common title for Christ is κύριος. O'Brien (*Philippians*, 462 n. 119) points out that the lack of the definite article suggests that σωτήρ is to be understood in a descriptive sense rather than as a title, although in the following note he admits that it would also have been heard as a title. Others suggest that it is used as a title; Collange, *Philippians*, 140; Hawthorne, *Philippians*, 169; Fee, *Philippians*, 380-81 n. 23. Some commentators point to the closest parallel in Paul being ὁ ῥυόμενος in 1 Thess 1:1 – Gnilka, *Philipperbrief*, 207; Müller, *Philipper*, 181.

[216] G. Fohrer, "σωτήρ in the Old Testament," *TDNT* 7 (1971) 1012-13.

[217] Michael, Philippians, 182-83; Hawthorne, *Philippians*, 171; O'Brien, *Philippians*, 462-63; Müller, *Philipper*, 181; Fee, *Philippians*, 381. Fee (*Philippians*,

the most apparent referent for the Philippians, who would not know the LXX.

A more immediate context for understanding σωτήρ within Greco-Roman culture was its application to the gods.²¹⁸ We find such use in the inscriptions from voluntary associations. Among the inscriptions connected to the associations of Zeus/Theos Hypsistos we have examples of the title. For example, we have a first century CE votive offering from Thessalonica dedicated to "Theos Hypsistos, Great Saviour" (Θεῶι Ὑψίστωι μεγίστῳ σωτῆρι; *IG* X/2 67). From elsewhere we have plentiful evidence for patron deities of voluntary associations bearing the title Saviour, especially Zeus (*Syll.*³ 985; *IG* II² 1291; *IG* IV 840; 841; *LSAM* 56; 65) and Sarapis and Isis (*IG* XI/4 1299). There is inscriptional evidence from various locales for associations of "Soteriastai"; *IG* II² 1343 (Athens, 37/36 BCE); *IG* XII/1 161 (Rhodes); Foucart 49 (Rhodes). The patron deity seems to have been Soteria (see *IG* II² 1343). In a decree of a Piraean ἔρανος we find the mention of the "sacred rites of Zeus Soter and of Herakles and of the Saviours" (*IG* II² 1291), while *Syll.*³ 985 (Philadelphi; I BCE) names Zeus and Hestia and "the other saviour gods" and later invokes "Saviour Zeus."²¹⁹

Some of the Macedonian associations seem to have adopted as a patron deity the heroized Thracian Horseman.²²⁰ The cult of the Thracian Horseman was one of the more popular of the indigenous cults in Macedonia, expressed primarily on funeral stelae.²²¹ The iconography of

---

381) suggests that Paul's audience was familiar with the use of σωτήρ in the contexts of both Emperor worship and the LXX; the latter is more unlikely.

²¹⁸ This would include the Emperor, who is frequently referred to as "Saviour" among his many titles, as were the Ptolemies in Egypt (Moulton and Milligan, *Vocabulary*, 621; W. Foerster, "σωτήρ in the Greek World," *TDNT* 7 [1971] 1004-12; A. D. Nock, "Soter and Euegertes," in *Essays on Religion in the Ancient World*, ed. Z. Stewart [Oxford: Clarendon 1972] 720-59; cf. V. M. Scramuzza, "Claudius Soter Euergetes," *HSCP* 51 [1940] 261-66). The cult of the Emperor is particularly well attested at Thessalonica (cf. Hendrix, "Thessalonians Honour Romans"). It is not as prominent at Philippi, although some interpreters use Thessalonica as a context for understanding σωτήρ in Philippians (Witherington, *Friendship and Finances*, 100; cf. Michael, *Philippians*, 183). Further on the Emperor cult at Philippi see Bormann, *Philippi*, 41-60.

²¹⁹ Barton and Horsley (*New Documents* 1, 27) note that the focus of this association is on present "this worldly" salvation.

²²⁰ Papazoglou, "Macedonia," 205; cf. 540 n. 106; see *IG* X/2 291; *CIL* III 704; IMakedD 920; Pilhofer 029/1.

²²¹ "The Thracian Horseman/Hero motif was depicted on thousands of grave monuments in Thrace and Macedonia" (V. A. Abrahamsen, "Pagan Funerary Practices in

this deity presents him on a horse, riding at full gallop, usually charging a wild animal such as a boar or a wolf with his spear.²²² The cult of the Thracian Horseman was particularly important at Philippi, where we find a nearby sanctuary along with numismatic evidence.²²³ Among the many epithets of this deity is the title "Saviour" (see *CCET* I no. 10).²²⁴ In Macedonia the cult of the Thracian Horseman was affected by a local belief in an afterlife that represented the dead as heroes.²²⁵ It may be that non-domestic slaves and freedmen in Macedonia "chose to be buried under the auspices of the Horseman/Hero, in hopes of an afterlife that was better than their earthly life."²²⁶ Some slaves may have formed associations to express these hopes.²²⁷

Although Paul's use of the epithet Saviour arguably derived from his knowledge of the LXX, among persons familiar with the use of this ascription for deities worshipped in associations it would have been

---

Northern Greece During the Early Christian Era," *Macedonian Studies* 6 [1989] 61; Pilhofer, *erste christliche Gemeinde*, 94; see *CCET, passim*). Most of the inscriptions are in Greek (Abrahamsen, "Pagan Funerary Practices," 62). See further R. F. Hoddinott, *The Tracians* (New York: Thames and Hudson, 1981) 169-75.

²²² S. Casson, *Macedonia, Thrace and Illyria: Their Relations to Greece from the Earliest Times Down to the Times of Philip son of Amyntas* (Oxford: Oxford University Press, 1926) 249. He was probably originally identified with the Thracian hero Rhesos, who fought in the Trojan war (Casson, *Macedonia, Thrace and Illyria*, 248).

²²³ See Pilhofer, *erste christliche Gemeinde*, 33-34. Pilhofer records the discovery near Philippi of a sanctuary to the Thracian Horseman, bearing the name Hero Auloneites, which dates to the Hellenistic period and was thriving in the time of the early Roman empire (Pilhofer, *erste christliche Gemeinde*, 33, cf. 93-100). This sanctuary may be connected to the association attested in Abdera, Thrace, not far from Philippi. For the latter see Poland, *griechischen Vereinswesens*, 223 and Poland B 66 = *CIL* III Suppl. 7378.

²²⁴ Collart, *Philippes*, 427; G. Kazarow, "Heros (thrakischer)," *RE Suppl.* 3 (1918) 1141. The Thracian horseman carried the title ἐπήκοος ("he who answers prayer"; see N. Hampartumian, *Corpus Cultus Equitis Thracii [CCET] IV: Moesia Inferior (Romanian Section) and Dacia* [EPRO 74; Leiden: Brill, 1979] 17); cf. the references to prayer in Philippians.

²²⁵ Papazoglou, "Macedonia," 205. Often the word ἥρως is added to the various epitaphs he is given.

²²⁶ Abrahamsen, "Pagan Funerary Practices," 65; cf. Collart, *Philippes*, 423. Abrahamsen notes that the workmanship on most of the Thracian Horseman inscriptions is simple, making it "fairly certain that they were used among the lower and middle strata" ("Rock Reliefs," 51). Upper rank men seem to have favoured a banqueting scene on their grave monument (Abrahamsen, "Pagan Funerary Practices," 64).

²²⁷ Abrahamsen, "Pagan Funerary Practices," 65.

rhetorically effective in a different way.²²⁸ Since hope for a better afterlife is the context in which Paul uses this title in Philippians, the title would have underscored this hope. Overall, this suggests that ascribing the designator "religious association" to the Philippian Christian community is entirely appropriate.

The extensive evidence for the connections between associations and the deceased in Philippi (and Macedonia more generally) leads Beare to conclude that, "[w]hen Paul came to Philippi, he would find ready hearers for a gospel of resurrection from the dead, and life eternal."²²⁹ Beare calls these associations "burial-clubs" as does Perdrizet, who points out that it is interesting to note the large number of funerary associations at Philippi, the first European city in which Christianity took root.²³⁰ In both cases they seem to indicate that the associations at Philippi are similar to the Roman *collegia funeriticia*. That they should be designated as such is not at all clear. Many religious and professional associations took care of the burial of their members without having that as a primary focus of their corporate life. In the case of most of the Macedonian associations, an existing religious association is benefacted (or founded) in order to commemorate the deceased after he or she has passed away. This practice is not the same as insuring a proper burial for the deceased and thus these associations should not be understood as funerary associations but rather as religious associations.²³¹

4. Conclusion

The Philippian Christian community is clearly a gender inclusive group in which women exercised some leadership capacity. As such, it is like a

---

²²⁸ Further evidence that this is a deliberate use of the epithet is suggested by the fact that in its context (Phil 3:18-21) Paul is directly countering the social practices of some voluntary associations, as we argued above.

²²⁹ Beare, *Philippians*, 9.

²³⁰ Beare, *Philippians*, 9; Perdrizet, "Inscriptions de Philippes," 318.

²³¹ In an earlier discussion we agreed with Kloppenborg ("Collegia and *Thiasoi*," 20-22) that associations which were formed for the sole purpose of burial of members probably did not exist before the second century CE, and even then the designation "funerary" association was a fiction of Roman law makers. The frequent mention of associations in burial contexts is a result of associations constituted for professional or religious reasons taking care of the burial of their own members. It may be the case that others have commissioned an association to carry out certain rites at their tomb, although this was not the principle *raison d'être* of the association.

religious voluntary association. The titles given to leaders at Philippi, ἐπίσκοπος and διάκονος, can be found among the leadership titles used in voluntary associations. At Philippi the Christians faced some of the same types of internal disharmony found among the voluntary associations. We noted Paul's concern that they distinguish themselves from the typical practices of the voluntary associations. Finance was another area in which we found both similarities with the associations and direct contrasts. The Philippians' collection and distribution of money figures prominently in the last chapter of the letter. The collecting of money itself coheres with the widespread practice in the associations, although we suggested that the disbursement of that money outside of the group was a significant difference, one that Paul highlights. Another financial consideration was benefaction, an issue that underlies Paul's careful negotiation of his gratitude for the Philippians' monetary gift. Overall, if the Philippian community is to be classified as analogous to a voluntary association, it is the religious associations rather than the professional associations that make the best analogue.

Chapter Six

The Thessalonian Christian Community

1. Paul's Letter to the Thessalonians

There is little doubt among New Testament scholars that Paul wrote 1 Thessalonians.[1] Most commentators place Paul in Corinth when he wrote to the Thessalonians, probably around 50/51 CE.[2] It is probably the first letter that we have from Paul.[3] Paul's primary purpose in writing to the Thessalonians is to encourage them to persevere and make progress in their Christian faith.[4] Paul seems to be addressing a number of issues that are bothering the Thessalonians and about which he has received word,[5] such as the fate of those Christians who have died before the parousia of

---

[1] For a summary of earlier arguments against Pauline authorship see Best, *Thessalonians*, 22-28.

[2] Bruce, *Thessalonians*, xxxiv-xxxv; D. J. Williams, *1 and 2 Thessalonians* (NIBC 12; Peabody: Hendrickson, 1992) 9-10; According to D. Lührmann Paul must have been in either Athens or Corinth when he wrote 1 Thessalonians ("The Beginnings of the Church at Thessalonica," in *Greeks, Romans, and Christians: Essays in Honour of Abraham J. Malherbe*, ed. D. L. Balch, W. A. Meeks, and E. Ferguson [Minneapolis: Fortress, 1990] 238).

[3] Some have argued for the authenticity of 2 Thessalonians and suggested that it was written before 1 Thessalonians. Adherents of this position argue along the lines that the "present" trouble in 2 Thess is presented as "past" in 1 Thess, the internal difficulties are presented as new in 2 Thess 3:11-12 but are familiar to all in 1 Thess, the autograph greeting makes most sense in a first letter (2 Thess 3:17-18), the Thessalonians do not need to be told of times and seasons (1 Thess 5:1) because 2 Thess 2:3-15 is already known, and Paul's direct responses (1 Thess 4:9, 13; 5:1) indicates that the Thessalonians raised questions based on 2 Thess (see T. W. Manson, "St. Paul in Greece: The Letters to the Thessalonians," *BJRL* 35 [1953] 438-47). However, in this work we do not treat 2 Thessalonians as an authentic letter of Paul.

[4] Plummer, *Thessalonians*, xviii.

[5] By using introductory formulae such as περὶ δὲ τῆς φιλαδελφίας (4:9), οὐ θέλομεν δὲ ὑμᾶς ἀγνοεῖν, ἀδελφοί, περὶ τῶν κοιμωμένων (4:13), and περὶ δὲ τῶν χρόνων καὶ τῶν καιρῶν (5:1) Paul seems to be responding to the Thessalonians directly. The issues he responds to may have been relayed through Timothy (1 Thess 3:6). However, A. J. Malherbe raises the possibility that Paul wrote an earlier letter to the Thessalonians (which was not the canonical 2 Thess) and the probability that the Thessalonians wrote back to him asking for advice ("Did the Thessalonians Write to Paul?" in *The Conversation Continues: Studies in Paul and John in Honour of J. Louis Martyn*, ed. R. Fortna and B. Gaventa [Nashville: Abingdon, 1990] 246-57).

Christ (4:13-18) and the signs preceding Jesus' return (5:1-11). Some have suggested that in 2:1-12 (and 2:17-20) Paul is responding to criticism that he and the other missionaries preached for financial gain, a charge supported by their hasty departure and failure to return.[6]

One contentious issue surrounding 1 Thessalonians is the unity of the letter. Some have proposed that 1 Thessalonians is in fact a composite of two letters, an earlier letter (2:13-4:2) having been inserted into a later letter (1:1-2:12 and 4:3-5:28).[7] This proposal is based on the presence in the canonical form of two "thanksgivings" (1:2-10; 2:13-16). The earlier letter reflects Paul's warmth for the community he has recently left, while the later letter is more didactic in tone, emphasizing Christian living and the Day of the Lord. Nevertheless, most scholars hold that 1 Thessalonians is a single letter, although some do suggest that material has been added to Paul's original letter.

The most frequently identified interpolation is the second thanksgiving (2:13-16). Arguments for this being an interpolation include the break in the material (2:13-16 does not fit the context and verses 12 and 17 seem to fit together well without the break), the unusual language, the presence of a second thanksgiving section, the veiled allusion to the destruction of Jerusalem in 70 CE (2:16b), and the strongly anti-Jewish tone that

---

[6] M. L. Soards, *The Apostle Paul: An Introduction to his Writings and Teaching* (New York and Mahwah: Paulist, 1987) 49-50; Bruce, *Thessalonians*, 27-28. A. J. Malherbe suggests that Paul's antithetical style is being used to address criticisms that were typical of wandering philosophers but he is careful to note that it is not possible to determine whether Paul is defending his own actions at Thessalonica (*Paul and the Thessalonians: The Philosophic Tradition of Pastoral Care* [Philadelphia: Fortress, 1987] 48). S. Walton suggests that no criticism of Paul exists at Thessalonica and that Paul is using the antithetical style "as a way of expanding and clarifying Paul's teaching" ("What Has Aristotle to do with Paul? Rhetorical Criticism and 1 Thessalonians," *TynBul* 46 [1995] 249). Such a position does not require the existence of external opponents of Paul at Thessalonica, as some have argued. Schmithals (*Paul and the Gnostics*,123-218) understands Paul to be responding to Jewish Christian Gnostics while Johanson (*To All the Brethren*, 58, 89-93, 164-65) understands Paul to be defending his message, and himself, in light of possible questions the Thessalonians themselves might raise as a result of the death of some of the community members. For a summary of this position in the work of Schmithals and Johanson see Walton, "Rhetorical Criticism," 240-42.

[7] Richard, *Thessalonians*, 11-19, 29-32; Murphy-O'Connor, *Paul*, 104-10. Schmithals' unlikely theory of 1 Thessalonians as a composite of four different letters is summarized by R. F. Collins ("A propos the Integrity of I Thes," *ETL* 55 [1979] 89-95) and Jewett (*Thessalonian Correspondence*, 33-36).

contradicts Romans 9-11.[8] This evidence suggests that this particular passage was added after Paul's death. It was inserted to reflect the developing tensions between non-Christian Jews and Christians after the Jewish war (66-70 CE).

Scholars who consider 2:13-16 to be authentic point out other features of the text. They argue that the concrete situation of opposition in 2:14 fits with the suggestion of suffering elsewhere in the letter (1:6; 2:2). They suggest that "imitation" (2:14) is a typical Pauline expression/motif, as is the liturgical or creedal language of 2:15. Finally, they point out that verse 17 fits no better after verse 12 than after verse 16.[9] It is not our intention to mediate this position nor to present compelling arguments of one over the other.[10] Although we tend towards the interpolation theory, there are instances in which 2:13-16 does seem to confirm the predominant picture we will be developing of the Thessalonian Christian community.[11] The omission of this passage from the canonical letter suggests that the remaining material can be viewed as one letter, not two, as the second thanksgiving section, the basis for the two-letter hypothesis, is no longer present.[12] Overall, it seems best to omit 2:13-16 from our discussion due to the controversy surrounding its authenticity.

The most contentious issue surrounding the Thessalonian correspondence is the authenticity of 2 Thessalonians. Strong arguments can be marshaled both for and against Pauline authorship of 2

---

[8] For details see B. A. Pearson, "1 Thessalonians 2:13-16: A Deutero-Pauline Interpolation" *HTR* (1971) 79-94; Richard, *Thessalonians*, 17-19; cf. Jewett, *Thessalonian Correspondence*, 36-41. H. Boers' form-critical study of 1 Thessalonians suggests that without 2:13-16 the letter has the form normative for letters of antiquity ("The Form-Critical Study of Paul's Letters: 1 Thessalonians as a Case Study," *NTS* 22 [1975-76] 151-52).

[9] See K. P. Donfried, "Paul and Judaism: I Thessalonians 2:13-16 as a Test Case," *Int* 38 (1984) 242-53; Jewett, *Thessalonian Correspondence*, 41.

[10] For an extensive survey of the various theories see Collins, "Integrity." A more recent survey and an extensive treatment of the passage is that of C. J. Schlueter, who argues that the passage is genuine and that Paul uses hyperbole with reference to the suffering of the Judeans in order to create solidarity between the Thessalonians and the Judean Christians (*Filling Up the Measure: Polemical Hyperbole in 1 Thessalonians 2:14-16* [JSNTSup 98; Sheffield: JSOT Press, 1994]).

[11] Namely, the reference to work; the reference to "your own fellow countrymen" who are distinguished from the "Judean Jews" and indicates that both the Thessalonian Christians and their persecutors are Gentiles, not Jews.

[12] Some scholars attribute 5:1-11 to a writer of the Lukan school who sought to correct false inferences drawn from 4:13-18. However, this position has not won general acceptance. See Jewett, *Thessalonian Correspondence*, 41-42 for a summary.

Thessalonians, and it is beyond the scope of our purpose to mediate between the two sides.[13] Murphy-O'Connor states that "[t]he arguments against the authenticity of 2 Thessalonians are so weak that it is preferable to accept the traditional ascription of the letter to Paul."[14] Nevertheless, for our purposes, we will rest our arguments on that which is almost universally held to be authentically Pauline, namely 1 Thessalonians.[15]

2. The Social Location of the Thessalonian Christians

a) The Thessalonians' Economic Situation

Paul gives a number of indications of the economic situation of the Thessalonians. In 2 Corinthians 8:1-5 Paul attempts to shame the Corinthians into contributing to the collection for the Jerusalem church by noting that the Macedonian Christians have given not only "according to their means" (κατὰ δύναμιν) but "beyond their means" (παρὰ δύναμιν, 2 Cor 8:1-5; cf. Rom 15:26-27). Paul was supported financially by the "Macedonians" while he was living in Corinth (2 Cor 11:9), although he is likely referring to the support given by the church at Philippi as that church was the "only one" that supported Paul in his work outside

---

[13] K. P. Donfried summarizes the primary points: "Factors most frequently mentioned in connection with the authenticity of 2 Thessalonians include: (1) the apparent literary dependence of 2 Thessalonians on 1 Thessalonians; (2) the tensions, if not contradictions, that are said to exist between 2 Thess. 2.3-12 and 1 Thess. 4.13-5.11; (3) the paucity of personal references and the formal, solemn tone of 2 Thessalonians; and (4) the references to forgery in 2 Thess. 2.2 and 3.17" ("2 Thessalonians and the Church of Thessalonica," in *Origins and Method: Towards a New Understanding of Judaism and Christianity. Essays in Honour of John C. Hurd*, ed. B. H. McLean [JSNTSup 86; Sheffield: JSOT Press, 1993] 130-31; cf. "The Theology of 2 Thessalonians" in *The Theology of the Shorter Pauline Epistles*, K. P. Donfried and I. H. Marshall [New Testament Theology; Cambridge: Cambridge University Press, 1993] 84-86): For more detail see M. J. J. Menken, *2 Thessalonians* (London and New York: Routledge, 1994) 27-43. A more detailed discussion of the history of scholarship is found in Jewett, *Thessalonian Correspondence*, 3-18 and Wanamaker, *Thessalonians*, 17-28.

[14] Murphy-O'Connor, *Paul*, 111; for details see ibid., 110-14.

[15] We are most persuaded by the distinct differences in the body of the 2 Thessalonians on the events surrounding the coming (parousia) of Jesus and the timetable for Jesus' coming ("thief in the night" in 1 Thess 5:2 verses Satan's "power, signs, lying wonders" in 2 Thess 2:9), and cautiously maintain that 2 Thessalonians is not a genuine letter of Paul. Donfried ("2 Thessalonians," 132-34) raises the interesting possibility that Timothy wrote the letter.

Macedonia (εἰ μὴ ὑμεῖς μόνοι, Phil 4:15).[16] The Thessalonians do not seem to have given financial aid to Paul personally.

Paul notes more specifically that the Philippians supported him financially while he was working in Thessalonica (Phil 4:16). This would coincide with the previous note (Phil 4:15) about the support beginning soon after his departure from Philippi, as Thessalonica was the next stop in Paul's travels along the Via Egnatia (1 Thess 2:2; cf. Acts 17:1). Interestingly, Paul does not mention this support when writing the Thessalonians. In fact, he seems to claim to have been supporting himself in 1 Thess 2:9, probably in an attempt to avoid shaming the Thessalonians.[17] Paul points out that he did not want to "be a burden" (ἐπιβαρέω) to the Thessalonians (2:9), not only indicating his reticence to rely on the Thessalonians' financial support for things such as food or lodging,[18] but the lack of a wealthy benefactor upon whom Paul could rely among the Thessalonian Christians (*contra* Acts 17:4). All this suggests that the Thessalonian Christians are not well off financially.[19]

There is some question as to whether Phil 4:16 indicates that Paul received help on more than one occasion while at Thessalonica or once at Thessalonica and on a number of occasions at other places. The text reads ὅτι καὶ ἐν Θεσσαλονίκῃ ἅπαξ καὶ δὶς εἰς τὴν χρείαν μοι ἐπέμψατε. Morris argues that ἅπαξ καὶ δίς is idiomatic for "more than once."[20] Since

---

[16] There is perhaps another reference to this support in Acts 18:5, wherein Paul is enabled to continue to be solely occupied with preaching upon the return of Silas and Timothy from Macedonia. Prior to this, he worked at his trade (Acts 18:1-4). See Bruce, *Philippians*, 153; O'Brien, *Philippians*, 533.

[17] Bruce (*Philippians*, 153) suggests that Paul is aiming to shame the Corinthian Christians in 2 Cor 11:8-9 but wants to refrain from doing so when writing 1 Thess. Alternatively, Bruce (*Philippians*, 153) suggests that the Philippians' gift was too small to eliminate the need for Paul to work, thus not worthy of mention (so Hawthorne, *Philippians*, 205). This latter suggestion is less likely.

[18] Wanamaker, *Thessalonians*, 103.

[19] Cf. Plummer, *Thessalonians*, 25. Paul is attempting to lay to rest any question about his motives for preaching. He was not preaching for his own gain, a fact his self-sufficiency underlines. Paul may even be indicating that he worked beyond the normal expectation of sunrise to sunset (R. F. Hock, *The Social Context of Paul's Ministry: Tentmaking and Apostleship* [Philadelphia: Fortress, 1980] 31).

[20] L. Morris, "ΚΑΙ ΑΠΑΧ ΚΑΙ ΔΙΣ," *NovT* 1 (1956) 205-08. He cites the LXX texts of Deut 4:13, 1 Kgs 17:39, Neh 13:20, and 1 Macc 3:30 and the quotation of Deut 4:13 in *1 Clement* 53.3 as uses of this expression. Morris is building on Frame, *Thessalonians*, 120-21. Morris makes it clear that rendering the phrase "twice" (Vincent, *Philippians*, 148; Michael, *Philippians*, 223) is too weak but "repeatedly" is too strong (so also Best, *Thessalonians*, 126).

it is used in the LXX without an initial καί Morris suggests that the καί in Phil 4:16 is added before the expression as a connective giving the following sense: "For both (when I was) in Thessalonica and more than once (in other places) you sent me gifts to meet my needs." Such a reading broadens the pattern of help the Philippians sent to Paul.[21] However, the same idiomatic expression, including the preceding καί is used in 1 Thess 2:18: διότι ἠθελήσαμεν ἐλθεῖν πρὸς ὑμᾶς, ἐγὼ μὲν Παῦλος καὶ ἅπαξ καὶ δίς. Morris suggests that the sentence can be translated with the καί as ascensive: "Because we wished to come to you, I Paul, and that more than once."[22] The καί cannot function here as a connective. This being so, it seems more likely that at Phil 4:16 the phrase would be better rendered, "for also (when I was) in Thessalonica you sent gifts, and that more than once, to meet my needs," and taken to indicate that on a number of occasions Paul received money from the Philippians while at Thessalonica.[23] This would confirm the social location of the Thessalonians among the poor. The financial contributions of the Philippians along with the necessity for Paul to work at his trade suggest that there was not even a patron of the Thessalonian Christians who would support Paul during his time among them.[24]

Early in 1 Thessalonians Paul makes reference to their receiving the word in much θλῖψις (1:6). While θλῖψις is often taken to mean "tribulation" or "persecution,"[25] Malherbe emphasizes that the context of

---

[21] Frame, *Thessalonians*, 121; Morris, "ΚΑΙ ΑΠΑΧ," 208; Martin, *Philippians*, 181; Gnilka, *Philipperbrief*, 178 n. 147; O'Brien, *Philippians*, 535; Müller, *Philipper*, 205; Witherington, *Friendship and Finances*, 130.

[22] Morris, "ΚΑΙ ΑΠΑΧ," 208. Cf. Wanamaker, *Thessalonians*, 121.

[23] So Lightfoot, *Philippians*, 166; Plummer, *Thessalonians*, 104; Beare, *Philippians*, 155; Collange, *Philippians*, 148; Hawthorne, *Philippians*, 205; Fee, *Philippians*, 445; Murphy-O'Connor, *Paul*, 102. Morris' concern in reading Phil 4:16 as indicating only one gift having been sent to Paul in Thessalonica seems to be to open the way for understanding Paul's stay in that city as very short. Although he does not say so, presumably this is to reconcile Paul's letter with the account in Acts 17:2, which seems to indicate only a three-week stay at Thessalonica (also Gnilka, *Philipperbrief*, 178). Our understanding of Phil 4:16 does not undermine the possibility that Paul received monetary gifts from the Philippians while elsewhere, as may be indicated in 2 Cor 11:9.

[24] Such was the case elsewhere. At Corinth Gaius seems to have benefacted Paul (Rom 16:23) and as did Phoebe at Cenchreae (Rom 16:1-2, although Phoebe's benefaction probably extended beyond Paul's stay at Cenchreae; see Whelan, "Amica Pauli," 84-85).

[25] Frame, *Thessalonians*, 82-83; Best, *Thessalonians*, 79; Bruce, *Thessalonians*, 15-16; Marshall, *Thessalonians*, 54; Wanamaker, *Thessalonians*, 81-82; cf. 1 Thess 2:14; Acts 17:5-9. J. M. G. Barclay suggests that the Thessalonians' θλῖψις (3:7; 1:6) is the

1:6 must be understood in light of the Thessalonians state at their reception of the gospel. He argues that θλῖψις indicates that the Thessalonians are experiencing distress over the acceptance of a new belief system and the consequential decisive break with their past. [26] However, Marshall points out that θλῖψις may indicate economic hardship, not persecution or psychological distress.[27] In writing of the contribution of the Macedonians to the Jerusalem collection in 2 Cor 8:1-5, Paul connects the Macedonians' θλῖψις to their "extreme poverty" (βάθους πτωχεία, 8:2), and then later notes that he does not want others to be eased at the expense of the Corinthians experiencing θλῖψις, which in this context indicates economic stress (2 Cor 8:13). This understanding of θλῖψις in 1 Thess 1:6 would suggest that the Thessalonian church accepted the gospel "in much poverty," and in so doing became imitators of Paul and his companions, who themselves were impoverished workers who had accepted the gospel. As a result, they became an example to others, not in their endurance of persecution, but in their acceptance of the gospel.[28]

---

mockery and abuse of the non-Christians who disparage a saviour who is so ineffective as to allow his worshippers to die ("Thessalonica and Corinth: Social Contrasts in Pauline Christianity," *JSNT* 47 [1992] 53-56; idem, "Conflict in Thessalonica," *CBQ* 55 [1993] 512-30). The divisions were exacerbated by the Thessalonians' tendency (stemming from their apocalyptic perspective) to treat non-believers as "outsiders" and protect themselves as a distinct society, particularly in "their offensive abandonment of common Greco-Roman religion" (Barclay, "Conflict," 514).

[26] Malherbe, *Paul and the Thessalonians*, 46-48. This idea is less prominent in his later commentary (Malherbe, *Thessalonians*, 115).

[27] Marshall, *Enmity in Corinth*, 234.

[28] *Contra* Wanamaker, *Thessalonians*, 81. Paul uses θλῖψις two other times in 1 Thessalonians. In 3:3-4, he indicates that Timothy is sent to them that they might not be moved by "these afflictions" (ἐν ταῖς θλίψεσιν ταύταις). If 1 Thess 2:13-16 is an interpolation, then the "afflictions" here are most clearly the experience of separation from Paul (2:17-20). If it is not an interpolation, then it might be the experience of persecution, but this persecution arose *after* they had already accepted the gospel (Malherbe, *Paul and the Thessalonians*, 47). The θλῖψις of 1 Thess 3:7 is clearly that which Paul experiences in the situation in which he now finds himself. Thus, the meaning of θλῖψις must be determined by its use in context, not by a predetermined notion; Wanamaker's contention that "[i]t is questionable that the same word would be used in two very different senses in the same general context of the letter" (*Thessalonians*, 81) ignores the fact that the meaning of words must always be determined in light of the context and an author is free to use the same words with different indications in any one piece of writing.

b) The Thessalonians as Manual Laborers

In the opening thanksgiving of 1 Thessalonians Paul presents the triad of "faith, hope, and love" with images of work: μνημονεύοντες ὑμῶν τοῦ ἔργου τῆς πίστεως καὶ τοῦ κόπου τῆς ἀγάπης καὶ τῆς ὑπομονῆς τῆς ἐλπίδος (1:3). The triad occurs again in 1 Thess 5:8: ἐνδυσάμενοι θώρακα πίστεως καὶ ἀγάπης καὶ περικεφαλαίαν ἐλπίδα σωτηρίας. In 1 Thess these three aspects of the Christian life resonate throughout the letter as Paul refers to each in a number of ways: πίστις (1:8; 3:2, 5, 6, 7, 10; cf. πιστεύω, 1:7; 2:4, 10, 13; 4:14), ἐλπίς (2:19, 4:13), ἀγάπη (3:6, 12; 5:13; cf. ἀγαπάω, 1:4; 4:9; ἀγαπητός, 2:8).[29]

Bossman is correct in his assessment that the statement of 1 Thess 1:3 reflects "Paul's reading of the assembly's standards," especially as they are repeatedly reaffirmed throughout the letter.[30] The triad of "faith, hope, and love" reflects the corporate values of the Thessalonians, as well as for others to whom they have become the example to be imitated.[31] Paul's thanksgiving statement serves as a word of praise "intended to create a positive emotion or *pathos* in the readers."[32] However, Bossman overlooks the significance of "work, labor, and steadfastness." Coupled with the assembly's standards, these too must reflect the "corporate values" of the Thessalonians. As such, they can be used to understand where their values lie.

Paul notes the Thessalonians' "endurance of hope" (ὑπομονῆς τῆς ἐλπίδος, 1:3). Since the Thessalonians have experienced some type of distress (θλῖψις, 1:6), Paul's words would underline the strength of their commitment to the Christian life. "Endurance" (ὑπομονή) can indicate "heroism" or inward strength in the face of outward difficulty. In the mythology of antiquity Heroes often underwent all kinds of stressful tasks in which they evidenced their courage and endurance.[33] Such heroic endurance would be familiar to Macedonians whose tombstones often make reference to or depict in relief two important heroes, the Thracian

---

[29] Elsewhere Paul presents the triad simply as "faith, hope, and love" (1 Cor 13:13; cf. Col 1:4-5; see Rom 5:1-5). Often two of the elements are linked; see D. M. Bossman, "Paul's Mediterranean Gospel: Faith, Hope, Love," *BTB* 25 (1995) 73.

[30] Bossman, "Paul's Mediterranean Gospel," 73.

[31] Bossman, "Paul's Mediterranean Gospel," 73, 75.

[32] Wanamaker, *Thessalonians*, 75.

[33] R. F. Collins, *The Birth of the New Testament: The Origin and Development of the First Christian Generation* (New York: Crossroad, 1993) 249 n. 21; Dibelius, *Thessalonicher/Philipper*, 3.

Horseman and Herakles.³⁴ Thus, the third element of Paul's triad would have been received as high praise for the Thessalonians.

This makes the first two elements of the triad more significant for our study of the social location of the Thessalonian Christians. The overall appeal of Paul's statement must surely resonate with the situation of the Thessalonians themselves. Paul begins with reference to their "work of faith" (ἔγρου τῆς πίστεως). The word ἔργον has clear connections with work, being the most frequently used word for such.³⁵ Paul uses it elsewhere in the letter to describe the work that the community's leaders do (5:3). The cognate verb ἐργάζομαι is used of manual labor, referring both to that of Paul and his companions while at Thessalonica (2:9) and that of the Thessalonians themselves (4:11). In 3:2 Paul describes Timothy as a "fellow-worker" (συνεργός).³⁶ Unlike Epaphroditus in Philippians, Timothy is not simply Paul's fellow-worker; he is sent with the recommendation of being "God's fellow-worker" in the gospel of Christ.³⁷

Paul makes reference to the Thessalonians' "labor of love" (κόπου τῆς ἀγάπης). Κόπος indicates more than manual labor: "it includes charitable

---

³⁴ According to Abrahamsen ("Pagan Funerary Practices," 61) there are literally thousands of depictions of the Thracian Horseman/Hero motif on grave monuments in Macedonia and Thrace (cf. Hoddinott, *Tracians*, 169-75). For examples from Macedonia see *IG* X/2 288, 289, *CIG* 2007f.

³⁵ Paul often uses ἔργον for that done in the Christian life, that done by non-Christians, and that done under the law. However, its basic meaning is manual labor (LSJ *s.v.*). The word ἔργον and its cognates is commonly employed not only in 1 Thessalonians and Philippians but throughout the Pauline corpus and the entire New Testament canon; ἔργον is used thirty-nine times in the Pauline epistles, nine times in Ephesians, Colossians, 2 Thessalonians, and twenty times in the Pastorals; Paul uses ἐργάζομαι twelve times, and it is used once in each of Ephesians and Colossians, four times in 2 Thessalonians, and not at all in the Pastorals. We cite the examples in 1 Thessalonians not as unique instances but in order to highlight what they might suggest about the audience in this letter. The absence of such words would in fact be a more significant piece of data, given Paul's tendency to use the word.

³⁶ In the disputed section of the letter (2:13-16) ἐνεργέω is used of God's work in the Thessalonians through his word (2:13).

³⁷ There are a number of readings of this verse in the manuscript evidence. The external evidence (esp. ℵ, A, and the diversity of versions) suggests καὶ διάκονον τοῦ θεοῦ is the original. However, the reading καὶ συνεργόν τοῦ θεοῦ (original reading of D, 33, some Old Latin mss, and Patristic writers) best explains the others, as a scribe would be more likely to object to Timothy being *God's* fellow-worker by either changing συνεργόν to διάκονον or deleting the words τοῦ θεοῦ (B, 1962); for a detailed discussion see Metzger, *Textual Commentary*, 631. The UBS committee gives the reading καὶ συνεργόν τοῦ θεοῦ a {B} rating.

toil of all kinds, and it implies more energy, persistence, and fatigue than mere 'work' (ἔργον)."[38] Paul uses κόπος two other times in 1 Thessalonians, in both instances with reference to the type of ministry Paul had among the Thessalonians (2:9; 3:5). The cognate verb κοπιάω is used of the community leaders (5:12).[39] Clearly, there is an emphasis on work in 1 Thessalonians.

Paul is particularly concerned to establish his *ethos* in the second part of the *exordium* of the letter: "You know what kind of men we proved to be among you for your sake" (1:5). This is elaborated in 2:1-12 where Paul notes his blameless moral conduct (2:3, 5-6, 9-10; cf. 4:1-7), his accountability towards God (2:5; cf. 4:1), and his encouragement and exhortation (2:7-8, 11-12; cf. 4:1, 18; 5:11).[40] In the midst of this he emphasizes the nature of his ministry among the Thessalonians: "For you remember our labor (τὸν κόπον) and toil (τὸν μόχθον), brethren; we worked night and day (νυκτὸς καὶ ἡμέρας ἐργαζόμενοι), that we might not burden any of you, while we preached to you the gospel of God" (2:9). In using the verb ἐργάζομαι, Paul is clearly indicating manual labor. The combination of κόπος and μόχθος indicates that the labor was physically challenging. Used together, they suggest "fatigue and weariness, hardship and distress."[41] Paul does not underplay but in fact highlights his own manual labor in the midst of establishing his *ethos*. Later Paul encourages the Thessalonians to continue to live in a manner pleasing to God "as you

---

[38] Plummer, *Thessalonians*, 8; LSJ *s.v.* Paul uses κόπος three times in 1 Thess and only seven times elsewhere (six in the Corinthian correspondence [1 Cor 3:8; 15:58; 2 Cor 6:5; 10:15; 11:23, 27] and once in Gal 6:17; cf. 2 Thess 3:8). The two words ἔργον and κόπος are only used in combination one other time by Paul, in 1 Cor 15:58, although the verb κοπιάω is used with the noun ἔργον in describing the Thessalonian leaders in 1 Thess 5:12-13; see 1 Cor 4:12 where κοπιάω is used with ἐργάζομαι; cf. Eph 4:28; Col 1:29 (ἐνεργέω).

[39] Paul uses κοπιάω eight times elsewhere: Rom 16:6, 12 (2x); 1 Cor 4:12; 15:10; 16:16; Gal 4:11; Phil 2:16.

[40] Cf. G. Lyons, *Pauline Autobiography: Towards a New Understanding* (SBLDS 73; Atlanta: Scholars Press, 1985) 189-201 for a detailed examination. Lyons concludes that "[t]he autobiographical remarks in 1 Thessalonians function parenthetically to remind Paul's converts of the Christian ethical values they share, as embodied in the ethos of their *typos*" (*Pauline Autobiography*, 221).

[41] Collins, *Birth*, 11. Together the words suggest that the labor continued on for some time, certainly longer than the three-week stay indicated by Acts 17.

learned from us" (4:1) and exhorts them to "work with your hands" (ἐργάζεσθαι ταῖς [ἰδίαις]⁴² χερσὶν ὑμῶν, 4:11).⁴³

In antiquity an artisan's life was not easy, but it was not the worst place to be in the social strata. Some artisans could rise to modest affluence and thus have money to spend. The majority could expect to earn enough each day for "a little bread and smoked fish," and thus feed their family, but savings were out of the question.⁴⁴ Artisans were lower rank and their work was considered slavish, even if they themselves were freeborn, as was the case with Paul. Bending over to work was considered a slavish position that no self-respecting elite person would willingly assume. A free man who took up a trade was viewed as having done something humiliating. Plying a trade was denigrated as it left no time for building friendships or developing one's virtue. Thus, artisans were considered incapable of attaining virtue or they were viewed as uneducated. Of course, many trades were harmful to the body, either by their requirement of physical exertion or by their sedentary character.

Artisans were "stigmatized as slavish, uneducated, and often useless" and "were frequently abused, often victimized, seldom if ever invited to dinner, and never accorded status."⁴⁵ Paul describes his own situation as

---

⁴² The word ἰδίαις is omitted in a number of important mss: the second corrector of א, B, the original hand of D, F G Ψ, 6, 104, 365, 1175, 1739, 1881, pc, sy^h. It is included in the Byzantine texts, along with the original hand of א, A, and the first corrector of D. The two readings have essentially equal weight in external evidence and internal criteria are not very helpful. The omission in the original would not much affect the meaning of the phrase.

⁴³ In doing so he uses a phrase similar to that of 1 Cor 4:12 where he states that he worked with his own hands (ἐργαζόμενοι ταῖς ἰδίαις χερσίν). There is a difference in the two uses. In 1 Cor 4:12 Paul's handwork is linked to his hardships as an apostle and serves as a contrast to the Corinthians' claim to wisdom and riches. In 1 Thessalonians Paul is not contrasting the recipients with himself.

⁴⁴ Hock, *Social Context*, 35; M. I. Finley, *The Ancient Economy* (Berkeley: University of California Press, 1973) 73. Lucian (*Fug.* 12) illustrates this well: "Their trades, however, were petty, laborious, and barely able to supply them with just enough" (LCL).

⁴⁵ Hock, *Social Context*, 36; cf. Joshel, *Work, Idenity, and Legal Status*, 63-69; P. Garnsey, "Non-slave Labor in the Roman World," in *Non-slave Labor in the Greco-Roman World*, ed. P. Garnsey, (Cambridge Philological Society Suppl. 6; Cambridge: Cambridge Philological Society, 1980) 35. MacMullen's "lexicon of snobbery" suggests that "[o]ccupations having to do with money or 'trade' are looked down on" (*Roman Social Relations*, 138-41; cf. 114-16; Grant, *Early Christianity*, 81). On later Jewish and Christian attitudes to various occupations see Grant, *Early Christianity*, 79-87. Cf. Plutarch's comment, "while we delight in the work [of craftsmen and artisans], we

enslavement (1 Cor 9:19) and a humiliation (2 Cor 11:7) and says he is without status (1 Cor 4:10) and reviled (1 Cor 4:12); probably much of this stems from his being an artisan.[46] Thus, Paul's claiming to work "night and day" and his "exhausting toil" (1 Thess 2:9) are not exaggerations but reflect the conditions of artisans in the first century. His chosen profession combined with his itinerancy probably accounts for his hardships recounted in the *peristasis* catalogues: hungry and thirsty (1 Cor 4:11; 2 Cor 6:5; 11:27), cold (2 Cor 11:27), naked (1 Cor 4:11; 2 Cor 11:27), and tired (2 Cor 6:5; 11:27).[47]

Despite this generally negative attitude towards manual labor, in 1 Thessalonians Paul's language about work reflects a more positive attitude, a clear indication of where to locate the Thessalonians on the social map of antiquity. We saw earlier that Paul's central message in 1 Thessalonians is to reaffirm to the Christians at Thessalonica that they are his "glory" and his "joy" (2:20). Throughout the letter Paul suggests that

---

despise the workman... for it does not of necessity follow that, if the work delights you with its graces, the one who wrought it is worthy of your esteem" (*Pericles* 1.4-2.2, LCL).

[46] Hock (*Social Context*, 66) is correct in suggesting that Paul's tentmaking cannot be attributed to "his taking up a rabbinic ideal of combining study of Torah with the practice of trade" and thus seen by him as positive. Rather, Paul saw his trade as a necessary, but not positive, part of his apostolic self-understanding – he was able to "boast in his weakness as an artisan" (Hock, *Social Context*, 67). This is due to Paul's social standing; Paul came from a rank which considered working at a trade "slavish and demeaning," namely, the provincial aristocratic class, and he reflects such an attitude in 1 Cor 9:19 and 2 Cor 11:7 (R. F. Hock, "Paul's Tentmaking and the Problem of His Social Class," *JBL* 97 [1978] 555-64). There are different functions between Paul's comments in 1 Cor 4:9-13 and those in 1 Thess 2:9 concerning his working with his hands. In 1 Cor 4:12 Paul is defending his practice and urges the Corinthians to imitate him in his humility as a means to overcoming the competition for honour (and thus the divisions) within the community. It is part of Paul's ideal that as a Christian he "boasts in his weakness." The gospel of Christ overturns the typical (for antiquity) categories of honour and shame. This is an important claim within a congregation composed of persons of mixed rank. In 1 Thess 2:9 and 4:11 Paul expresses no defense of the practice of manual labour but assumes that the community will not question his own or their own participation in it. The rhetorical function of 1 Thess 2:9 in its context illustrates the intimate relationship that Paul and his coworkers shared with the Thessalonians. It is part of his *ethos*; their motives were not impure (2:5-6) and they did not act improperly (2:9-10). This is in contrast to Corinth where Paul's manual labor seems to have been understood as Paul acting "improperly," although an impropriety of a different sort.

[47] The artisan's life explains Paul's need to rely on the patronage of others such as Phoebe (Rom 16:1-2; Whelan, "Amica Pauli") and the Philippian church (Phil 4:10-20; 2 Cor 11:9).

they share his own social level and are themselves manual workers.[48] To be placed in such a low ranking category as manual worker if one occupied a higher rank would represent not praise but denigration and dishonour; certainly it would be grounds to reject Paul and his message. In fact, it would represent a challenge to one's honour that could not go unanswered. Paul would not gain friends but make enemies with such bold claims if they were being made among the elite. Thus, the Thessalonians must be among the lower rank persons of ancient society. That Paul does not disparage but rather commends work confirms that the Thessalonians are themselves manual workers.[49]

Presumably Paul and the Thessalonians worked at the same trade or trades within the same general area, thus facilitating contact between Paul and the Thessalonians.[50] And it was "while" at work that Paul preached the

---

[48] Those who understand the Thessalonians to be manual workers include Frame, *Thessalonians*, 6; Rigaux, *Thessaloniciens*, 521; Best, *Thessalonians*, 176; Hock, *Social Context*, 42-47; Meeks, *First Urban Christians*, 64-5; Jewett, *Thessalonian Correspondence*, 120-21; Russell, "Social Problem," 111-12; Schöllgen, "sozialstruktur," 76; Kloppenborg, ""ΦΙΛΑΔΕΛΦΙΑ," 267; Murphy-O'Connor, *Paul*, 117; de Vos, *Community Conflicts*, 154; Malherbe, *Thessalonians*, 65. Jewett (*Thessalonian Correspondence*, 120) points out that this was noted as early as the nineteenth century by G. Lünemann, *Critical and Exegetical Handbook to the Epistles of St. Paul to the Thessalonians* (Edinburgh: T. & T. Clark, 1880) 123. Cf. R. Jewett, "Tenement Churches and Communal Meals in the Early Church: The Implications of a Form-Critical Analysis of 2 Thessalonians 3:10," *BR* 38 (1993) 23-31 who shows that early Christians in Rome were mostly slaves and lower rank manual workers.

[49] Barclay ("Conflict," 519) argues against Jewett's view (*Thessalonian Correspondence*, 118-23) that the Thessalonians were impoverished manual workers as it is based on "somewhat flimsy evidence." He suggests that "all that Paul's injunctions show is that *he* assumes that work means work with one's hands. This is hardly a reliable basis for a social profile of the congregation." ("Conflict," 519 n. 23, his emphasis). He overlooks the fact that in identifying himself and the Thessalonians with handwork there are clear social indicators implied for the first century audience. Were they not in such a class Paul would lose his point in the negative reaction to his rhetoric by those who considered themselves to be above this particular social location. Cf. Hock, who notes that moral philosophers who write on work are often "encouraging those who were not privileged, that is the urban poor, to work for their living" (*Social Context*, 44).

[50] Hock (*Social Context*, 46-47) suggests that Paul's injunction to "work with your hands" (1 Thess 4:11) is meant to encourage the Thessalonian workers to choose suitable occupations. It is odd that, given his description of tradespeople working together at the same trade, and a Pauline missionary strategy of preaching while working, that Hock would not conclude that the Thessalonians already have a chosen profession, one that they share with Paul and with one another. Rather than look for a reason why Paul needs to "instruct" and "remind" the Thessalonians to find suitable work (Hock, *Social Context*,

gospel[51] and presumably made his initial converts. Thus, the core of the Thessalonian community was comprised of hand-workers who shared Paul's trade.[52] Unfortunately, Paul does not state the nature of his manual labour in 1 Thessalonians or elsewhere. However, Acts 18:3 suggests that Paul was a σκηνοποιός.[53] It has a basic meaning of "tentmaker," but since tents were made primarily of leather, it could indicate that Paul was more generally a leather worker.[54]

As an itinerant worker Paul probably worked in one of the local shops at Thessalonica. Since Paul was there "night and day" he would have used the opportunity to share his gospel message with fellow-workers and customers, the former being the most likely candidates for proselytizing.[55]

---

43), the passage can be understood as an encouragement to continue what they are already doing. This certainly fits better with the context (4:9-12).

[51] The participial clause in 1 Thess 2:9 is best translated, "working day and night we proclaimed to you the gospel of God" (Collins, *Birth*, 220 n. 69).

[52] Cf. Acts 19:9 where Luke refers to Paul, upon having left the synagogue at Ephesus, teaching in the σχολή. While this is usually thought to be a lecture hall, and thus evidence for Paul being a wandering philosopher, Malherbe (*Social Aspects*, 90) observes that the word is a common designation for a guildhall. Such guildhalls were frequently named after the patron of the guild. Thus, Luke might be presenting a picture of the early church at Ephesus as a guild that meets in the σχολή of Tyrannos (Liebenam, *Organisation*, 272 n. 4; Ellis, *Pauline Theology*, 139). While in Ephesus Paul not only teaches but works at his trade suggesting frequent contact with workers who could have formed the core of the Ephesian church (Malherbe, *Social Aspects*, 90-91).

[53] According to Lüdemann, Acts 18:2-3 and Paul's connection in Corinth with Aquila and Pricilla is "a singular and quite untendentious report" suggesting that the tradition of Paul the σκηνοποιός is fairly reliable. G. Lüdemann, *Early Christianity According to the Traditions in Acts: A Commentary* (Minneapolis: Fortress, 1987) 198.

[54] Hock, *Social Context*, 20-21, 72. W. Michaelis ("μιμέομαι, κτλ," *TDNT* 4 [1967] 394) notes that some patristic writers read σκυτοτόμος ("leather-worker") for σκηνοποιός at Acts 18:3 (see also BAGD *s.v.*). Goat hair was used to make fabric that could be weaved into, among other things, tents (Michaelis, "μιμέομαι," 394). Thus, some (F. F. Bruce, *Paul: Apostle of the Heart Set Free* (Grand Rapids: Eerdmans, 1977) 36; Theissen, *Social Setting*, 105) have suggested that Paul was a weaver. However, as Raymond Collins (*Birth*, 12) points out, the rabbis despised weaving so it is an unlikely trade for Paul to take up. Within the range of leather working, Paul was probably not a tanner as Jews considered it to be an unclean occupation. Murphy-O'Connor (*Paul*, 117) accepts the traditional ascription of "leather-worker" suggesting that "there must have been a considerable demand for tents and other leather articles in a city which had so many traveling merchants."

[55] Cf. de Vos, *Community Conflicts*, 153: n. 110. On Paul's use of the workshop in his mission strategy see further R. F. Hock, "The Workshop as a Social Setting for Paul's Missionary Preaching." *CBQ* 41 (1979) 438-43. For a brief overview of the talking while working in antiquity see also Collins, *Birth*, 13-14. Socrates is said to have

Such workers were likely already involved in some form of professional association. If Paul "worked with his hands" as a leather worker, he might be drawn to such an association. Although no leather-workers' guilds are attested in Macedonia, there is evidence for them elsewhere. For example, a first-century CE inscription from Phrygia (*IGRR* 907) records honours bestowed by "the most venerable guild of leather-workers." In Lydia an association of leather-workers set up an honourary inscription at a member's tomb (*SEG* XXIX1183). At Termessus (Pisidia) a guild of leather-workers erected a statue to their benefactor (IPisidia 93).[56]

3. The Thessalonians and the Voluntary Associations

a) Leadership Structure

Within the Macedonian voluntary association inscriptions, as with associations generally, we noted that a number of different officials are attested, although there is no consistency in the terms used for these officials. Turning to 1 Thessalonians we see that there is clearly some leadership in the Thessalonian Christian community. Paul makes reference to unnamed leaders by encouraging the Thessalonians "to respect those who labour among you and are over you (προϊσταμένους) in the Lord and admonish you, and to esteem them very highly in love because of their work" (5:12-13). Paul uses a general designation for such leaders as those who are "over" others (προϊστημι), indicating a group of persons who have a special function within the congregation.[57]

---

conversed with Simon the shoemaker in Simon's workshop (see Hock, "Workshop," 438); tradition has it that Socrates spent much of his time in a variety of workshops (Xenophon, *Mem.* 4.2.1-39; 3.10.1-15) and in the marketplace (Plato, *Ap.* 17C). In this way, philosophical discourse was kept open and public. It became less so when Plato and Antisthenes chose to teach in the gymnasia.

[56] Guilds associated with the leather trade are also attested at Thyatira, Mitylene, Ephesos, Philadelphia (see R. J. Forbes, *Studies in Ancient Technology*, vol. 5 [Leiden: Brill, 1966²] 57) and Rome and Ostia (Forbes, *Ancient Technology*, 54-55).

[57] Rigaux, *Thessaloniciens*, 576-78; Best, "Bishops and Deacons," 372; cf. Laub, "Gemeindegründer," 33; Hainz, *Ekklesia*, 38-39. Wanamaker's suggestion that they are patrons and exercise authority by virtue of their wealth is unlikely as they are not named and thus not honoured (unlike the other illustrations he uses; *Thessalonians*, 193; also Jewett, *Thessalonian Correspondence*, 103). Such patronage is discouraged in 1 Thess 4:9-12. The designation ὁ προεστώς can be used as a title, as is found in an inscription from an association (συμβίωσις) of male worshippers of the Dioscurii: καὶ τῇ

Paul uses the cognate verb of κόπος to refer to one of the responsibilities of these leaders The noun occurs twice elsewhere in the letter, once for Paul's manual labor among the Thessalonians (2:9) and once for his work at the formative stages of the community (3:5). It is likely that the leaders at Thessalonica continued with both kinds of activity, the manual labor alongside community members and the labor of community formation.[58] If so, the leaders of the Thessalonians are like the leaders of many voluntary associations. They are chosen from within the association itself and carry on with their everyday tasks as workers while having some authority in official meetings of the association. It reflects a willingness on Paul's part to allow his Christian communities to develop locally and without a preconceived notion of "church leadership" imposed upon them.[59] That the leaders in the community are unnamed does not indicate that Paul does not know them so much as that the leadership positions might have rotated on a monthly or yearly basis, as was common in the associations. Paul leaves them unnamed so that the general exhortation will be applicable to any who are in a position of leadership.[60]

b) Internal Community Relationships

Locating the Thessalonian Christian community in the context of the voluntary associations helps explain Paul's injunction that the Thessalonians νουθετεῖτε τοὺς ἀτάκτους (5:14).[61] Ἄτακτος and its cognates can have various meanings including "moral wrong-doing," "idleness from work," and "disorderliness."[62] Some commentators understand ἄτακτος in 1 Thess 5:14 to mean "lazy" or "idle" (that is, those who will not work) based on Paul's injunction in 4:11 and references to the idle in 2 Thess 3:6-11.[63] If this is the case, then it is clear that Paul is

---

Διοσκουριτῶν συμβιώσει ἀνδρῶν, προεστῶτος Τελεσφορίωνος, γραμματεύοντος Ἀκληπιάδου (*CIG* 3540, Pergamon; Ellis, *Pauline Theology*, 135).

[58] Not simply "Christian" κόπος, as Hainz seems to suggest (*Ekklesia*, 43-44).

[59] Laub, "Gemeindegründer," 32.

[60] Cf. Laub points out that Paul does not address the leaders directly but addresses the entire community ("Gemeindegründer," 32-33; also Hainz, *Ekklesia*, 47).

[61] Paul singles out the "fainthearted" and the "weak" as being in need of special attention.

[62] See LSJ *s.v.*; Moulton and Milligan, *Vocabulary*, 89; cf. C. Spicq, "Les Thessaloniciens 'inquiets' étaient-ils des paresseux?" *StTh* 10 (1956) 1-8.

[63] Milligan, *Thessalonians*, 152-54; Frame, *Thessalonians*, 196-97; W. Neil, *The Epistle of Paul to the Thessalonians* (MNTC; London: Hodder and Stoughton, 1950) 124;

writing to those whom others in the group could reasonably expect to be working, namely, other workers. As such, it fits well within the context of a workers' association, particularly those of the same trade (and perhaps even the same workshop) for whom the lack of a number of fellow-workers would require increased output on their behalf and would certainly strain community relations.[64]

Best, *Thessalonians*, 230 (who seems uncertain); Bruce, *Thessalonians*, 122-23; Wanamaker, *Thessalonians*, 196-97; Williams, *Thessalonians*, 96-97. The only New Testament occurrence of ἄτακτος is 1 Thess 5:14. In the New Testament 2 Thess 3:7 is the only occurrence of ἀτακτέω and 2 Thess 3:6 and 11 the only occurrences of ἀτάκτως. Those who understand ἀτάκτως/ἀτακτέω in 2 Thess 3:6-12 as "disorderly" include Rigaux, *Thessaloniciens*, 704-05; Bruce, *Thessalonians*, 205; Jewett, *Thessalonian Correspondence*, 104-05; Collins, *Birth*, 94; Menken, *2 Thessalonians*, 130-33; Williams (*Thessalonians*, 144) uses "idle" and "disorderly" interchangeably. Donfried suggests that it is best rendered "ill-ordered" or "not well-ordered," and indicates a problem within the congregation of some claiming a charismatic authority which places them in leadership over others ("2 Thessalonians," 141-42; Russell, "Social Problem," 107-08). Since there are obvious contextual references to manual labor (3:7-8, 10, 12), and since ἀτάκτως/ἀτακτέω is used in contexts of manual labor for "idle" or "non-workers" (Moulton and Milligan, *Vocabulary*, 89) this would seem to be the most obvious reference point in this passage (so Frame, *Thessalonians*, 299; Neil, *Thessalonians*, 192-93; Masson, *Thessaloniciens*, 112; Best, *Thessalonians*, 333-34; Wanamaker, *Thessalonians*, 282). The writer is addressing those who refuse to work, and exhorts them to work for their living (3:12). Delling notes that it is not just a reference to laziness but to an avoidance of work obligations through other tasks (what we might term procrastination); "outside Christianity the verb, when applied to work, does not in the first instance lay emphasis on sloth but rather on an irresponsible attitude to the obligation to work" ("ἄτακτος, κτλ.," *TDNT* 8 [1972] 48). This seems to be the way Richard understands it (*Thessalonians*, 379). For speculations on why some of the Thessalonian Christians might have given up working (based on the assumption that 2 Thess is authentic) see Malherbe, *Paul and the Thessalonians*, 101 (they have become cynic preachers), Russell, "Social Problem," 108 (due to unemployment at Thessalonica), Marshall, *Thessalonians*, 223 (disdain for manual labor), B. W. Winter, "'If Any Man Does Not Wish to Work...' A Cultural and Historical Setting for 2 Thessalonians 3:6-16," *TynBul* 40 (1989) 312 (their reliance upon benefaction), Barclay, "Conflict," 522-24 (undertaking aggressive evangelism).

[64] This is how we understood the use of the cognates in 2 Thess 3:6-12 (see previous note) but it need not carry the same meaning here. "There is nothing in the immediate context of our verse [1 Thess 5:14] to suggest which meaning Paul has in mind; that he uses the root in one sense on a later occasion does not imply that he must have so used it earlier when on *a priori* grounds there is an equally probable meaning" (Best, *Thessalonians*, 230; cf. Richard, *Thessalonians*, 270). These comments are even more apropos if we are considering the works of two different writers.

A number of scholars understand ἄτακτος to indicate undisciplined or disorderly actions or persons.⁶⁵ In general, the word indicates "standing against the order or nature of God," and in military contexts it is used of those who would not follow commands or who broke rank.⁶⁶ The use in 1 Thessalonians suggests to some commentators that a number of the Thessalonian Christians have given up working and are trespassing social boundaries because they perceive the parousia to be near.⁶⁷ Jewett suggests that they are "obstinate resisters of authority" and turns to 2 Thess 3:6-15 to suggest that they have given up their occupations and are relying on other members of the congregation for support.⁶⁸ Jewett is correct that "[t]here is no evidence in this passage that the motivation of their behavior was laziness," a false inference, he suggests, from Paul's own example of his self-sufficiency.⁶⁹ Neither does Jewett make a strong case that the ἄτκατοι are directly challenging the leadership of the Christian community, an inference based on military contexts.⁷⁰

In almost all interpretations the eschatological context determines for the interpreter who Paul addresses as the ἄτκατοι in 1 Thess 5:14, although generally 2 Thessalonians is immediately introduced into the argument.⁷¹ Such an exegetical move is not necessary. The context of 1

---

⁶⁵ Plummer, *Thessalonians*, 94; Rigaux, *Thessaloniciens*, 582-83; Marshall, *Thessalonians*, 150; Jewett, *Thessalonian Correspondence*, 104-05; Collins, *Birth*, 94; Richard, *Thessalonians*, 270; Malherbe, *Thessalonians*, 317. A close connection was often made between laziness and disorderliness so the term might indicate both. Collins suggests that this group of "disorderly" were the "only distinct group of Thessalonians identified by Paul" (*Birth*, 95, citing also Holtz, *Thessalonicher*, 250-15; U. Schnelle, "Die Ethik des 1. Thessalonicherbriefes," in *The Thessalonian Correspondence*, ed. R. F. Collins [BETL 87; Louvain: Louvain University Press, 1990] 299), but this assumes a technical designation for ἄτακτοι and overlooks Paul's reference to the leaders in 5:12, as well as the "faint-hearted" and "weak" in 5:14.

⁶⁶ Plummer, *Thessalonians*, 94; Jewett, *Thessalonian Correspondence*, 104.

⁶⁷ Marxsen 1979:71; Jewett, *Thessalonian Correspondence*, 104-05.

⁶⁸ Jewett, *Thessalonian Correspondence*, 105.

⁶⁹ Jewett, *Thessalonian Correspondence*, 105.

⁷⁰ The best evidence comes from the reference in 5:12 to leaders who admonish the Thessalonians (νουθετουντας ὑμας) and the injunction that the Thessalonians admonish (νουθετεῖτε) the ἄτακτοι in 5:14 (not mentioned by Jewett). This is tenuous at best and Paul's words in both verses need to be seen as directed to the congregation as whole. The first reference need not indicate that the function of the leaders is to admonish the idle.

⁷¹ Cf. Richard, *Thessalonians*, 270. Jewett (*Thessalonian Correspondence*, 135-47) gives a lengthy analysis of a number of models that have been used to understand the community situation at Thessalonica. Jewett himself suggests that the sociological designation of a millenarian movement best describes the Thessalonian Christians

Thess 5:12-22 and the shift at 5:11 from the *probatio* to the *peroratio* means that the preceding discussion of eschatology need not frame the discussion of the ἄτκατοι in 1 Thessalonians.[72] In fact, 1 Thess 5:12-22 seems to be concerned with internal community relationships and one cannot simply bracket out the ἄτκατοι as a separate problem. They are part of Paul's concern that the members of the community coexist well together, encouraging one another (5:11, 14) and the leaders (5:12), being considerate of others ("faint-hearted," "weak"), and worshipping God properly, not in a context of personal piety (as the following is most often read) but of communal piety:

> Rejoice always, pray constantly, give thanks in all circumstances; for this is the will of God in Christ Jesus for you. Do not quench the Spirit, do not despise prophesying, but test everything; hold fast to what is good, abstain from every form of evil. (5:16-22)

(*Thessalonian Correspondence*, 161-71). The most telling point against Jewett's hypothesis is his admission that "the Thessalonian situation is rather atypical of other millenarian movements" in that opposition and the death of some members led to a "crisis of morale" (*Thessalonian Correspondence*, 176). One would expect, as Jewett points out, that this would intensify the movement, as it does in millenarian movements generally. Moreover, although Jewett suggests much of the letter is addressed to issues raised by the presence of the ἄτακτοι they are only singled out as a problematic group near the end of the letter, very briefly and among the "faint-hearted" and "weak," *all* of whom the Thessalonians are told to be patient with. This is hardly what one would expect for such a group of troublemakers as Jewett constructs. Jewett himself assumes that apocalypticism is the dominant theme not only of the letter but within the congregation. However, this is based more on his reading of 2 Thess, which he understands to be authentic. Thus, he describes the Thessalonians as, for example, "a charismatic, apocalyptic congregation in the Greco-Roman culture that had experienced a world-shaking conversion from paganism" (*Thessalonian Correspondence*, 141). This mixed description assumes both that charism and apocalypticism was unknown outside of Christian/Jewish circles (untrue) and that "world-shaking conversion" has to do with such beliefs rather than a reconfiguring of previous social relationships. He chides some scholars for assuming that the Thessalonian Christians were an amorphous, low-intensity community (*Thessalonian Correspondence*, 141), but his own assumptions indicate that they must have been fairly dull lot as pagans! Jewett points out the modern church models read back in to the Thessalonians' situation by other scholars but does not seem to have escaped it himself; his model seems to be that of modern North American evangelicals converted from nominal Christian backgrounds and now focused on the soon coming return of Jesus.

[72] The same is true of 2 Thess 3:6-13.

With this communal context in mind, we turn to the voluntary associations.[73] A number of inscriptions show that the voluntary associations often struggled with the problem of disorderly behavior, so much so that legislation was introduced to limit it, and fines and corporal punishment were used to enforce the legislation. For example, the second century CE rule of the Iobakkoi (*IG* II² 1368; Athens) uses the verb ἀκοσμέω, a synonym of ἀτακτέω,[74] in reference to those who disrupt a meeting.

> If anyone begins a fight or if someone is found disorderly (εὑρεθῇ τις ἀκοσμῶν), or if someone comes and sits in someone else's seat or is insulting or abuses someone else... the one who committed the insult or the abuse shall pay to the association 25 drachmae and the one who was the cause of the fight shall pay the same 25 drachmae or not come to any more meetings of the Iobakkoi until he pays. (lines 72-83)

In lines 136-146 ἀκοσμέω is used again in a similar context. Anyone who causes a disturbance at a meeting is indicated by the touch of an officials θύρος[75] and is required to leave the feast. Should one so designated refuse to leave, "bouncers" (ἵπποι) were in place to remove physically such persons, who then also became liable to the same punishment stipulated earlier for those who fight.

In the regulations of the mysteries of Andania (*IG* V/1 1390; 96 BCE) there is a section entitled "Concerning the Disorderly" (ἀκοσμούντων) which reads,

---

[73] de Vos (*Community Conflicts*, 157-73, esp. 166-68) links the use of ἄτακτοι to voluntary associations, but does so in terms of associations involved in civil disobedience as a response to repression, not in terms of internal disruptions within the group itself. However, the evidence for professional associations undertaking civil action is quite limited; see Fisher, "Roman Associations," 1222; Kloppenborg, "Collegia and Thiasoi," 19-20.

[74] That ἀτακτέω and ἀκοσμέω can be used synonymously can be seen in Suidas' *Lexicon* entry for ἄκοσμα which lists simply "ἀπρεπῆ, ἄτακτα." Plutarch uses the cognates synonymously in describing the universe, noting that there is nothing unplaced or unorganized (ἄτακτον οὐδ᾽ ἀκατακόσμητον) left over to crash into the existing worlds (*Def. Orac.* 424 A, LCL). In describing one who must evidence repentance Philo notes that a person must avoid "great gatherings" (τοὺς τῶν πολλῶν θιάσους) since "a crowd (ὄχλος) is another name for everything that is disorderly (ἄτακτον), indecorous (ἄκοσμον), discordant (πλημμελές), culpable (ὑπαίτιον)" (*Praem. Poen.* 20, LCL). When writing of matter and its relationship to God, Origen refers at one point to matter being in a state of confusion and disorder (ἦν δὲ ἄτακτος ἡ ὕλη καὶ ἀκόσμητος, *Philocal.* 24.1), using the words as synonyms.

[75] It is unclear whether this is a simple touch or a significant blow.

whenever the sacrifices and mysteries are celebrated, let everyone keep silent and listen to the things announced. And let the officers flog the disobedient and those who live indecently and prevent them from (participating) in the mysteries" (lines 39-41).

Such inscriptions give some indication of the type of disturbances that could occur at a meeting (fighting, disruptions of order and ceremony, abuse of others), along with guidance on how to deal with such disturbances (fines and floggings).[76] Paul's use of ἄτακτοι indicates that some in the Thessalonian Christian community are disorderly, but this is not a challenge to the leadership from a "breakaway" group. It involves disruptions and disturbances within the context of worship.[77] Paul's injunction, "see that none of you repays evil for evil, but always seek to do good to one another and to all," following his "be patient with them all"

---

[76] In Macedonia a gymnasiarchal law from Beroea legislates against disobedient, unruly behavior using the word ἀτακτέω (text published by J. M. R. Cormack, "The Gymnasiarchal Law of Beroea," in *Ancient Macedonia* 2, ed. B. Laourdas and Ch. Makaronas [Institute for Balkan Studies 155; Thessalonica: Institute for Balkan Studies, 1977] 139-50; cf. Horsley, *New Documents* 4, 104). From Amphipolis the fragment of a military code from *ca.* 200 BCE seems to refer to the need to control soldiers who are intent on looting (*SEG* XXXX no. 524 fr. A, col. 2, lines 1-3; cf. Spicq, "Thessaloniciens," 6 and nn. 2 and 3). Problems with the disorderly occurred within the public cults. A fourth century BCE regulation for the festival of the Artemisia requires that the presidents of the games conduct the games in a just manner and fine those who are disorderly (τὸν ἀτακτέοντα; *IG* XII/9 189; Eretria). In a public procession from the temple of Athena (*CIG* 3599, Ilion, II BCE) the regulations stipulate that "there are to be appointed two men who are to take care that there is good order [in the procession] and those who have been appointed are to have power to beat with a rod those who are disorderly (τοὺς ἀτακτοῦντας)" (lines 27-29). One frequently meets the "rod-bearers" in the inscriptions from public cults and private associations, and even, according to Acts 16:35, 38, at Philippi where the magistrates use them as a go-between with the jailer.

[77] Cf. Spicq, "Thessaloniciens," 11-12; B. Reicke, "Thessalonicherbriefe," *RGG* 6 (1962) cols. 851-53. Reicke also connects the ἄτακτοι to the associations, but does so in the context of their eschatological enthusiasm ("Schwärmerei"), and particularly Paul's reference to "drinking" in 1 Thess 5:7 (*Diakonie, Festfreude, und Zelos in Verbindung mit der altchristlichen Agapenfeier* [Uppsala Universitets Årsskrift 1951, 5; Uppsala and Wiesbaden: Lundequist and Harrassowitz, 1951] 242-43, 247). He moves quickly to emphasize that the ἄτακτοι were also lazy and living the "parasitic" life, drawing almost immediately upon 2 Thess 3:6-16 (pp. 243-44). He concludes, "dass die soziale Unordnung in Thessalonich ein Ausdruck der eschatologischen Überspanntheit war, oder der Schwärmerei" (p. 245). Later in the same work Reicke details the community problems encountered in the associations (*Diakonie*, 321-38), but does not tie it in explicitly to his earlier discussion of Paul's Christian communities ("Zum Teil fällt das Licht rückwärts auf die oben behandelten paulinischen Briefe," *Diakonie*, 338).

(including the ἄτακτοι) indicates that verbal admonishing should suffice to stem disorderliness rather than fines and flogging.

In 1 Thess 4:11 Paul encourages the Thessalonians φιλοτιμεῖσθαι ἡσυχάζειν.[78] In doing so he uses a term frequent in association inscriptions but he gives it a different nuance. The verb φιλοτιμέομαι, and the cognate noun, φιλοτιμία, are used in association inscriptions in contexts quite different from injunctions to "live quietly." These words are used for the competition and rivalry for honour within the association itself.[79] The quest for honours was promoted as a means of encouraging members to contribute more and more lavishly to the social practices of the association. For example, in *IG* II² 1263 (Piraeus, 300 BCE) the secretary of an association is honoured with the erection of a statue, "so that also the others shall be zealous for honour (φιλοτιμῶνται) among the members, knowing that they will receive thanks from the members deserving of benefaction" (lines 27-31).[80] In the second century CE at Athens an association of male friends (ἔφανον σύναγον φίλοι ἄνδρες) proclaimed, "let the association increase by zeal for honour" (αὐξανέτω δὲ ὁ ἔρανος ἐπὶ φιλοτειμίαις, *IG* II² 1369). For Paul, in contrast, the "quest for honour" is found in a community of mutual co-existence, not a life of competition with one another for honour.[81]

Thus, although there are some similarities between the Thessalonian Christian community and the voluntary associations, Paul reflects a desire for a community *ethos* different from that found in the associations. It is still significant that Paul *uses* voluntary association language to produce this different community *ethos*. Paul uses association language self-consciously to encourage a different type of social control (without fines

---

[78] Paul uses φιλοτιμέομαι in two other places, in Rom 15:20 of preaching the gospel and 2 Cor 5:9, of pleasing God.

[79] Cf. Kloppenborg, "Egalitarianism," 258. Φιλοτιμία can be used to describe the benefaction itself; see *IG* II² 1292 (Attica, III BCE) where crowns are awarded to the treasurer and secretary of the association of Sarapistai "so that there will be a rivalry among everyone to strive for honour"; cf. *IG* II² 1314 (Piraeus, 213/12 BCE); 1315 (Piraeus, 211/10 BCE); *IG* XII/5 606 (Ceos, III BCE); IDelos 1519 (153/52 BCE).

[80] Cf. *IG* II² 1271 (a *thiasos* in Piraeus 298/97 BCE); 1273.A (a *thiasos* in Piraeus 222/21 BCE); 1277 (a *koinon* in Athens, 278/77 BCE); 1292 (a *koinon* in Athens, c. 250 BCE).

[81] *Contra* the usual understanding of 1 Thess 4:11 as referring to individuals who should not rely on the support of others in the church: Milligan, *Thessalonians*, 55; Frame, *Thessalonians*, 163; Plummer, *Thessalonians*, 66; Neil, *Thessalonians*, 87-88; Best, *Thessalonians*, 177-78; Bruce, *Thessalonians*, 91-93; Wanamaker, *Thessalonians*, 164; Williams, *Thessalonians*, 78.

or floggings). Such usage suggests that the Thessalonian Christian community shares the same discursive field as the associations and is best placed within that field. That is, despite these differences in community relationships, they are still analogous to the voluntary associations.

c) Further Implications for Community Structure

The context of the voluntary associations raises an intriguing possibility concerning Paul's comments in 1 Thessalonians 1:9b, where he conveys to the Thessalonians the report that he has heard about them from others: "how you turned to God from idols, to serve a living and true God."[82] Most interpreters of 1 Thessalonians seem to understand the second person plural in 1:9b as a reference to individual conversion experiences initiated by Paul's preaching.[83] Ἐπιστρέφω literally means to "turn" or "turn back." It can be used with an ethical sense of obligation to do something that one has been asked or required to do (which can be acted upon or ignored)[84] or in the religious sense of turning to a deity.[85] In the LXX it is found particularly in the phrase ἐπιστρέφειν... κύριον (θεόν). Although it is rare in Paul, he does use it for conversion experiences in 2 Cor 3:16 (turning to the Lord, a citation from Exod 34:34) and in Gal 4:9

---

[82] Πῶς should be taken not as "how," that is as a description of the method of their becoming Christian, but as "that," indicative of their having done so (Best, *Thessalonians*, 81-82).

[83] We found no instances in which this was expressed, but it was certainly implied in the comments of many exegetes, esp. P. Perkins, "1 Thessalonians and Hellenistic Religious Practices," in *To Touch the Text: Biblical and Related Studies in Honour of Joseph A. Fitzmyer, S.J.*, ed. M. Hooker and P. Kobelski (New York: Crossroad, 1989) 325-34. Some, such as Williams (*Thessalonians*, 33, 35), suggest that a confirmation of the Acts account can be found here, thus indicating individual conversions. Holtz suggests that one can see behind 1:9 a mission sermon with an emphasis on monotheism like that in *Joseph and Aseneth*, a text which focuses on the conversion of an individual (*Thessalonicher*, 62). Malherbe looks to the LXX background of ἐπιστρέφω and discusses, among other passages, Hos 5:4, 6:1, and Joel 2:13, all of which involve the conversion of Israel *as a whole* to God (*Thessalonians*, 119). He draws upon the philosophical schools and ends up presenting an overall sense of individual conversions.

[84] See Moulton and Milligan, *Vocabulary*, 246; cf. G. Bertram, "στρέφω, κτλ.," *TDNT* 7 (1971) 722-23.

[85] Bertram, "στρέφω," 722-25; Richard, *Thessalonians*, 53.

(for Christians turning back to idols). The word ἐπιστρέφω "is a suitable word to express the change from one faith to another."[86]

As such, it is possible that Paul is referring to the collective experience of an already formed group of Thessalonians.[87] If Paul did preach among workers of the same trade (as we have suggested), they were undoubtedly part of a professional association of "handworkers" of the same trade and were thus involved in "idolatrous" worship.[88] Rather than envision a scenario in which Paul converted a number of individuals over time, a picture encouraged by the usual reading of Acts, we could imagine that over time Paul managed to persuade the members of the existing professional association to switch their allegiance from their patron deity or deities "to serve a living and true God."[89] In this case 1 Thessalonians 1:9b would be better paraphrased "you all turned (collectively) to God from idols."

The introduction of a new deity to an association is attested in a few cases in antiquity (e.g., *Syll.*[3] 985; *IG* X/2 255). Old allegiances die hard, and it would take some time to replace former patron deities with a new deity since in associations there would be no need for an exclusive switch;

---

[86] Best, *Thessalonians*, 82. For individual conversions see for example Acts 3:19; 11:21; 14:15; 15:19; 26:18. A collective conversion might be envisioned in Acts 9:35 "all the residents of Lydda and Sharon saw him, and they turned (ἐπέστρεψαν) to the Lord."

[87] Cf. Collins (*Studies*, 295) notes that in 1 Thess 1:6 (*sic*, 1:7) Paul calls the Thessalonians an example (singular) to other churches, indicating that "[i]t is not the believing individuals as such who are cited as examples for the believers of the Grecian provinces, rather it is the belief of the church as such which is exemplary."

[88] In antiquity εἴδωλον does not always carry such a pejorative sense and Gentiles often used it to describe that upon which they focused their worship (LSJ *s.v.*; Moulton and Milligan, *Vocabulary*, 183; F. Büchsel, "εἴδωλον, κτλ.," *TDNT* 2 [1964] 375-77).

[89] Kloppenborg suggests the transformation of an existing trade association at Thessalonica, although he does not pursue this idea ("ΦΙΛΑΔΕΛΦΙΑ," 276; cf. Kloppenborg, "Edwin Hatch," 235); cf. R. M. Evans, "Eschatology and Ethics: A Study of Thessalonica and Paul's Letters to the Thessalonians" (unpublished Th.D. Dissertation, Basel University, 1967) 89; Others who assume that the Thessalonians are a voluntary association include L. Fatum, "Brotherhood in Christ: A Gender Hermeneutical Reading of 1 Thessalonians," in *Constructing Early Christian Families: Family as Social Reality and Metaphor*, ed. H. Moxnes (London and New York: Routledge, 1997) 183-215; B. Ehrman, *Early Christian Writings*, 263 (although he also ties the community structure to the synagogue); de Vos, *Community Conflicts*, 164. de Vos suggests that "[t]o the average Thessalonian, the Christian community probably would have resembled a *thiasos*" (*Community Conflicts*, 153 n. 110), but he does not explore the details of the connections outside of civic disruptions by associations. He does allow for Kloppenborg's suggestion of a "converted trade *thiasos*."

more than one deity could be worshipped. For this reason there is no clear example of a voluntary association converting to the worship of a new deity accompanied by the disregarding of earlier allegiances. That the Thessalonians have done so stands out as unique. Perhaps this is the reason that they have been noted among other believers and that they have become a paradigm for imitation (1 Thess 1:7-9).

We may explain the lack of analogues in antiquity as a result of the aggressive missionary impulse of Pauline Christianity being a unique feature in antiquity as other groups were not concerned with conversion.[90] Groups that did undertake the worship of another god often broke away from earlier deities slowly as they were not faced with the same monotheistic demands that Paul's Christianity brought with it. While it is true that the text does not indicate the turning of an entire group to the veneration of Jesus, neither does it indicate what is assumed by most: individual conversions. The possibility of a group "conversion" should not be discounted too quickly.

Another intriguing possibility arises from the suggestion that the Thessalonian Christian community was formed as a professional association of "handworkers," perhaps tentmakers or leather-workers. If this were the case, we would expect that the group would be composed primarily of males, since women would not be members of an association of artisans in a trade dominated by males[91] even if they worked in the same occupation.[92] Most interpreters do not read 1 Thessalonians this way, but rather see the group as including both men and women.[93]

---

[90] M. Goodman, *Mission and Conversion: Proselytizing in the Religious History of the Roman Empire* (Oxford: Clarendon, 1994); S. McKnight, *A Light Among the Gentiles: Jewish Missionary Activity in the Second Temple Period* (Minneapolis: Fortress, 1991); summarized in Ascough, *Voluntary Associations*, 158-61.

[91] Waltzing, *corporations Professionnelles*, 1.348; Whelan, "Amica Pauli," 75-76; Schmeller, *Hierarchie und Egalität*, 48; Kloppenborg, "Collegia and *Thiasoi*," 25.

[92] S. Pomeroy, *Goddesses, Whores, Wives, and Slaves: Women in Classical Antiquity* (New York: Dorset, 1975) 201. Women could serve as *patrons* of all-male guilds, although they did not participate in them (see Kloppenborg, "Collegia and *Thiasoi*," 25; Whelan, "Amica Pauli," 76). Honourifics given to a woman patron by an association do not necessarily indicate that she is a member in the association (Waltzing, *corporations Professionnelles*, 1.349).

[93] This is particularly obvious in newer works which tend to translate ἀδελφός inclusively as "brothers and sisters"; see NRSV; Hainz, *Ekklesia*, 41 n. 5, 45; M. McGehee, "A Rejoinder to Two Recent Studies Dealing with 1 Thessalonians 4:4," *CBQ* 51 (1989) 82-89; Richard, *Thessalonians*, 128 and *passim*; Lührmann, "Beginnings," 247. We have little doubt that Paul elsewhere uses ἀδελφός inclusively and support such

There are some indications in 1 Thessalonians that the community was composed primarily of men. Clearly, there is no indication of women in the community and no advice is given to women, children, or families. Most telling is Paul's command to each member of the community: εἰδέναι ἕκαστον ὑμῶν τὸ ἑαυτοῦ σκεῦος κτᾶσθαι ἐν ἁγιασμῷ καὶ τιμῇ, μὴ ἐν πάθει ἐπιθυμίας καθάπερ καὶ τὰ ἔθνη τὰ μὴ εἰδότα τὸν θεόν, τὸ μὴ ὑπερβαίνειν καὶ πλεονεκτεῖν ἐν τῷ πράγματι τὸν ἀδελφὸν αὐτοῦ (4:4-6). This passage has created much difficulty for commentators. Any interpretation rests on the precise meaning of σκεῦος in the context of this passage.[94] Quite literally the word indicates "vessel, tool, utensil,"[95] but Paul is probably using it euphemistically. Three suggestions have been put forth: "wife,"[96] "body,"[97] and "male genitalia."

Wanamaker summarizes the latter position: "it seems better to understand σκεῦος as connoting the human body in its sexual aspect, that is, as a euphemism for the genitalia."[98] This is how it is used as a

---

translations. For the reasons given below it is better translated as "brothers" in 1 Thessalonians.

[94] Although this is not the only problem in the passage; see Collins, *Studies*, 299.

[95] LSJ s.v.

[96] Reading "to take a wife for himself" (RSV). Best, *Thessalonians*, 161-62); Frame, *Thessalonians*, 149-50; C. Maurer, "σκεῦος," *TDNT* 7 (1971) 365-67; Meeks, *First Urban Christians*, 228 n. 130; Collins, *Studies*, 313; O. L. Yarbrough, *Not Like the Gentiles: Marriage Rules in the Letters of Paul* (SBLDS 80; Atlanta: Scholars Press, 1985) 69-73; Holtz, *Thessalonicher*, 157-58; Malherbe, *Paul and the Thessalonians*, 51; idem, *Thessalonians*, 227. See further those cited by Collins, *Studies*, 311-12. J. M. Bassler uses 1 Corinthians 7:36-38 as background and suggests that in 1 Thessalonians 4:4 σκεῦος refers to a virgin and indicates that the Thessalonians should stay celibate, even if betrothed to another ("Σκεῦος: A Modest Proposal for Illuminating Paul's Use of Metaphor in 1 Thessalonians 4:4," in *The Social World of the First Christians: Essays in Honour of Wayne A. Meeks*, ed. L. M. White and O. L. Yarbrough [Minneapolis: Fortress, 1995] 61).

[97] Reading "to gain mastery over his body" (NEB; NIV). So Plummer, *Thessalonians*, 59-60; Dibelius, *Thessalonicher/Philipper*, 21; Neil, *Thessalonians*, 79-80; Rigaux, *Thessaloniciens*, 504-06; Morris, *Thessalonians*, 124; Marxsen, *Thessalonicher*, 60-61; Richard, *Thessalonians*, 198 (Morris, Marxsen, and Richard note the suggestion of sexual control); M. McGehee, "A Rejoinder to Two Recent Studies Dealing with 1 Thessalonians 4:4," *CBQ* 51 (1989) 82-89. See further the list in Collins, *Studies*, 312.

[98] Wanamaker, *Thessalonians*, 152. Cf. BAGD s.v.; J. M. Reese, *1 and 2 Thessalonians* (NTM 16; Wilmington: Michael Glazier, 1979) 44; J. Whitton, "A Neglected Meaning for *skeuos* in 1 Thessalonians 4.4," *NTS* 28 (1982) 142-43; Bruce, *Thessalonians*, 83; Marshall, *Thessalonians*, 108-09; Williams, *Thessalonians*, 72 (cautiously), and especially Donfried, "Cults of Thessalonica," 341-42 and T. Elgvin,

translation for כלי in the LXX of 1 Samuel 21:5, where David assures the priest of Nob that "the young men's vessels are holy" in response to a question about whether they have kept themselves from women.[99] It is attested in such uses in non-biblical Greek.[100]

The passage itself is clearly placed in the context of sexual misconduct, and Paul enclosing his words with references not only to ἁγιασμός (4:3, 7) but to πορνεία (4:3) and ἀκαθαρσία (4:7), the latter two often used in contexts of sexual immorality.[101] Donfried places the text within the larger cultic context of Thessalonica:

> All of this suggests that Paul is very deliberately dealing with a situation of grave immorality, not too dissimilar to the cultic temptations of Corinth. Thus, Paul's severe warnings in this section, using the weightiest authorities he possibly can, is intended to distinguish the behavior of the Thessalonian Christians from their former heathen and pagan life which is still much alive in the various cults of the city.[102]

The interpretation of σκεῦος as "genitalia" seems to be the one that best takes account of the textual data.[103] One cannot simply assume that although the pronouns used are masculine, the instruction to control (κτᾶσθαι) the genitalia "would apply equally to women."[104] The understanding of sexuality in antiquity seems to mitigate this. In the understanding of the ancients' "ideology of sexual hierarchy" it was assumed that "at the masculine end of the scale stood strength and control, at the feminine end weakness and vulnerability."[105] As Dale Martin points out with respect to 1 Corinthians 7:36-38,

> Paul's exclusive address to the young man thus reveals his assumption of the male-female hierarchy of strength. He addresses the one who has power, the man, and delegates to him the responsibility for doing what

---

"'To Master His Own Vessel'. 1 Thess 4.4 in Light of New Qumran Evidence," *NTS* 43 (1997) 604-19. *Contra* McGehee ("Rejoinder," 82 n. 2) who suggests that this interpretation "has not been persuasive."

[99] See Bruce, *Thessalonians*, 83.

[100] See Maurer, "σκεῦος," 359; BAGD *s.v.*

[101] Murphy-O'Connor, *Paul*, 125; Donfried, "Cults of Thessalonica," 341; cf. Fatum, "Brotherhood in Christ," 189.

[102] Donfried, "Cults of Thessalonica," 341-42.

[103] It is clear that each of the options has problems; Collins, *Studies*, 299, 314.

[104] Wanamaker, *Thessalonians*, 153.

[105] D. B. Martin, *The Corinthian Body* (New Haven and London: Yale University Press, 1995) 226-27.

needs to be done in the woman's best interest (at least according to Paul's point of view). The weaker of the two, the woman, cannot be relied upon to make a decision for herself.[106]
Women were assumed to be more easily consumed by desire and more willing to give in to it. Control in such situations rested with the male. Due to their own physiology, women lacked the ability to control their own sexual desires.[107] Thus, when Paul speaks of controlling the genitalia (σκεῦος) it would be addressed to the males, who physiologically were thought to have the ability to do so.[108]

That the Thessalonian Christian community is primarily a group of males finds some support in Fatum's recent essay.[109] Fatum begins by noting that both 1 Thessalonians and the audience to which it is addressed are "defined by androcentric values and social conventions and organized in terms of the patriarchal structures so characteristic of urban society in Graeco-Roman Antiquity."[110] She uses 1 Thess 4:3-8 to show how exclusively male is Paul's exhortation in the letter. Although she understands σκεῦος as "wife," she notes that "the power to interpret gender and to administer sexuality" was "generally accepted as a male prerogative."[111]

Fatum draws back from arguing that the community was only males: "Historically we may assume, of course, as stated already, that women were among the converts in Thessalonica." She points to Acts 17:4 but immediately shows one cannot rely on the veracity of the Acts account.[112] She reasons that women in the community are embedded in the lives of men such that when Paul addresses the Thessalonians "they are not among the brothers of Christ; individually they are not members of the new community." As such, women are "invisible in Christ" and "their socio-sexual presence among the brothers is, virtually, a non-presence."[113] If it is the case that the Thessalonian Christian community was primarily

---

[106] Martin, *Corinthian Body*, 227.

[107] See further the discussion in Martin, *Corinthian Body*, 219-28.

[108] Cf. "With the Stoics, Paul shares the belief that the complete extirpation of desire is both possible and preferable, even within sexual relations in marriage"; D. B. Martin, "Paul Without Passion: On Paul's Rejection of Desire in Sex and Marriage," in *Constructing Early Christian Families: Family as Social Reality and Metaphor*, ed. H. Moxnes (London and New York: Routledge, 1997) 207.

[109] Fatum, "Brotherhood in Christ," 183-97.

[110] Fatum, "Brotherhood in Christ," 184.

[111] Fatum, "Brotherhood in Christ," 191.

[112] Fatum, "Brotherhood in Christ," 192-93.

[113] Fatum, "Brotherhood in Christ," 194.

composed of males, then this particular community was atypical among Christian communities known from Paul's letters, such as those communities at Corinth, Philippi, and Rome.

3. Conclusion

In this and the previous chapters we have used the voluntary associations as a means to understand some of the exegetical issues in both Philippians and 1 Thessalonians. In doing so, we illustrated some of Paul's language by reference to the typicalities of association language. We saw that some of the community features of the both of the Macedonian Christian communities find ready analogies in the voluntary associations. Overall, this investigation helps us to understand better, and often in new ways, both Paul and his practices, and the practices and structure of the groups to which he writes.

At a number of points in our discussion we showed that aspects of Paul's understanding of the Macedonian communities can be found in the inscriptions of the voluntary associations Elsewhere we suggested that Paul's concepts and language contrast with that typical of the voluntary associations. In some cases Paul uses the practices of the associations in his attempts to nuance the Macedonian's self-understanding as communities. In doing so Paul's starting point is voluntary association language and organization. All of this suggests that both Paul and the Macedonian Christian communities share the same discursive field as the voluntary associations. Although there is no one association inscription that has all the features of either Philippians or 1 Thessalonians (and thus no one association that is exactly the same), the comparative process reveals that on the social map of antiquity the associations provide a ready analogue for understanding the community structure of the Paul's Macedonian Christian communities.

Appendix

Jewish Communities In Macedonia

In giving attention to the voluntary associations as a background for understanding Pauline community formation, we do not want to disparage the importance of Judaism and the synagogues for understanding early Pauline Christianity. It is important to note that in the case of the Macedonian context there is very little evidence for the presence of Jews and God-fearers during the first century CE. Despite this, large communities of both are continually affirmed.[1] Papazoglou's comments are typical: "We do not know when the first Jews were established in Macedonia; yet by the mid-first century A.D. there were at Philippi, Thessalonike and Beroia fairly numerous Jewish communities grouped around their synagogues."[2] However, Papazoglou's evidence comes primarily from the book of Acts.[3] Since it is generally recognized that Acts

---

[1] Such methodological assumptions occur with respect to other sites. For example, although we have no evidence for the presence of a Jewish population in Troas during the first century CE C. J. Hemer assumes there to have been many Jews there ("Alexandria Troas," *TynBul* 26 [1976] 95). He then goes on to suggest that Luke did not describe the founding of the Christian community at Troas (Acts 16:8) because it was not representative of *Paul's* policy and method (Hemer, "Alexandria Troas," 95). He does not consider the possibility that it was not representative of *Luke's* assumptions about Paul's method precisely because there was no Jewish community there. It is perplexing that in the face of such evidence, and the lack of evidence in Paul, that Luke's presentation is still assumed to reflect accurately Paul's missionary strategy.

[2] Papazoglou, "Macedonia," 207. J. Nehama attributes the growth of the Jewish population in Thessalonica to the general dispersion of Jews in the Hellenistic period, concluding that "Thessalonique en avait reçu un grand nombre et elle devient ainsi un des centres les plus prépare l'avènement du christianisme" (*Histoire des Israélites de Salonique* 1 *La Communaute Romaniote – Les Sefaradis et leur Dispersion* [Thessalonica: Molho, 1935] 15). However, he simply assumes this based on a general movement of Jews from the east to the west and especially the presence of Jews in Alexandria; cf. "Il est donc à présumer que..." (p. 10), "Il est à présumer qu'ils..." (p. 13).

[3] Papazoglou, "Macedonia," 541 n. 116. Also Lightfoot, *Biblical Essays*, 242-45; Nehama, *Histoire des Israélites*, 31-44; Schürer, *History of the Jewish People*, 3/1:65. Acts seems to be the basis upon which many scholars make the assumption that there existed at Thessalonica (and Philippi) a substantial Jewish community. An exception is W. Schenk who notes that there is no archaeological evidence for Jews at Philippi and suggests that the only indication of Jews at Philippi is if Phil 3:2-19 can be connected

itself cannot always be relied upon for historical accuracy in many details,[4] this conclusion seems tenuous. In this appendix we will put forth reasons why, given the available data, we find it unlikely that at their core the Macedonian Christian communities had a significant number of Jewish adherents.

1. Literary and Archaeological Evidence

A review of the literary evidence provides little support for the existence of Jews in first century CE Macedonia. The primary reference comes from Philo's record of a letter from Herod Agrippa (37-44 CE) to Caligula which notes that most provinces in Rome's control include a Jewish population, listing among them Macedonia (*Leg. Gai.* 281-82):

> Concerning the holy city I must now say what is necessary. It, as I have already stated, is my native country, and the metropolis not only of the one country of Judaea but also of many, by reason of the colonies which it has sent out from time to time into the bordering districts of Egypt, Phoenicia, Syria in general, and especially that part of it which is called Coelo-Syria and also with those more distant regions of Pamphylia, Cilicia, the greater part of Asia Minor as far as Bithynia, and the furthermost corners of Pontus. And in the same manner into Europe, into Thessaly, and Boeotia, and Macedonia, and Aetolia, and Attica, and Argos, and Corinth and all the most fertile and wealthiest districts of Peloponnesus, and not only are the continents full of Jewish colonies, but also all the most celebrated islands are so too; such as Euboea, and Cyprus, and Crete. I say nothing of the countries beyond the Euphrates, for all of them except a very small portion, and Babylon, and all the satrapies around, which have any advantages whatever of soil or climate, have Jews settled in them.

Agrippa's point, however, is to indicate how widespread Judaism has become, and, in arguing for Caligula's benefaction of Jerusalem, wants to underline the point that "it corresponds well to the greatness of your good fortune, that, by conferring benefits on one city, you should also benefit ten thousand others, so that your renown may be celebrated in every part of the habitable world, and many praises of you may be combined with thanksgiving" (Philo, *Leg. Gai.* 284). The comments are so general that Agrippa (or Philo in recreating the letter) may simply have affirmed a Macedonian Jewish

---

with Phil 1:28-30, a possibility he does not explore and one that is unlikely ("Der Philipperbrief in der neueren Forschung (1945-85)," *ANRW* II.25.4 [1987] 3289).

[4] See E. Haenchen, *The Acts of the Apostles: A Commentary* (Oxford: Blackwell, 1971) 90-116; Lüdemann, *Early Christianity*, 1-16, cf. 179-88.

community with little knowledge to the contrary.⁵ Josephus notes that the Jews in Alexandria bear the title "Macedonians," but the connection is through the granting of separate quarters and certain privileges (ἰσοπολιτεία) to the Jewish community on a par with those granted to the Macedonians (*Ap.* 2.4.36; *Bell.* 2.488).⁶ He does not indicate a Jewish presence in Macedonia.

Overall, the literary evidence outside of Acts does not offer strong support for the existence of a large Jewish population in Macedonia.⁷ Levinskaya provides a more hopeful picture when she concludes that epigraphic evidence from Macedonia "supports the picture we can obtain from the book of Acts."⁸ However, the epigraphical evidence is only slightly more informative and Levinskaya is overly optimistic.⁹ One significant inscription comes from Stobi, in the north western part of the province, and dates to the third century CE (*CIJ* 694).¹⁰ The inscription records Claudius Tiberius Polycharmos' donation of a synagogue. This patron's *tria nomina* indicates that he is a citizen and a friend of Rome.¹¹

---

⁵ Cf. Lührmann, "Church at Thessalonica," 239.

⁶ Here Josephus notes that Alexander the Great granted these; elsewhere he suggests they came though Ptolemy Soter (*Ant.* 12.7-8) or through Alexander and reaffirmed by Ptolemy (*Bell.* 2.487-88).

⁷ Schürer (*History of the Jewish People*, 3/1.64) and I. A. Levinskaya (*The Book of Acts in its Diaspora Setting* [BAFCS 5; Grand Rapids: Eerdmans, 1996] 154) only note the reference in Philo. Nehama (*Histoire des Israélites*, 21-24) notes Philo (without giving the reference) along with a sibylline oracle (no reference, although his description is of an oracle about the general dispersion of the Jews). In support he also points to Strabo ("Livres VII à X"), Seneca (no reference), and Josephus ("Livre V"). I was unable to locate the references in Seneca, nor could I locate his points of reference in Strabo. The Josephus reference "nous apprendons que les Juifs avaient combattu dans les phalanges d'Alexandre et s'y étaient distingués" (*Histoire des Israélites*, 24) although this does not make them Macedonians (again, I could not locate the reference). Nehama (*Histoire des Israélites*, 24) mentions a Macedonian general under Alexander named Mossolamos, but this person seems rather to have been a Jew of Alexandria (see *Ap.* 1.200-04; cf. *Ant.* 13.4.74-76).

⁸ Levinskaya, *Book of Acts*, 195.

⁹ My own consideration of the evidence was completed before the publication of Levinskaya, *Book of Acts*, 154-57. We both consider the same basic evidence but draw differing conclusions. She maintains that the evidence affirms the picture in Acts of Jews in first century CE Macedonia; I am less convinced. For my review of Levinskaya's book see *TJT* 14 (1998) 268-69.

¹⁰ On Stobi itself see J. Wiseman, "The City in Macedonia Secunda," in *Villes et peuplement dans l'Illyricum protobyzantin* (Palais Farnese: Ecole Française de Rome, 1984) 289-313.

¹¹ Names with the Tiberius-Claudius combination are frequent from the time of the Emperor Claudius (Tiberius Claudius Nero Germanicus, 41-54 CE) and especially common in the second half of the first century and the first half of the second. The Greek cognomen Polycharmos is not common, and Achyrios may be of Semitic origin. See the discussion in M. Hengel, "Die Synagogeninschrift von Stobi," *ZNW* 57 (1966) 151-52; cf. N. Vulić, "Inscription grecque de Stobi," *BCH* 56 (1932) 294.

He may be Jewish, or more likely a "Jewish sympathizer."[12] Certainly he is wealthy, and uses his wealth to benefit the Jewish community. If he is not a Jew then he acts in much the same way that the Capernaum centurion of Luke 7:5 is said to act; "he loves our people, and it is he who built our synagogue for us."[13] The synagogue dedicated by Polycharmus (Synagogue I) had walls, with geometric frescoes and the repeated legend Πολύχαρμος ὁ πατὴρ εὐχήν ("Polycharmos, the father [has fulfilled] a vow"). Πατήρ, along with the feminine μήρηρ, were honourary titles given to rich patrons of synagogues.[14] In this case only part of the family villa is donated for use as a synagogue, the remainder continues to be available to Polycharmus' family.[15] At the very least this shows a significant number of Jews in third century CE Stobi, enough that a designated meeting area is required. Unfortunately, this tells us little of the first century CE, although the synagogue may have been extent at that time.

Two tomb inscriptions from Beroea provide fairly late evidence for Jews there. *CIJ* 694a reads Μημούρηων [᾿Ι]ωάνο [υ] κὲ Ἀνδρέου τοιὼς Παριγορίου and probably dates from the fifth century CE.[16] It has a depiction of a menorah and a lulab on the right side and either an open scroll or the ark of the covenant on the left.[17] The second inscription dates from the fifth century CE and is the epitaph of a woman set up by her son-in-law (*CIJ* 694b). The inscription stipulates that if the tomb is opened the offender will be required "to pay to the most holy synagogue one silver pound." The payment of fines to a synagogue or a religious association as a way of protecting the tomb from tomb robbers was common in antiquity.[18] These two inscriptions are too late to be considered as strong evidence for Jews in Macedonia in the first century CE.

---

[12] This is possible by the third century, when the designation of such occurs more frequently in the literary and epigraphic record.

[13] Hengel, "Synagogeninschrift," 164; cf. Acts 10:1-2.

[14] See Hengel, "Synagogeninschrift," 176-77.

[15] His ownership of a villa large enough to accommodate a synagogue attests to Polycharmus' wealth. It is not possible to determine the social location of the membership of the synagogue, although it is unlikely to have been solely composed of upper rank people and in fact is probably of a mixed type.

[16] As it stands the text indicates a tomb of John and Andrew. However the exact reading of this text is disputed. D. Feissel (*Recueil des inscriptions chrétiennes de Macédoine du III*ᵉ *au VI*ᵉ *siècle* [BCH Supplement 8; Athens and Paris: Ecole Française D'Athènes; Diffusion de Boccard, 1983] 294) suggests only one deceased person, reading ᾿Ιωσῆς ᾿Αλεξανδρεούς, with which Levinskaya (*Book of Acts*, 157) agrees. The interpretation of τοιὼς is uncertain.

[17] See further Feissel, *inscriptions chrétiennes*, 294 (pl. 65); Levinskaya, *Book of Acts*, 157.

[18] The warning itself would not deter thieves, but those who stood to gain financially from violations would probably be fairly vigilant in watching over the tombs. This particular fine is not steep (see Feissel, *inscriptions chrétiennes*, 295).

Three tomb inscriptions from Thessalonica have been identified as possibly being Jewish. *CIJ* 693 (= *IG* X/2 633) reads Μημόριον Ἀβραμηο(υ) καὶ τῆς συνβίου αὐτοῦ Θεοδότης ("In memory of Abraham and his wife Theodote") and dates from the second century CE. It has no distinct Jewish symbols other than the names and may be a Christian epitaph.[19] *CIJ* 693b reads κύριος μεθ᾿ ἡμῶν ("The Lord is with us," thought to be a paraphrase of Psalm 46:8, 12) and appears with a symbol of a menorah on a sarcophagus.[20] The marble door of a tomb at Thessalonica (*CIJ* 693c) reads Βενιαμῆς ὁ καὶ Δομέτιος ("Benjamin, the one also called Domitios").[21] These inscriptions raise the possibility that ethnic Jews were living at Thessalonica by the second or third century CE. Since they were found in the early Christian necropolis to the east of Thessalonica they may be Jewish-Christian.[22] While they may show a Jewish population in Thessalonica, more likely they show that some Christian Jews moved to the city.

Although *IG* X/2 72 is included in *CIJ* (693d) we do not consider it to be Jewish. This controversial inscription is inscribed Θεῶι Ὑψίστωι κατ᾿ ἐπιταγὴν ΙΟΥΕΣ. The controversy arises over the meaning of the final letters before the break in the inscription. Some scholars suggest that the letters ΙΟΥΕΣ "may be an attempt to transliterate the name of Jahwe" in the genitive,[23] although others call this into question.[24] Habicht restores it

---
[19] Levinskaya, *Book of Acts*, 155.

[20] B. Lifshitz notes that the formula has not been found in Jewish inscriptions but is frequent in Christian epigraphy ("Prolegomenon," in *Corpus of Jewish Inscriptions: Jewish Inscriptions from the Third Century B.C. to the Seventh Century A.D. I: Europe*, ed. P. J.-B. Frey [New York: KTAV, 1975] 75). A second sarcophagus has the symbol of a menorah. R. S. Kraemer points out that the deceased might be Christian Jews ("Jewish Tuna and Christian Fish: Identifying Religious Affiliation in Epigraphic Sources," *HTR* 84 [1991] 141-62. 151).

[21] Levinskaya (*Book of Acts*, 155) incorrectly attributes this to the second sarcophagus of *CIJ* 963b.

[22] Levinskaya, *Book of Acts*, 155; cf. Kraemer, "Jewish Tuna," 151. Evidence from elsewhere attests to the possibility of Christians continuing to use Jewish symbolism; see Kraemer, "Jewish Tuna," 151. *CIJ* 84 (Italy) has a depiction of a menorah alongside the Christian Chi-Rho symbol. Some dedications from Greece depicting both crosses and menorahs on them have been found and lamps with depictions of menorahs have been found in Christian catacombs. However, there is evidence of Christians and Jews buried side by side in Cilicia, with the same curse formula being used by both to protect the graves (L. H. Feldman, *Jew and Gentile in the Ancient World: Attitudes and Interactions from Alexander to Justinian* (Princeton: Princeton University Press, 1993) 362; L. H. Kant, "Jewish Inscriptions in Greek and Latin," *ANRW* II.20.2 (1987) 685-86; cf. Kraemer, "Jewish Tuna," 160-61).

[23] Roberts, Skeat, and Nock, "Guild of Zeus Hypsistos," 65; cf. Ch. Avezou and Ch. Picard, "Inscriptions de Macédoine et de Thrace," *BCH* 37 (1913) 100; A. Plassart, "La Synagogue juive de Délos," *RB* 11 (1914) 529 n. 5; R. E. Witt, "The Egyptian Cults in Ancient Macedonia," in *Ancient Macedonia* 1, ed. B. Laourdas and Ch. Makaronas

as the Roman name Ἰού(λιος) (but gives no indication what name might be abbreviated Ἐσ).[25] This is affirmed by Feissel and Sève who point out that the name of the dedicator is necessary.[26] We would agree that the ending does not likely refer to the Jewish God. No other example of the use of the deity's name in the genitive after κατ' ἐπιταγήν could be found except for *IG* V/1 245 where there is no reference to the deity in the dative beforehand. Thus the name of the dedicator is most likely.[27] It seems unlikely, moreover, that a Jewish group would transliterate the name YHWH rather than use a euphemism like κύριος, lest someone, Jewish or not, audibly pronounce the sacred name (which would be likely in a period in which most people read out loud, even to themselves).

Nevertheless, some arguments are still put forth for the Jewish provenance of this Macedonian inscription on the basis of its dedication to Theos Hypsistos. Ὕψιστος was a common epitaph of God in the LXX and the writings of Hellenistic Judaism.[28] Furthermore, a number of scholars argue that in the Bosporus the cult of Theos Hypsistos was an offshoot of Judaism.[29] This argument then gets extended to other regions, including Macedonia. In the majority of instances the influence of Judaism in the use of Theos Hypsistos (and even Zeus Hypsistos) has been called into

---

(Thessalonica: Institute for Balkan Studies, 1970) 328 n. 13; D. Feissel and M. Sève, "Inscriptions de Macédoine," *BCH* 112 (1988) 455; *CIJ* 693d (B. Lifshitz).

[24] P. Perdrizet, "Némésis," *BCH* 38 (1914) 91 n. 2; P. M. Nigdelis, "Synagoge(n) und Gemeinde der Juden in Thessaloniki: Fragen aufgrund einer neuen jüdischen Grabinschrift der Kaiserzeit," *ZPE* 102 (1994) 297-306. 1994:298 n. 5; Pilhofer, *erste christliche Gemeinde*, 184-85 n. 111.

[25] C. Habicht, "Review of *IG* X/2," *Gnomen* 46 (1974) 491.

[26] Feissel and Sève, "Inscriptions de Macédoine," 455.

[27] Levinskaya suggests that this possibility "should be considered seriously" (*Book of Acts*, 155 n. 9).

[28] Cf. M. Simon, "Theos Hypsistos," in *Ex Orbe Religionum: Studia Geo Widengren*, ed. C. J. Bleeker, S. G. F. Brandon, and M. Simon (Studies in the History of Religions 21; Leiden: Brill, 1972) 372-76; Levinskaya, *Book of Acts*, 111-13. It is used quite rarely by Philo and Josephus, suggesting that it needed to be used with care lest their non-Jewish readers misunderstand it to indicate not the monotheistic God of the Jews but the top deity in a hierarchy of gods; see Trebilco, *Jewish Communities*, 129-30.

[29] See for example E. H. Minns, *Scythians and Greeks: A Survey of Ancient History and Archaeology of the North Coast of the Euxine from the Danube to the Caucasus* (Cambridge: Cambridge University Press, 1913) 621-22. The argument is summarized in J. Ustinova, "The *Thiasoi* of Theos Hypsistos in Tanais," *HR* 31 (1991) 159-60 and Trebilco, *Jewish Communities*, 139. Some suggest that ὕψιστος worked for the Jewish community as an invitation to syncretism by which they might bring Gentiles into monotheistic Judaism as converts (see Simon, "Theos Hypsistos," 376). On the problems with the use of the concept of "syncretism" in scholarly discourse see Levinskaya, *Book of Acts*, 197-205. Levinskaya suggests that in the Bosporus there is no syncretism; rather, those who worship Theos Hypsistos are Gentile "God-fearers" (*Book of Acts*, 113-14).

question.³⁰ The primary argument against such influence is the wide use of ὕψιστος in non-Jewish contexts, where no Jewish influence is likely.³¹ Kraabel examines a number of inscriptions from the areas of Lydia, Phrygia, and Ionia and concludes that "the epithet ὕψιστος, when it appears in Asia Minor, can never be taken, by itself, as proof that the text is Jewish."³² Ustinova reaches a similar conclusion in her study of the ὕψιστος inscriptions from the θίασος of Tanais in the Bosporus,³³ as does Tačeva-Hitova for Thrace, Moesia, and the Balkan region.³⁴

---

³⁰ See Roberts, Skeat, and Nock, "Guild of Zeus Hypsistos"; A. T. Kraabel, "Ὕψιστος and the Synagogue at Sardis," *GRBS* 10 (1969) 81-93; T. Drew-Bear, "Local Cults in Graeco-Roman Phrygia," *GRBS* 17 (1976) 248; Horsley, *New Documents* 1, 25-29; M. Tačeve-Hitova, "Dem Hypsistos geweihte Denkmäler in den Balkanländern," *Balkan Studies* 19 (1978) 59-75; idem, *Eastern Cults in Moesia Inferior and Thracia (5th Century BC - 4th Century AD.)* (EPRO 95; Leiden: Brill, 1983) 203-15; Trebilco, *Jewish Communities*; Ustinova, "*Thiasoi* of Theos Hypsistos"; Pilhofer, *erste christliche Gemeinde*, 186-88.

³¹ See Roberts, Skeat, and Nock, "Guild of Zeus Hypsistos," 64-69.

³² Kraabel, "Ὕψιστος," 91. The same is true of the use of ἀρχισυνάγωγος and συναγωγή in inscriptions, neither of which alone prove Jewish provenance (Poland, *griechischen Vereinswesens*, 355-58; Kraemer, "Jewish Tuna," 147-48; Horsley, *New Documents* 4, no. 113). Levinskaya (*Book of Acts*, 92-93) summarizes the evidence for ὕψιστος with the intention of showing that the use of ὕψιστος was not in widespread use in non-Jewish contexts. However, her limited evidence is determined in part by her own assumption that every instance in which a deity is not named must be Jewish and in her comparison of epigraphic texts with the Jewish LXX, where ὕψιστος is used "over one hundred and ten times." However, the actual epigraphical instances of ὕψιστος in inscriptions that are identified as Jewish on other grounds is quite limited and no more widespread than the confirmed non-Jewish uses. Later (*Book of Acts*, 99-100) she assumes that non-Jews would be thoroughly familiar with the Jewish use, a tenuous suggestion at best. Cf. her later suggestion that ὕψιστος "was spread through its occurrence in the Septuagint" (*Book of Acts*, 109), indicating the a widespread non-Jewish readership of the LXX.

³³ Ustinova, "*Thiasoi* of Theos Hypsistos," 159-65. Levinskaya (*Book of Acts*, 108) disputes Ustinova's conclusion based on her *assumption* of the Jewish provenance of all inscriptions dedicated to Theos Hypsistos. Her own re-examination of a third-century CE text commonly attributed to a θίασος of adherents of Sabazios "the Most High god" is unconvincing (*Book of Acts*, 88-92). The letters identifying this inscription with a θίασος of Sabazios are fragmentary (ΘΙΑ---ΣΕΒΑΖΙ | ΑΝΟΣΘΗ---ΤΟΥΤΑΣ). Levinskaya suggests that they reflect personal names and indicate an inscription set up by Jews or God-fearers. Her disallowance of the common reconstruction θίασος Σεβαζιανός is based on the grammatical rarity of adjectives with θίασος and the absence of the adjective σεβαζιανός in our sources. However, neither grammatical rarities nor *hapax legomena* are uncommon in epigraphy. Her own interpretation has to overlook the use of καὶ one line earlier which is normally interpreted as introducing the final name of the list of adherents. In her reconstruction it introduces the final few names, itself an odd grammatical move.

³⁴ Tačeve-Hitova, "Hypsistos," 1978; *idem*, *Eastern Cults*, 190-215.

Although the use of ὕψιστος is not out of keeping with the God of the Jews, its presence does not necessarily indicate Jewish influence.[35] It is used as an epithet of Zeus in Macedonian inscriptions (and inscriptions elsewhere). In fact, the cult of Zeus Hypsistos was widely diffused in Macedonia and may even have originated there (see further below).[36] The title ὕψιστος "belongs to the language of private dedications," not to public cult.[37] Three voluntary association inscriptions from Macedonia make explicit reference to an association: οἱ συνήθεις ἐπιμεληταί from Edessa (IEdessa 3), οἱ συνελθόντες θρησκευταί from Pydna (IPydna 1), and ἡ συνήθεια from Thessalonica (*IG* X/2 933).[38] The connection of ὕψιστος with private dedications is confirmed by inscriptions from elsewhere.[39] Inscriptions from Macedonia which mention Zeus Hypsistos are generally simple dedicatory inscriptions, but show the distribution of the associations to be primarily in the eastern part of the province: in Elimia (IMaked 7, 16, 27), Kalliani (IMaked 3, 21, 22), Eordaea (IMaded 90), Edessa (IEdessa 1 and 2, IMakedD 6, 7, 38), Idomene,[40] Anydron (IAnydron 1), Agrosykia,[41] Beroea (IBeroea 1),[42] Pydna (IPydna 1),

---

[35] Cf. A. B. Cook, *Zeus: A Study in Ancient Religion* (Cambridge: Cambridge University Press, 1925) 890; L. M. White, "Visualizing the 'Real' World of Acts 16: Toward Construction of a Social Index," in *The Social World of the First Christians: Essays in Honour of Wayne A. Meeks*, ed. L. M. White and O. L. Yarbrough (Minneapolis: Fortress, 1995) 256-57 n. 67.

[36] For more on Zeus Hypsistos (especially bibliography) see S. Düll, *Die Götterkulte Nordmakedoniens in römischer Zeit* (Münchener archäologische Studien 7; Munich: Fink, 1977) 205 n. 20, 428.

[37] Roberts, Skeat, and Nock, "Guild of Zeus Hypsistos," 59.

[38] The fragmentary nature of this inscription makes its association with Zeus Hypsistos somewhat questionable. See further Roberts, Skeat, and Nock, "Guild of Zeus Hypsistos," 57 n. 27 and Edson, "Cults of Thessalonica," 187.

[39] For example see *P.Lond.* 2710. Sixteen inscriptions from the θίασος of adherents of θεὸς ὕψιστος have been found in the Bosporus region, fifteen of them in Tanais: *CIRB* 1260, 1260a, 1261, 1277, 1278, 1279, 1280, 1281, 1282, 1283, 1284, 1285, 1286, 1287, 1289, 1231 (probably from Gorgippia); see overview in Levinskaya, *Book of Acts*, 111; Minns, *Scythians and Greeks*, 620-25. A particularly interesting example is a votive stele found at Panormos near Kyzikos in Mysia and dates from II CE (*IBM* 4.2.153 no. 1007; see Cook, *Zeus*, 881-82 no. 21). Below a relief of Zeus, Artemis (or Hecate or Dionysus), and Apollo is a low relief depiction of a banquet scene involving six men with a cup-bearer, a musician, a dancing girl, and a mime. The text reads "I Thallos, the name-giver [of the *thiasos*], duly presented the relief to Zeus Most High and to the Place [where the *thiasotai* assemble]" (text and translation in Cook, *Zeus*, 882).

[40] Tačeve-Hitova, "Hypsistos," 70 no. 2.

[41] See M. B. Hatzopoulos, *BE* (1991) 502 no. 394; P. Chrysostomou, *ArchDelt* 39 (1984) *chron.* 263-64.

[42] A second dedication to Zeus Hypsistos found in Beroea is reported by Cormack ("Dedications," 21-23 and pl. 1.2; also published by Tačeve-Hitova, "Hypsistos," 72 no. 12). The stele is badly worn, but Cormack reads on the gable Διὶ ὑψίστῳ, which is

Thessalonica (*IG* X/2 62), Mésiméri,[43] Anthemonte (IAnthemonte 1), Trebeni,[44] and near Philippi.[45] The association of Zeus Hypsistos at Pydna (IPydna 1) has a number of functionaries including λογιστεύοντος, ἄρχοντος, ἀρξισυνάγογος, πρὶν Πιερίωνος, προστάτος, γραμματέως. This is probably true for other associations of Zeus Hypsistos.

The earliest known dedications to Zeus Hypsistos are found in Edessa, Macedonia (IEdessa 1 and 2). The two identical dedications by Zolius, son of Alexander, on behalf of his children date from the early part of the second century BCE and indicate a man of some means.[46] Another ancient dedication to Zeus Hypsistos comes from Anthemonte (IAnthemonte 1). It may even be the case that the main sanctuary of this city was devoted to Zeus Hypsistos at this time.[47]

The early attestation for the cult of Zeus Hypsistos in Macedonia suggests that it is a native cult of Macedonia that spread throughout the Mediterranean world.[48] The early inscriptions from Edessa, along with the early dedications to Zeus Hypsistos at both Eordaea and Elimia (see above; both south of Edessa), suggest that the "cradle of the cult" of Zeus Hypsistos is the region around Mt. Bermion and Mt. Barnous that

---

confirmed by the relief of an eagle not unlike that of the dedications to Zeus Hypsistos from Edessa. In commenting on the inscriptions now in the museum at Verria (Boroea) Cormack notes that there are "a dozen or so votive inscriptions, including some to Zeus Hypsistos," but he does not say how many ("Progress Report on the Greek Inscriptions of the Trite Meris for *IG* X," in *Ancient Macedonia* 1, ed. B. Laourdas and Ch. Makaronas, [Thessaloniki: Institute for Balkan Studies, 1970] 194).

[43] Unpublished but noted in Hatzopoulos and Loukopoulou, *Recherches*, 51 n. 4; Salonica Museum inv. no. 1745.

[44] Tačeve-Hitova, "Hypsistos," 74 no. 20.

[45] White, "Visualizing," 256 n. 67. Although White identifies its provenance as Philippi, it was actually found 15 km south east of Philippi, in the province of Thrace (Pilhofer, *erste christliche Gemeinde*, 185 n. 13). For an overview of the wider distribution of Zeus Hypsistos inscriptions throughout the ancient Mediterranean world see Roberts, Skeat, and Nock, "Guild of Zeus Hypsistos," 56-59 or Cook, *Zeus*, 876-90. Tačeve-Hitova, *Eastern Cults*, 192-203 has collected dedications to Theos or Zeus Hypsistos from Thrace, the neighbouring province of Macedonia.

[46] Roberts, Skeat, and Nock, "Guild of Zeus Hypsistos," 60-62. Altogether we have six dedications to Zeus Hypsistos from Edessa. A mid first century CE inscription is clearly that of an association (οἱ συνήθεις ἐπιμεληταί, IEdessa 3), with the others probably, but not definitely, being somehow affiliated with an association of sorts.

[47] Hatzopoulos and Loukopoulou, *Recherches*, 64, cf. 51.

[48] Roberts, Skeat, and Nock, "Guild of Zeus Hypsistos," 61, 72; Papazoglou, "Macedonia," 204; S. Pelekides, "Ἀνασκαφὴ Ἐδέσσης," *ArchDelt* 9 (1923) 269; Pilhofer, *erste christliche Gemeinde*, 182-85. However, when the epithet was used in other locations it most often indicates the supreme deity of that particular area rather than the worship of the Macedonian Zeus/Theos Hypsistos. Thus, in Syria it meant *Ba'al-šamin* and in Samaria it meant YHWH (Cook, *Zeus*, 889; Trebilco, *Jewish Communities*, 128). Levinskaya (*Book of Acts*, 88) disputes the evidence for this in Syria.

encompasses these areas.[49] This accords well with Cook's suggestion that the epithet Hypsistos "had originally a literal rather than an metaphorical sense" and was associated with a mountain cult of Zeus. Zeus is the obvious choice as deity, as he was universally seen as the supreme Olympian god throughout the Greek world.[50] However, he had a special significance for the people of Macedonia as he fathered Makedon, the eponymous ancestor of the people.[51] The fact that the inscription from Edessa in 51 CE (IEdessa 3) mentions an association of Zeus Hypsistos suggests that such associations originated fairly early in Macedonia.[52]

All this evidence suggests that when examining the inscriptions dedicated to Theos Hypsistos from Macedonia we would do well to follow Trebilco's suggestion that "an inscription using 'Theos Hypsistos' is to be regarded as Jewish *only* if there are clear signs of Jewish provenance and no indications that it might be pagan."[53] In the case of the Macedonian inscriptions there is no evidence that there was a Jewish influence behind the cult associations of either Zeus Hypsistos or Theos Hypsistos.[54] The epithet was probably widely used because it concentrated all "powers in the hands of one deity, thought of as reigning over all from an exalted station in the skies."[55] It represents the trend in the Greco-Roman world towards monotheism and the need for a deity that had world-wide or even cosmic authority.[56]

We can conclude that in Macedonia neither the cult of Zeus Hypsistos or Theos Hypsistos was connected with Judaism. Thus, the presence of inscriptions to Zeus/Theos Hypsistos in Macedonia, particularly in Thessalonica, cannot be used to confirm a large population of Jews living in the region or in Thessalonica itself. That many inscriptions give the

---

[49] Hatzopoulos and Loukopoulou, *Recherches*, 64.

[50] Cook, *Zeus*, 876.

[51] "The district of Macedonia took its name from Macedon the son of Zeus and Thyia, Deucalion's daughter, as Hesiod says: 'And she conceived and bare to Zeus who delights in the thunderbolt two sons, Magnes and Macedon, rejoicing in horses, who dwell round about Pieria and Olympus.... and Magnes again (begot) Dictys and godlike Polydectes'." (Constantinus Porphyrogenitus [905-59 CE], *de Them.* 2 p. 48B, in Hesiod, LCL, p. 156-57).

[52] For other cult titles of Zeus see N. G. L. Hammond and G. T. Griffith, *A History of Macedonia 2: 550-336 B.C.* (Oxford: Claredon, 1979) 164 n. 2.

[53] Trebilco, *Jewish Communities*, 133, my emphasis; cf. Pilhofer, *erste christliche Gemeinde*, 188.

[54] The exception might be *IG* X/2 72, discussed above. Those who see the divine name at the end of the inscription use it to show Jewish influence, but this reading is unlikely.

[55] Roberts, Skeat, and Nock, "Guild of Zeus Hypsistos," 67-68; cf. Trebilco, *Jewish Communities*, 132.

[56] Kraabel, "Ὕψιστος," 92-93.

deity the epithet ὕψιστος is more likely due to Macedonia being the birthplace of this usage.

Two other pieces of epigraphic evidence for Jews at Thessalonica are somewhat more significant as indicative of a Jewish presence in Macedonia. The first is a bilingual Greek and Hebrew inscription which includes the Greek text of Numbers 6:22-27 from the Samaritan Pentateuch rather than the LXX (*CIJ* 693a). This quotation is framed above and below with "Blessed be our God forever" in Hebrew (לעולם ברוך אלהינו) and was dedicated by a man and his family who "made this" (ποιήσαντι). It is unclear whether that which was made was a synagogue building or the inscription.[57] The text probably dates from the fifth or sixth century CE.[58] Lifshitz suggests that the name of the "Samaritan Tower" at Thessalonica indicates that the Samaritans were known at Thessalonica for a long time.[59] On the other hand, Schürer doubts that this inscription indicates the existence of a Samaritan community at all.[60] Overall, it is unlikely that it reflects a large Jewish population in first century CE Thessalonica as it is of such a late date.

The final piece of evidence is the most substantial for the presence of a Jewish community at Thessalonica. *SEG* XLIV 556 comes from a second or third century CE sarcophagus and includes a warning that re-use of the sarcophagus will result in a fine of 75,000 denarii to the synagogues (ταῖς συναγωγαῖς). Levinskaya points out that there were "several Jewish communities" (or at least enough Jews to form more than one synagogue) although "it is impossible to say whether the Jewish congregations in Thessalonica had a unified organization or were completely independent of each other."[61] Although this evidence is closer to the first century, it is still inconclusive as evidence for a large number of Jews in Thessalonica at that time.

At Philippi there is a singular tombstone inscription that mentions a synagogue (Pilhofer 387a). Although it has been noted as tacit support for the existence of a Jewish community at Philippi during the time of Paul,[62] the inscription itself dates from the late third or early fourth century or later.[63] Thus, its support of Luke's account is tenuous at best. In fact,

---

[57] Schürer, *History of the Jewish People*, 3/1.67; Levinskaya, *Book of Acts*, 156.

[58] J. Purvis, "The Paleography of the Samaritan Inscription from Thessalonica," *BASOR* 221 (1976) 121-23.

[59] Lifshitz, "Prolegomenon," 71.

[60] Schürer, *History of the Jewish People*, 3/1.67.

[61] Levinskaya, *Book of Acts*, 156.

[62] Koukouli-Chrysantaki, "Colonia Iulia Augusta Philippensis," 34.

[63] Koukouli-Chrysantaki, "Colonia Iulia Augusta Philippensis," 33; Pilhofer, *erste christliche Gemeinde*, 232. Koukouli-Chrysantaki ("Colonia Iulia Augusta Philippensis,"

Pilhofer points out that in 1359 inscriptions from Philippi there are no Jewish symbols or names and no indication of Jews, nor is there any literary evidence for the presence of Jews in the city.[64]

Given the lack of solid archaeological or literary evidence it seems wise to be more cautious in assessing the Jewish presence in Macedonia in the first century CE than has often been the case. What evidence does exist is late and not particularly informative as to the size of the Jewish community in the various locales. An argument from silence is never a strong one, and we would not want categorically to state that there were no Jews in Macedonia, particularly Thessalonica and Philippi, in the first century CE as archaeologists may still unearth important information. However, the state of our present knowledge suggests that if there were any Jews in first century CE Macedonia they seem to be neither well-established nor "fairly numerous." It seems unlikely that the core of the Christian communities at Thessalonica and Philippi is to be found among Jews and/or God-fearers, as the significant lack of any indication of the presence of Jews in 1 Thessalonians and Philippians confirms.

2. Evidence From Paul's Letters

A number of features of 1 Thessalonians suggest that Paul's audience was not composed of a significant number of Jews. The primary evidence comes from 1 Thess 1:9 where Paul notes that the Thessalonians "turned to God from idols to serve a living and true God." This verse indicates that prior to their conversion the Thessalonians had been involved in worshipping idols and thus were not Jews or God-fearers.[65] Furthermore, in 1 Thessalonians Paul gives no special attention to Jewish persons or

---

35) notes a late third or early fourth century CE inscription mentioning a Smyrnean named Simon who "may" be part of a Jewish community.

[64] Pilhofer, *erste christliche Gemeinde*, 232-33. However, this leads him to conclude that the Jewish community at Philippi was very small and financially weak, although it did have some σεβόμενοι, including some women (Pilhofer, *erste christliche Gemeinde*, 233-34). This reflects his basic assumption of the veracity of Acts.

[65] Paul would not describe Jews (or God-fearers) as turning from idols to God. Holtz suggests that Paul is referring to the time before they became "God-fearers" and attached themselves to the synagogue, but this is an unlikely interpretation which relies on the account of Acts 17:1-4 (*Thessalonicher*, 10). Note also that if 2:14-16 is taken as authentic then Paul's distinction between the Thessalonians' persecution by their "own countrymen" (ὑπὸ τῶν ἰδίων συμφυλετῶν) and the persecution of those in Judea by "the Jews" (ὑπὸ τῶν Ἰουδαίων) suggests that the Thessalonians are not themselves Jewish (nor in conflict with a Jewish group). "Fellow countrymen" (συμφυλέται) occurs nowhere else in the New Testament, although "fellow-citizens" (συμπολῖται) is used at Eph 2:19.

practices, and there is little use of the Old Testament. Plummer lists eight possible cases where reference to the LXX may occur,[66] none of which are obviously "deliberate." Thus, "[a]lthough, consciously or unconsciously, [Paul] sometimes uses the language of the LXX, yet he nowhere quotes the O.T., which would have little interest for imperfectly instructed Macedonian converts."[67] While we cannot say absolutely that there were no Jewish persons at Thessalonica it does seem that "Gentiles formed the bulk of the Thessalonian Church."[68] If there were any Jews and "God-fearers" in the congregation their presence was small enough that their Jewish background does not seem to be a factor in the overall ethos of the congregation.[69] As Lührmann states, "no reader of this letter would think of former Jews among the Thessalonians if they had not been so informed by Luke."[70]

In Philippians there is little evidence that there was a significant Jewish presence within the Philippian Christian community;[71] there are no clear allusions to the Hebrew scripture[72] and the proper names in the letter are Greek and Latin (Epaphroditus, Syntyche, Euodia, Clement). Although

---

[66] Plummer, *Thessalonians*, xx-xxii. The references are 2:4 (Jer 12:3); 2:16 (Gen 15:16; Dan 8:23); 2:19 (Prov 16:31; cf. Exek 16:12, 23:42); 4:5 (Ps 78[79]:6; Jer 10:25 [cf. 9:3]); 4:6 (Deut 32:32; Ps 93[94]:1); 4:8 (Ezek 37:14); 5:8 (Is 59:17; Wis 5:18); 5:22 (Job 1:1, 2:3).

[67] Plummer, *Thessalonians*, xiv; cf. Collins, *Birth*, 105.

[68] Plummer, *Thessalonians*, xvi.

[69] Most commentators acknowledge the predominance of Gentiles in the congregation, while allowing for a few Jews (usually based on the account in Acts): Eadie, *Thessalonians*, 12-13; Frame, *Thessalonians*, 3-4; Plummer, *Thessalonians*, xvi; Rigaux, *Thessaloniciens*, 20; Best, *Thessalonians*, 5; Laub, "Gemeindegründer," 18, 20; Bruce, *Thessalonians*, xxii-xxiii; Jewett, *Thessalonian Correspondence*, 118-19; Wanamaker, *Thessalonians*, 85; de Vos, *Community Conflicts*, 146-47.

[70] Lührmann, "Church at Thessalonica," 239. As Plummer asserts with regard to the Jews and "God-fearers" who converted according to Acts 17, "there is no trace of them in these two Epistles" (*Thessalonians*, 24). Best notes that "[t]he variant reading of the Western text of Acts 17.4, 'many of the God-fearers and a large number of Gentiles', is probably an attempt to minimize the difference between Acts and 1 Th" (*Thessalonians*, 5).

[71] The Gentile composition of the Philippian church was argued as early as 1833 and is now generally accepted; see Jewett, "Conflicting Movements," 372 n. 1.

[72] D. Dormeyer is certainly overly optimistic in suggesting that "[i]f all converted Philippians have learned the Hebrew Bible, self-evidently they have learned the metaphor of the Old Testament" ("The Implicit and Explicit Readers and the Genre of Philippians 3:2-4:3, 9-9: Response to the Commentary of Wolfgang Schenk," *Semeia* 48 [1989] 47-59). I rather doubt that in the short period that Paul remained with them the Philippians would have learned much more than a superficial awareness of some of the primary themes of the Old Testament in so far as they intersected with Paul's understanding of Christianity. Any vague references to the Hebrew scripture would very likely not have been noted by the Philippian Christians.

Paul's letter to the Philippians has no real indication of the presence of Jews in the church, it does polemicize against those who advocate Jewish practices (Phil 3:2-17). Certainly Paul holds no high praise for these opponents in Phil 3:2-17 as he introduces them by immediately censuring their character and their practices. That these opponents are involved in some kind of Jewish practices is clear from Paul's third censure. Paul coins a term, κατατομή, which is an obvious play on the word περιτομή ("circumcision"),[73] suggesting that Paul's opponents were advocating circumcision. Immediately following this warning Paul draws attention to the "true" circumcision being found in Christ.[74] In order to become circumcised one must be uncircumcised to begin with – namely, not already Jewish.

Paul is presenting arguments to counter a group that advocates Christian participation in Jewish circumcision practices. Two primary proposals have been put forth as to the identity of these opponents: non-Christian Jews and Jewish-Christian Judaizers. Most scholars take one or the other of these positions, although they nuance it variously. Without rehearsing all of the contours of the debate here we will note that we understand Paul to have been referring to Judaizing Christian missionaries in Phil 3:2-3.[75] During Paul's ministry he was often confronted with Judaizing Christians to whom he was required to respond (e.g., in Galatia and in Corinth). If there is no significant group of Jews in Philippi, these Judaizing missionaries must be coming from the outside and planning to target Gentile converts to Christianity. Paul gives no indication in his letter that these opponents have already adversely affected the Philippian

---

[73] Beare, *Philippians*, 104.

[74] In using ἡμεῖς ἐσμεν Paul is including the Philippians in his own group.

[75] For a summary of the debate concerning the nature of Paul's opponents see O'Brien, *Philippians*, 26-35 or Hawthorne 1983:xliv-xlvii, although these two reach different conclusions. Hawthorne understands them to be Jews whereas O'Brien sees them as Jewish Christians. Other supporters of the "Judaizing Christians" theory are C. L. Mearns, "Early Eschatological Development in Paul: The Evidence of I and II Thessalonians," *NTS* 27 (1980-81) 194-204; Perkins, "Philippians," 90-91; Tellbe, "Sociological Factors," 98-100 (Tellbe prefers to call them "agitators" rather than opponents). Some scholars maintain that the entire third chapter of Philippians (vv. 2-21) is aimed at three different groups: the "evil workers" (2-3), the "perfectionists" (12-16), and the enemies of the cross of Christ (18-19) (see the summary in Fitzgerald, "Philippians," 323). We maintain that chapter three deals primarily with two different groups of opponents, the first addressed in 3:2-16 and the second in 3:18-21, with 3:17 serving as a bridge between Paul's addressing of the two groups (the nature of the second group is not Jewish); see Jewett, "Conflicting Movements," 376-87 and idem, "Epistolary Thanksgiving," 40-49 (although we disagree with his identification of who the opponents are); *pace* H. Koester ("The Purpose of the Polemic of a Pauline Fragment (Philippians III)," *NTS* 8 [1961-62] 317-32) and Mearns ("Eschatological Development," 194-204) who argue that Phil 3:1-21 reflects a single group of Judaizers.

congregation or are now present at Philippi.[76] He is warning them of potential danger, not censuring them for actions already past (as was the case when he wrote Galatians).[77] Thus, Paul's invective against those who maintain Jewish practices seems more likely to be aimed at Christian Judaizers whom Paul anticipates coming to Philippi in order to show discontent among the worshippers there.

Paul's description of his Jewish background is presented in Philippians 3:4-6 in a way easily understandable to those who have only cursory knowledge of Judaism, particularly a Judaism presented by Judaizing Christians. Paul's lack of development of the place of the Law suggests that his references to it and to his blamelessness before it are more idealization and caricature (Phil 3:4-11). Paul has no need to nuance his comments because his audience was not steeped in the nuances of the Law. Paul uses the Law, as he does all references to his former status in Judaism, as part of his list of achievements. This list is impressive even without understanding the nuances. What Paul wants to present as more impressive to his audience is his giving up this derived honour for something even greater. All of this evidence argues against the early church in Philippi being formed from a Jewish group or its "sympathizers" (as Acts 16:13-15 would suggest). At least at the time of Paul's writing, his audience is predominantly Gentile.[78]

3. Evidence From Acts

It is axiomatic in New Testament studies that the Book of Acts is a secondary source for the life and ministry of Paul.[79] Nevertheless, many scholars admit that there may be some reliable tradition embedded in the account of Acts. In seeking to determine the extent of the Jewish presence within the Macedonian Christian communities we will examine carefully those elements that may or may not confirm the picture we have formed from the literary and archaeological evidence and from the letters of Paul. The method employed by Lüdemann proves helpful for the attempt to determine which of the details in Acts can be accepted as reliable.[80]

---

[76] Cf. Fee, *Philippians*, 294; Jewett, "Conflicting Movements," 382.

[77] Nevertheless, Paul sees these Judaizers as a real threat; he is not simply holding up the Jews as a cautionary example (Murphy-O'Connor, *Paul*, 228; *pace* Garland, "Composition and Unity," 165-66; Hawthorne, *Philippians*, 125).

[78] White, "Morality Between Two Worlds," 205-06; so also Barth, *Philipper*, 8; Gnilka, *Philipperbrief*, 3 (who also allows for a few individual Jews in the congregation); Schenk 1987:3289.

[79] See J. Knox, *Chapters in a Life of Paul* (Macon: Mercer University Press, 1987²).

[80] Lüdemann, *Early Christianity*.

Lüdemann examines the content of Acts to determine what material is redactional, what is from the tradition Luke received, and what is historical. The framework of Acts is secondary and Luke has compressed into a single account incidents that may have happened on separate visits to a city. However, many of the incidents themselves may reflect reliable data.

Luke makes it clear that Paul's initial preaching in Thessalonica takes place in the synagogue of the Jews (Acts 17:1-3). He has only moderate success among the Jews themselves, but a great number of God-worshippers and rich women respond positively to Paul's message. The entire passage resonates with Lukan redaction. Luke's use of συναγωγή in Acts 17:1 is most often taken to indicate the presence of a physical building; elsewhere in Luke-Acts it is clear that this is what Luke envisions (Luke 4:14-15, 16-30, 31-38; 7:5; 11:43; 20:46; Acts 18:7).[81] However, given the problematic nature of the evidence for the existence of physical synagogue buildings and a clear organization within the synagogue, Luke is probably embellishing his accounts. While the debate is sure to continue, for our purposes we note that one cannot use Luke alone to support the existence of a synagogue at Thessalonica; independent confirmation is necessary. It is precisely this independent confirmation that is lacking, as we saw above.

Acts 17:4 suggests that along with some Jews who were persuaded to join Paul and his companions there were "a great many of the devout Greeks and not a few of the leading women." The "devout Greeks," or "God-fearers" as they have come to be called, are most likely created by Luke in order to fit into his narrative pattern of Paul converting Jews and "God-fearers."[82] The phrase "leading women" probably indicates women of wealth and some high standing, precisely those whom we did not find evidence for in the text of 1 Thessalonians. As Lüdemann points out, their presence in the text "seems to be redactionally suspect because of the parallels" in Acts 17:12 which tells of the conversion of well-to-do women at Beroea and Acts 13:50 in which "the Jews" of Antioch of Pisidia stir up

---

[81] Rarely does Luke's use of συναγωγή clearly indicate a reference to the congregation (Acts 13:43; perhaps Luke 8:41). Elsewhere he notes Jesus or the apostles "entering" synagogues, which seems to indicate a building designated as such; Luke 6:6; 12:11; 13:10; Acts 9:20; 13:5, 14; 14:1; 17:10, 17; 18:19. Other references are made to speaking "in" the synagogues: Acts 15:21; 18:4; 19:8. The remaining references are slightly more vague, but still seem to indicate a physical location ("the synagogue") rather than the assembled community: Luke 21:12; Acts 6:9; 9:2; 22:19; 24:12; 26:11.

[82] A. T. Kraabel, "The Disappearance of the 'God-Fearers'," *Numen* 28 (1981) 113-26; R. S. MacLennan and A. T. Kraabel, "The God-Fearers – A Literary and Theological Invention," *BARev* 12/5 (1986) 46-53, 64. For an overview of the discussion see Ascough, *Pauline Churches*, 16-20.

women of high standing against Paul and Barnabas.[83] It is a Lukan tendency to mention conversions from among the upper classes,[84] or, alternatively, given the temporal separation between the writing of 1 Thessalonians (50s) and Acts (80s), it may be the case that by Luke's time a number of higher status women have become part of the Thessalonian community.

One of the Thessalonians named in the Acts account bears some attention. The name Jason (Acts 17:5-9) was a common Greek name, "after the Thessalonian hero who led the Argonauts in quest of the Golden Fleece."[85] This person may be Jewish: "Hellenistic Jews living in the Diaspora frequently adopted approximative homonyms as a moniker while dealing with the Hellenistic world," in this case as a derivative of Joshua or Jeshua.[86] Thus, some commentators assume Jason is Jewish,[87] an assumption which is strengthened if this is the same Jason as that mentioned in Rom 16:21. There Paul refers to Jason as being among his "kinsmen" (οἱ συγγενεῖς μου) presumably indicating that he is Jewish.[88] However, since Jason was a common Greek name in antiquity, the Jason of Acts 17:5-9 might be a Gentile if he is not the same person Paul mentions in Rom 16:21.[89]

Malherbe points out that, in the Acts account of the founding of the Thessalonian church, Jason's house (οἶκος) becomes the base for Paul's work *after* he separates from the synagogue, suggesting that Jason is to be understood as a Gentile.[90] That Jason was host to Paul, his companions, and perhaps to the Thessalonian Christians, as well as his posting bond for

---

[83] Lüdemann, *Early Christianity*, 185-86; cf. 156. These leading women become stock figures in Luke's drama, unlike Lydia in Acts 16, of whom the reader is given much more detail, lending some authenticity to the narrative (although not without some Lukan redaction).

[84] See Haenchen, *Acts of the Apostles*, 507; R. I. Pervo, *Profit with Delight: The Literary Genre of the Acts of the Apostles* (Philadelphia: Fortress, 1987) 77-78. Pervo suggests that this is part of Luke's "propagandistic fiction"; "[t]he upward mobility of many new religions encourages fictional propaganda about their adherents' social status" (Pervo, *Profit with Delight*, 79).

[85] F. F. Bruce, *The Acts of the Apostles* (London: Tyndale Press, 1951) 326.

[86] Collins, *Birth*, 230 n. 200.

[87] For example, Bruce, *Acts of the Apostles*, 32; C. S. C. Williams, *A Commentary on the Acts of the Apostles* (BHNTC. London: Adam and Charles Black, 1964²) 198.

[88] J. D. G. Dunn, *Romans 9-16* (WBC 38B; Waco: Word, 1988) 909; J. A. Fitzmyer, *Romans: A New Translation with Introduction and Commentary* (AB 33; New York: Doubleday, 1993) 738.

[89] So Malherbe, *Paul and the Thessalonians*, 15-17; Meeks, *First Urban Christians*, 63; cf. Haenchen, *Acts of the Apostles*, 507 n. 9.

[90] Malherbe, *Paul and the Thessalonians*, 13-14. Jason's οἶκος might have served as the meeting place of a synagogue, but this is less likely in the context.

Paul and his companions suggests that Jason has some wealth.[91] Malherbe goes on to point out that this is precisely the type of convert Luke would present in his account: "socially prominent and well-off converts."[92] This observation calls some aspects of Luke's account into question. Nevertheless, that a house could function as a workshop[93] suggests that Acts might provide some reflection of the social location of the Thessalonian Christians that we detected in 1 Thessalonians. As handworkers they would have had a place in which to carry out their work. This place might have been Jason's house (whether or not he posted bond for Paul and his companions).[94] Overall, Luke's picture of the founding of the Thessalonian community provides little help in determining the social status of the Thessalonian congregation. We must conclude that there is little to be gained for our study from the Acts accounts.[95]

The Lukan account of the travels of the early Christian missionaries places Paul and Silas in the city of Philippi during Paul's second journey. They are passing through the city on their way to points further east. At this point in Luke's narrative the first "we" passage begins. Although some have used this as evidence that Luke is here recording his own observations, others have suggested that these are the observations of an

---

[91] Malherbe, *Paul and the Thessalonians*, 15-16.

[92] Malherbe, *Paul and the Thessalonians*, 16.

[93] See Hock, *Social Context*, 32-33. Malherbe describes what the workshop in which Paul worked would be like if it were attached to someone's household (*Paul and the Thessalonians*, 17-20). It was not a *domus* but an *insula*, which had shops on street level and living quarters above and behind.

[94] Although generally skeptical of Acts, Collins (*Birth*, 15) includes Jason among the first converts of Thessalonica. He then assumes that Jason was not a leather worker, and questions Malherbe's suggestion of Jason's house as a workshop, citing in support Gaius in Corinth (Rom 16:23) and Lydia in Philippi (Acts 16:14-15), neither of whom worked at the same trade as Paul. However, these latter examples betray Collin's bias towards uniformity in Paul's missionizing tendencies. We would rather suggest that each locale determine Paul's strategy and the nature of the resulting community. Only in 1 Thessalonians does Paul make a *direct* connection between his manual labor and the type of people who make up his audience.

[95] In his brief study of Luke's account of the founding of the Thessalonian church in Acts 17:1-9, Lührmann concludes that while some of the details of the story are confirmed in general by Paul's letters, showing that Luke did have some information, much of the story is modeled on what Luke thought Paul usually did: preaching in the synagogue, some success, rejection by the Jews, leaving the city ("Church at Thessalonica," 237-41). Cf. Collins (*Birth*, 36) describes Luke's presentation in Acts 17 as "an account whose language and episodic presentation are characteristic of Luke. His narrative focus leads him to focus more on the adventures of Paul, his hero, than to give a detailed description of what actually happened in Thessalonica. He is more interested in the conversion of some Gentiles and the Jews' growing hostility to the gospel than he is in the real situation of the church at Thessalonica."

unnamed source writer whom Luke has incorporated into his narrative, although not without changes.⁹⁶

The word commonly used for a Jewish place of meeting in the early first century was προσευχή, so it is noteworthy that in the only place that Luke uses such a designation – Acts 16:13, 16 – the passage is full of ambiguity as to the Jewishness of the scene.⁹⁷ The usual conclusion often drawn from Acts 16 that there existed at Philippi a Jewish community rests on weak foundations and ambiguous language. A number of features of the text deserve some attention. Acts 16:13 records that on the Sabbath Paul and his companions went out of the city to where they thought that there was a place of prayer (προσευχή) by the river. Most commentators have suggested that the meeting that the missionaries came upon was in fact a gathering of Jews. Since προσευχή is the designation for a Jewish place of worship in the first century and earlier, a number of commentators understand Luke to be here referring to a "house" of prayer, not just a place of prayer.⁹⁸

While προσευχή often refers to a building, it can indicate outdoor meetings, the most likely sense in Acts 16:13. Many who understand προσευχή in this way maintain that Paul attended a Jewish service.⁹⁹ It was not a synagogue meeting, since only women were in attendance. A synagogue required a *minyan*, a quorum of ten adult males who must be present for congregational prayer and public reading of the scripture.¹⁰⁰ It is also interesting to note that while προσευχή can indicate a Jewish place of prayer there are some cases where it is used of a pagan place of

---

⁹⁶ I tend towards this latter position. Such a position makes best sense of the civic pride reflected in the well-attested reading πρώτη τῆς μερίδος Μακεδονίας πόλις in Acts 16:12 (see R. S. Ascough, "Civic Pride at Philippi: The Text-Critical Problem of Acts 16.12," *NTS* 44 [1998] 93-103). However, I think that the identification of the "we" source with "Luke" himself is tenuous and not likely insofar as the text of Acts 16 seems to reflect some traditions with an overlay of Lukan concerns.

⁹⁷ That is, where he uses συναγωγή there is mention of "Jews," leaving the type of gathering clear in the mind of the reader. Such is not the case at Philippi. Elsewhere in Acts Luke uses προσευχή as "prayers" but nowhere else as "place of prayer": 1:14; 2:42; 3:1; 6:4; 10:4, 31; 12:5.

⁹⁸ So H. Greeven, "εὔχομαι, κτλ. D. Prayer in the Synagogue," *TDNT* 2 (1964) 808; Haenchen, *Acts of the Apostles*, 499; J. Munck, *The Acts of the Apostles: A New Translation with Introduction and Commentary* (AB 31. New York: Doubleday, 1967) 161.

⁹⁹ Bruce, *Acts of the Apostles*, 314; Neil 1973:181; Dillon 1990:753.

¹⁰⁰ On this requirement see *m Meg.* 4.3; J. M. Reynolds, R. Tannenbaum, and K. T. Erim, *Jews and God-fearers at Aphrodisias: Greek Inscriptions With Commentary* (Proceedings of the Cambridge Philological Society, Supplementary vol. 12; Cambridge: Cambridge Philological Society, 1987) 28-29; F. F. Bruce, *The Book of the Acts* (NICNT; Grand Rapids: Eerdmans, 1988²) 310 n. 37.

prayer.¹⁰¹ This makes Luke's use of προσευχή somewhat ambiguous. Luke notes that the missionaries "supposed"¹⁰² that this was a "Jewish" meeting (Acts 16:13). He does not confirm that it was so.¹⁰³ This ambiguity may be due to Luke's own desire to muddy the situation.

It is possible, certainly beyond proof, that Luke is aware that the riverside meeting at Philippi was not Jewish at all. Luke's ambiguous use of προσευχή may be deliberate. It allows him to preserve his pattern of Paul's missionary strategy (to Jews first, then to Gentiles) for those who would understand προσευχή in its Jewish sense. At the same time, it maintains the sense of his source material, which indicates that it was a pagan meeting. Since there is no mention of a synagogue at Philippi in Luke's sources, Luke needs to be cautious in too boldly stating the existence of such a meeting.¹⁰⁴ The familiarity of the reader with the situation would determine how προσευχή was understood. The description in Acts is not conclusive one way or another.¹⁰⁵

Other indications of the Jewish origins of the Philippian Christian community in Acts 16 can be called into question. The placing of the initial contact between Paul and his converts "on the Sabbath day" (Acts 16:13) is probably Lukan. Luke uses the phrase τῇ ἡμέρᾳ τῶν σαββάτων here, at Luke 4:16, and Acts 13:14. He uses (τῇ) ἡμέρᾳ τοῦ σαββάτου at Luke 13:14, 16 and 14:5. The notion that Jesus and his followers observe

---

¹⁰¹ BAGD *s.v.*; noted in Greeven, "εὔομαι," 808. Levinskaya summarizes the evidence (*Book of Acts*, 213-25). She maintains that the non-Jewish cases of προσευχή can all be interpreted differently than is usual. To do this she either emends a text so that προσευχή is not actually the word in question or stretches the evidence to suggest that it "is not impossible" that the inscription is Jewish. In each case she merely raises possibilities without actually proving anything. One's presuppositions will determine how one interprets the evidence (as do hers in this case). For a more balanced discussion of the methodological problems see Kraemer, "Jewish Tuna," 144-47.

¹⁰² Νομίζω, used with the infinitive, LSJ *s.v.*

¹⁰³ The difficulty of the proper interpretation of Acts 16:13 is compounded by a text critical problem. A number of readings for ἐνομίζομεν προσευχήν are found in the various manuscripts, with no single reading having strong support. The later Byzantine text reads ἐνομίζετο which would be translated "according to custom," thus removing the uncertainty of the missionaries about the nature of the meeting. Metzger notes the problems and possible solutions (*Textual Commentary*, 447). While the UBS committee opted for the reading ἐνομίζομεν προσευχὴν εἶναι, they only did so as it is "the least unsatisfactory solution" to a problem which is "well-nigh baffling."

¹⁰⁴ Although I am equally skeptical about the existence of a synagogue at Thessalonica (and Beroea), Luke's shift back to the term συναγωγή in Acts 17 is due to the much more schematic nature of his sources for the remainder of Macedonia.

¹⁰⁵ In Luke-Acts (and the New Testament) the only other place where προσευχή is used as "place of prayer" is in reference to the temple in a citation from Is 56:7: καὶ ἔσται ὁ οἶκος μου οἶκος προσευχῆς (Luke 19:45; par. Mark 11:17; Matt 21:13).

the Sabbath is certainly a Lukan one (Luke 4:31; 6:6; 13:10; 23:56; Acts 15:44; 17:2; 18:4).[106]

Luke notes that the first Christian convert at Philippi, Lydia, was a "worshipper of God" (σεβομένη τὸν θεόν, Acts 16:14). Most commentators take this phrase to indicate that Lydia was a non-Jewish synagogue worshipper or at least sympathetic to Judaism.[107] The designation for Lydia as a "Jewish sympathizer" is assumed to go back to tradition. This assumption is based on the establishment of προσευχή as a "place of prayer for Jews," and thus may be ill-founded. It is equally possible that Luke has at his disposal a tradition of a devout woman who became Paul's first convert in Philippi. The term can in fact indicate that Lydia was a "godly woman."[108] In order to preserve this tradition Luke may have introduced her in terms of a worshipper of God when in fact she was a worshipper of a deity or deities other than the Jewish God. As with the mention of a προσευχή, σεβομένη τὸν θεόν may have been used in order not to disrupt Luke's pattern of presenting Paul approaching first the Jews and then the Gentiles.[109]

In light of Luke's redactional tendencies and his choice of language it seems probable that he has embellished a tradition of Paul's first contacts

---

[106] The length of the stay of the missionaries in Philippi is left ambiguous: ἡμέρας τινάς (Acts 16:12). Haenchen (*Acts of the Apostles*, 494; cf. Munck, *Acts of the Apostles*, 161) suggests that it really refers to the time between their arrival and the first Sabbath, not the length of the entire stay. The genitive absolute that begins the healing story is a Lukan transitional phrase (Lüdemann, *Early Christianity*, 180). The story wreaks havoc on the chronology if it is taken to have occurred on the same day that the missionaries first visited the προσευχή, since Paul would have been in jail at the same time he was at the river. That Luke does not explicitly place the healing of the possessed girl on the Sabbath and that the girl follows Paul and Silas for many days (πολλὰς ἡμέρας, 16:18) indicates that the missionaries went to the place of prayer on a number of consecutive days, not just the Sabbath.

[107] Haenchen, *Acts of the Apostles*, 494; Bruce, *Book of the Acts*, 311; Williams, *Acts of the Apostles*, 194; Thomas, "Place of Women," 118; Martin, *Philippians*, 8; Beare, *Philippians*, 11.

[108] Pointed out but rejected by Haenchen, *Acts of the Apostles*, 494.

[109] The existence of a Jewish community in Thyatira of Asia Minor is no evidence for the religious affiliation of Lydia, yet it continues to be used in proving Lydia's status as Jewish sympathizer (e.g., Bruce, *Book of the Acts*, 311). First, we have no way of knowing how long ago she had left that city. If she was a former slave, she may have not been in Thyatira since being a small child. Second, many other cults flourished in Thyatira, including those of Asclepius, Dionysus, Artemis, and Isis, suggesting that Lydia's devotion might have been towards one of many deities, if her former residence is use to establish the nature of her piety. Witt notes that "The woman Lydia from Thyatira came from a Lydian city which depicted on its coins Isis standing with sistrym and sceptre.... Isis in an inscription is named 'Lydia' (*VS* [= *SIRIS*] 371)" (*Isis in the Graeco-Roman World* [Aspects of Greek and Roman Life; London: Thames and Hudson, 1971] 322, n. 28).

at Philippi. It seems certain that the missionaries encountered a group of women gathered for the worship of a deity.[110] Although Luke's language leaves open the possibility of understanding this as a Jewish gathering, a close look at the language suggests that it is ambiguous at best, despite Luke's reliance upon a fairly substantial set of sources.[111] Since elsewhere Luke clearly places Paul in the synagogue, the situation at Philippi must be somewhat different. I would suggest that Luke's source makes it clear that there is no Jewish community at Philippi, yet Luke does his best to fit the origins of the Christian community in this city into his own pattern of Paul going first to the Jews and then to the Gentiles.[112] For our purposes, we can conclude that Luke's presentation of the origins of the church at Philippi does not undermine our contention that the Philippian Christian community did not contain a significant number of Jews, nor was it necessarily based on the model of the synagogue.

4. Conclusion

In this appendix we have argued that the assumption that in first century CE Macedonia there existed a large group of Jews and God-fearers who would form the backbone of the Christian communities has little literary and archaeological evidence to support it. In both 1 Thessalonians and Philippians there are no clear references to Jews or things Jewish. While not the basis of our investigation, it does provide further justification for the seeking of analogous community formations in groups other than the synagogues.

---

[110] Schenk suggests that Luke constructs the gathering of women for his own literary purpose, but does not say what that purpose might be ("Philipperbrief," 328). If it were pure fabrication, with no tradition in Luke's sources, it is difficult to understand why Luke would invent a women's meeting, rather than a mixed gender meeting.

[111] That is, Luke's account of Paul at Philippi is more substantial than his summary descriptions of Paul's activities elsewhere in Macedonia (Acts 17). The reference to Paul and Silas advocating Jewish practices that were unlawful for the Romans to accept (Acts 16:21) has little bearing on the argument that the religious gathering was Jewish, as this charge is probably Lukan redaction and not necessarily a reflection on the actual charges brought against the missionaries. The other mention of Philippi is Acts 20:6. Luke reports that after the Feast of Unleavened Bread Paul and his companion(s) sailed from Philippi (Philippi itself was landlocked; its port was Neapolis, 16 km to the south-east on the Via Egnatia). Lüdemann (*Early Christianity*, 221) notes that this is probably Lukan as "Luke loves to incorporate Jewish feasts in his work for the purpose of dating (cf. [Acts 20:] v.16)." It does not suggest the existence of a Jewish community in Philippi.

[112] None of this proves conclusively that Luke is embellishing a tradition of non-Jewish origins for the Christian community at Philippi. We simply raise these points to show the ambiguity of Luke's language and to challenge those who to confidently make assertions on the basis of Acts.

Bibliography

Abrahamsen, Valerie Ann. "Christianity and the Rock Reliefs at Philippi." *BA* 51 (1988) 46-56.

_____. "Pagan Funerary Practices in Northern Greece During the Early Christian Era." *Macedonian Studies* 6 (1989) 58-72.

_____. *Women and Worship at Philippi: Diana/Artemis and Other Cults in the Early Christian Era*. Portland, ME: Astarte Shell Press, 1995.

_____. "Women At Philippi: The Pagan and Christian Evidence." *JFSR* 3 (1987) 17-30.

Adkins, Arthur W. M. *Merit and Responsibility: A Study in Greek Values*. Oxford: Clarendon, 1960.

Alexander, Loveday. "Hellenistic Letter-Forms and the Structure of Philippians." *JSNT* 37 (1989) 87-101.

_____. "Paul and the Hellenistic Schools: The Evidence of Galen." In *Paul in His Hellenistic Context*, ed. Troels Engberg-Pedersen, 60-83. Minneapolis: Fortress, 1995.

Alföldy, G. "Collegium-Organisation in Intercisa." *AAntHung* 6 (1958) 177-98.

Applebaum, Shimon. "The Organization of the Jewish Communities in the Diaspora." In *The Jewish People in the First Century: Historical Geography, Political History, Social, Cultural and Religious Life and Institutions*, ed. S. Safrai and M. Stern, 464-503. CRINT 1. Assen and Philadelphia: VanGorcum and Fortress, 1974.

Arnaoutoglou, Ilias. "Associations and Patronage in Ancient Athens." *Ancient Society* 25 (1994) 5-17.

_____. "Between *koinon* and *idion*: Legal and Social Dimensions of Religious Associations in Ancient Athens." In *Kosmos: Essays in Order, Conflict and Community in Classical Athens*, ed. P. Cartledge, P. Millett, and S. von Reden, 68-83. Cambridge: Cambridge University Press, 1998.

_____. "ΑΡΧΕΡΑΝΙΣΤΗΣ and its Meaning in Inscriptions." *ZPE* 104 (1994) 107-10.

Ascough, Richard S. "An Analysis of the Baptismal Ritual of the *Didache*." *StLtg* 24 (1994) 201-13.

_____. "Associations, Voluntary." In *Eerdmans' Dictionary of the Bible*, ed. David Noel Freedman, 117-18. Grand Rapids: Eerdmans, 2000.

_____. "Benefaction Gone Wrong: The 'Sin' of Ananias and Sapphira in Context." In *Text and Artifact in the Religions of Mediterranean Antiquity: Essays in Honour of Peter Richardson*, ed. Stephen G. Wilson and Michel Desjardins, 91-110. ESCJ 9. Waterloo: Wilfred Laurier University Press, 2000.

_____. "Civic Pride at Philippi: The Text-Critical Problem of Acts 16.12." *NTS* 44 (1998) 93-103.

_____. "The Completion of a Religious Duty: The Background of 2 Cor 8:1-15." *NTS* 42 (1996) 584-99.

_____. "Local and Translocal Relationships Among Voluntary Associations and Early Christianity." *JECS* 5 (1997) 223-41.

_____. "Matthew and Community Formation." In The *Gospel of Matthew in Current Study: Studies in Memory of William G. Thompson, S.J.*, ed. David E. Aune, 96-126. Grand Rapids and Cambridge: Eerdmans, 2001.

_____. "Recent Books on Philippi." *TJT* 13 (1997) 72-77.

_____. "Review of P. Wick, *Der Philipperbrief: Der formale Aufbau des Briefs als Schlüssel zum Verständnis seines Inhalts* (BWANT 7/15; Stuttgart: Kohlhammer, 1994)." *JBL* 114 (1995) 750-52.

_____. "The Thessalonian Christian Community as a Professional Voluntary Association." *JBL* 119 (2000) 311-28.

_____. "Voluntary Associations and Community Formation: Paul's Macedonian Christian Communities in Context." Unpublished Ph.D. dissertation, University of St. Michael's College, Toronto School of Theology, 1997.

_____. *What Are They Saying About the Formation of Pauline Churches?* Mahwah: Paulist, 1998.

Ausbüttel, Frank M. *Untersuchungen zu den Vereinen im Westen des römischen Reiches.* FAS 11. Kallmünz: Michael Laßieben, 1982.

Avezou, Ch., and Ch. Picard. "Inscriptions de Macédoine et de Thrace." *BCH* 37 (1913) 84-154.

Bakirtzis, Charalambos and Helmut Koester. *Philippi at the Time of Paul and After His Death.* Harrisburg: Trinity Press International, 1998.

Baldwin, Barry H. "Strikes in the Roman Empire." *CJ* (1964) 75-76.

Bandini, V. *Appunti sulle corporazioni romane.* Fondazione Guglielmo Castelli 14. Milan: Giuffrh, 1937.

Barclay, John M. G. "Conflict in Thessalonica." *CBQ* 55 (1993) 512-30.

_____. "Thessalonica and Corinth: Social Contrasts in Pauline Christianity." *JSNT* 47 (1992) 49-74.

Bardtke, Hans. "Der gegenwärtige Stand der Erforschung der in Palästina neu gefundenen hebräischen Handschriften, 44: Die Rechtsstellung der Qumran-Gemeinde." *TLZ* 86 (1961) 93-104.

Barrett, C. K. *The New Testament Background: Selected Documents.* 2nd edition. San Francisco: Harper Collins, 1987.

Bartchy, S. Scott. "Undermining Ancient Patriarchy: The Apostle Paul's Vision of a Society of Siblings." *BTB* 29 (1999) 68-78.

Barth, Gerhard. *Der Brief an die Philipper.* ZB NT 9. Zürich: Theologischer Verlag, 1979.

Barton, S. C., and G. H. R. Horsley. "A Hellenistic Cult Group and the New Testament Churches." *JAC* 24 (1981) 7-41.

Bassler, Jouette M. "Σκεῦος: A Modest Proposal for Illuminating Paul's Use of Metaphor in 1 Thessalonians 4:4." In *The Social World of the First Christians: Essays in Honor of Wayne A. Meeks*, ed. L. Michael White and O. Larry Yarbrough, 53-66. Minneapolis: Fortress, 1995.

Batten, Alicia J. "The Moral World of Greco-Roman Associations." Unpublished paper presented at the Canadian Society of Biblical Studies Annual Meeting, Laval, Quebec, May 24, 2001. To be published in *Cultic Groups, Guilds, and Collegia: Associations in the Ancient World*, ed. John S. Kloppenborg and McLean B. Hudson.

Beare, F. W. *A Commentary on the Epistle to the Philippians.* London: Adam and Charles Black, 1959.

Beck, Roger. "The Mysteries of Mithras." In *Voluntary Associations in the Graeco-Roman World*, ed. John S. Kloppenborg and Stephen G. Wilson, 176-85. London and New York: Routledge, 1996.

Berry, Ken L. "The Function of Friendship Language in Philippians 4:10-20." In *Friendship, Flattery, and Frankness of Speech: Studies on Friendship in the New Testament World*, ed. John T. Fitzgerald, 107-24. NovTSup 82. Leiden/New York/Köln: Brill, 1996.

Bertram, Georg. "στρέφω, κτλ." *TDNT* 7 (1971) 722-23.

Best, Ernest. "Bishops and Deacons: Philippians 1,1." *SE* 4 (1968) 371-76.

_____. *The First and Second Epistles to the Thessalonians*. London: Black, 1972.

Bevan, Edwyn Robert. "Mystery Religions." In *The History of Christianity in the Light of Ancient Knowledge: A Collective Work*, 83-115. London and Glasgow: Blackie and Sons, 1929.

Black, David Alan. "The Discourse Structure of Philippians: A Study in Textlinguistics." *NovT* 37 (1995) 16-49.

Boak, A. E. R. "The Organization of Guilds in Greco-Roman Egypt." *TAPA* 68 (1937) 212-20.

Boers, Hendrikus. "The Form-Critical Study of Paul's Letters: 1 Thessalonians as a Case Study." *NTS* 22 (1975-76) 140-58.

Bömer, Franz. *Untersuchungen über die Religion der Sklaven in Griechenland und Rom*. 4 Vols. Akademie der Wissenschaften und der Literatur. Wiesbaden: Steiner, 1958-63.

Bonnard, P. *L'épître de saint Paul aux Philippiens et l'épître aux Colossiens*. CNT 10. Neuchâtel: Delachaux, 1950.

Bonner, Cambell. *Studies in Magical Amulets, Chiefly Graeco-Egyptian*. Ann Arbor: University of Michigan Press, 1950.

Borgen, Peder. "'Yes,' 'No,' 'How Far?': The Participation of Jews and Christians in Pagan Cults." In *Paul in His Hellenistic Context*, ed. Troles Engberg-Pedersen, 30-59. Minneapolis: Fortress, 1995.

Bormann, Lukas. *Philippi: Staat und Christengemeinde zur Zeit des Paulus*. NovTSup 78. Leiden: Brill, 1995.

Bossman, David M. "Paul's Mediterranean Gospel: Faith, Hope, Love." *BTB* 25 (1995) 71-78.

Böttger, P. C. "Die eschatologische Existenz der Christen. Erwägungen zu Philipper 3.20." *ZNW* 60 (1969) 244-63.

Brady, Thomas A. "The Reception of the Egyptian Cults by the Greeks (330-30 B.C.)." In *Sarapis and Isis: Collected Essays*, 7-88. Chicago: Ares, 1978. Repr. of the 1935 edition.

Braun, H. *Qumran und das Neue Testament*. 2 Vols. Tübingen: Mohr Siebeck, 1966.

Briant, P. "Les iraniens d'Asie Mineure après la chut de l'empire achéméide." *DHA* 11 (1985) 167-95.

Brissonius, B. *Antiquitatum ex iure civili selectarum libri quattuor*. Leipzig, 1741.

Brooten, Bernadette J. *Women Leaders in Ancient Synagogues: Inscriptional Evidence and Background Issues*. Brown Judaic Studies 36. Chico: Scholars Press, 1982.

Broughton, T. Robert S. "Roman Asia Minor." In *An Economic Survey of Ancient Rome*. Vol. 5, ed. Tenny Frank, 499-916. Baltimore: Johns Hopkins University Press, 1938.

Brown, Raymond E., and John P. Meier. *Antioch and Rome: New Testament Cradles of Catholic Christianity*. New York: Paulist, 1983.
Bruce, F. F. *1 & 2 Thessalonians*. WBC 45. Waco: Word, 1982.
_____. The Acts of the Apostles. London: Tyndale Press, 1951.
_____. *The Book of the Acts*. NICNT. Grand Rapids: Eerdmans, 1988².
_____. *Paul: Apostle of the Heart Set Free*. Grand Rapids: Eerdmans, 1977.
_____. *Philippians*. NIBC 11. Peabody: Hendrickson, 1983.
Buckler, William H. "Labour Disputes in the Province of Asia." In *Anatolian Studies: Presented to Sir William Mitchell Ramsay*, ed. William H. Buckler and W. M. Calder, 27-50. Manchester: Manchester University Press, 1923.
Burford, Alison. *Craftsmen in Greek and Roman Society*. Aspects of Greek and Roman Life. London and Ithaca: Thames & Hudson and Cornell University Press, 1972.
Burkert, Walter. *Ancient Mystery Cults*. Cambridge and London: Harvard University Press, 1987.
_____. *Greek Religion*. Cambridge: Harvard University Press, 1985.
Burtchaell, James T. *From Synagogue to Church: Public Services and Offices in the Earliest Christian Communities*. Cambridge and New York: Cambridge University Press, 1992.
Byrne, Brendan. "The Letter to the Philippians." In *The New Jerome Biblical Commentary*, ed. Raymond E. Brown, Joseph A. Fitzmyer, and Roland E. Murphy, 791-97. Englewood Cliffs, NJ: Prentice Hall, 1990.
Campbell, J. Y. "The Origin and Meaning of the Christian Use of the Word ΕΚΚΛΗΣΙΑ." *JTS* 49 (1948) 130-43.
_____. "ΚΟΙΝΩΝΙΑ and Its Cognates in the New Testament." *JBL* 51 (1932) 352-80.
Campenhausen, Hans von. *Ecclesiastical Authority and Spiritual Power in the Church of the First Three Centuries*. London: Adam and Charles Black, 1969.
Capper, Brian J. "Paul's Dispute with Philippi: Understanding Paul's Argument in Phil 1-2 from his Thanks in 4.10-20." *TZ* 49 (1993) 193-214.
Carpinelli, Francis Giordano. "'Do This as *My* Memorial' (Luke 22:19): Lucan Soteriology of Atonement." *CBQ* 61 (1999) 74-91.
Carter, Warren. *Matthew and the Margins: A Sociopolitical and Religious Reading*. Maryknoll: Orbis, 2000.
Casson, Stanley. *Macedonia, Thrace and Illyria: Their Relations to Greece from the Earliest Times Down to the Times of Philip son of Amyntas*. Oxford: Oxford University Press, 1926.
Cenival, Françoise. Les associations religieuses en Egypte d'après les documents démotiques. 2 Vols. Publications de l'Institut français d'archéologie orientale du Caire. Bibliothèque d'étude, vol. 46. Caire: Institut français d'archéologie orientale, 1972.
Chadwick, Henry. "The Silence of Bishops in Ignatius." *HTR* 43 (1950) 169-72.
Chapouthier, Fernand. "Némésis et Niké." *BCH* (1924) 287-303.
_____. "Un troisième bas-relief du théâtre de Philippes." *BCH* 49 (1925) 239-44.
Chilton, Bruce. "The Eucharist: Exploring Its Origins." *BRev* 10/6 (1994) 36-43.
Clarke, Andrew D. *Serve the Community of the Church: Christians as Leaders and Ministers*. First-Century Christians in the Graeco-Roman World. Grand Rapids and Cambridge: Eerdmans, 2000.

Clemente, Guido. "Il patronato nei collegia dell'imperio romano." *SCO* 21 (1972) 142-229.
Cohn, Max Conrat. *Zum römischen Vereinsrecht: Abhandlungen aus der Rechtsgeschichte.* Berlin: Weidmann, 1873.
Cole, Susan Guettel. "Greek Cults." In *Civilization of the Ancient Mediterranean: Greece and Rome*, ed. Michael Grant and Rachel Kitzinger, 887-908. New York: Charles Scribner's Sons, 1988.
Collange, Jean-François. *The Epistle of Saint Paul to the Philippians.* London: Epworth, 1979.
Collart, Paul. "Inscriptions de Philippes." *BCH* 57 (1933) 313-79.
_____. *Philippes, ville de Macédonia, depuis ses origines jusqu'à la fin de la l'époque romaine.* Thèse. Université de Genève 85. Paris: Boccard, 1937.
Collins, J. N. *Diakonia: Re-interpreting the Ancient Sources.* New York: Oxford University Press, 1990.
Collins, Raymond F. "A propos the Integrity of I Thes." *ETL* 55 (1979) 67-106.
_____. *The Birth of the New Testament: The Origin and Development of the First Christian Generation.* New York: Crossroad, 1993.
_____. *Studies on the First Letter to the Thessalonians.* Louvain: Louvain University Press, 1984.
Cook, Arthur Bernard. *Zeus: A Study in Ancient Religion.* Cambridge: Cambridge University Press, 1925.
Cormack, James M. R. "Dedications to Zeus Hypsistos at Beroea." *JRS* 31 (1941) 19-23.
_____. "The Gymnasiarchal Law of Beroea." In *Ancient Macedonia* 2, ed. Basil Laourdas and Ch. Makaronas, 139-50. Institute for Balkan Studies 155. Thessalonica: Institute for Blakan Studies, 1977.
_____. "L. Calpurnius Piso." *AJA* 48 (1944) 76-77.
_____. "Progress Report on the Greek Inscriptions of the Trite Meris for *IG* X." In *Ancient Macedonia* 1, ed. Basil Laourdas and Ch. Makaronas, 193-202. Thessalonica: Institute for Balkan Studies, 1970.
Cotter, Wendy J. "The Collegia and Roman Law: State Restrictions on Voluntary Associations 64 BCE - 200 CE." In *Voluntary Associations in the Graeco-Roman World*, ed. John S. Kloppenborg and Stephen G. Wilson, 74-89. London and New York: Routledge, 1996.
_____. "Our *Politeuma* is in Heaven: The Meaning of Phil. 3.17-21." In *Origins and Method: Towards a New Understanding of Judaism and Christianity. Essays in Honour of John C. Hurd*, ed. Bradley H. McLean, 92-104. JSNTSup 86. Sheffield: JSOT Press, 1993.
_____. "Women's Authority Roles in Paul's Churches: Countercultural or Conventional?" *NovT* 36 (1994) 350-72.
Countryman, L. William. "Patrons and Officers in Club and Church." In *SBL 1977 Seminar Papers*, ed. P. J. Achtemeier, 135-43. SBLASP 11. Missoula: Scholars Press, 1977.
Crosby, Michael H. *House of Disciples: Church, Economics, & Justice in Matthew.* Maryknoll: Orbis, 1988.
Dahl, Nils A. "Euodia and Syntyche in Philippians." In *The Social World of the First Christians: Essays in Honor of Wayne A. Meeks*, ed. L. Michael White and O. Larry Yarborough, 3-15. Minneapolis: Fortress, 1995.

_____. *Studies in Paul: Theology for the Early Christian Mission*. Minneapolis: Augsburg, 1977.
Dailey, Thomas F. "To Live or Die: Paul's Eschatological Dilemma in Philippians 1:19-26." *Int* 44 (1990) 18-28.
Danker, Frederick W. "Associations, Clubs, Thiasoi." *ABD* 1 (1992) 501-03.
_____. *Benefactor: Epigraphic Study of a Graeco-Roman and New Testament Semantic Field*. St. Louis: Clayton, 1982.
_____. "On Stones and Benefactors." *Currents in Theology and Mission* 8 (1981) 351-56.
Danker, Frederick, and Robert Jewett. "Jesus as the Apocalyptic Benefactor in Second Thessalonians." In *The Thessalonian Correspondence*, ed. Raymond F. Collins, 486-98. BETL 87. Leuven: Leuven University Press, 1990.
Dareste, Rodolphe, Bernard Haussoullier, and Théodore Reinach, eds. *Récueil des inscriptions juridiques grecques: Texte, traduction, commentair*. SJ 6. Rome: "L'Erma" Di Bretschneider, 1965.
Dassmann, E. "Hausgemeinde und Bischofsamt." In *Vivarium: Festschrift Theodor Klauser zum 90. Geburtstag*, 82-97. JAC Ergänzungsband 11. Münster: Aschendorff, 1984.
Daube, David. "Review of P. W. Duff, *Personality in Roman Private Law* (London: Cambridge University Press, 1938)." *JRS* 33 (1943) 86-93 and 34 (1944) 125-35.
d'Escurac-Doisy, H. "Notes sur le phénomène associatif dans le monde paysan à l'époque du Haut-Empire." *AntAfr* 1 (1967) 59-71.
de Robertis, F. M. *Il fenomeno associativo nel mondo romano dai collegi della repubblica alle corporazioni del basso impero*. Naples: Liber Scientifica edifice, 1955.
_____. *Storia delle corporazioni e del regime associativo nel mondo romano*. 2 Vols. Bari: Adriatica editrice, 1934.
de Rossi, Giovanni Battista. *La Roma sotteranea cristiana*. Rome: Cromo-litografia Pontificia, 1864-77.
de Vos, Craig Steven. *Church and Community Conflicts: The Relationships of the Thessalonian, Corinthian and Philippian Churches*. SBLDS 168. Atlanta: Scholars Press, 1999.
de Witt, Norman W. "Organization and Proceedure in Epicurean Groups." *CP* 31 [1936] 205-11.
Dehandschutter, Boudewijn. "Polycarp's Epistle to the Philippians: An Early Example of 'Reception'." In *New Testament in Early Christianity*, ed. Jean-Marie Sevrin, 275-91. BETL 86. Leuven: Leuven University Press, 1989.
Deissmann, G. Adolf. *Bible Studies: Contributions Chiefly From Papyri and Inscriptions to the History of the Language, the Literature, and the Religion of Hellenistic Judaism and Primitive Christianity*. Edinburgh: T. & T. Clark, 1901.
_____. *Light From the East: The New Testament Illustrated by Recently Discovered Texts of the Greco Roman World*. New York: George H. Doran, 1927[2].
Delling, Gerhard. "σύζυγος." *TDNT* 7 (1971) 748-50.
_____. "ἄτακτος, κτλ." *TDNT* 8 (1972) 47-48.
Dibelius, Martin. *An die Thessalonicher I, II. An die Philipper*. HNT 11. Tübingen: Mohr, 1937[3].
Dill, Samuel. *Roman Society from Nero to Marcus Aurelius*. London: Macmillan, 1905.

Dodds, E. R. *The Greeks and the Irrational.* Berkeley and Los Angeles: University of California Press, 1966.
Dombrowski, B. W. "היחד in IQS and τὸ κοινόν: An Instance of Early Greek and Jewish Synthesis." *HTR* 59 (1966) 293-307.
Donfried, Karl P. "2 Thessalonians and the Church of Thessalonica." In *Origins and Method: Towards a New Understanding of Judaism and Christianity. Essays in Honour of John C. Hurd,* ed. Bradley H. McLean, 128-44. JSNTSup 86. Sheffield: JSOT Press, 1993.
_____. "The Cults of Thessalonica and the Thessalonian Correspondence." *NTS* 31 (1985) 336-56.
_____. "Paul and Judaism: I Thessalonians 2:13-16 as a Test Case." *Int* 38 (1984) 242-53.
_____. "The Theology of 2 Thessalonians." In *The Theology of the Shorter Pauline Epistles,* ed. Karl P. Donfried and I. Howard Marshall, 81-113. New Testament Theology. Cambridge: Cambridge University Press, 1993.
Dormeyer, Detlev. "The Implicit and Explicit Readers and the Genre of Philippians 3:2-4:3, 9-9: Response to the Commentary of Wolfgang Schenk." *Semeia* 48 (1989) 47-59.
Doughty, Darrell J. "Citizens of Heaven: Philippians 3.2-21." *NTS* 41 (1995) 102-22.
Dow, Sterling. "The Egyptian Cults in Athens." *HTR* 30 (1937) 183-232.
Drew-Bear, Thomas. "An Act of Foundation from Hypaipa." *Chiron* 10 (1980) 509-36.
_____. "Local Cults in Graeco-Roman Phrygia." *GRBS* 17 (1976) 247-68.
Duff, P. W. *Personality in Roman Private Law.* London: Cambridge University Press, 1938.
Duling, Dennis C. "The Matthean Brotherhood and Marginal Scribal Leadership." In *Modelling Early Christianity: Social-Scientific Studies of the New Testament in Its Context,* ed. Philip F. Esler, 159-82. London: Routledge, 1995.
_____. "Social-Scientific Small Group Research and Second Testament Study." *BTB* 25 (1995) 179-93.
Düll, Siegrid. *Die Götterkulte Nordmakedoniens in römischer Zeit.* Münchener archäologische Studien 7. Munich: Fink, 1977.
Duncan-Jones, Richard. *The Economy of the Roman Empire: Quantitative Studies.* New York: Cambridge University Press, 1974.
Dunn, James D. G. *Romans 9-16.* WBC 38B. Waco: Word, 1988.
Dupont, Florence. *Daily Life in Ancient Rome.* Oxford: Blackwell, 1992.
Dupont, Jacques. *The Salvation of the Gentiles: Studies in the Acts of the Apostles.* New York: Paulist, 1979.
Eadie, John. *Commentary on the Greek Text of the Epistles of Paul to the Thessalonians.* London: Macmillan, 1877.
Ebner, Martin. *Leidenslisten und Apostelbrief: Untersuchungen zu Form, Motivik und Funktion der Peristasenkataloge bei Paulus.* FB 66. Würzburg: Echter, 1991.
Edson, Charles. "Cults of Thessalonica (Macedonica III)." *HTR* 41 (1948) 153-204.
Edwards, Douglas R. *Religion and Power: Pagans, Jews and Christians in the Greek East.* New York: Oxford University Press, 1996.
Edwards, H. J. "Commerce and Industry." In *A Companion to Greek Studies,* ed. Leonard Whibley, 518-30. New York and London: Hafner, 1963[3].

Ehrman, Bart D. *The New Testament: A Historical Introduction to the Early Christian Writings.* New York and Oxford: Oxford University Press, 1997.
Elgvin, Torleif. "'To Master His Own Vessel.' 1 Thess 4.4 in Light of New Qumran Evidence." *NTS* 43 (1997) 604-19.
Elliott, John H. *What is Social-Scientific Criticism?* GBS. Minneapolis: Fortress, 1993.
Ellis, E. Earle. *Pauline Theology: Ministry and Society.* Grand Rapids: Eerdmans, 1989.
Engberg-Pedersen, Troels. "Stoicism in Philippians." In *Paul in His Hellenistic Context,* ed. Troels Engberg-Pedersen, 256-90. Minneapolis: Fortress, 1995.
Ernst, Josef. "Von der Ortsgemeinde zur Grosskirche – dargestellt an den Kirchenmodellen des Philipper- und Epheserbriefes." In *Kirche im Werden: Studien zum Thema Amt und Gemeinde im Neuen Testament,* ed. Josef Hainz, 123-42. Munich: Schöningh, 1976.
Evans, Robert M. "Eschatology and Ethics: A Study of Thessalonica and Paul's Letters to the Thessalonians." Unpublished Th.D. Dissertation, Basel University, 1967.
Fatum, Lone. "Brotherhood in Christ: A Gender Hermeneutical Reading of 1 Thessalonians." In *Constructing Early Christian Families: Family as Social Reality and Metaphor,* ed. Halvor Moxnes, 183-215. London and New York: Routledge, 1997.
Fee, Gordon D. *Paul's Letter to the Philippians.* NICNT. Grand Rapids: Eerdmans, 1995.
Feissel, Denis. *Recueil des inscriptions chrétiennes de Macédoine du IIIe au VIe siècle.* BCH Supplement 8. Athens and Paris: Ecole Française D'Athènes; Diffusion de Boccard, 1983.
Feissel, Denis and Michel Sève. "Inscriptions de Macédoine." *BCH* 112 (1988) 449-66.
Feldman, Louis H. *Jew and Gentile in the Ancient World: Attitudes and Interactions from Alexander to Justinian.* Princeton: Princeton University Press, 1993.
Ferguson, Everett. *Backgrounds of Early Christianity.* Grand Rapids: Eerdmans, 1987.
Ferguson, William Duncan. *The Legal and Governmental Terms Common to the Macedonian Greek Inscriptions and the New Testament.* Historical and Linguistic Studies Second Series 2/3. Chicago: Chicago University Press, 1913.
Ferguson, William Scott. "The Attic Orgeones." *HTR* 37 (1944) 61-140.
_____. *Hellenistic Athens: An Historical Essay.* London: MacMillan, 1911.
_____. "Review of Bernhard Laum, *Stiftungen in der griechischen und römischen Antike: Ein Beitrag zur antiken Kulturgeschichte* (Leipzig: Teubner, 1914)." *CP* 11 (1916) 109-10.
_____. "Review of Franz Poland, *Geschichte des griechischen Vereinswesens* (Leipzig: Teubner, 1909)." *CP* 5 (1910) 228-30.
Finley, M. I. *The Ancient Economy.* Berkeley: University of California Press, 1973.
Fisher, Nicholas R. E. "Greek Associations, Symposia, and Clubs." In *Civilization of the Ancient Mediterranean: Greece and Rome,* ed. Michael Grant and Rachel Kitzinger, 1167-97. New York: Charles Scribner's Sons, 1988.
_____. "Roman Associations, Dinner Parties, and Clubs." In *Civilization of the Ancient Mediterranean: Greece and Rome,* ed. Michael Grant and Rachel Kitzinger, 1199-225. New York: Charles Scribner's Sons, 1988.
Fitzgerald, John T. "Philippians, Epistle to the." *ABD* 5 (1992) 318-26.
_____. "Philippians in the Light of Some Ancient Discussions of Friendship." In *Friendship, Flattery, and Frankness of Speech: Studies on Friendship in the New*

Testament World, ed. John T. Fitzgerald, 141-60. NovTSup 82. Leiden, New York, Köln: Brill, 1996.

Fitzmyer, Joseph A. "Jewish Christianity in Acts in the Light of the Qumran Scrolls." In *Studies in Luke-Acts*, ed. L. E. Keck and J. L. Martyn, 233-57. Nashville: Abingdon, 1966.

_____. *Romans: A New Translation with Introduction and Commentary*. AB 33. New York: Doubleday, 1993.

Flanagan, Neal. "A Note on Philippians 3,20-21." *CBQ* 18 (1956) 8-9.

Foerster, Werner. "σωτήρ in the Greek World." *TDNT* 7 (1971) 1004-12.

Fohrer, Georg. "σωτήρ in the Old Testament." *TDNT* 7 (1971) 1012-13.

Forbes, Clarence Allen. "Ancient Athletic Guilds." *CP* 50 (1955) 238-52.

Forbes, R. J. *Studies in Ancient Technology*. Vol. 5. Leiden: Brill, 1966².

Foucart, Paul. *Des Associations Religieuses chez les Grecs: Thiases, Éranes, Orgéons*. Paris: Klincksieck, 1873.

Fowler, William W. "Club." *EncBrit* 6 (1910¹¹) 564-68.

Fraikin, Daniel. "Introduction of Sarapis and Isis in Opus." *Numina Aegaea* 1 (1974) 1-3.

Frame, James E. *A Critical and Exegetical Commentary on the Epistles of St. Paul to the Thessalonians*. ICC. Edinburgh: T. & T. Clark, 1912.

Fraser, Peter Marshall. *Rhodian Funerary Monuments*. Oxford: Clarendon Press, 1977.

Garland, David E. "The Composition and Unity of Philippians: Some Neglected Literary Factors." *NovT* 27 (1985) 141-73.

Garland, Robert. *The Piraeus: From the Fifth to the First Century B.C.* London: Duckworth, 1987.

Garnsey, Peter. *Ideas of Slavery from Aristotle to Augustine*. The W. B. Stanford Memorial Lectures. Cambridge and New York: Cambridge University Press, 1996.

_____. "Non-slave Labour in the Roman World." In *Non-slave Labour in the Greco-Roman World*, ed. Peter Garnsey, 34-47. Cambridge Philological Society Suppl. 6. Cambridge: Cambridge Philological Society, 1980.

Garnsey, Peter, and Richard Saller. *The Roman Empire: Economy, Society and Culture*. London: Duckworth, 1987.

Gaston, Lloyd. "Pharisaic Problems." In *Approaches to Ancient Judaism*, ed. Jacob Neusner, 85-100. New Series 3. Atlanta: Scholars Press, 1993.

Gaventa, Beverly Roberts. *First and Second Thessalonians*. Interpretation. Louisville: Westminster John Knox, 1998.

Georgi, Dieter. "The Early Church: Internal Jewish Migration or New Religion." *HTR* 88 (1995) 35-68.

_____. *The Opponents of Paul in Second Corinthians*. Philadelphia: Fortress, 1986.

Gillman, Florence M. *Women Who Knew Paul*. Collegeville: Liturgical Press, 1992.

Ginsburg, M. "Roman Military Clubs and Their Social Functions." *TAPA* (1940) 149-55.

Gnilka, J. *Der Philipperbrief*. HThK 10/3. Freiburg: Herder, 1980³.

Goodman, Martin. *Mission and Conversion: Proselytizing in the Religious History of the Roman Empire*. Oxford: Clarendon, 1994.

Grant, Robert M. *Early Christianity and Society: Seven Studies*. New York: Harper and Row, 1977.

Greenfield, J. "The Marzeah as a Social Institution." *Acta Antiqua Academiae Hungaricae* 22 (1974) 451-55.

Greeven, Heinrich. "εὔομαι, κτλ. D. Prayer in the Synagogue." *TDNT* 2 (1964) 800-08.

Gschnitzer, Fritz. "Eine persiche Kultstiftung in Sardeis und die 'Sippengötter' Vorderasiens." In *Im Bannkreis des Alten Orients: Studien zur Sprach- und Kulturgeschichte des Alten Orients und seines Ausstrahlungsraumes*, ed. W. Meid and H. Trenkwalder, 45-54. Innsbrucker Beiträge zur Kulturwissenschaft 24. Innsbruck: Institut Für Sprachwissenschaft der Universität Innsbruck, 1986.

Guterman, S. L. *Religious Toleration and Persecution in Ancient Rome*. London: Aiglon Press, 1951.

Habicht, Christian. "Review of *IG* X/2." *Gnomen* 46 (1974) 484-92.

Haenchen, Ernst. *The Acts of the Apostles: A Commentary*. Oxford: Blackwell, 1971.

Hainz, Josef. "Die Anfänge des Bischofs- und Diakonenamtes." In *Kirche im Werden: Studien zum Thema Amt und Gemeinde im Neuen Testament*, ed. Josef Hainz, 91-107. Munich: Schöningh, 1976.

_____. *Ekklesia: Strukturen paulinischer Gemeinde-Theologie und Gemeinde-Ordnung*. BU 9. Regensburg: F. Pustet, 1972.

_____. *Koinonia: "Kirche" als Gemeinschaft bei Paulus*. BU 16. Regensburg: Pustet, 1982.

Hammond, N. G. L., and G. T. Griffith. *A History of Macedonia 2: 550-336 B.C.* Oxford: Claredon, 1979.

Hampartumian, Nubar. *Corpus Cultus Equitis Thracii (CCET) IV: Moesia Inferior (Romanian Section) and Dacia*. EPRO 74. Leiden: Brill, 1979.

Hanson, John S. "The Dream/Visions Report and Acts 10:1 - 11:18." Unpublished Ph.D. Diss., Harvard University, 1978.

Hardy, E. G. *Studies in Roman History 1*. London and New York: Sonnenschein and MacMillan, 1906.

Harland, Philip A. "Claiming a Place in *Polis* and Empire: The Significance of Imperial Cults and Connections Among Associations, Synagogues and Christian Groups in Roman Asia (c. 27 BCE – 138 CE). Unpublished Ph.D. dissertation, University of Toronto, 1999.

_____. "Honouring the Emperor or Assailing the Beast: Participation in Civic Life Among Associations (Jewish, Christian and Other) in Asia Minor and the Apocalypse of John." *JSNT* 77 (2000) 99-121.

_____. "Honours and Worship: Emperors, Imperial Cults and Associations at Ephesus (First to Third Centuries C.E.)." *SR* 25 (1996) 319-34.

_____. "Spheres of Contention, Claims of Preeminence: Rivalries Among Associations in Sardis and Smyrna." Unpublished paper presented at the Annual Meeting of the Canadian Society of Biblical Studies, Laval, Quebec, May 24, 2001.

Harnack, Adolf von. "On the Origin of the Christian Ministry." *Expositor* 3/5 (1887) 321-43.

Hatch, Edwin. *The Influence of Greek Ideas on Christianity*. The Hibbert Lectures, 1888. London: Williams and Norgate, 1891.

_____. *The Organization of Early Christian Churches: Eight Lectures*. Bampton Lectures. London: Rivingtons, 1881.

Hatzopoulos, M. B., and L. D. Loukopoulou. *Recherches sur les marches orientales des temenides (Anthemonte-Kalindoia) i*. Meletemata 11. Athens: De Boccard, 1992.

Hawthorne, Gerald F. *Philippians*. WBC 43. Dallas: Word, 1983.

Heineccius, Johann Gottlieb. *De collegiis et corporibus opificum*. Halae Magdeburgicae: Litteris C. Henchelii, 1723.

Heinrici, Georg. "Die Christengemeinden Korinths und die religiösen Genossenschaften der Griechen." *ZWT* 19 (1876) 465-526.
Hemer, Colin J. "Alexandria Troas." *TynBul* 26 (1976) 79-112.
Hendrix, Holland L. "Benefactor/Partonage Networks in the Urban Environment: Evidence from Thessalonica." *Semeia* 56 (1992) 39-58.
_____. "Thessalonians Honor Romans." Unpublished Th.D. Thesis, Harvard University, 1984.
Hengel, Martin. *Judaism and Hellenism: Studies in their Encounter in Palestine During the Early Hellenistic Period.* Philadelphia: Fortress, 1974.
_____. "Die Synagogeninschrift von Stobi." *ZNW* 57 (1966) 145-83.
Herrmann, Peter. "Mystenvereine in Sardeis." *Chiron* 26 (1996) 315-48.
Heyob, Sharon Kelly. *The Cult of Isis Among Women in the Graeco-Roman World.* EPRO 51. Leiden: Brill, 1975.
Hicks, E. L. "On Some Political Terms Employed in the New Testament." *CR* 1 (1887) 4-8, 42-46.
Hirschfeld, Otto. "Der praefectus vigilum in Nemausus und die Feuerwehr in den römischen Landstädten." In *Gallische Studien*, part 3. Wein: C. Gerold's sohn, 1884. Repub. in *Kleine Schriften* (Berlin: Weidmann, 1913) 96-111.
Hock, Ronald F. "Paul's Tentmaking and the Problem of His Social Class." *JBL* 97 (1978) 555-64.
_____. *The Social Context of Paul's Ministry: Tentmaking and Apostleship.* Philadelphia: Fortress, 1980.
_____. "The Workshop as a Social Setting for Paul's Missionary Preaching." *CBQ* 41 (1979) 438-50.
Hoddinott, R. F. *The Tracians.* New York: Thames and Hudson, 1981.
Hoey, A. S. "Rosaliae Signorum." *HTR* 30 (1937) 15-35.
Holtz, Traugott. *Der erste Brief an die Thessalonicher.* EKK 13. Zürich: Benziger, 1986.
Horsley, G. H. R. *New Documents Illustrating Early Christianity: A Review of the Greek Inscriptions and Papyri.* NewDocs 1. North Ryde, Australia: Ancient History Documentary Research Centre, Macquarie University, 1981.
_____. *New Documents Illustrating Early Christianity: A Review of the Greek Inscriptions and Papyri published in 1978.* NewDocs 3. North Ryde, Australia: Ancient History Documentary Research Centre, Macquarie University, 1983.
_____. *New Documents Illustrating Early Christianity: A Review of the Greek Inscriptions and Papyri Published in 1979.* NewDocs 4. North Ryde, Australia: Ancient History Documentary Research Centre, Macquarie University, 1987.
_____. *New Documents Illustrating Early Christianity: Linguistic Essays.* NewDocs 5. North Ryde, Australia: The Ancient History Documentary Research Centre, Macquarie University, 1989.
_____. "The Inscriptions of Ephesos and the New Testament." *NovT* 34 (1992) 105-68.
_____. "The Politarchs." In *The Book of Acts in Its First Century Setting 2: The Book of Acts in Its Graeco-Roman Setting*, ed. David W. J. Gill and Conrad Gempf, 419-31. Grand Rapids and Carlisle: Eerdmans and Paternoster, 1994.
Horsley, G. H. R. and John A. L. Lee. "A Preliminary Checklist of Abbreviations of Greek Epigraphic Volumes." *Epigraphica* 56 (1994) 129-69.
Hugédé, N. *Saint Paul et la Grèce.* Paris: Les Belles Lettres, 1982.

Jaczynowska, Maria. *Les associations de la jeunesse romaine sous le Haut-Empire.* Wroclaw: Zaklad Narodowy Im Ienia Ossolinskisch, 1978.

———. "Le caratteristiche delle associazioni della gioventù romana (collegia iuvenum)." *AIV* 134 (1975/76) 359-81.

Jeffers, James S. *The Greco-Roman World of the New Testament: Exploring the Background of Early Christianity.* Downers Grove: InterVarsity Press, 1999.

Jeremias, Joachim. *Jerusalem in the Time of Jesus: An Investigation into Economic and Social Conditions During the New Testament Period.* Philadelphia: Fortress, 1969.

Jervis, L. Ann. "1 Corinthians 14:34-35: A Reconsideration of Paul's Limitation of the Free Speech of Some Corinthian Women." *JSNT* 58 (1995) 51-74.

Jewett, Robert, "Conflicting Movements in the Early Church as Reflected in Philippians." *NovT* 12 (1970) 362-90.

———. "The Epistolary Thanksgiving and the Integrity of Philippians." *NovT* 12 (1970) 40-53.

———. "Tenement Churches and Communal Meals in the Early Church: The Implications of a Form-Critical Analysis of 2 Thessalonians 3:10." *BR* 38 (1993) 23-43.

———. *The Thessalonian Correspondence: Pauline Rhetoric and Millenarian Piety.* Foundations and Facets. Philadelphia: Fortress, 1986.

Johanson, Bruce C. *To All the Brethren: A Text-Linguistic and Rhetorical Approach to 1 Thessalonians.* ConBNT 16. Stockholm: Almqvist & Wiksell, 1987.

Johnson, Luke Timothy. *The Literary Function of Possessions in Luke-Acts.* SBLDS 39. Missoula: Scholars Press, 1977.

Jones, A. H. M. "The Economic Life of the Towns of the Roman Empire." In *La Ville: Deuxième partie: Institutions économiques et sociales,* vol. 2, ed. Jean Firenne, 161-94. Recueils de la Société Jean Bodin 7. Brussels: éditions de la Libraire Éncyclopédique, 1955.

Jones, C. P. "A Deed of Foundation from the Territory of Ephesos." *JRS* 73 (1983) 116-25.

Jones, Nicholas F. *The Associations of Classical Athens.* Oxford: Oxford University Press, 1999.

Josaitis, Norman F. *Edwin Hatch and Early Church Order.* Gembloux: Éditions J. Duculot, 1971.

Joshel, Sandra R. *Work, Identity, and Legal Status at Rome: A Study of the Occupational Inscriptions.* Norman and London: University of Oklahoma Press, 1992.

Judge, E. A. *The Social Pattern of Christian Groups in the First Century: Some Prolegomena to the Study of New Testament Ideas of Social Obligation.* London: Tyndale, 1960.

Juster, Jean. *Les Juifs dans l'empire romain: Leur Condition Jurdique, Économique et Sociale.* Paris: Paul Geuthner, 1914.

Kant, L. H. "Jewish Inscriptions in Greek and Latin." *ANRW* II.20.2 (1987) 671-713.

Kaye, Bruce N. "Eschatology and Ethics in 1 and 2 Thessalonians." *NovT* 17 (1975) 47-57.

Kaysar, F. *Recueil d'inscriptions grecques et latins (non funéraires) d'Alexandrie Impériale (Ier - III^{er} s. apr. J.-C.).* Bibliothèque d'étude 108. Cairo: Institut Français d'archéologie orientale du Caire, 1996.

Kazarow, G. "Heros (thrakischer)." *RE Suppl.* 3 (1918) 1132-48.

Kennedy, H. A. A. "The Financial Coloring of Phil. 4.15-18." *ExpTim* 12 (1900-1901) 43-44.

Klauck, Hans-Josef. "Die Hausgemeinde als Lebensform im Urchristentum." *MTZ* (1981) 32:1-15.

_____. *Hausgemeinde und Hauskirche im frühen Christentum.* SBS 103. Stuttgart: Katholisches Bibelwerk, 1981.

_____. *Herrenmahl und hellenistischer Kult: Eine religionsgeschichtliche Untersuchung zum ersten Korintherbrief.* NTAbh 15. Münster: Aschendorff, 1982.

_____. "Lord's Supper." *ABD* 4 (1992) 362-72.

_____. *The Religious Context of Early Christianity: A Guide to Graeco-Roman Religions.* SNTW. Edinburgh: T. & T. Clark, 2000.

Klinghardt, Matthias. *Gemeinschaftsmahl und Mahlgemeinschaft. Soziologie und Liturgie frühchristlicher Mahlfeiern.* Texte und Arbeiten zum neutestamentlichen Zeitalter 13. Tübingen and Basel: Francke, 1996.

Kloppenborg, John S. "Collegia and *Thiasoi*: Issues in Function, Taxonomy and Membership." In *Voluntary Associations in the Graeco-Roman World*, ed. John S. Kloppenborg and Stephen G. Wilson, 16-30. London and New York: Routledge, 1996.

_____. "Edwin Hatch, Churches and *Collegia*." In *Origins and Method: Towards a New Understanding of Judaism and Christianity. Essays in Honour of John C. Hurd*, ed. Bradley H. McLean, 212-38. JSNTSup 86. Sheffield: JSOT Press, 1993.

_____. "Egalitarianism in the Myth and Rhetoric of Pauline Churches." In *Reimagining Christian Origins: A Colloquium Honoring Burton L. Mack*, ed. Elizabeth A. Castelli and Hal Taussig, 247-63. Valley Forge: Trinity Press International, 1996.

_____. "Status und Wohltätigkeit bei Paulus und Jakobus." In *Von Jesus zum Christus – Christologische Studien: Festgabe für Paul Hofmann zum 65. Geburtstag*, ed. Rudolf Hoppe and Ulrich Busse, 127-54. Berlin and New York: Walter de Gruyter, 1998.

_____. "ΦΙΛΑΔΕΛΦΙΑ, ΘΕΟΔΙΔΑΚΤΟΣ and the Dioscuri: Rhetorical Engagement in 1 Thessalonians 4.9-12." *NTS* 39 (1993) 265-89.

Kloppenborg, John S. and B. Hudson McLean, eds. *Cultic Groups, Guilds, and Collegia: Associations in the Ancient World.* In preparation.

Kneissl, P. "Die Entstehung und Bedeutung der Augustalität." *Chrion* 10 (1980) 291-326.

_____. "Die utriclairii. Ihre Rolle im gallo-römischen Transportwesen und Weinhandel." *BJ* 181 (1981) 79-99.

Knox, John. *Chapters in a Life of Paul.* Macon: Mercer University Press, 1987[2].

Koester, Helmut. "The Purpose of the Polemic of a Pauline Fragment (Philippians III)." *NTS* 8 (1961-62) 317-32.

Kornemann, Ernst. "Collegium." *PW* 4/1 (1900) 380-479.

Koukouli-Chrysantaki, Chaido. "Colonia Iulia Augusta Philippensis." In *Philippi at the Time of Paul and After His Death*, ed. Charalambos Bakirtzis and Helmut Koester, 5-35. Harrisburg: Trinity Press International, 1998.

Kraabel, A. T. "Paganism and Judaism: The Sardis Evidence." In *Diaspora Jews and Judaism: Essays in Honor of, and in Dialogue with, A. Thomas Kraabel*, ed. J. Andrew Overman and Robert S. MacLennan, 237-56. South Florida Studies in the History of Judaism 41. Atlanta: Scholars Press, 1992.

_____. "The Disappearance of the 'God-Fearers'." *Numen* 28 (1981) 113-26.

_____. "Ὕψιστος and the Synagogue at Sardis." *GRBS* 10 (1969) 81-93.
Kraemer, Ross S. "Jewish Tuna and Christian Fish: Identifying Religious Affiliation in Epigraphic Sources." *HTR* 84 (1991) 141-62.
Kurz, K. "Methodische Bemerkungen zum Studium der Kollegien im Donaugebiet." *AAntHung* 8 (1960) 133-44.
La Piana, Georg. "Foreign Groups in Rome During the First Century of the Empire." *HTR* 20 (1927) 183-354.
Lampe, Peter. "Das korinthische Herrenmahl im Schnittpunkt hellenistisch-römischer Mahlpraxis und paulinischer Theologia Crucis (1 Kor 11,17-34)." *ZNW* 82 (1991) 183-213.
Laub, Franz. "Paulus als Gemeindegründer (1 Thess)." In *Kirche im Werden: Studien zum Thema Amt und Gemeinde im Neuen Testament*, ed. Josef Hainz, 17-38. Munich: Schöningh, 1976.
Laum, Bernhard. *Stiftungen in der griechischen und römischen Antike: Ein Beitrag zur antiken Kulturgeschichte*. Leipzig: Teubner, 1914.
Leicht, P. "Lineamenti della introduzione storica al diritto corporativo." In *Atti del primo convegno di studi sindacali e corporativi*, 65-78. Rome, 1930.
_____. "Ricerche sulle corporazioni professionali in Italia dal secolo V all' XI." *RAL* 12 (1936) 195-241.
Lemerle, Paul. *Philippes et la Macédoine orientale à l'epoque chrétienne et byzantine*. BEFAR 158. Paris: Boccard, 1945.
_____. "Inscriptions latines et grecques de Philippes." *BCH* 59 (1935) 126-65.
Lane, Eugene N. "Men: A Neglected Cult of Roman Asia Minor," *ANRW* 2.18.3 (1990) 2161-74.
Leon, Harry J. *The Jews of Ancient Rome: Updated Edition*. Peabody: Hendrickson, 1995.
Levine, Lee I. *Roman Caesarea: An Archaeological-Topological Study*. Jerusalem: Institute of Archaeology, Hebrew University of Jerusalem, 1975.
Levinskaya, Irina A. *The Book of Acts in its Diaspora Setting*. BAFCS 5. Grand Rapids: Eerdmans, 1996.
Liebenam, W. *Zur Geschichte und Organisation des römischen Vereinswesens: Drei Untersuchungen*. Leipzig: Teubner, 1890.
Lietzmann, Hans. *An die Korinther I/II*. Revised by W. G. Kümmel. HNT 9. Tübingen: Mohr Siebeck, 1969[5].
Lifshitz, Baruch. "Prolegomenon." In *Corpus of Jewish Inscriptions: Jewish Inscriptions from the Third Century B.C. to the Seventh Century A.D. I: Europe*, ed. P. Jean-Baptiste Frey, 1-97. New York: KTAV, 1975.
Lightfoot, J. B. *Biblical Essays*. London: Macmillan, 1893.
_____. *Saint Paul's Epistle to the Philippians*. London: Macmillan, 1881[6].
Lincoln, Andrew T. *Paradise Now and Not Yet: Studies in the Role of the Heavenly Dimension in Paul's Thought with Special Reference to His Eschatology*. SNTSMS 43. Cambridge: Cambridge University Press, 1981.
Linderski, Jerzy. "Der Senat und die Vereine." In *Gesellschaft und Recht im griechisch-römischen Altertum*, 94-132. Deutsche Akademie der Wissenschaften zu Berlin 52. Berlin: Akademie Verlag, 1968.
_____. "Suetons Bericht über die Vereinsgesetzgebung unter Caesar und Augustus." *ZGR* 79 (1962) 322-28.

Loening, Edgar. *Die Gemeindeverfassung des Urchristentums: Eine Kirchenrechtliche Untersuchung*. Halle: Niemeyer, 1888.
Louis, Paul. *Ancient Rome at Work: An Economic History of Rome from the Origins to the Empire*. London and New York: Kegan Paul, Trench, Trubner and Knopf, 1927.
Louw, Johannes P., and Eugene A. Nida. *Greek-English Lexicon of the New Testament Based on Semantic Domains*. 2 Vols. New York: United Bible Society, 1988.
Lüdemann, Gerd. *Early Christianity According to the Traditions in Acts: A Commentary*. Minneapolis: Fortress, 1987
Lüderitz, Gert. "What is the Politeuma?" In *Studies in Early Jewish Epigraphy*, ed. J. W. van Henten and P. W. van der Horst, 183-225. AGJU 21. Leiden, New York, Köln: Brill, 1994.
Lührmann, Dieter. "The Beginnings of the Church at Thessalonica." In *Greeks, Romans, and Christians: Essays in Honor of Abraham J. Malherbe*, ed. David L. Balch, Everett Ferguson, and Wayne A. Meeks, 237-49. Minneapolis: Fortress, 1990.
Lünemann, Gottlieb. *Critical and Exegetical Handbook to the Epistles of St. Paul to the Thessalonians*. Edinburgh: T. & T. Clark, 1880.
Luter, A. Boyd, and Michelle V. Lee. "Philippians as Chiasmus: Key to the Structure, Unity and Theme Questions." *NTS* 41 (1995) 89-101.
Lyons, George. *Pauline Autobiography: Towards a New Understanding*. SBLDS 73. Atlanta: Scholars Press, 1985.
MacLennan, Robert S., and A. T. Kraabel. "The God-Fearers – A Literary and Theological Invention." *BARev* 12/5 (1986) 46-53, 64.
MacMullen, Ramsay. *Roman Social Relations 50 B.C. to A.D. 284*. New Haven and London: Yale University Press, 1974.
_____. "A Note on Roman Strikes." *CJ* 58 (1962) 269-71.
MacMullen, Ramsay, and Eugene N. Lane, ed. *Paganism and Christianity 100-425 C.E.: A Sourcebook*. Minneapolis: Fortress, 1992.
Malherbe, Abraham J. "Did the Thessalonians Write to Paul?" In *The Conversation Continues: Studies in Paul and John in Honor of J. Louis Martyn*, ed. R. Fortna and B. Gaventa, 246-57. Nashville: Abingdon, 1990.
_____. *The Letters to the Thessalonians: A New Translation with Introduction and Commentary*. AB 32B. New York: Doubleday, 2000.
_____. *Paul and the Thessalonians: The Philosophic Tradition of Pastoral Care*. Philadelphia: Fortress, 1987.
_____. "Paul's Self-Sufficiency (Philippians 4:11)." In *Friendship, Flattery, and Frankness of Speech: Studies on Friendship in the New Testament World*, ed. John T. Fitzgerald, 125-39. NovTSup 82. Leiden, New York, Köln: Brill, 1996.
_____. *Social Aspects of Early Christianity*. Philadelphia: Fortress, 1983².
Malina, Bruce J. *Christian Origins and Cultural Anthropology: Practical Models for Biblical Interpretation*. Atlanta: John Knox, 1986.
_____. "Early Christian Groups: Using Small Group Formation Theory to Explain Christian Organizations." In *Modelling Early Christianity: Social-Scientific Studies of the New Testament in its Context*, ed. P. F. Esler, 96-113. London: Routledge, 1995.
Malinowski, Francis X. "The Brave Women of Philippi." *BTB* 15 (1985) 60-64.
Mannzmann, Anneliese. *Griechische Stiftungsurkunden: Studie zu Inhalt und Rechtsform*. Fonts et Commentationes 2. Münster: Aschendorff, 1962.

Manson, T. W. "St. Paul in Greece: The Letters to the Thessalonians." *BJRL* 35 (1953) 438-47.
Mantel, H. "The Nature of the Great Synagogue." *HTR* 60 (1967) 69-91.
Marshall, I. Howard. *1 and 2 Thessalonians*. NCBC. Grand Rapids: Eerdmans, 1983.
Marshall, Peter. *Enmity in Corinth: Social Conventions in Paul's Relations with the Corinthians*. WUNT 2.23. Tübingen: Mohr Siebeck, 1987.
Martin, Dale B. *The Corinthian Body*. New Haven and London: Yale University Press, 1995.
_____. "Paul Without Passion: On Paul's Rejection of Desire in Sex and Marriage." In *Constructing Early Christian Families: Family as Social Reality and Metaphor*, ed. Halvor Moxnes, 201-15. London and New York: Routledge, 1997.
_____. *Slavery as Salvation: The Metaphor of Slavery in Pauline Christianity*. New Haven and London: Yale University Press, 1990.
Martin, Ralph P. *Philippians*. NCBC. London: Oliphants, 1976.
Marxsen, Willi. *Der erste Brief an die Thessalonicher*. ZBK NT 11/1. Zurich: Theologischer Verlag, 1979.
Masson, Charles. *Les Deux Épitres de Saint Paul aux Thessaloniciens*. Neuchâtel and Paris: Delachaux & Niestle, 1957.
Matthias, B. "Zur Geschichte der römischen Zwangsverbände." In *Festschrift zum fünfzigjährigen Doctorjubiläum von Dr. H. v. Buchka*. Rostock: Universität Rostock, 1891.
Maué, Hermann C. *Der praefectus fabrum: ein Beitrag zur Geschichte des römischen Beamtentums und des Collegialwesens während der Kaiserzeit*. Halle: Niemeyer, 1887.
Maurer, C. "σκεῦος." *TDNT* 7 (1971) 359-67.
McCready, Wayne O. "*Ecclesia* and Voluntary Associations." In *Voluntary Associations in the Graeco-Roman World*, ed. John S. Kloppenborg and Stephen G. Wilson, 59-73. London and New York: Routledge, 1996.
McGehee, Michael. "A Rejoinder to Two Recent Studies Dealing with 1 Thessalonians 4:4." *CBQ* 51 (1989) 82-89.
McKnight, Scot. *A Light Among the Gentiles: Jewish Missionary Activity in the Second Temple Period*. Minneapolis: Fortress, 1991.
McLean, Bradley H. "The Agrippinilla Inscription: Religious Associations and Early Church Formation." In *Origins and Method: Towards a New Understanding of Judaism and Christianity. Essays in Honour of John C. Hurd*, ed. Bradley H. McLean, 239-70. JSNTSup 86. Sheffield: JSOT Press, 1993.
_____. "For the Love of Dionysos: Five Forms of Dionysias Devotion." Unpublished Paper, 1995.
_____. "The Place of Cult in Voluntary Associations and Christian Churches on Delos." In *Voluntary Associations in the Graeco-Roman World*, ed. John S. Kloppenborg and Stephen G. Wilson, 186-225. London and New York: Routledge, 1996.
_____. "Trade Guilds of Lydia and Phrygia." Unpublished essay of 1995, prepared for *Cultic Groups, Guilds, and Collegia: Associations in the Ancient World*, ed. John S. Kloppenborg and Bradley H. McLean.
Mearns, Christopher L. "Early Eschatological Development in Paul: The Evidence of I and II Thessalonians." *NTS* 27 (1980-81) 137-57.

Meeks, Wayne A. *The First Urban Christians: The Social World of the Apostle Paul.* New Haven: Yale University Press, 1983.

———. "The Man From Heaven in Paul's Letter to the Philippians." In *The Future of Early Christianity: Essays in Honor of Helmut Koester,* ed. Birger A. Pearson, 329-36. Minneapolis: Fortress, 1991.

———. *The Moral World of the First Christians.* LEC 6. Philadelphia: Westminster, 1986.

———. "The Urban Environment of Pauline Christianity." In *SBL 1980 Seminar Papers,* ed. P. J. Achtemeier, 113-22. SBLASP 19. Chico: Scholars, 1980.

Meiggs, Russell. *Roman Ostia.* Oxford: Clarendon, 1960.

Mendelsohn, I. "Guilds in Ancient Palestine." *BASOR* 80/4 (1940) 17-21.

———. "Guilds in Babylonia and Assyria." *JAOS* 60 (1940) 68-72.

Mengel, B. *Studien zum Philipperbrief: Untersuchungen zum situativen Kontext unter besonderer Berücksichtigung der Frage nach der Ganzheitlichkeit oder Einheitlichkeit eines paulinischen Briefes.* WUNT 2/8. Tübingen: Mohr Siebeck, 1982.

Menken, Maarten J. J. *2 Thessalonians.* London and New York: Routledge, 1994.

Merkelbach, Reinhold. "Zwei Texte aus dem Sarapeum zu Thessalonike." *ZPE* 10 (1973) 45-54.

Metzger, Bruce M. *A Textual Commentary on the Greek New Testament.* London: United Bible Societies, 1971.

Meyer, Marvin W., ed. *The Ancient Mysteries: A Sourcebook. Sacred Texts of the Mystery Religions of the Ancient Mediterranean World.* San Francisco: Harper and Row, 1987.

Michael, John Hugh. *The Epistle of Paul to the Philippians.* Moffatt NT Commentary. London: Hodder and Stoughton, 1928.

Michaelis, Wilhelm. "μιμέομαι, κτλ." *TDNT* 4 (1967) 659-74.

Miller, E. C. "Πολιτεύεσθε in Philippians 1.27: Some Philological and Thematic Observations." *JSNT* 15 (1982) 86-96.

Milligan, George. *St. Paul's Epistles to the Thessalonians: The Greek Text with Introduction and Notes.* London: Macmillan, 1908.

Minns, Ellis H. *Scythians and Greeks: A Survey of Ancient History and Archaeology of the North Coast of the Euxine from the Danube to the Caucasus.* Cambridge: Cambridge University Press, 1913.

Mitchell, Alan C. "'Greet the Friends by Name:' New Testament Evidence for the Greco-Roman *Topos on Friendship.*" In *Greco-Roman Perspectives on Friendship,* ed. John T. Fitzgerald, 225-62. SBLRBS 34. Atlanta: Scholars Press, 1997.

Mommsen, Theodor. *De collegiis et sodaliciis Romanorum. Accedit inscriptio lanuvina.* Kiel: Libraria Schwersiana, 1843.

Monti, G. *Le corporazione nell'evo antico e nell'evo medioevo.* Bari, 1934.

Morris, Leon. *The First and Second Epistles to the Thessalonians.* NICNT. Grand Rapids: Eerdmans, 1959.

———. "ΚΑΙ ΑΠΑΧ ΚΑΙ ΔΙΣ." *NovT* 1 (1956) 205-08.

Moulton, James Hope, and George Milligan. *The Vocabulary of the Greek New Testament Illustrated from the Papyri and Other Non-literary Sources.* London: Hodder and Stoughton, 1914-29.

Müller, A. "Sterbekassen und Vereine mit Begräbnisfürsorge in der römischen Kaiserzeit." *Neue Jahrbücher für das klassische Altertum, Geschichte und deutsche Literatur* 15 (1905) 183-201.

Müller, Jac. J. *The Epistles of Paul to the Philippians and Philemon*. NICNT. Grand Rapids: Eerdmans, 1955.

Müller, Ulrich B. *Der Brief des Paulus an die Philipper*. THK 11/I. Berlin: Evangelische Verlagsanstalt, 1993.

Munck, Johannes. *The Acts of the Apostles: A New Translation with Introduction and Commentary*. AB 31. New York: Doubleday, 1967.

Murphy-O'Connor, Jerome. *Paul: A Critical Life*. Oxford: Clarendon, 1996.

Nanos, Mark D. *The Mystery of Romans: The Jewish Context of Paul's Letter*. Minneapolis: Fortress, 1996.

Nehama, J. *Histoire des Israélites de Salonique 1: La Communaute Romaniote – Les Sefaradis et leur Dispersion*. Thessalonica: Molho, 1935.

Neil, William. *The Epistle of Paul to the Thessalonians*. MNTC. London: Hodder and Stoughton, 1950.

Neubecker, F. *Vereine ohne Rechtsfähigkeit*. Leipzig, 1908.

Neumann, K. J. *Der römische Staat und die allgemeine Kirche bis auf Diocletian*. Leipzig: Veit, 1890.

Nigdelis, P. M. "Synagoge(n) und Gemeinde der Juden in Thessalonica: Fragen aufgrund einer neuen jüdischen Grabinschrift der Kaiserzeit." *ZPE* 102 (1994) 297-306.

Nilsson, Martin P. *Cults, Myths, Oracles, and Politics in Ancient Greece*. Lund: Gleerup, 1951.

_____. *The Dionysiac Mysteries of the Hellenistic and Roman Age*. Lund: Gleerup, 1957.

Nock, A. D. *Conversion: The Old and the New in Religion from Alexander the Great to Augustine of Hippo*. Oxford: Oxford University Press, 1933.

_____. "The Historical Importance of Cult-Associations." *CR* (1924) 105-09.

_____. "Soter and Euegertes." In *Essays on Religion in the Ancient World*, ed. Zeph Stewart, 720-59. Oxford: Clarendon 1972.

_____. "Studies in the Graeco-Roman Beliefs of the Empire." *JHS* 45 (1925) 84-101.

O'Brien, Peter T. *The Epistle to the Philippians: A Commentary on the Greek Text*. NIGTC. Grand Rapids: Eerdmans, 1991.

Osiek, Carolyn. *What Are They Saying About the Social Setting of the New Testament?* New York and Mahwah: Paulist, 1992[2].

Oster, R. "Holy Days in Honour of Artemis." In *New Documents Illustrating Early Christianity: A Review of the Greek Inscriptions and Papyri Published in 1979*, ed. G. H. R. Horsley, 74-82. NewDocs 4. North Ryde, Australia: Ancient History Documentary Research Centre, Macquarie University, 1987.

Palmer, D. W. "'To Die is Gain' (Philippians 1:21)." *NovT* 17 (1975) 203-18.

Panayotou, Anna, and P. Chrysostomou. "Inscriptions de la Bottiée et de l'Almopie en Macédoine." *BCH* 117 (1993) 359-400.

Pancirolus, G. *De magistratibus municipalibus et corporibus artificium*. Genf, 1623.

Papazoglou, Fanoula. "Macedonia Under the Romans." In *Macedonia: 4000 Years of Greek History and Civilization*, ed. M. B. Sakellariou, 192-207. Athens: Ekdotike Athenon S.A, 1988.

_____. "Quelques aspects de l'histoire de la province de Macédoine." *ANRW* II.7.1 (1979) 302-69.
Paton, W. R. and E. L. Hicks. *The Inscriptions of Cos.* Oxford: Clarendon, 1891.
Pearson, B. A. "1 Thessalonians 2:13-16: A Deutero-Pauline Interpolation." *HTR* (1971) 79-94.
Pelekides, S. "'Ανασκαφὴ 'Εδέσσης." *ArchDelt* 9 (1923) 259-69.
Pennacchietti, F. A. "Nuove iscrizion i di Hierapolis Frigia." *Atti della Accademia delle Scienze de Torino* 101 (1966) 287-328.
Perdrizet, Paul. "Inscriptions de Philippes: Les Rosalies." *BCH* 24 (1900) 299-333.
_____. "Némésis." *BCH* 38 (1914) 89-100.
_____. "Syriaca, part 2." *RArch* 35 (1899, 3rd ser.) 34-53.
Perkins, Pheme. "Christology, Friendship and Status: The Rhetoric of Philippians." In *SBL 1987 Seminar Papers*, ed. Kent H. Richards, 509-20. SBLASP 26. Atlanta: Scholars Press, 1987.
Pervo, Richard I. *Profit with Delight: The Literary Genre of the Acts of the Apostles.* Philadelphia: Fortress, 1987.
Peterlin, D. *Paul's Letter to the Philippians in the Light of Disunity in the Church.* NovTSup 79. Leiden/New York/Köln: Brill, 1995.
Peterman, Gerald W. "'Thankless Thanks': The Epistolary Social Convention in Philippians 4:10-20." *TynBul* 42 (1991) 261-70.
Pfister, F. "Épiphanie." *RESuppl* 4 (1924) 278-323.
Picard, Ch., and Ch. Avezou. "Le testament de la prêtresse Thessalonicienne." *BCH* 38 (1914) 38-62.
Pickard-Cambridge, Arthur W. *The Dramatic Festivals of Athens.* Revised by J. Gould and D. M. Lewis. Oxford: Clarendon, 1968².
_____. *The Theatre of Dionysus in Athens.* Oxford: Clarendon, 1940.
Pilhofer, Peter. *Philippi. Band I. Die erste christliche Gemeinde Europas.* WUNT 87. Tübingen: Mohr Siebeck, 1995.
_____. *Philippi. Band II. Katalog der Inschriften von Philippi.* WUNT 119. Tübingen: Mohr Siebeck, 2000.
Plassart, André. "La Synagogue juive de Délos." *RB* 11 (1914) 523-34.
Platnerus, E. *De collegiis opificum (Disputatio I und II).* Leipzig, 1709.
Pleket, H. W. "Some Aspects of the History of the Athletic Guilds." *ZPE* 10 (1973) 197-227.
Plummer, Alfred. *A Commentary on St. Paul's Epistle to the Philippians.* London: Robert Scoll, 1909.
_____. *A Commentary on St. Paul's First Epistle to the Thessalonians.* London: Roxburghe, 1918.
Poland, Franz. *Geschichte des griechischen Vereinswesens.* Leipzig: Teubner, 1909.
Pomeroy, Sarah. *Goddesses, Whores, Wives, and Slaves: Women in Classical Antiquity.* New York: Schocken, 1975.
Portefaix, Lilian. *Sisters Rejoice: Paul's Letter to the Philippians and Luke-Acts as Received by First-Century Philippian Women.* ConBNT 20. Stockholm: Almqvist & Wiksell, 1988.
Preisigke, Friedrich. *Namenbuch enthaltend alle griechische, lateinischen, ägyptischen, hebräischen, arabischen, und sonstigen semitischen und nichsemitischen Menschennamen.* Amsterdam: Hakkert, 1967. Repr. of 1922 edition.

Purvis, J. "The Paleography of the Samaritan Inscription from Thessalonica." *BASOR* 221 (1976) 121-23.
Radin, Max. *Legislation of the Greeks and Romans on Corporations*. Columbia University: Tuttle, Morehouse & Taylor, 1910.
Rajak, Tessa, and D. Noy. "*Archisynogogoi*: Office, Title and Status in the Greco-Roman World." *JRS* 83 (1993) 75-93.
Rapske, Brian. *The Book of Acts and Paul in Roman Custody*. BAFCS 3. Grand Rapids and Carlisle: Eerdmans and Paternoster, 1994.
Reed, Jeffrey T. "Philippians 3:1 and the Epistolary Hesitation Formulas: The Literary Integrity of Philippians, Again." *JBL* 115 (1996) 63-90.
Reese, James M. *1 and 2 Thessalonians*. NTM 16. Wilmington: Michael Glazier, 1979.
Reicke, Bo. "Constitution of the Primitive Church." In *The Scrolls and the New Testament*, ed. K. Stehdahl, 143-56. New York: Harper, 1957.
_____. *Diakonie, Festfreude, und Zelos in Verbindung mit der altchristlichen Agapenfeier*. Uppsala Universitets Årsskrift 1951, 5. Uppsala and Wiesbaden: Lundequist and Harrassowitz, 1951.
_____. "Thessalonicherbriefe." *RGG* 6 (1962) cols. 851-53.
Reilly, Linda. *Slaves in Ancient Greece: Slaves from Greek Manumission Inscriptions*. Chicago: Ares, 1978.
Rein, W. "Collegium." *PW* 2 (1842) 493-501.
Renan, Ernest. *The Apostles*. New York: Carleton, 1866.
Reumann, John. "Church Office in Paul, Especially in Philippians." In *Origins and Method: Towards a New Understanding of Judaism and Christianity. Essays in Honour of John C. Hurd*, ed. Bradley H. McLean, 82-91. JSNTSup 86. Sheffield: JSOT Press, 1993.
_____. "Contributions of the Philippian Community to Paul and to Earliest Christianity." *NTS* 39 (1993) 438-57.
_____. "Philippians, Especially Chapter 4, as a 'Letter of Friendship': Observations on a Checkered History of Scholarship." In *Friendship, Flattery, and Frankness of Speech: Studies on Friendship in the New Testament World*, ed. John T. Fitzgerald, 83-106. NovTSup 82. Leiden, New York, Köln: Brill, 1996.
_____. "The Theologies of 1 Thessalonians and Philippians: Contents, Comparison, and Composite." In *SBL 1987 Seminar Papers*, ed. Kent H. Richards, 521-36. SBLASP 26. Atlanta: Scholars Press, 1987.
Reynolds, Joyce M., Robert Tannenbaum, and Kenan T. Erim. *Jews and God-fearers at Aphrodisias: Greek Inscriptions With Commentary*. Proceedings of the Cambridge Philological Society, Supplementary vol. 12. Cambridge: Cambridge Philological Society, 1987.
Rhomiopoulou, Katerina. "New Inscriptions in the Archaeological Museum, Thessalonica." *Ancient Macedonian Studies in Honor of Charles F. Edson*, ed. Harry J. Dell, 299-305. Thessalonica: Institute for Balkan Studies, 1981.
Rice, David G., and John E. Stambaugh, eds. *Sources for the Study of Greek Religion*. SBLSBS 14. Missoula: Scholars, 1979.
Richard, Earl J. *First and Second Thessalonians*. Sacra Pagina 11. Collegeville: Liturgical Press, 1995.

Richardson, G. Peter. "Early Synagogues as Collegia in the Diaspora and Palestine." In *Voluntary Associations in the Graeco-Roman World*, ed. John S. Kloppenborg and Stephen G. Wilson, 90-109. London and New York: Routledge, 1996.
Rigaux, B. *Les épîtres aux Thessaloniciens*. EBib. Paris: Lecoffre, 1956.
Robbins, Vernon K. *Exploring the Texture of Texts: A Guide to Socio-Rhetorical Interpretation*. Valley Forge: Trinity Press International, 1996.
Robert, Louis. "Hellenica V, Inscriptions de Philippes publiées par Mertzidès." *RPh* 13 (1939) 136-50.
Roberts, C. H., T. C. Skeat, and A. D. Nock. "The Guild of Zeus Hypsistos." *HTR* 29 (1936) 39-88.
Robinson, David M. "Inscriptions from Macedonia." *TAPA* 69 (1938) 43-76.
Rohde, Joachim. *Urchristliche und frühkatholische Ämter: Eine Untersuchung zur früchristlichen Amtsentwicklung im Neuen Testament und bei den apostolischen Vätern*. Theologische Arbeiten 33. Berlin: Evangelische Verlagsanstalt, 1976.
Rose, H. J. "Feralia." *OCD* (1970^2) 434.
_____. "Parentalia." OCD (1970^2) 781.
Ruppel, W. "Politeuma. Bedeutungsgeschichte eines staatsrechtlichen Terminus." *Philologus* 82 (1927) 268-312, 433-54.
Russell, R. "The Idle in 2 Thess 3.6-12: An Eschatological or a Social Problem?" *NTS* 34 (1988) 105-19.
_____. "Pauline Letter Structure in Philippians." *JETS* 25 (1982) 295-306.
Salač, A. "Inscriptions du Pangée de la région Drama-Cavalla et de Philippes." *BCH* 47 (1923) 49-96.
Saldarini, Anthony J. *Matthew's Christian-Jewish Community*. Chicago: University of Chicago Press, 1994.
Salmon, George. "The Christian Ministry." *Expositor* 4 (1887) 2-27.
Sampley, J. Paul. *Pauline Partnership in Christ*. Philadelphia: Fortress, 1980.
_____. "Societas Christi: Roman Law and Paul's Conception of the Christian Community." In *God's Christ and His People: Studies in Honour of N.A. Dahl*, ed. Wayne A. Meeks and J. Jervell, 158-74. Oslo: Universitetsforlaget, 1977.
San Nicolò, Mariano. *Äegyptisches Vereinswesen zur Zeit der Ptolemäer und Römer*. 2 Vols. Münchener Beiträge zur Papyrusforschung und antiken Rechtsgeschichte 2. Heft. Munich: C. H. Beck, 1913-15.
_____. "Zur Vereinsgerichtsbarkeit im Hellenistischen Aegypten." In *Epitymbion*, ed. H. Swoboda, 255-99. Reichenberg: Stiepel, 1927.
Sanday, W. "The Origin of Christian Ministry. II. Criticism of Recent Theories." *Expositor* 5 (1887) 97-114.
Sass, G. "Zur Bedeutung von δοῦλος bei Paulus." *ZNW* 40 (1941) 24-32.
Schenk, Wolfgang. *Die Philipperbriefe des Paulus. Kommentar*. Stuttgart: Kohlhammer, 1984.
_____. "Der Philipperbrief in der neueren Forschung (1945-85)." *ANRW* II.25.4 (1987) 3280-313.
Schiess, Traugott. *Die römischen* collegia funeraticia *nach den Inschriften*. München: Ackermann, 1888.
Schlier, Heinrich. "κέρδος, κτλ." *TDNT* 3 (1965) 672-73.
Schlueter, Carol J. *Filling Up the Measure: Polemical Hyperbole in 1 Thessalonians 2:14-16*. JSNTSup 98. Sheffield: JSOT Press, 1994.

Schmeller, Thomas. *Hierarchie und Egalität: Eine sozialgeschichtliche Untersuchung paulinischer Gemeinden und griechisch-römischer Vereine.* SBS 162. Stuttgart: Katholisches Bibelwerk, 1995.

Schmidt, Karl L. "ἐκκλησία." *TDNT* 3 (1965) 501-36.

Schmithals, Walter. *Paul and the Gnostics.* New York: Abingdon, 1972.

Schmitt-Pantel, Pauline. "Évergétisme et Mémoire du Mort: À propos des fondations de banquets publics dans les cités grecques à l'époque hellénistique et romaine." In *La mort, les morts dans les sociétés anciennes,* ed. Gherardo Gnoli and Jean-Pierre Vernant, 177-88. Cambridge: Cambridge University Press, 1982.

Schneider, C. "Zur Problematik des Hellenistischen in den Qumrantexten." In *Qumranprobleme, Vorträge des Leipziger Symposions über Qumranprobleme vom 9. bis 14. Oktober 1961,* ed. H. Bardtke, 299-314. Berlin: Akademie Verlag, 1963.

Schnelle, Udo. "Die Ethik des 1. Thessalonicherbriefes." In *The Thessalonian Correspondence,* ed. Raymond F. Collins, 293-305. BETL 87. Louvain: Louvain University Press, 1990.

Schoedel, William R. "Ignatius, Epistles of." *ABD* 3 (1992) 384-87.

Schöllgen, G. "Hausgemeinden, *oikos*-Ekklesiologie, und monarchischer Episkopat." *JAC* 31 (1988) 74-90.

_____. "Was wissen wir über die Sozialstruktur der paulinischen Gemeinden?" *NTS* 34 (1988) 71-82.

Schulz-Falkenthal, Heinz. "Zur Frage der Entstehung der römischen Handwerkerkollegien." *WZ* 14 (1965) 55-64.

_____. "Zur Frage der organisatorischen Vorbilder für den korporativen Zusammenschluss in den *collegia opificium* und ihr Verhältnis zu den mittelalterlichen Zünften." *WZ* 19 (1970) 41-50.

_____. "Gegenseitigkeitshilfe und Unterstützungstätigkeit in den römischen Handwerkergenossenschaften." *WZ* 20 (1971) 59-78.

_____. "Zur Lage der römischen Berufskollegien zu Beginn des 3. Jhs. u.Z. (die Privilegien der centonarii in Solva nach einem Reskript des Septimius Severus und Caracalla)." *WZ* 15 (1966) 285-94.

_____. "Zur politischen Aktivität der römischen Handwerkerkollegien." *WZ* 21 (1972) 79-99.

_____. "Römische Handwerkerkollegien im Dienst der städtischen Gemeinschaft und ihre Begünstigung durch staatliche Privilegien." *WZ* 22 (1973) 21-35.

Schürer, Emil. *The History of the Jewish People in the Age of Jesus Christ (175 B.C. - A.D. 135). A New English Version.* 3 Vols. Rev. and ed. G. Vermes, F. Millar, M. Black, and M. Goodman. Edinburgh: T. & T. Clark, 1979-87.

Scramuzza, Vincent M. "Claudius Soter Euergetes." *HSCP* 51 (1940) 261-66.

Seland, Torrey. "Philo and the Clubs and Associations of Alexandria." In *Voluntary Associations in the Graeco-Roman World,* ed. John S. Kloppenborg and Stephen G. Wilson, 110-27. London and New York: Routledge, 1996.

Sellew, Philip. "Religious Propaganda in Antiquity: A Case from the Sarapeum at Thessalonica." *Numina Aegaea* 3 (1980) 15-20.

Sherwin-White, A. N. *The Letters of Pliny: A Historical and Social Commentary.* Oxford: Clarendon, 1966.

Sifakis, G. M. *Studies in the History of Hellenistic Drama.* University of London Classical Studies 4. London: Athlone, 1967.

Sigonius, C. *De antiquo iure civium Romanorum, Italiae, provinciarum, ac Romanae iurisprudentiae iudicis libri XI*. Frankfurt a. M, 1593.
Silva, Moises. *Philippians*. Wycliffe Exegetical Commentary. Chicago: Moody, 1988.
Simon, M. "Theos Hypsistos." In *Ex Orbe Religionum: Studia Geo Widengren*, ed. C. J. Bleeker, S. G. F. Brandon, and M. Simon, 372-85. Studies in the History of Religions 21. Leiden: Brill, 1972.
Smallwood, E. Mary. *The Jews Under Roman Rule*. SJLA 20. Leiden: Brill, 1976.
Smith, Dennis E. "The Egyptian Cults at Corinth." *HTR* 70 (1977) 201-31.
_____. "Meals and Morality in Paul and His World." In *SBL 1981 Seminar Papers*, ed. Kent H. Richards, 319-39. SBLASP 20. Chico: Scholars Press, 1981.
Smith, Jonathan Z. *Drudgery Divine: On the Comparison of Early Christianities and the Religions of Late Antiquity*. Chicago: University of Chicago Press, 1990.
Snyder, Graydon F. *First Corinthians: A Faith Community Commentary*. Macon: Mercer University Press, 1992.
Soards, Marion L. *The Apostle Paul: An Introduction to his Writings and Teaching*. New York and Mahwah: Paulist, 1987.
Sohm, Rudolph. *Kirchenrecht*. 2 Vols. Berlin: Von Duncker & Humblot, 1923.
Sokolowski, Franciszek. *Lois sacrées des cités grecques*. École française d'Athènes. Travaux et mémoires, fasc. 18. Paris: E. de Boccard, 1969.
_____. "Propagation of the Cult of Sarapis and Isis in Greece." *GRBS* 15 (1974) 441-48.
Sordi, Marta. *The Christians and the Roman Empire*. London and Sydney: Croom Helm, 1983.
Spicq, C. "Les Thessaloniciens 'inquiets' étaient-ils des paresseux?" *StTh* 10 (1956) 1-13.
Stambaugh, John E., and David L. Balch. *The New Testament in Its Social Environment*. LEC 2. Philadelphia: Westminster, 1986.
Stevenson, George H. "Clubs, Roman." *OCD* (1970^2) 255-56.
Stöckle, A. "Berufsvereine (griechische)." *RE Suppl* 4 (1924) 155-211.
Stowers, Stanley K. "Friends and Enemies in the Politics of Heaven: Reading Theology in Philippians." In *Pauline Theology I: Thessalonians, Philippians, Galatians, Philemon*, ed. Jouette M. Bassler, 105-21. Minneapolis: Fortress, 1991.
Strathmann, H. "πόλις, κτλ." *TDNT* 4 (1967) 516-35.
Streeter, B. H. *The Primitive Church: Studied With Special Reference to the Origins of Christian Ministry*. Hewlett Lectures for 1928. London: Macmillan, 1929.
Suggs, M. Jack. "Concerning the Date of Paul's Macedonian Ministry." *NovT* 4 (1960) 60-68.
Tačeve-Hitova, Margarita. "Dem Hypsistos geweihte Denkmäler in den Balkanländern." *Balkan Studies* 19 (1978) 59-75.
_____. *Eastern Cults in Moesia Inferior and Thracia (5th Century BC - 4th Century AD.)*. EPRO 95. Leiden: Brill, 1983.
Tafrali, O. *Topographie de Thessalonique*. Paris: Geuthner, 1913.
Tarn, William W., and G. T. Griffith. *Hellenistic Civilisation*. London: Edward Arnold, 1952^3.
Tellbe, Mikael. "The Sociological Factors Behind Philippians 3.1-11 and the Conflict at Philippi." *JSNT* 55 (1994) 97-121.
Theissen, Gerd. *Social Reality and the Early Christians: Theology, Ethics, and the World of the New Testament*. Minneapolis: Fortress, 1992.

_____. *The Social Setting of Pauline Christianity: Essays on Corinth*. Philadelphia: Fortress, 1982.
Thiering, B. E. "*Mebaqqer* and *Episkopos* in Light of the Temple Scroll." *JBL* 100 (1981) 59-74.
Thomas, W. Derek. "The Place of Women in the Church at Philippi." *ExpTim* 83 (1972) 117-20.
Tod, Marcus N. "Clubs, Greek." *OCD* (1970²) 254-55.
_____. "Macedonia. Inscriptions." *Annual of the British School at Athens* 23 (1918-19) 67-97.
_____. *Sidelights on Greek History: Three Lectures on the Light Thrown By Greek Inscriptions on the Life and Thought of the Ancient World*. Oxford: Blackwell, 1932.
Townsend, John T. "Missionary Journeys in Acts and European Missionary Societies." In *SBL 1985 Seminar Papers*, ed. Kent H. Richards, 433-37. SBLASP 24. Atlanta: Scholars Press, 1985.
Trebilco, Paul R. *Jewish Communities in Asia Minor*. SNTSMS 69. Cambridge and New York: Cambridge University Press, 1991.
Tuckman, B. W. "Development Sequence in Small Groups." *Psychological Bulletin* 63 (1965) 384-99.
Ustinova, J. "The *Thiasoi* of Theos Hypsistos in Tanais." *HR* 31 (1991) 150-80.
Vaage, Leif E. "Religious Rivalries and the Struggle for Success: Jews, Christians, and Other Religious Groups in Local (Urban) Settings (63 BCE - 330 CE)." Unpublished Paper Presented to the Annual Meeting of the Canadian Society of Biblical Studies, Montreal, Quebec, 1995.
van Nijf, Onno M. *The Civic World of Professional Associations in the Roman East*. Dutch Monographs on Ancient History and Archaeology 17. Amsterdam: Gieben, 1997.
Vermes, G. *The Dead Sea Scrolls in English*. London: Penguin, 1987³.
Vidman, Ladislaus. *Isis und Sarapis bei den Griechen und Römern: Epigraphische Studien zur Verbreitung und zu den Trägern des ägyptischen Kultes*. RVV 29. Berlin: De Gruyter, 1970.
Vincent, M. R. *The Epistles to the Philippians and to Philemon*. ICC. Edinburgh: T. & T. Clark, 1897.
Voutiras, Emmanuel. "Berufs- und Kultverein: Ein ΔΟΥΜΟΣ in Thessalonike." *ZPE* 90 (1992) 87-96.
Vulič, N. "Inscription grecque de Stobi." *BCH* 56 (1932) 291-98.
Walker-Ramish, Sandra. "Graeco-Roman Voluntary Associations and the Damascus Document: A Sociological Analysis." In *Voluntary Associations in the Graeco-Roman World*, ed. John S. Kloppenborg and Stephen G. Wilson, 128-45. London and New York: Routledge, 1996.
Wallace-Hadrill, Andrew. "Patronage in Roman Society: From Republic to Empire." In *Patronage in Ancient Society*, ed. Andrew Wallace-Hadrill, 63-87. Leicester-Nottingham Studies in Ancient Society 1. London and New York: Routledge, 1990.
Walton, Steve. "What Has Aristotle to do with Paul? Rhetorical Criticism and 1 Thessalonians." *TynBul* 46 (1995) 229-50.
Waltzing, J. -P. *Étude Historique sur les corporations Professionnelles chez les Romains depuis les origines jusqu'a la chute de l'Empire d'Occident*. 4 Vols. Mémoire

couronne par l'Academie royale des Sciences, des Lettres et des Beaux-Arts de Belgique. Louvain: Peeters, 1895-1900.

Wanamaker, Charles A. *The Epistles to the Thessalonians: A Commentary on the Greek Text.* NIGTC. Grand Rapids: Eerdmans, 1990.

Watson, Duane F. "Rhetorical Analysis of Philippians and Its Implications for the Unity Question." *NovT* 30 (1988) 57-88.

Weaver, P. R. C. *Familia Caesaris: A Social Study of the Emperor's Freedmen and Slaves.* Cambridge: Cambridge University Press, 1972.

Weinfeld, Moshe. *The Organizational Pattern and the Penal Code of the Qumran Sect: A Comparison With Guilds and Religious Associations of the Hellenistic Period.* NovT et orbis antiquus 2. Göttingen: Vandenhoeck & Ruprecht, 1986.

Whelan, Caroline F. "Amica Pauli: The Role of Phoebe in the Early Chruch." *JSNT* 49 (1993) 67-85.

White, L. Michael. *Building God's House in the Roman World: Architectural Adaptation Among Pagans, Jews and Christians.* ASOR Library of Biblical and Near Eastern Archaeology. Baltimore: Johns Hopkins University Press, 1990.

———. "Morality Between Two Worlds: A Paradigm of Friendship in Philippians." In *Greeks, Romans, and Christians: Essays in Honor of Abraham J. Malherbe,* ed. David L. Balch, Wayne A. Meeks, and Everette Ferguson, 201-15. Philadelphia: Fortress, 1990.

———. "Visualizing the 'Real' World of Acts 16: Toward Construction of a Social Index." In *The Social World of the First Christians: Essays in Honor of Wayne A. Meeks,* ed. L. Michael White and O. Larry Yarbrough, 234-61. Minneapolis: Fortress, 1995.

Whitton, J. "A Neglected Meaning for *skeuos* in 1 Thessalonians 4.4." *NTS* 28 (1982) 142-43.

Wick, Peter. *Der Philipperbrief: Der formale Aufbau des Briefs als Schlüssel zum Verständnis seines Inhalts.* BWANT 7/15. Stuttgart: Kohlhammer, 1994.

Wiens, Devon H. "Mystery Concepts in Primitive Christianity and in its Environment." *ANRW* II.23.2 (1980) 1248-84.

Wilcken, U. *Griechische Ostraka.* Leipzig: Von Gisecke & Devrient, 1899.

Wild, Robert A. *Water in the Cultic Worship of Isis and Sarapis.* EPRO 87. Leiden: Brill, 1981.

Wilken, Robert L. *The Christians as the Romans Saw Them.* New Haven and London: Yale University Press, 1984.

———. "Collegia, Philosophical Schools, and Theology." In *The Catacombs and the Colosseum: The Roman Empire as the Setting of Primitive Christianity,* ed. Stephen Benko and John J. O'Rourke, 99-120. Valley Forge: Judson, 1971.

Williams, C. S. C. *A Commentary on the Acts of the Apostles.* BHNTC. London: Adam and Charles Black, 1964².

Williams, David John. *1 and 2 Thessalonians.* NIBC 12. Peabody: Hendrickson, 1992.

Williams, Margaret H. "The Structure of Roman Jewry Re-considered – Were the Synagogues of Ancient Rome Entirely Homogeneous?" *ZPE* 104 (1994) 129-41.

Wilson, Stephen G. "Voluntary Associations: An Overview." In *Voluntary Associations in the Graeco-Roman World,* ed. John S. Kloppenborg and Stephen G. Wilson, 1-15. London and New York: Routledge, 1996.

_____. "ΟΙ ΠΟΤΕ ΙΟΥΔΑΙΟΙ: Epigraphic Evidence for Jewish Defectors." In *Text and Artifact in the Religions of Mediterranean Antiquity: Essays in Honour of Peter Richardson*, ed. Stephen G. Wilson and Michel Desjardins, 354-71. ESCJ 9. Waterloo: Wilfred Laurier University Press, 2000.

Wilson, Thomas. *St. Paul and Paganism*. Edinburgh: T. & T. Clark, 1927.

Winter, Bruce W. "'If Any Man Does Not Wish to Work....' A Cultural and Historical Setting for 2 Thessalonians 3:6-16." *TynBul* 40 (1989) 303-15.

Wiseman, James. "The City in Macedonia Secunda." In *Villes et peuplement dans l'Illyricum protobyzantin*. Palais Farnese: Ecole Française de Rome, 1984.

Witherington III, Ben. *Friendship and Finances in Philippi: The Letter of Paul to the Philippians*. The New Testament in Context. Valley Forge: Trinity Press International, 1994.

Witt, R. E. "The Egyptian Cults in Ancient Macedonia." In *Ancient Macedonia* 1, ed. Basil Laourdas and Ch. Makaronas, 324-33. Thessalonica: Institute for Balkan Studies, 1970.

_____. *Isis in the Graeco-Roman World*. Aspects of Greek and Roman Life. London: Thames and Hudson, 1971.

Woodhead, A. G. *The Study of Greek Inscriptions*. Cambridge and New York: Cambridge University Press, 1981^2.

Woodward, A. M. "Inscriptions from Beroea in Macedonia." *Annual of the British School at Athens* 18 (1911-12) 133-65.

Wright, N. T. "Putting Paul Together Again: Toward a Synthesis of Pauline Theology (1 and 2 Thessalonians, Philippians, and Philemon)." In *Pauline Theology 1: Thessalonians, Philippians, Galatians, Philemon*, ed. Jouett M. Bassler, 183-211. Minneapolis: Fortress, 1991.

Youtie, Herbert C. "A Note on Edson's Macedonica III." *HTR* 42 (1949) 277-78.

Ziebarth, Erich Gustav Ludwig. *Das griechische Vereinswesen*. Stuttgart: S. Hirzel, 1896.

Zuckerman, Constantine. "Hellenistic Politeumata and the Jews: A Reconsideration. Review of *The Jews in Hellenistic and Roman Egypt: The Struggle for Equal Rights*, by Aryeh Kasher." *Scripta classica Israelica: Yearbook of the Israel Society for the Promotion of Classical Studies* 8/9 (1988) 171-85.

Indexes

1. Modern Authors

Abrahamsen   136, 138, 170
Arnaoutoglou   16
Ascough   11, 12, 74, 150, 209
Ausbüttel   3, 4, 5, 6, 7, 71

Barclay   167-68, 174
Barton   13, 65, 69
Batten   65
Beare   143, 160
Berry   142
Best   203
Black   116, 123
Bormann   9, 154, 158
Bossman   169
Buckler   18

Campbell   73
Carter   11, 13
Cenival   7
Clarke   12
Collins, J.   82, 83
Collins, R.   73, 175, 185, 208
Cook   200
Cotter   42, 43, 45, 78, 134, 135, 148
Countryman   8, 106
Crosby   11

Dahl   125, 145
Danker   51
Dassmann   131
d'Escurac-Doisy
de Robertis   6
de Rossi   7
de Vos   149, 175, 181, 185
Dibelius   130
Donfried   188
Dormeyer   203
Doughty   146
Dow   58, 105

Duff   6
Duling   10, 11

Ehrman   11, 12
Ernst   133

Fatum   189
Fee   112
Feissel   196
Ferguson, W.   5
Fisher   15
Foucart   4, 58

Garland   116
Garnsey   123
Gaston   3
Georgi   75
Gnilka   112
Goodman   186
Gschnitzer   89

Habicht   195
Haenchen   211
Hainz   72, 82, 104, 133, 157
Harland   91
Hatch   82, 83
Hawthorne   204
Hemer   191
Hendrix   61
Heyob   59
Hock   174
Holtz   184, 202
Horsley   x, 13, 65, 69, 80, 111

Jewett   145, 174, 179-80
Jones, N.   7
Judge   8

Klauck   9, 75, 87, 88

Klinghardt 9
Kloppenborg 9, 10, 21, 45, 55, 60, 74, 105, 160, 185
Kornemann 5
Kraabel 197

La Piana 95
Lampe 9
Laum 5
Lee, J. x
Lee, M. 116
Levinskaya 193, 197, 201, 210
Liebenam 4
Lietzmann 75, 81
Lifshitz 195, 201
Lightfoot 113, 132
Lincoln 148
Lüdemann 205, 212
Lüderitz 148, 149
Lührmann 203, 208
Luter 116

MacMullen 172
Malherbe 112, 162, 163, 175, 184, 208
Malinowski 135
Marshall, I. 168
Martin, D. 123, 188, 189
McKnight 186
McLean 10, 56
Meeks 8, 13, 87, 91, 92, 104, 106, 107, 111, 146
Mendelsohn 102
Milligan 82
Mommsen 4, 7
Morris 166-67
Moulton 82
Murphy-O'Connor 165, 175

Nehama 191
Neumann 74
Nilsson 100

O'Brien 74, 155, 157, 204
Osiek 110

Papazoglou 54, 191

Perdrizet 160
Peterlin 138
Peterman 141, 157
Pilhofer x, 9, 202
Plummer 76, 203
Poland 5, 68, 71

Reumann 130, 131, 139
Richard 179
Roberts 3
Russell 110, 116

Saldarini 10
Sampley 140-42
San Nicolò 5
Sass 123
Schlueter 164
Schmeller 9, 56, 59
Schmidt 75
Schmithals 163
Schöllgen 59, 111
Schulz-Falkenthal 6
Schürer 201
Sève 196
Smith, J. Z. 1, 2,
Sordi 8
Streeter 133

Tačeve-Hitova x, 197
Tellbe 149
Tod 3, 92
Townsend 104, 106
Trebilco 200
Tuckman 83

Ustinova 196, 197

van Nijf 7
Vincent 155

Walton 163
Waltzing 5, 56
Wanamaker 168, 187
Weaver 127, 128
Whelan 55
White 199
Wick 116

Wilken 8, 9, 92
Williams, C.
Williams, D. 184
Williams, M. 102
Wilson, S. 9, 51

Witherington 134
Witt 211

Ziebarth 5
Zuckermann 148

2. Ancient Texts

a) Hebrew Bible / LXX

Genesis
  15:16 203

Exodus
  34:34 184

Numbers
  6:22-27 201

Deuteronomy
  4:13 166
  32:32 203

1 Samuel
  21:5 188

1 Kings
  17:39 166

Nehemiah
  13:20 166

Job
  1:1 203
  2:3 203

Psalms
  46:8 195
  46:12 195
  78:6 203
  93:1 203

Proverbs
  16:31 203
  56:7 210

Isaiah
  59:17 203

Jeremiah
  9:3 203
  10:25 203
  13:3 203

Ezekiel
  16:12 203
  23:42 203
  37:14 203

Daniel
  8:23 203

Hosea
  5:4 184
  6:1 184

Joel
  2:13 184

Wisdom of Solomon
  5:18 203

1 Maccabees
  3:30 166

b) New Testament

Matthew
4:23	75
5:25-26	61
6:2	75
6:5	75
8:36	119
9:35	75
10:17	75
12:9	75
13:54	75
16:18	72
16:26-30	69
16:26	119
18:17	72
21:13	210
23:6-12	134
23:13-26	75
23:34	75

Mark
11:17	210
14:22-26	69

Luke
4:14-15	206
4:16-30	206
4:16	210
4:31-38	206
4:31	211
6:6	206, 211
7:5	194, 206
8:41	206
9:25	119
11:43	206
12:11	206
13:10	206, 211
13:14	210
13:16	210
14:5	210
15:15	147
19:14	147
20:46	206
21:12	206
22:17-20	69
23:56	211

Acts
1:14	209
2:42	70, 209
2:44	30
2:46	70
3:1	209
3:19	185
4:32	30
6:1-12	70
6:4	209
6:9	206
9:2	206
9:20	206
9:35	185
10:1-11:18	97
10:1-2	194
10:4	209
10:31	209
11:26	29
12:5	209
12:7-10	97
13:5	206
13:14	206, 207
13:43	206
13:50	206
14:1	206
15:21	206
15:44	211
16:8	191
16:11-15	23
16:11-40	112
16:12	209, 211
16:13-15	205
16:13	209, 210
16:14-15	125, 208
16:14	211
16:16	209
16:18	211
16:21	212
17	171, 203, 208, 212
17:1-9	111
17:1-4	202
17:1-3	206
17:1	166, 206
17:2	167, 211
17:4	166, 189, 206
17:5-9	207

Indexes

17:6	147	16:5	72, 105
17:8	147	16:6	136, 171
17:10	206	16:7	136
17:12	206	16:12	136, 171
17:17	206	16:13	103
18:1-4	166	16:16	72, 105
18:2-3	174	16:21	207
18:2	135	16:23	88, 167, 208
18:3	174	16:25	70
18:4	206, 211		
18:5	166	1 Corinthians	
18:7	206	1-4	60
18:18	135	1:2	72, 105, 107
18:19	206	1:10-17	104
18:26	135	1:11	136
19:8	206	2:1	70
19:9	174	3:5	129
20:1-2	115	3:8	171
20:6	212	3:15	119
20:16	212	4:1	70
20:28	129, 131	4:8	155
21:39	147	4:9-13	173
22:19	206	4:10	173
22:28	147	4:11	173
23:1	147	4:12	171, 172, 173
23:11	97	4:17	106
24:12	206	5:1-2	70
26:11	206	5:9-13	70
26:28	29	6	60
27:18	119	6:1-8	144
		6:1-11	60
Romans		6:12-20	70
1:1	122	7:17	72, 105, 106
2:4	155	7:36-38	188
3:25	70	8-10	60, 88, 91
5:1-5	169	8:1-13	99
9:1-11	164	8:10	88
9:23	155	9	106
10:12	155	9:19	173
13	91	10:14	88
13:4	129	10:23-11:1	99
15:8	129	10:32	72
15:16	133	11-14	60
15:26-27	150, 165	11:16	72, 105, 106
16:1-2	167, 173	11:17-34	60
16:1	72, 105, 129, 135	11:18	72, 105
16:3	135	11:23-26	69

12:28	138	Galatians	
13:13	169	1:10	122
14:26-33	143	1:13	72
14:34-35	143	1:22	72, 105
15:9	72	2:17	129
15:10	171	3:28	124
15:20	183	4:9	184
15:51	70	4:11	171
15:58	171	6:17	171
16:16	171		
16:19	72, 105, 135	Ephesians	
		2:12	147
2 Corinthians		2:19	202
2:15-2:13	106	3:7	129
3:6	129	4:28	171
3:16	184	6:5	67
4:7	155	6:6	122
5:9	183	6:21	129
6:4	129		
6:5	171, 173	Philippians	
6:10	155	1-2	145
7:9	119	1:1-3:1	115
8	106, 150	1:1	70, 79, 80, 122, 123, 129-32
8:1-15	104, 150		
8:1-12	118	1:3-11	117
8:1-5	165, 168	1:5	117, 140, 152
8:1-4	111	1:7	140
8:1-2	150, 152	1:8	139
8:1	72, 105	1:10	70
8:2	155, 168	1:11	120
8:3	151	1:15-18	144, 145
8:2	155	1:15	144
8:9	155	1:19-26	139
8:13	168	1:20	144
9:1-5	104	1:21	119
10-13	106	1:22	120
10:15	171	1:26	115
10:16	40	1:27	77, 78, 117, 135, 147, 148
11:3	67, 70		
11:7	173	1:28-30	192
11:8-9	153, 166	1:28	144, 145
11:9	151, 165, 167, 173	1:30	144
11:15	129	2:1	140, 141
11:17	173	2:2	141
11:23	129, 171	2:2-4	139
11:27	173	2:3	144
11:28	72, 105	2:5	143

2:6-11	70, 115, 139, 143, 146, 147	4:10	151, 152
		4:11-13	154
2:13	139	4:11	154, 155
2:14	143	4:14-20	120
2:16	171	4:14	140, 153
2:17	70	4:15-16	117
2:19	123	4:15-18	120
2:21	145	4:15	120, 141, 152, 153
2:22	123, 145	4:16	141, 151, 154, 166, 169
2:24	115		
2:25-30	138	4:17	120, 156
2:25	124, 138, 141	4:18	121, 124
3	145	4:19	121, 141, 155
3:1-4:3	115	4:21-23	115
3:1-21	204	4:12	70
3:1-17	145	4:14	118
3:1-11	149	4:15	72
3:1-2	115	4:16	167
3:2-21	146	4:19	118
3:2-19	191	4:22	127
3:2-17	204		
3:2-16	204	Colossians	
3:2-3	204	1:4-5	169
3:2	147	1:7	124, 129
3:3-6	205	1:23	129
3:4-11	205	1:25	129
3:6	72	1:29	171
3:7-8	119	3:22	67
3:8	120	4:12	122, 124
3:9	156		
3:10	140, 142, 143	1 Thessalonians	
3:13	120	1:1-2:12	163
3:17	204	1:1	72, 73, 157
3:18-21	146, 149, 204	1:2-10	163
3:19	146, 147	1:3	169
3:20-21	115, 147, 149	1:6	164, 167-68, 169, 185
3:20	77, 78, 146, 147, 148, 149	1:7-9	186
		1:7	169, 185
3:21	146	1:8	169
4:1	139, 144, 153	1:9	184-85, 202
4:2	124, 134, 141	2:1-12	163, 170
4:3	125, 126, 135	2:2	164, 166
4:4-7	115	2:3-12	165
4:8-9	115	2:3	171
4:10-20	82, 104, 115, 116, 120, 139, 141, 151, 154, 173	2:4	169, 203
		2:5-6	171, 173
		2:7-8	171

2:9-10	171, 173	5:1	162
2:9	166, 170, 171, 173, 174, 177	5:2	165
		5:3	170
2:10	169	5:7	182
2:11-12	171	5:8	203
2:12	163, 164	5:11	171, 180
2:13-4:21	163	5:12-22	180
2:13-16	163, 164, 168, 170	5:12-13	171, 176
2:13	169, 170	5:12	171, 179, 180
2:14	105, 164	5:13	169
2:15	164	5:14	177, 179, 180
2:16	163, 164, 203	5:16-22	180
2:17-20	163, 164, 168	5:22	203
2:17	163		
2:18	167	2 Thessalonians	
2:19	153, 169, 203	2:2	165
2:20	173	2:3-15	162
3	71	2:9	165
3:2	129, 169, 170	2:13	117
3:3-4	168	2:3-15	162
3:5	169, 170, 177	3:6-16	182
3:6	162, 169	3:6-13	180
3:7	168, 169	3:6-12	177
3:8	129	3:6-11	177, 179
3:10	169	3:7	177
3:12	129, 169	3:11-12	162
4:1-8	70	3:12	177
4:1-7	171	3:17	165
4:1	171, 172		
4:3-5:28	163	1 Timothy	
4:3-8	189	1:1-2	91
4:3	188	3:2	129
4:4-6	187	3:8	171
4:4	187, 188	5:1	132
4:5	203	5:2	132
4:6	67, 129, 203	5:17	132
4:8	203	5:19	132
4:9-12	174, 175		
4:9	162	2 Timothy	
4:11	170, 172, 173, 174, 177, 183	2:24	122
		4:19	135
4:12	46		
4:13-5:11	165	Titus	
4:13-18	163, 164	1:5	132
4:13	162, 169	1:7	129
4:14	169	1:11	119
5:1-11	162, 164	3:1	91

Philemon
23   124

James
1:1   122

1 Peter
2:9   134
2:11-17   91
2:25   129
4:16   29

2 Peter
1:1   122

Jude
1   122

c) Eary Christian Writings

1 Clement   106, 126
60-61   91

Clement of Alexandria
Stromata
3.6.53.1   126

Didache   8, 69
9-10   70

Epistle of Barnabas
19.8   30

Eusebius
Hist. Eccl.
6.19, 16   107
7.32, 27   107
10.1   107

Origen
Contra Celsum
1.1   7
3.2.3   107
8.17   7
8.47   7

Philocal.
24.1   181

Polycarp
Philippians
3:2   115
12.3   91
14.1   137

Martyrdom of Polycarp
10.2   91

Tertullian
Apologia
39   107

Histories
4.83   37

d) Other Greco-Roman and Jewish Writings

Alexander Severus
Historia Augusta, Vita Alexander
49   7

Apuleius
19   96

Aristides
Sacred Talks
2.394   37

Aristotle
Ethica Nicomachea
11.52   30
5.4.13   118-19

Caesar
De Bello Civili
3.103   23

Cicero
De Officiis
1.16.51   30
1.150-51   121-22

In L. Pisonem
40.96 23

Dead Sea Scrolls
1QS
6.12-20 130

CD
1.9 29
13.7-9 130

Digesta
47.22 15, 29, 87

Dio Cassius
60.6.6-7 43
60.6.6 43

Diogenes Laertius
Epicurus
10.11 30

Gaius
Institutes
4 29

Herodotus
8.138.1 27

Josephus
Antiquitates
12.7-8 193
13.4.74-75 193
Bellum Judaicum
2.487-88 193
2.488 193

Contra Apionem
1.200-04 193
2.4.36 193

Lucian
Alexander sive Pseudomantis
10 41

Fugitivi
12 172

De Peregrini Morte
11 107

Mishnah
m.Meg.
4.3 209

Pausanias
2.4.6 97
3.14.4 38
10.38.13 37

Petronius
Satyricon 49

Philo
De Abrahamo
235 30

De Ebrietate
14 103
20 103

De Praemiis et Poenis
20 181

De Vita Cont. 37

De Vita Mosis
1.28.156 30

In Flaccum
4 24, 87, 147
136 24, 147

Legatio ad Gajum
281-82 192
284 192
311-12 24, 147

Plato
Apologia
17 176

Epinomis
985C 34

Leges
    909-10A   34

Respublica
    4.424a   30
    5.449c   30

Pliny
  Epistulae
    10.33.3   44
    10.34.1   44
    10.92   44
    10.93   45
    10.96   44, 108

Plutarch
  De Defectu Oraculorum
    424   181

  De Pericles
    1.4-2.2   172-73

Porphyry
  De Antro Nympharum
    15   68

Strabo
    4.1.4   36
    12.8.14   38

Seutonius
  De Vita Caesarum
    "Augustus"
    32.1   43

Tertullian
  Apologia
    38-39   7

Theophrastus
  de causis Plant.
    1.13.11   27

  Hist. Plant.
    6.6.4   27

Thucidides
    3.82-84   16
    8.54   16
    8.65   16

Tosephta
  t.Hul.
    2.3   103

Varro
  R.R.
    2.1.16   147

Xenophon
  Memorabilia Socratis
    3.10.1-15 176
    4.2.1-39   176

e) Inscriptions and Papyri

BGU
    1074   44, 99

Cagnat
I
    682   89

CCCA
I
    456   89

CCET
I
    10   159

CIRB
    1231   198
    1260   198
    1261   198
    1277   198
    1278   198
    1279   198
    1280   198
    1281   198
    1282   198
    1283   198

1284	198
1285	198
1286	198
1287	198
1289	198

CMRDM

4.137	38

CIG

1793	82
1800	82
2000f	25, 54, 71, 80, 170
2082	23
2562	34
3037	82, 83
3496	22
3599	86, 182
5853	17, 95, 109, 159
5866	78

CIJ

84	195
693	80, 195, 201
694	80, 193, 194

CIL

II

5812	56

III

611	23
633	20, 51, 54, 64, 71, 72, 79, 125
656	26, 150
664	21
703	26, 28, 54, 71, 150
704	26, 27, 28, 54, 71, 150, 158
707	26, 28, 150
870	56
1303	57
7378	159
7437	56
9585	245

V

992	56
2072	57
8307	56

VI

261	56
377	56
641	24
642	23-24
2193	43
2239	57
10109	57
10234	24, 46
10423	57
24627	57

IX

2480	57
4697	57

X

5907	56

XI

5223	57

XIV

2112	11, 24, 45, 63, 86

Foucart

48	153
49	158
51	55
55	55
56	153
59	62
64	153
65	153

IAcanthus

1	x, 20, 23, 54

IAlexandria(K)

65	58
70	58
91	80

Indexes

IAmphipolis	
1	x, 25, 54, 58
IAnthemonte	
1	x, 199
IAnydron	
1	x, 52, 198
IApamBith	
35	55
IBeroea	
1	x, 52, 58, 198
2	x, 23, 25
3	xi, 25
IBM	
4.2.153	198
ICos	
36	33
IDelos	
1016	65
1061	153
1519	63, 64, 74, 150, 153, 183
1520	24, 64, 70, 153
1521	63, 108, 153
1522	55, 81, 153
1523	153
1774	24
1778	24
2081	153
2710	108
IEdessa	
1	xi, 198. 199
2	xi, 198, 199
3	xi, 52, 198, 199, 200
IEphesus	
22	99
24	35, 70
27	36
444	135
454	135
899	70
900	70
901	70
903	70
906	70
2078	135
2079	135
2080	135
3214	33
3803	32
IFayum	
I	
9	80
15	78
II	
121	77
IG	
II^2	
337	41, 93
1134	99
1177	42, 94
1256	125, 153
1263	64, 144, 150, 153, 183
1265	64
1271	62, 64, 144, 153, 183
1273	17, 62, 150, 153, 183
1275	29, 84, 87, 143
1277	153, 183
1278	62, 153
1283	94, 125
1284	64
1291	64, 142, 144, 153, 158
1292	57, 62, 64, 144, 150, 153, 182, 183
1297	40, 55, 125, 142, 150, 153
1298	63, 125
1314	153, 183
1315	153, 183
1317	64, 94, 144, 153, 156
1323	64, 125
1325	64, 87
1326	87

1327	62, 64, 87, 142, 144, 153	IX/1	
		486	82
1328	87	670	56, 142
1329	62, 64, 125, 150, 153		
1333	64	X/2	
1334	153	58	20, 31, 52, 72, 82
1335	64	62	199
1337	150	67	20, 156
1339	63, 64, 100	68	72
1343	62, 68, 70, 153, 158	72	195, 200
1361	87, 100, 134, 143	192	20, 51, 72, 89
1363	64	220	20, 53, 72, 89
1365	40	244	20
1366	38, 39, 55, 67, 70, 125	255	20, 31, 35, 36, 58, 79, 97, 134, 185
1368	24, 63, 64, 70, 85, 86, 100, 125, 142, 143, 145, 181	259	26, 71, 79
		260	26, 28, 71, 79, 146, 153, 156
1369	29, 30, 40, 64, 85, 86, 144, 150, 183	261	79
1375	150	288	25, 52, 72, 80, 170
1390	64	289	25, 72
2347	55, 153	291	21, 25, 71, 158
2354	55	309	23, 53, 71, 79, 96
2499	125	480	53
2948	87	503	25, 79
2950	64	506	52, 71, 79
2951	64	633	195
4636	70	860	71
4637	70	933	71, 198
IV		XI/4	
774	82	1061	62, 99
824	82	1216	57
840	33, 54, 125, 153, 158	1217	57
841	34, 54, 158	1218	57
		1219	57
V/1		1220	57
245	196	1221	57
1390	55, 63, 70, 86, 143, 153, 181	1222	57
		1227	57
		1299	25, 31, 37, 70, 96, 158
VII			
33	94	XII/1	
687	56	127	30
688	56	155	62, 63
2482	98	161	156
2485	99	677	64

736	156	IKyme	
937	62	30	29
		45	62
XII/3			
248	39	IIlion	
329	81	10	64
330	33, 142, 156		
1098	29	*ILS*	
		4966	43
XII/5			
606	62, 150, 156	IMagnMai	
		98	70, 134
XII/7		99	97
58	40	100	70, 151
515	33	109	82
		215	96
XII/9		217	82
189	182		
		IMaked	
XIV		3	198
1890	80	7	198
2304	80	16	198
		21	198
IGL		22	52, 198
1989	80	27	198
1990	80	90	198
2298	80		
		IMakedD	
IGRR		3	23
782	80	6	198
796	56	7	198
907	135, 176	38	198
1020	41	58	23
1095	40	284	72
		920	26, 27, 71, 158
IKalambaki		1104	20, 62, 71, 79, 156
1	xi, 23, 65		
		IMylasa	
IKalkhedon		861	64
13	64	942	64
IKilikiaBM		IPergamon	
2.201	76	297	100
		319	100
IKnidos		320	100
23	64	485	65, 70

IPisidia		53	70
93	176	56	153
		65	158
IPriene			
174	64, 153	LSCG	
195	70	77	70
201	64	124	134
205	70	171	41
IPydna		LSCGSup	
1	xi, 52, 53, 54, 58, 72, 79, 80, 198	91	67
		LSS	
ISardBR		91	70
22	89		
		MAMA	
ISmyrna		5	35
218	135	264	62
653	64		
713	24	Μουσεῖον	
715	135	93	82, 83
721	135	100	83
IThessalonica		OGIS	
1	xi, 20, 25, 71	50	62, 77, 99
2	xi, 23, 71, 79, 80	51	63, 77
3	xi, 23, 71	143	78
		145	78
ITralleis		611	80
1	38	614	80
LSAM		P.Cairo.Dem	
1	64, 153	30605	63, 108
2	64	30606	61, 63, 84, 86
7	64		
8	153	P.Cair.Zenon	
9	70, 143	59034	37
11	153		
13	153	P.Enteuxeis	
15	153	20	108
19	70	21	108
20	37		
23	64	P.Karanis	
34	42	575	108
38	153		
48	134	P.Lillie.Dem.	
50	70	29	108

Indexes

P.Lond.		B 186	81
2193	84, 85, 90		
2710	24, 108, 143, 198	*RIG*	
		33	94
P.Mich.Tebt.		993	57
32	78	1226	82
243	24, 63, 68, 70, 86, 108	1307	94
244	24, 70, 86, 108		
248	108	*SEG*	
		III	
P.Oxy.		674	30, 108
2476	99		
2610	99	XVI	
		931	148
P.Paris			
42	77	XXIX	
		1183	176
P.Petri		1184	135
III.42	156	1195	29
P.Rainer		XXXVII	
V.23	108	559	25, 71
P.Ryl.		XXXX	
580	108	524	182
Pilhofer	x	XLIV	
029	26, 27, 28, 54, 158	556	201
091	20		
095	54, 71, 79	*SIRIS*	
133	26, 28, 146, 150	80	57
142	79	81	57
143	54, 79	82	57
144	54	122	20, 52, 62, 72
145	54	123	52, 62, 72, 79
147	79	124	20, 52, 72, 79
209	20, 62, 72, 79	371	211
338	52, 54, 71, 72, 136	426	57
339	72, 136		
340	54, 58	*Syll.*³	
350	20	694	70, 98
387	201	704	99
697	20, 21, 71	985	35, 39, 55, 65, 66, 158, 185
Poland		1009	64, 70, 153
B 66	159	1012	64
B 79	8	1014	64

1024	24, 70, 85	1149	35
1044	39	1150	35
1128	35	1150	35
1140	23, 24, 71	1151	35
1147	35	1153	35
1148	35		

3. Subjects

Ἀδελπηός   see Brotherhood
Agdistis   35, 89
Ahura Mazda   89
Altar   100
Anubis   21,
Aphrodite   21, 41, 124
Apollo   39, 41, 198
Ἀρχισυνάγωγος   79-80, 197
Artemis   36, 41, 150, 182, 198, 211
Artisans   12, 22, 50, 53, 93, 98, 118, 129, 172, 173
Asiani   23, 53, 71
Asclepius   21, 41, 107, 211
Associations, definition of   3
Ἄτακτος   177-84
Athena   182
Athletes   22
Attis   22
Authorities   61

Bakers   18
Bankers   18
Banquets   see Meals
Baptism   69
Barbers   17, 18
Bendis   94
Benefaction   see Patronage
Brotherhood   10, 76-77, 90, 98
Builders   18
Burial   21, 24, 26, 29, 33, 45, 46, 56, 78, 80

Carpenters   18
Charity   25
Clement   125, 126, 203
Collection, Paul's   150, 152

Collegia   20, 24, 42
Commerce   50
Court   see Legal action
Crown   153
Cupid   22
Cybele   22

Dead Sea Scrolls   81, 101-02, 130
Decree   15, 41
Dedication   20, 100
Demeter   23, 42, 57, 87, 94, 98
Διάκονος   82-83, 129-32, 137, 138, 161
Diana   21, 136, 138
Didache   69
Dining associations   16
Dining hall   25
Dionysus   21, 25, 56, 71, 77, 87, 132, 145, 146, 198, 211
Dionysiac artists   22, 62, 77, 98, 99, 107
Dioscurii   176
Disruptions   17, 42, 86, 143, 144, 179, 181
Dreams   28, 34, 36, 37, 38, 97
Drinking   17, 24, 85, 86, 90, 143, 147, 182
Dyers   18

Ἐκκλησία   21, 72-75, 105, 136-37
Emperor   20, 22
Encomium   118
Epaphroditus   124, 128, 203
Epicureans   29
Epigraphy   4
Ἐπίσκοπος   80-81, 129-32, 138, 161

Ἔρανος 5, 44
Erastus 88, 103
Ἑταιρεία 16
Eucharist 69
Euodia 125, 127, 128, 134, 135, 138, 143, 144, 145, 203
Exclusivity 88

Familia Caesaris 127, 128
Fictive kinship 10, 76
Finances 25, 63, 79, 84, 85, 86, 104, 115, 121, 127, 149-57, 161, 163, 165-66
Fines 68, 86, 143, 182, 183
Fire fighters 44
Foreigners 16, 17, 22, 38, 42, 44, 93, 95
Friendship 29, 30, 87, 112, 117, 139-40, 142, 152, 156, 183
Fullers 18
Funerals *see Burial*
Funerary association 11, 21, 27, 160

Gladiators 22
God-fearers 191, 194, 196, 202, 203, 206, 211, 212
Great mother 24, 82

Herakles 21, 25, 58, 80, 158, 170
Hermes 21, 82
Hero 21, 25, 146
Hestia 35
Honourific practices 12, 19, 20, 22, 23, 51, 55, 57, 62-64, 88-89, 145, 183, 186
Honour / shame 25, 49, 123, 146, 165-66, 173-74
Horseman, Thracian 54, 158-59, 169-70
Household 8, 11, 21,
Hymn 69, 70, 115, 143, 146
Hypsistos 19, 21, 52, 58, 80, 84, 85, 158, 196-201

Iobakkoi 85, 143, 145, 181
Isis 20, 21, 31, 37, 42, 57, 95, 96, 97, 107, 134, 136, 138, 158

Jason 207-08
Judaizers 115

Κοινωνέω, -ία 120, 140-43, 157
Kore 98

Leadership 12, 79-83, 129, 176-77
Leather-worker 175, 176, 186
Legal action 60, 86, 144
Letter 36, 108
Liber and Libera 31, 58
LXX 73-74, 105, 123, 130, 157, 166-67, 184, 188, 197, 201
Lydia 23, 125, 208, 211
Marketplace 118-22, 128
Mars 54
Marzeah 102
Matthew, Gospel of 10, 72, 73, 75
Meals 15, 24, 26, 31, 46, 60, 69, 70, 79, 80, 91, 131, 143, 147, 159
Membership 15, 20,
Memorial 25, 32-33, 53
Men (Tyranos) 38, 40, 55, 67, 68
Merchants 12, 16, 17, 22, 23, 74, 93, 95, 129
Mining associations 16
Mithras 68
Money *see Finances*
Moral conduct 65-70, 171, 184, 188
Muses 33
Mysteries 1

Nemesis 21, 54
Nike 54

Opponents of Paul 144-45
Oracles 28, 34
Ὀργεῶνες 5, 87

Papyri 15
Parentalia 26, 150
Patron 16, 20, 21, 40, 51, 52, 62, 108, 153, 167, 176
Patronage 34, 61-63, 118, 122, 150, 154
Peculium 48

Philosophical school 1, 8
Φῦλαι 15
Phoebe 135, 153, 167
Piety 85
Pirates 16
Prison 144, 152, 154
Political action 42, 44
Πολίτευμα 77-78, 146-49
Poseidon 34, 38, 39
Poverty 118, 167
Prayer 69, 70
Πρεσβύτερος 132
President 84
Prisca 135
Processions 21
Προσευχή 209-11
Purple-dyers 22, 25, 72
Pythagoreans 29

Regulations 169
Riots *see Political action*
Rivalry 88-89, 144, 145, 150
Rod-bearers 86, 182
Rosalia 26-28, 54, 145, 150, 153, 156

Sabazios 89
Sachypsis 77
Sacrifice 15, 85
Salutatio 62
Samaritan 201
Sarapis 20, 21, 31, 36, 37, 51, 57, 95, 96, 97, 98, 134, 158
Sarapistai 96, 105
Saviour 157-60, 168
Senatusconsultum 45
Septuagint *see LXX*
Shipowners 16
Silversmiths 23, 65, 72
Σκεῦος 187-89
Slaves 12, 47- 50, 52, 60, 67, 122-23, 127, 132, 138, 159, 172

Social status 47-51, 117, 173
Social mobility 50
Societas 120, 140-42
Souregethes 22
Statutes 15
Sylvanus 21, 23, 51, 64
Synagogue 1, 8, 11, 12, 80, 91, 101-02, 112, 133, 175, 191, 193, 194, 201, 206-11
Syntyche 125, 127, 128, 134, 135, 138, 143, 144, 203
Tanners 18,
Temple 21, 31
Tentmaker 175, 186
Terminology 71, 105
Therapeutai 37
2 Thessalonians 114, 162, 164-65, 179, 180
Θίασος 5, 71, 107
Θλῖψις 118, 140, 167-68, 169
Tomb 26, 76, 169, 194, 195
Trade 17, 72, 93, 118, 120, 121, 172, 178
Trade guilds 5, 11, 16,
Treasurer 63, 79, 133

Vinyard 26, 28
Visions 28, 34
Votives 20,

Women 31, 34-35, 40, 47, 52, 54, 55, 56, 57, 58, 63, 66, 71, 125, 134-38, 160, 186, 187, 189, 206, 207
Work 12, 164, 169-76, 177, 186, 208

Yoke-makers 23

Zeus 19, 21, 34, 35, 38, 39, 41, 52, 58, 66, 77, 78, 80, 84, 85, 158, 196, 198-200

4. Place Names

Acanthus 23
Aetolia 192
Agrosykia 198
Aigiale 33
Alexandria 58, 78, 87, 95, 193
Alistrati 19, 156
Ambrakia 82
Amisus 44
Amphipolis 23, 24, 25, 58, 182
Anatolia 127
Andania 181
Anthemonte 199
Antioch (Psidia) 206
Antioch (Syria) 11
Anydron 52, 198
Apulia 94
Argos 98, 192
Athens 7, 16, 29, 38, 41, 55, 57, 68, 85, 87, 93, 94, 96, 98, 140, 142, 145, 162, 181, 183
Attica 55, 183, 192

Beirut 24
Beneventum 98
Beroea 23, 25, 52, 80, 194, 198, 199, 206, 210
Bithynia 26, 44, 107, 192
Boeotia 56, 78, 192
Bosporus 196, 197
Bostra 81
Britain 7

Caesarea Maritima 88, 103, 117
Cairo 102
Campania 94
Canopus 98
Cenchrea 153, 167
Ceos 183
Chalcedon 41
Chalcis 98
Cilicia 192
Citium 55
Colossae 153

Corinth 22, 60, 88, 90, 97, 98, 103, 104, 110, 150, 153, 162, 165, 167, 188, 190, 192, 204
Cos 33
Crete 34, 78, 192
Cyprus 41, 99, 192

Dacia 96
Danube 7
Dead Sea 8
Delos 16, 24, 30, 31, 37, 55, 57, 64, 70, 81, 94, 95, 96, 98, 108, 153, 183
Dion 27
Dyrrachium 23

Edessa 23, 52, 198, 199, 200
Egypt 5, 7, 15, 30, 41, 57, 78, 80, 84, 85, 86, 95, 98, 112, 127, 158, 192
Elimia 198, 199
Embona 156
Eordaea 198, 199
Ephesus 22, 33, 35, 36, 87, 111, 128, 144, 145, 151
Epirus 98
Eresos 134
Eretria 182
Erythrae 100
Euobea 192

Fayum 78

Galatia 75, 204
Gaul 7
Germany 7
Gorgippia 198

Hagios Mamas 25

Iberia 7
Idomene 198
Illion 182
Ionia 197
Isthmos 41
Italy 7, 80, 94, 195

Jerusalem 104, 150, 168, 192

Kalambaki 19, 23
Kalauria 34, 55
Kalliani 18, 52, 198
Kanata 81
Kassandreia 25
Knidos 64
Kyme 29
Kyzikos 57, 82, 83

Lanuvium 11, 86
Lesbos 55
Lycia 38, 78
Lydda 185
Lydia 28, 89, 176, 197

Magnesia 97, 134
Magnesia ad Maeander 104, 150
Manshiyeh 77
Mantinea (Arcadia) 57
Maroneia 52
Megara 94
Mésiméri 199
Metropolis (Lydia) 82
Miletus 134
Mitylene 132
Moesia 197
Myconos 81, 85

Nag Hammadi 8
Neapolis (Macedonia) 212
Napoca 56
Nicomedia 44
Nicopolis 56
Nob 188
North Africa 7, 96
Nysa 99

Opus 20, 31, 36, 96, 134
Ostia 43, 109, 151

Palestine 102, 103
Pamphylia 192
Panamaros (Caria) 77
Peloponnesus 192
Pergamon 98, 99, 100, 177

Perinthus 80
Pessionos (Phrygia) 23
Philadelphia (Egypt) 90
Philadelphia (Lydia) 35, 55, 65, 66
Philippi 19, 22, 26, 27, 52, 64, 75, 112, 113, 137, 138, 145, 146, 150, 152, 158, 160, 182, 190, 199, 201, 202, 205, 208, 210, 211, 212
Phoenicia 192
Phrygia 28, 78, 176, 197
Physcos 56, 142
Piraeus 17, 41, 42, 64, 84, 86, 94, 134, 142, 156, 158, 183
Podgora 19
Pompeii 78
Pontus 41, 192
Priene 96, 153
Proussotchani 19
Puteoli 95
Pydna 52, 53, 58, 78, 198, 199

Raktcha 19
Reussilova 19, 150
Rhodes 55, 64, 95, 108, 156, 158
Rome 7, 17, 22, 42, 43, 55, 57, 91, 94, 95, 96, 98, 99, 103, 117, 124, 128, 132, 151, 190

Samothrace 22, 24
Sardis 89
Selian 19, 26, 150
Sharon 185
Sicily 94
Smyrna 24, 137
Sounion 38, 39, 67
Stobi 19, 193, 194
Syria 127, 192

Tanis 197, 198
Tebtunis 84, 86
Teos 94, 98
Termessus (Pisidia) 176
Thebes 98
Thera 33, 34, 81, 142, 156
Thessalonica 19, 20, 22, 23, 25, 26, 30, 32, 36, 51, 53, 58, 75, 80, 82, 96, 104,

110, 111, 113, 145, 153, 156, 162, 166, 177, 188, 198, 199, 201, 206, 208, 210
Thessaly   192
Thrace   26, 80, 81, 197
Thyatira   22
Tralles   38

Trebeni   199
Troas   191
Troezen   82
Tyre   17, 95, 109, 151

Veneventum   98

www.ingramcontent.com/pod-product-compliance
Lightning Source LLC
Chambersburg PA
CBHW072022240426
43667CB00044B/2123